THE RETAIL FLORIST

BUSINESS

PETER B. PFAHL, Ph.D.

Professor of Floriculture, Emeritus
The Pennsylvania State University

P. BLAIR PFAHL, JR.

Retail Florist
Cleveland, Ohio

THE INTERSTATE
Printers & Publishers, Inc.
Danville, Illinois

THE RETAIL FLORIST BUSINESS, Fourth Edition.
Copyright © 1983 by The Interstate Printers & Publishers,
Inc. All rights reserved. Prior editions: 1968, 1973, 1977.
Printed in the United States of America.

Library of Congress Catalog Card No. 82-81934

ISBN 0-8134-2250-7

To Edythe and Robert

PREFACE

The retail florist industry in the United States is a complex structure of many retail establishments, most of which are classified as small shops employing from 1 to 10 employees. Each retail florist is an individual and no two of them operate their shops in the same manner. We often speak of an "average" florist or a "typical" florist, but there really is no such person.

In this book the authors have tried to present material of benefit to several groups of people. Primarily, the volume is a textbook to be used by college, high school, and vocational students who expect to become retail florists or work in the retail florist industry. It was also planned to aid retail florists who are already in the business, by presenting new ideas on the management and operation phase of the retail florist industry.

Many florists have different ways of doing things in their shops, and this book does not try to present all of the ideas. It essentially summarizes activities and provides several ideas and ways of doing each of the many jobs involved in operating and managing a retail florist shop.

The reader should keep in mind that not all of the ideas presented in this book will be applicable to all florists. Each florist must try out the ideas, adopt the beneficial ones, and discard the ones which do not seem pertinent.

The authors do not profess to know everything about the retail florist industry. They are presenting ideas from the senior author's 31 years of teaching Retail Flower Store Management to future florists and from his personal experiences and observations gained from his close association for over 30 years with many retail florists. Prior to this time he worked in a retail florist shop for several years in the Pittsburgh area. The co-author is a retail florist in Cleveland, Ohio. His day-to-day practical experiences in the field round out the complete view of the retail florist industry.

As there is very little published material in this field, it is the authors' hope that this book will be of value to all of you who are training to become retail florists as well as those of you who are already in the retail florist business. This text could be used to advantage as a training manual for new employees.

This fourth edition brings the reader up-to-date on management practices of the eighties.

PETER B. PFAHL

P. BLAIR PFAHL, JR.

ACKNOWLEDGMENTS

The authors gratefully acknowledge the assistance and advice of William Curtis, Dr. Elwood Kalin, Professor Paul Krone (now deceased), Herbert Mitchell, Jennifer Brown, Dr. Dennis Wolnick, Florists' Transworld Delivery Association, TELEFLORA, Inc., Florafax Association, and the many others whose names appear as references in the book. Appreciation is also given to the *Florists' Review, The Exchange,* and the *Southern Florist and Nurseryman* for the articles used as references for this book. Pictures are acknowledged by the name of the shops; those not marked are courtesy of the Agricultural Photographic Department, The Pennsylvania State University.

CONTENTS

◈ *PART ONE* ◈
BUSINESS MANAGEMENT

ᴖᴖ *PART TWO* ᴖᴖ
FLORAL DESIGN

 PART ONE

BUSINESS MANAGEMENT

 *Chapter 1*

INTRODUCTION

Everybody loves flowers and enjoys having them in the home. Flowers seem to speak a language of their own. The following fable written by Dr. M. E. John, The Pennsylvania State University, will illustrate the point:

> Something was different. I sensed it as I entered the living room. No one else was there. Everything seemed to be in its place. Yet I knew something had been added. Soon my eyes turned to the coffee table where someone had placed a bouquet of flowers. At once I recognized that this was the cause of the change. As I sat down in my chair I could feel their effect. My spirits were lifted. I felt cheerful and everything seemed right with the world. All of this caused me to stop and ponder as to why these flowers have such power. They cannot speak as we speak. They cannot move. Yet somehow they have a great influence over our moods. . . . Somehow they touch us when we are unaware. At times when one is depressed they pull man out of himself and broaden his outlook. Yes, flowers really speak: not English, or Spanish, or Chinese, but their own language—a language without words, but one with the universal meaning of love, beauty and cheer. This is what gives them power.

The retail florist business is based on the love of flowers.

The retail florist industry is comprised of many small businesses, in contrast to the trend towards consolidation in other retail industries. Figures from the U.S. Department of Agriculture and the Society of American Florists indicate that in 1979 there were 30,000*

---

*Various sources list between 25,000 and 32,000 retail florists, depending on whether or not they include green plant stores and mass markets. The best estimate for legitimate retail florists in the United States in 1980 is approximately 30,000. The 1977 Census of Retail Trade showed 29,375 retail florists, to which can be added a 10 per cent increase for 1980 according to marketing economists.

Figure 1-1. A flower arrangement says "Welcome" in a customer's home.

retail florists in the United States, grossing $3.1 billion annually. Compare this with three shops in 1800. (The 1982 FTD Flower Business Fact Book shows sales moving from $1.9 billion in 1976 to $3.3 billion in 1980.) In 1979, 47 per cent of sales were for funerals, 25 per cent for weddings and special occasions, 19 per cent for hospitals, and 9 per cent for everyday use. Two out of every three florists have businesses with annual gross sales of less than $100,000, accounting for less than one-third the total sales of the industry. In the United States the average retail florist with a payroll in 1977 had $108,854 in sales—quite an increase over $52,202 reported in 1963. The average shop without a payroll had $24,020 in 1977. In 1977 the total average sales per single unit shop in the United States was $108,350. One-fourth of the businesses are medium in size with sales of $150,000 to $250,000, and only one in nine florists is considered a "large" florist with annual sales over $500,000.

In 1979 in the United States there were over 75 retail florists who grossed a million dollars.

Only 1 out of every 11 flower shops has a paid manager. Most of the retail florist shops are family businesses with the owner as the manager, assisted by a spouse, often plus a son or daughter.

The florist business has changed considerably since the end of World War II. There have been major changes which have had a significant impact on retail florists. Some of the crucial changes have been:

1. The increased occurrence of "Please Omit."
2. The growing number of small, informal weddings.
3. The temporary furor arising from the claim—later proved to be false—that flowers could be dangerous to hospital patients.
4. The fantastic increase in demand for potted plants.
5. Diversification.
6. More holidays.
7. The increased involvement by nonflorist outlets with floral products.

This last change will most likely have the greatest long-range impact on florists. Studies have indicated that nearly 40 to 60 cents out of each dollar spent on floriculture items was spent in nonflorist retail establishments. In the sense that the nation's nearly 30,000 retail florists are essentially more artistic than business- or sales-minded, the mass market outlet offering the impulse item is a useful, complementary service. This will be discussed later in Chapter 16, the chapter on merchandising.

The business is no longer just one of raising and selling flowers with particular emphasis on funeral flowers. The retail florist business today is one of designing and service. In many shops the majority of flowers are arranged rather than being sent out as just loose cut flowers in a box. They are designed, delivered, and charged.

Retail florists are merchants, fundamentally occupied in buying and selling. They sell services as well as merchandise, and the words "sentiment," "service," "emotion," and "artistry" are all important in this specialized business. The florist business is really like no other business *because* florists specialize in many operations of design, service, and selling. The service is just as important as the artistry that goes with it. The florist must also consider sentiment and take into consideration the feelings of others. A hostess' request that a florist "do" the flowers is a golden opportunity to show off special talents. The creative possibilities are limitless to demonstrate once again the flower shop's services in a professional manner.

Retail florists are important to the economy of the United States. They need to know modern merchandising methods that will sell their merchandise most efficiently and most profitably. Successful retail florists are those who are competent to carry on a large-scale promotion to compete for the consumer's dollar. The success of any business is measured by its profits. In the retail florist shop the profits are due to the successful management of the business by the manager or owner.

The retail florists of the United States conduct about 75 per cent of their business by telephone—many of their customers are only names and voices. To serve these customers, florists provide considerable extra service. For example, 84 per cent offer some form of flowers-by-wire service, 95 per cent extend credit to their customers, and 80 per cent provide free delivery. They also offer advice and help customers choose appropriate flowers for weddings and funerals. All of these services cost money, adding to the overall costs of operation as discussed in Chapter 6. Most florists have a tradition of services, including delivery, gift wrapping, reminder service for anniversaries and birthdays, check cashing, charge accounts, and civic services.

Flowers also play a role in the economy of many European countries although they seem to be more integrated as a part of everyday life in certain countries. The average amounts spent on flowers and plants by one person in 1975 are as follows: Switzerland—$32.00; West Germany—$28.50; the Netherlands—$23.15; Sweden—$19.53; France—$9.75; Italy—$8.75; and Great Britain—$4.15. The approximate per capita consumption in the United States was $14.00 annually.

The retail florist business is considered an easy-entry industry. It is easy to get into with a moderate investment, and it is easy to get out. Although there are approximately 30,000 retail florists in the

Figure 1-2. The interior of a modern retail flower shop. (Courtesy, York Florist, Washington, D.C.)

country today, some areas are uncrowded. Competition is keen in the large cities, but there are hundreds of communities in the United States that could support flower shops where competition does not exist. Past experience has shown that it takes approximately 10,000 people to support a retail flower shop adequately. In many communities, however, this ratio is considerably lower. The total area to be served and the purchasing power of the people are important points. Many other factors must be considered, so that the ratio of 1 to 10,000 is only a tentative figure.

The U.S. Department of Agriculture Crop Reporting Service reported in 1981 that the greatest quantity of flowers produced in the 28 largest flower-producing states was as follows: 422,000,000 stems roses, 382,000,000 carnations, 307,000,000 chrysanthemums including standards and pompons, and 285,000,000 stems gladioli. Sales values for these crops are not available at this time. Stems of import cut flowers have risen from 3.3 per cent of the total in 1971 to 40.6 per cent in 1981, according to the U.S. Department of Agriculture Statistical Report for 1981 for floriculture crops.

The tradition of the majority of a florist's customers being women continues. In a recent survey it was shown that 63 per cent of the customers were female and only 37 per cent male. Only 16 per

cent of the florists interviewed felt their percentage of male customers was increasing.

There is much to attract people into the retail flower business.
The average flower shop is an attractive place in which to work, and,
in general, is a business that requires relatively little capital to get
started. It is a business in which several members of the family can
work at regular or irregular intervals without extensive training. It is
also a business where the owner can be his/her own boss.

There are unattractive features as well. The sale of flowers is
irregular from day to day and the supply of flowers is seasonal. The
flowers are perishable and as such constitute a certain amount of
risk. Probably the two greatest disadvantages to the retail florist
business are the long working hours and the relatively low wages for
employees. However, these may be offset by the enjoyment of working with flowers and being one's own boss.

Today not only must retail florists be good designers, but they
must also be experts in sales, merchandising, and, particularly, in
business management. In this book we will first discuss the elements
of being a florist and methods for managing a retail florist shop, and
conclude with the fundamentals of flower arrangement and good
design which are so important to the success of any retail florist.

Chapter 2

QUALIFICATIONS OF A
RETAIL FLORIST

What are the qualifications of a retail florist? *What is a retail florist?* You know that a retail florist is one who sells flowers and designs floral arrangements. But there is more to being a florist than just this. A retail florist must be skilled in designing, managing a business, buying, selling, providing services, and advising customers. Sylvia Valencia once said that if she were asked for a definition of a florist, she would have to say: "A florist is a composite of the doctor, the lawyer, and the minister because each day he is truthfully required to act in the capacity of advisor to many." So, to be a florist, you should have at your fingertips the knowledge of the correct protocol for formal dining, weddings, and for sympathy flowers. Be aware of the basic differences in what is permitted by various churches in the way of flowers for altar decorations and for formal services. Be ready to inform your customers on all matters pertaining strictly to flowers, their care, and how they should be used. In other words, as a retail florist, you should be a knowledgeable person who is ready to give information and service when it is requested.

There are, however, certain other qualifications which you should possess to be successful. Although you may not have all of these, you should be able to meet at least three-fourths of the 12 qualifications for being a retail florist which follow.

QUALIFICATIONS

1. **Be a good businessperson.** Know how to run your business and make a profit. Every retailer, whether florist or not, is in business to make money and not just for the fun of it.

Figure 2-1. Future retail florists learning the art of flower arranging and the mechanics of retail design.

2. **Be an artist** and have the ability to design. It is the design work going out to the customer which forms the foundation for your reputation. Of the many florists in the country, it is usually the ones whose arrangements are above average that are the most successful. In a large shop where all the designers are hired, an owner may feel it is unnecessary to know how to design. This is a fallacy—sooner or later the customer will want to see the owner's work or ask for specific suggestions and ideas. Therefore, the ability to design is as vital to a successful florist as is being a good businessperson.

3. **Have enough capital** to get started and to keep going for two years without profit. During the first six to nine months in the business you will just make enough to cover expenses and maybe pay yourself a small salary. The profits will not be realized until the second or third year. Have enough cash on hand to pay for supplies and merchandise, to carry growing accounts receivable, and to establish a good credit rating, in addition to paying for your own living.

4. **Be a good buyer.** Careful buying is necessary in order to achieve a fair profit from the business.
5. **Be really interested in your business.** You should have the love for, and appreciation of, flowers. It is not enough just to want to make money; you must like working with flowers.
6. **Have the ability to meet people** and to talk to them. You must know how to cater to the general public, and like it! To be above average as a florist you must be a good salesperson, not simply an order taker.
7. **Know how to advertise.** You must know how much to spend on advertising, when to advertise, what to say, and which media to use. You should also know how to arrange the store attractively and to set up good window displays which attract customers into the shop. These are all a part of advertising.
8. **Know how to train and handle employees.** You must keep them satisfied with their jobs and with one another. You must know how to train them so they will be an asset to the business and how to handle them properly so that you will get the maximum amount of work from each one. Satisfied employees who will stay with you reduce the trouble and expense of finding and training new personnel. Employee turnover should be kept to a minimum.
9. **Have experience.** The best advice anyone can give you if you want to become a florist is *get some experience and work for another florist for at least a year* before going into business for yourself. We say at least a year so that you will have the experience of going through all of the florists' holidays. There are nine main ones, each of which is different. It would be preferable to work several years with another florist, but one year's experience should be the absolute minimum. This type of training will enable you to gain knowledge of the types of flowers and materials handled throughout the year in the retail flower shop and the sort of flowers that customers prefer and why they prefer them. You can learn about both wholesale and retail prices and how they fluctuate throughout the year. Other knowledge you will gain includes sales methods, buying procedures, record keeping, customer relations, and stock control. If you keep your eyes open and are observant, you can learn a lot in a year's time. Many new businesses fail the first year

because of the inexperience of the owner. (See Voigt's report from Dun and Bradstreet, Chapter 11.)

10. **Be a merchandiser.** In today's economy, if you want to get your fair share of the consumer's dollar, you must know how to merchandise your product. There is more to it than just *selling* flowers; this will be discussed later in detail.

11. **Have a thorough knowledge of the plants and flowers that you handle.** Know how to take care of them and make them last longer in your own shop as well as in the customer's home. People will bring all sorts of questions on horticulture to you and expect you to be able to answer them. You may not know all the answers, but you should know those concerning the specific materials you sell. Because of the foliage plant boom of recent years it is essential to be well informed on the care of house plants.

12. **Participate in civic affairs.** It is very important to take an interest and an active part in community life. You are not expected to join all civic organizations and drives, but you should be active in some. Also join and help support your own trade associations so you will know what is going on within the industry.

All of these qualifications are important and most of them will be discussed in detail in other chapters in this book.

TRAINING

Most retail florists of today were trained for the business by working in a flower shop for many years. This was the way they gained experience, and it is part of the training you need now. However, as the small retail florist is not a specialist in one thing only, training is vital in many more operations than just floral designing.

A formal college education is not essential for the successful operation of a retail floral shop, *but it is highly desirable.* A major in floriculture will give you a background of fundamental knowledge in botany, chemistry, and physiology, as well as in the growing, care, and keeping quality of cut flowers and pot plants. Also, you will learn the rudiments of floral design and the management of a retail florist shop. By augmenting the program with courses in accounting, bookkeeping, salesmanship, psychology, business ethics, marketing, and merchandising you will have a good foundation for the retail florist business. In addition, a session at one of the design schools located throughout the country would be very beneficial. These de-

Figure 2-2. Practice makes perfect for future retail florists.

sign schools are also a *must* for high school students who do not go to college or junior college but want to become retail florists.

A good basic education is essential for your success as a retail florist, but upon completion of any kind of academic training, whether it be a college degree in floriculture or business management or a high school diploma, you must obtain specialized training and experience by working in a retail florist shop.

These, then, are some of the main qualifications that you should have or develop to become a successful retail florist. With these go the prerequisite of any successful business—*hard work*. The retail florist works long hours and must work hard to show a profit at the end of the year.

If you are planning to go into business for yourself, there is a check list which you may obtain from the Small Business Administration, Washington, D.C. 20008. Go over this in detail and fill in all the questions honestly so that you can properly analyze your chances for success. There are about 100 questions under the following headings: "(1) Are you the type? (2) What are your chances of success? (3) How much capital will you need? (4) Should you share ownership with others? (5) Where should you locate? (6) Should you buy a going business? (7) Are you qualified to supervise buying and selling? (8) How will you price your products and services? (9) What selling methods will you use? (10) How will you manage personnel? (11) What records will you keep? (12) What laws will affect you? (13) What other problems will you face? (14) Will you keep up-to-date?" Just thinking about each of these questions will help in planning your future in the retail florist business.

The life of a retail florist is a good one and, for the owner, a rewarding one financially and personally. The product is one of the best liked products in the world, and most of a florist's efforts will result in bringing cheer and happiness to others as well as providing a good living. The opportunities for women in this field are excellent.

Chapter 3

TYPES OF RETAIL FLOWER SHOPS

The retail flower shop as we know it today has been in existence only about 90 years. Flowers were sold originally from the greenhouse to the people who came to buy them. As designing of flowers became necessary, one end of the greenhouse or the headhouse was set apart for the designing and sale of floral pieces.

At about the same time, some greenhouse producers of flowers began to market the flowers through local grocery stores. The retail sale of flowers was simply an adjunct of the local general store. It was not long before separate retail flower shops began to spring up all over the country, leading to the retail florist industry of today.

Most of the 30,000 retail florist shops in the United States today would fall into 1 of 14 categories or types. Many of them are what we call "average shop" florists, but some of them are more specialized. However, even the so-called "average florists" differ from one another.

About half of retail florists are retail-only (buy everything they sell). A survey taken by *The Exchange* in 1963, but still of interest as the percentages have changed very little, showed that 53.5 per cent of retail florists were retail-only and 46.5 per cent were retail-growers. The following percentages of each group as classified by location indicate a strong correlation between where they locate and whether they have incorporated a greenhouse operation.

	Retail-Only	*Retail-Growers*
Downtown	35.2	5.1
Suburban	56.0	72.1
Rural	8.8	22.8

The heavy concentration of shops of both types in the suburban areas with a much smaller percentage of shops (primarily retail-only) in the downtown area, may account for the remarks heard from time to time that there are too many retail florists in the business today. Many areas, however, still are not adequately served by the retail florist industry.

CATEGORIES OF FLOWER SHOPS

Which type of shop should you choose? Let's look at a few of the details concerning 14 different types of retail flower shops in existence today.

Average Shop

This is the category in which the majority of shops belong, and the one which is the hardest to describe and typify. The shop is small to medium in size as far as gross volume of business and number of employees are concerned. It will have moderate prices and average-to-good designs. It has a large clientele with at least half of these as telephone customers. These shops are found in small towns, suburban areas, and occasionally in the downtown area in our cities. The hours that they stay open may be long and often irregular. The supply of flowers on hand is usually just enough to make a nice display, but not large. The quality must be medium to good. In a small town, the florist will be acquainted with all of the customers, and there will be very few strangers. Credit will be extended to almost anyone who requests it. The average shop is often a family shop with husband, wife, son or daughter, and maybe one other employee. The owner is usually the manager, buyer, and often the designer because the average retail flower shop in the United States today is a small shop with few employees, not a large shop with a manager and a dozen employees. As the census figures show, the majority of retail florists in the United States are under $100,000 in gross volume of sales (Chapter 1). Over 50 per cent of the customers will charge their flowers. The business includes many services including packing, designing, delivery, charging, and advice on the best and most appropriate flowers for all occasions. Even in the "average shop" category no two florists are exactly alike.

High Class Shop

This shop is often found in the suburban areas catering to people who have more than an average income and are willing to spend money on flowers. The prices will be high, and so will the quality of the merchandise. Only merchandise of top quality would be permitted to leave this type of shop. This is closely controlled at all times. The artistry in design must be the best in the industry because that is what the customers will expect for their money. Most of the clientele will be regular customers, who will charge their flowers and usually telephone their orders. It has been estimated that at least 80 per cent of this group will have a charge account. The shop hours will be definite, more regular, and not as long as in certain other types of shops. The customers are willing to spend money, but they will be more exacting in their likes and dislikes. There must be no duplicating of designs for funerals, parties, weddings, etc. This type of business will also include many services such as credit, delivery, and advice, as well as outstanding work in design. In selling, patience is required because many of the customers will be "fussy" about their orders and may take quite a while to make up their minds as to what they want. Others will be very precise and definite about their orders. The owner must have originality and a good imagination to be able to suggest unusual designs to the customer. Extra services will be required, such as keeping the customers' personal name cards on hand to send with funeral and other orders and maintaining an up-to-date reminder card file system of birthdays and anniversaries. These time-consuming services are eventually paid for by the customers in the markup. The shop will be attractive and kept up-to-date, and the rental will be high.

Cash-and-Carry Shop

A cash-and-carry shop is usually a downtown shop utilizing a small area for its operation. This might be a subway shop, or a small shop in an office building; however, there are many others in small shops on the main and side streets. The majority of the business will be from transient trade with few regular customers. The business will be mostly cash-and-carry with a minimum of charge accounts and delivery. However, as experience has shown that a retail florist cannot exist on cash-and-carry sales alone, some regular customers must be cultivated. Requests for design or make-up work will be at a minimum, so that only a small workroom will be necessary. The prices on the merchandise will be low and the quality medium to good. The success of the business depends on volume, so window streamers and displays which catch the eye of the passerby are essential. The hours are usually quite regular and determined by the other merchants in the area. The shop must be located where plenty of foot traffic passes the store.

Retail-Grower Combination Florist

Surveys have shown that 46.5 per cent of our florists are retail-growers. (See Figures 3-1 and 3-2.) This includes many florists who have just one small greenhouse as well as florists with many greenhouses. Their operations are quite different depending upon their size. However, they all have several things in common. One of the greatest advantages is the fact that they can advertise that they grow their own flowers. The implication is that everything in the shop is fresh. Actually, they may only raise 2 per cent of their merchandise, or as much as 80 per cent of it—none are able to raise 100 per cent of the flowers they sell. In fact, it doesn't pay to raise roses on a small scale. Research workers tell us that a rose grower must have at least 10,000 plants in the greenhouse to make the operation profitable. Other advantages retail-growers enjoy are: first and most important—being able to buy a larger quantity of plants at one time, being able to make up their planters instead of buying them ready-made, increasing profits in the spring by using bedding plants grown in their own greenhouses, raising novelty items for the shop which may be hard to get on the market, and quick access to a few extra flowers needed for a particular arrangement. The use of one or more greenhouses or conservatories for an open house before Christmas or Easter is an excellent promotion. If there is space, the florist can build good will by staging a flower show. The greenhouse also offers an excellent opportunity for growing and storing foliage plants for weddings and other decorating jobs.

There are, of course, some disadvantages to being a retail-grower. The florist must have training as a grower as well as a designer, including the know-how to take care of potted plants in the

Figure 3-1. A modern retail-grower florist. (Courtesy, Frederick's Flowers, Souderton, Pa.)

Figure 3-2. A flower shop with an all glass front and a conservatory greenhouse. (Courtesy, Penny Hill Flowers, Wilmington, Del.)

greenhouse as well as in the home. More investment is necessary for this type of business, since greenhouse construction is expensive. Usually one part of the business carries the other financially, and most of these florists do not keep adequate records to tell which is making the money. If the retail shop gets the attention, the greenhouse will suffer or vice versa. Theoretically, the retail shop should pay (on paper) for the flowers used from the greenhouse at the regular market price. However, often the paper work and book-keeping are not worth the time and effort as most of the shops are small to medium in size. Another disadvantage is that a retail-grower florist usually must be located out of the cities and suburban business districts because of zoning laws, rents, and taxes. The hours are usually irregular and long, because many people feel they can call a greenhouse anytime at night or on Sundays and find someone there. This type of shop can be very successful in a small town. Prices are usually average and quality good. Retail florists who have a garden center in connection with the shop would fit into this category.

College Town Shop

A retail florist shop in a college town is usually an average shop with certain special functions. The prices are usually moderate and the design work is average to good. The moderate prices are necessitated by the salaries of the faculty and the spending money of the students. The shop should correlate its advertising, promotion, and sales to the activities of the school. Window displays should tie in with college functions. Corsages should be cultivated for the dances and centerpieces for sorority and fraternity parties. A good rapport should be established between the florist and the students. A majority of the design work will be corsages and decorations. The hours will usually be fairly regular. About half of the customers will pay cash. Many college town florists have encouraged "will calls" for the corsages to cut down on the enormous expense of delivery time spent trying to deliver flowers to the girls in the residence halls. The extent of holiday work will depend on whether the students are in school or have gone home for the vacation so the time table of the college must be studied ahead of time to plan accurately. There will usually be plenty of telephone or wire orders both incoming and outgoing for Mother's Day and other holidays, depending upon the activities of the student population.

Hotel Shop

A hotel flower shop is a very specialized type of retail flower shop. Sometimes it is a branch store of another shop, or it may be a complete shop in itself. The rent is usually quite high, and the shop is small with limited space for a design area and for storage. The refrigerator and store must be well stocked at all times, because much of the work will be rush work. The majority of the customers will pay cash and often will take the merchandise with them. Thus, there must be plenty of cut flowers on hand as well as several made-up gift pieces in attractive containers. The designer must be able to design a piece quickly while the customer waits. Many customers in a hotel shop will be men, so a large supply of red roses must be kept on hand, as this is the flower most commonly purchased by them. Although many men who are frequent customers are learning about flowers, the majority of men who enter a flower shop always ask for red roses—they don't seem to know that any other flowers exist. Many also know that red roses signify "love," and that is what they wish to say with the flowers. Prices will be high due to the high rental, and the quality of the flowers should be excellent. Most shops do not open early in the morning, but often stay open at night. Many are open on Sunday. The funeral work in a hotel shop will be at a minimum unless the store is an old established firm with many regular charge account customers. The operation of the hotel flower shop will be determined by the type of hotel—whether it is a resident hotel with permanent guests or a downtown hotel with mostly transient guests.

Figure 3-3. A hotel flower shop. (Courtesy, Buning The Florist, Inc., Fort Lauderdale, Fla.)

Hospital Shop

A hospital flower shop is usually a small shop located in the lobby of a hospital. Sometimes it may be a florist shop in the vicinity of the hospital specializing in hospital arrangements. It may be a branch of a regular shop or a part-time shop operated by a person who has another income or business. The shop space will be limited and most orders will be for small hospital arrangements in containers. There will be very little funeral or decoration business. There should be gift novelties, novelty flower arrangements, baby novelties, and small vase arrangements on hand at all times. Merchandise must be well displayed for the customer to see, because there will be plenty of spontaneous or impulse buying by people coming to visit someone in the hospital. The business will be mostly cash-and-carry. Most hospitals today require flowers to be in containers, so there will not be many loose flowers sold. Most containers should be inexpensive and the prices for the merchandise will be moderate. People will spend more money on hospital flowers if they see them already arranged and on display. Bright flowers should be used for men and pastels for women. Do not stock many flowers with pollen or strong fragrance or odors which may cause discomfort to the patient. A good many pot plants are sold for hospital orders. Comic books, crayons, toys, puzzles, books, and other items which will delight youngsters who are hospitalized should be kept in stock to use in arrangements. Small arrangements, novelties, and pot plants in the range of $7.50 to $22.00 will be the best sellers in most hospital flower shops.

Apartment House Shop

The retail florist shop located in an apartment house is another specialized type. It is usually small to medium in size with a small workroom with quite a high rental involved. It must be kept attractive at all times with made-up arrangements in the display refrigerator. It is comparable to a high class suburban shop except for size, with high prices and high quality merchandise. The majority of customers will be regular ones who charge their flowers. There will be very little transient trade and very little cash-and-carry business. A large part of the business will be funeral, wedding, gift, and decoration work for private parties. The apartment house shop will probably be in a fairly large city, making advertising very important. People may not even know there is a florist shop in the apartment building unless it is well advertised. Space may be a problem requiring arrangements for ample storage areas or rooms somewhere in the basement. Getting to the delivery truck entrance to load deliveries may also be a problem. It is important to cultivate the other tenants and those of neighboring buildings to encourage them to become regular customers—a good word-of-mouth reputation is essential. It should be possible to build up a good centerpiece and party decoration business. High prices will be charged for the flowers, designs, and services rendered. Quality merchandise must be used at all times to build a good reputation. Regular hours, which are not too long, will usually prevail in an apartment flower shop.

Mall or Shopping Center Shop

Most of the newer shopping centers being constructed today are called "malls," large complexes including many businesses both large and small. This new type of florist shop is quite different from most shops. The rental is usually very high and may require a percentage of the gross sales be paid in addition to the rent, as well as contributing a share for advertising—the contract must be carefully studied. Space is usually limited, and it may be necessary to rent another area for storage. This type of business will depend mainly on volume sales from the foot traffic of the mall / center. Attractive displays, prices on merchandise, and cash-and-carry sales will help to bring the customers inside. For the first few years, until the shop is established, there will not be many telephone or charge customers, nor much funeral work. Specials are very good, according to some florists who have been successful in opening a branch store in a shopping center. Also, specials bring people into the store where they are exposed to attractive displays of other merchandise and impulse items, promoting extra sales. Browsing should be encouraged in these shops.

One of the drawbacks to this type of operation is the hours which usually must conform to the mall hours. This often means staying open until 9:00 or 10:00 P.M., although opening time may be 10:00 A.M. or noon. One of the big assets is ample, and usually free, parking. This type shop carries different merchandise than the average florist, and is involved in more group promotions and advertising. Shopping is more leisurely. Due to the limited floor space, the make-up work must usually be done in the rear of the sales area. Many shopping center florists carry as large a gift line as space permits. There are many problems to this type of business, such as a fair rental, extra costs, types of merchandise to handle, credit policies, salary schedules due to odd hours, and other factors. Many of these are still unsolved because this type of florist is relatively new. It is best not to expect to make money the first three years while the business is being established.

Before choosing a particular center, analyze the developer's market analysis to be sure the center will attract the sort of customers sought. Basically, there are three types of shopping centers or malls—neighborhood, community, and regional. The International Council of Shopping Centers, Washington, D.C., can assist in this decision.

Kiosk

This is becoming increasingly popular in shopping malls. It is vital to check out the mall carefully. Determine the foot traffic count in the mall area itself. Many florists feel that a mall should have at least a traffic count of 90,000 to 100,000 people per week. Another point to consider is the area needed in the mall to conduct this amount of business. The consensus of opinion from florists who have been successful is that an area of 350 to 400 square feet is needed in a desirable location within the mall.

Department Store Florist

Another type of retail florist shop can be found in some of our larger department stores, in which the florist leases floor space. Although the sales area may be large, the workroom may be small. The merchandise must be good quality at moderate prices, and volume sales are needed. There will be plenty of foot traffic in the store, and the florist must persuade a good share of the people to buy. There will be many impulse sales. Mass displays and cash-and-carry specials are useful. Made-up pieces should be kept in the display refrigerator at all times. Browsing should be encouraged and everything should be priced.

There are advantages and disadvantages to the department store flower shop. The contract must be analyzed carefully to be sure that all of the profits do not go to the store. The hours must conform to those of the store, requiring special permission to work in the store after hours on special occasions or at holiday times. The shop will never be open on Sundays. This can be a problem with Sunday weddings and funerals. Although all store personnel must be given discounts, their purchases should give a large enough increase in volume to offset the lower profit margin. A big advantage is having no costs for billing customers nor any bad debts, since the store pays all bookkeeping charges and assumes the responsibility of collecting all accounts. Often the store will supply paper and bags for wrapping and carrying the merchandise. The store will usually keep the windows clean, carry out the trash, and keep the place painted. The flower shop can tie in with the bridal salon and may attract a great deal of wedding work. There will be more gift items and cash-and-carry sales than funeral work until a reputation has been established with some of the regular customers in the store. There will be very few telephone customers at first. There are problems in this type of operation, but the florist who knows what is in the contract and how to *merchandise* flowers will succeed. Among others, the problems will include: competing with the gift and artificial flower departments of the store, working after hours on funeral or wedding work, buying in quantity but carefully, avoiding the store receiving all the profits, and supplying too many flowers to other departments without getting a proper markup. A clear understanding must be reached whether deliveries will be made with the department store's or the florist's equipment and personnel.

Bachman's European Flower Market

The European Flower Market (EFM), which has been developed and patented by Bachman's in Minneapolis and is being handled by the Pillsbury Company, can be adapted for retail florist shops as well as supermarkets and malls or as a branch of the retail florist shop. (See Figure 3-4.) This innovation in cut flower merchandising keeps flowers fresh by using a uniform blanket of cool air. The EFM Boutique holds approximately 20 bunches of cut flowers, has 17.4 square feet of refrigerated display area, and is 15 inches deep. Open on all sides, it allows the customer complete accessibility to the flowers for their cash-and-carry purchases. Proper display and ease of purchase is essential to any merchandising program. The success of this will be dependent upon physical facilities as well as location, including how much transient trade passes the unit. Bachman's claim that the best success in merchandising of flowers is to handle high quality flowers and that this is the secret to the success of these "Bouquet Boutiques." As of 1980, sales of these units seem to be

Figure 3-4. A Bouquet Boutique. (Courtesy, Bachman's European Flower Market, Bloomington, Minn.)

sluggish. How successful these boutiques eventually become only time will tell.

Mini-shop

These shops are just 10′ × 20′ and are pre-built by a company with headquarters in Seattle, Washington. They are built for convenience, speed, and economy to serve the customer instantly. They are successful in high density areas, such as shopping centers, where they sell cameras and film as well as fresh and permanent flowers and pot plants. Costs are cut down because there is no delivery, no charging, and little design work.

Supermarket

Although many florists consider supermarkets handling flowers as being competitors, many of them are in the flower business as a sideline to the food and other items. A retail florist might co-operate with the supermarket by actually handling the cut flowers and pot plants rather than having some inexperienced novice handling them and giving out wrong information on the care of plants. As supermarkets are getting into most aspects of a retail flower shop, they could be considered a new type, the fourteenth.

We have discussed some of the features of the various types of retail flower shops in the United States. However, there are many shops which are combinations of two or more of these. Also, when asked to describe a typical florist shop it is impossible, because there is really no such thing as a typical retail florist. Each florist is different, even those which we call "average" florists.

LEASING

Large department stores, to provide better customer services and conveniences, are leasing more and more departments, especially those requiring a high degree of specialization. Retail florists are a natural for this new leasing venture, but must carefully weigh all the factors before starting into this type of a business. Consider the following factors: (1) Pick a store that has a place in the community and does a good job of filling community needs. (2) Determine whether the store is a prestige store or one concerned with price? (3) Aim for the downtown base store, not one with many small branches. (4) Only consider a large suburban branch if the main store has just one or two, but keep in mind long hours of 10 to 12 hours every day. (5) Make sure the store's position is clearly defined. Be sure you know what it will cost. The advantages and disadvantages to leasing a store in a department store are similar to those just discussed under "Department store retail florist."

You have certain advantages to offer the department store, and these should be presented and discussed when coming to any business agreement with the store:

1. The leased flower shop can add prestige to the store.
2. It gives the store additional customer convenience.
3. It adds to the store's fashion leadership.
4. Flower buyers are consistent customers and will help to build overall store traffic.
5. Flower departments are a natural source for display material.
6. Flowers-by-wire or telephone will give the department store a unique service not open to other competing stores.

SOLE OWNERSHIP OR PARTNERSHIP

There are three forms of ownership for retail florist businesses. The most common form is that of individual ownership or proprietorship. The second one, in which quite a few businesses fall, is that of a partnership of two (or occasionally more) partners. The third category is that of a corporation; not too many retail florists are large enough to find it economically advantageous to incorporate. Corporations will not be discussed in this book, as the laws are so complicated that this must be accomplished only with the help of an attorney.

Before making a decision on which type of ownership you will use, consider the advantages and disadvantages of each.

The advantages of a proprietorship are as follows:

- Everything is in your hands as the owner—you are your own boss.
- You have full freedom of action.
- You do not share the profits.

The disadvantages of a proprietorship are as follows:

- You, as owner, are personally liable for all debts.
- You probably have limited personal assets restricting your borrowing power.

᪐ You probably do not possess all the talents for selling, book-keeping, and management, as well as designing.

᪐ Unless the family is capable of carrying on, the business usually is discontinued when the owner dies.

The advantages of a partnership are as follows:

᪐ A second viewpoint will tend to prevent rash actions.

᪐ The personal assets of the partners provide a broader base for obtaining capital.

᪐ Two people might be a great success together where singly they might fail if the talents of one offset the deficiencies of the other.

The disadvantages of a partnership are as follows:

᪐ Each partner is individually responsible for all business debts.

᪐ Each partner is responsible for the business commitments of the other.

᪐ The death of a partner automatically dissolves the business.

᪐ Working together closely can result in disagreements, creating friction between the partners.

Before going into a partnership, think it over carefully and be sure you know the habits, honesty, and management abilities of your prospective partner. You might be better off on your own. Each individual case is different and must be studied by all parties concerned.

As a prospective retail florist, you must decide on the type of a retail florist shop you wish to operate and also on the form of ownership which will be most advantageous to you.

SHOP NAME

Selecting the name of your florist shop is another important consideration. Many florists use their own name because they feel it is a real advantage to keep their name constantly in the public eye and have people associate their name with that of a good, reliable retail florist shop. Others will take the name of the street, section of town, name of the city, hotel, or shopping center. Select the name which will give the best publicity and result in establishing a profitable business.

Careful consideration of the advantages and disadvantages of each type of retail florist shop, form of ownership, and manner of naming the shop is essential and will reduce the number of headaches later on in the business.

Chapter 4

SITE AND LOCATION

One of the most important aspects you must consider in establishing a retail florist shop is the location. This single factor can often make the difference that spells success or failure. Many failures in the flower business occur because the owner didn't investigate thoroughly enough to determine the need for a florist shop in the community chosen. Location does not entail the mere physical site of the shop, but includes the city or community, the people, their incomes, their habits, the competition, the availability of suppliers, and other factors. The location should be decided on a practical businesslike basis. All too often a person's home town may already have enough or even too many retail florists. Although the figure of one florist per 10,000 people is often quoted, there are too many other considerations and variables to take into account to make it practical to really use this figure except as a general guide. Other considerations would be the earning power or average income of the residents, growth rate of the community, type of industries, nationalities of the people, per capita retail sales, and the extent to which the people seem flower-minded. Will they spend money for flowers? This is the ultimate goal.

A good location is the major element necessary to insure your success. The factors to be considered in selecting a location can be divided into two main categories: (1) selection of the city and (2) the location within the city. These will both be discussed in detail.

SELECTING THE CITY

Select the city or community very carefully by studying and analyzing the community, its business, and its people. Much of the information can be obtained from the local government, chamber of commerce, sales tax figures, and census figures.

Investigate first the people in the community and surrounding areas who are to be potential customers. It is important to correlate the population of the area to the number of existing retail florist shops. Consider the national origin of the residents, because some groups are more inclined to buy flowers than others. A breakdown of population by religion will also give an indication of flower-purchasing habits. Ethnic groups can strongly influence the type of designs that will be a major part of the business. The attitude of your prospective customers toward flowers is very important and will greatly determine the success or failure of your shop. It is also vital to determine whether or not the community is progressive.

Consider next the businesses and industries in the community. How many are there? If there is only one which goes into a slump, it will affect your business almost immediately. Several businesses and diversified industries in a community lead to a more stable economy. The kinds of businesses are important because they indicate the type of people in the area. Of course, if you locate in a strictly residential area, there will not be any business to consider.

The income of the people in the community is another factor. Usually figures are available to give the average income or median income level of the people in the community. Also determine whether most of the people are in the same income bracket, or if there is a wide range between the high- and low-income levels. However, do not give undue importance to the income levels—people in all income brackets love flowers and their willingness to buy may be influenced by their attitudes toward flowers and their national origins. In some locations you might have higher potential sales in a low-income area than you would in a different high-income area.

A study of the existing flower shops is essential. Are they well managed and operated? Are they successful and making money? What is the reputation of each shop and its owner? What is the appearance of these shops? What is the quality of the merchandise and the quality of their designs? How many shops are there that will be competitors? Are the present florists an integral part of the community life? All of these things should be considered to see if you can successfully compete with the existing retail flower shops in the area. Your chances of success may depend upon these factors.

Another factor that will help you decide on the city is the per capita sales of the area. You may not be able to get the figures for florists only, but you can get either the per capita sales figure or the total sales figures from the local business bureau or from local governmental records. Although per capita sales for flowers will vary considerably from one city to another, it is usually found that, on the average, ½ of 1 per cent of all retail sales in a community will be for flowers. Thus, you can figure the amount spent on flowers in the area and, with the number of retail florists, have some idea of the average gross for each shop. Another way to evaluate the existing florists' shops as to their gross return is to figure that each full-time employee accounts for from $40,000 to $60,000 gross sales. The average is $50,000, but the better shops aim for $60,000 gross volume of sales per *full-time* employee.

Transportation facilities are also important because you handle such a perishable product. You need to be near either the flower market or production area, or you must have good transportation available between it and your shop. If the community is isolated from such facilities, it may not be a good location unless wholesale florist trucks service it daily or several times a week.

The last factor is whether or not you think you can make money in this community. A complete analysis of all of these factors is necessary to determine if you think your business will be successful.

LOCATING WITHIN THE CITY

After you have decided upon the city, it is necessary to choose the specific location.

First, find the progressive part of the town. Check on the area where the established businesses are modernizing and seem most forward-looking. Don't locate in an area which is going downhill.

It is usually preferable to locate your shop in or near a business district. Even in a highly residential suburb, there will usually be a few stores; it is wise, and often necessary due to zoning, to locate with them. The alternative is to choose a large piece of property on a well-traveled street where you can offer ample free parking. Whether or not the location is in the business district may, in the final analysis, be determined by the type of shop the florist expects to operate.

Parking is another factor to consider unless you are in a shopping center, where plenty will be provided. It will not be your responsibility or concern if you locate in a hospital, hotel, or department store. But, for most of our regular retail florists, parking is a real problem, especially in the cities, and must be considered. It will be ideal if you can provide parking on your own property, whether just a few spaces or a half acre. In the city you may want to consider being near the municipal parking lots / garages or on a street with

Figure 4-1. A flower shop with parking facilities provided. (Courtesy, Royer's Flowers, Lebanon, Pa.)

plenty of parking meters. If the shop is in a residential area, be sure there is some convenient parking nearby even though the majority of the orders will be by phone. A certain number of customers will drive to the shop and want to see the store, the displays, and the merchandise. Therefore, it is important to provide adequate parking facilities for the convenience of the customers.

If you decide to build a retail flower shop on a drive-in site, the following points may be helpful:

1. Fast traffic or congested areas do not produce drop-in traffic for the drive-in retailer—traffic averaging 35 to 45 miles per hour is preferable.

2. A stop sign slows traffic.
3. A street where left turns are permitted increases the number of directions from which a site may be approached.
4. Sites at intersections of two streets are classified as far corner, near corner, or inside location which means between the corners; far corner site is preferred as it provides greater visibility.
5. The quicker the customer recognizes a site as a drive-in retailer, the better. A drive-in site should have adequate frontage—at least 100 feet for a park-and-shop drive-in; on a highway 300 feet is preferred.
6. The site should be deep enough to allow adequate parking at peak periods.
7. The site should be easy to enter and leave.
8. Parking space should be sufficient to allow ease of parking, turning around, and backing.
9. Zoning regulations should be such as to permit the sign to be seen.
10. Avoid fast traffic and congested areas.
11. Avoid areas that have a great deal of competition for customers from the same flow of traffic.
12. Do not locate on a hillside or on the inside of a curve on a highway.
13. Do not locate too close to the road as it may be widened later.

When you are considering a specific site within the city, check out the tax assessment—it may be more than you can afford—and zoning regulations that apply. Zoning laws vary widely but may cover the following:

ᥫ Restrict areas in which businesses may be located.
ᥫ Require fireproof construction (not frame) in central fire district.
ᥫ Prohibit greenhouse with retail shop.
ᥫ Regulate how close to the property lines you can build.
ᥫ Restrict sizes, types or placement of signs.
ᥫ Prohibit displays on the sidewalk, limiting or hindering impulse and holiday sales.

A survey of the foot traffic passing the location is important for most types of shops. In a downtown area try to locate on the side of the street where people walk. Figures indicate that the following number of persons will pass a downtown shop in cities of various sizes: for a city of 2,500 to 25,000, 372 per hour or up to 4,464 per day can be expected; for a city of 50,000 to 250,000, 1,791 per hour or up to 21,492 per day; and for a city of above 250,000 population, 3,500 per hour, or as many as 42,000 per day.

Try to locate on the shady side of the street. The sun streaming in the display window will wilt the flowers very quickly. An awning may help part of the day, but, as it reduces the effectiveness of the window display, it is not the best idea.

Another factor you must consider is the rent or the mortgage payments if you are buying or constructing your own building. Make sure the rent is comparable to others in the area. As a rule of thumb, most retail florists do not allow more than 3 to 4 per cent of their gross volume of sales for rent. This is a good reason to try to estimate the expected gross sales before going into business. The utilities should not exceed 2 per cent of the gross volume of sales.

Delivery is an important part of the business, so be sure that there is adequate space, preferably in the rear of the store or at the side, for loading or unloading your truck and for receiving shipments. Handling these operations through the front door is inconvenient to both customers and staff and is time-consuming. Check out the laws regarding standing trucks if the store opens on an alley, municipal parking lot, or side street.

One final factor in selecting the site is to check the condition of nearby buildings. Be sure they are in good repair, neat, and attractive, as this will enhance your reputation. The architectural style of the neighboring buildings will influence the design you plan for your store front. (See Chapter 7.)

If your reason for selecting a site is to relocate your business, be sure to consider whether your present customers will follow you to the new location.

BUYING A BUSINESS

If you decide to buy a business, you should consider many of the previously mentioned factors even though the actual site and location are already established. Many of those factors should be studied before investing money in the business. A thumbnail guide to buying a business would be the following:

1. Don't be too anxious to buy.
2. Find out why the business is for sale.

3. Seek advice from a lawyer and have an accountant go over the books.
4. Be sure to examine the gross volume sales figures, net returns, and net profit after taxes, and ask to see the owner's income tax report for the past two years.
5. Beware of hidden liens, mortgages, and back taxes.
6. Find out if the employees are staying with the business or going to a competitor.

Purchasing an existing business has certain advantages which you should not overlook, as follows:

- The volume of business and the potential can be measured.
- The store and fixtures are already set up.
- There is an established clientele.
- The inventory of stock is ready for business.
- There may be benefits from obtaining a long-term, low-cost lease.

There also are disadvantages to buying a business which you should be aware of:

- The business may be going downhill through mismanagement or for other reasons.
- The neighborhood may be changing.
- The business may have agreements with employees involving heavy fixed operating expenses.
- Too much of the trade may be tied up with the personality of the former owner.
- The good will may be overpriced, resulting in too high a purchase price.
- The net profit may be too low in relation to the gross volume of sales.

BUYING A SECOND SHOP

When you buy another flower shop to add to your business operations, the following factors should be considered:

1. Is there any merchandise listed in the inventory which is on a consignment basis?
2. How well have the fixed assets been maintained and repaired?
3. What are the conditions of the mortgage on the property?

4. Are there any contingent liabilities not listed by the seller?
5. What are the employment contracts with the employees and what about vacations and employee benefits?
6. What are the legislative laws and restrictions on the physical aspects of the property?
7. What future changes are planned for the area?
8. What percentage of the inventory is really salable?
9. Is there a competent manager for the second shop?
10. Will this second shop compete unprofitably with the parent shop?
11. How much capital will be needed to modernize the shop?
12. What is the present reputation of the shop? If it is unsatisfactory, how much will it cost to change?

Adherence to the right answers to the foregoing factors will provide greater assurance that the purchase of another flower shop has the best possible chance of being a good business move.

Whether one starts a new business or purchases an existing florist shop, the consideration of the site and location is one of the most important factors to the success of a retail florist.

An informative brochure, "Using Census Data to Select a Store Site," Small Marketers Aid No. 154, is available from the Small Business Administration, Washington, D.C.

Chapter 5

COST OF STARTING IN BUSINESS

The retail florist business is an easy-entry business. It is a freely competitive industry, which does not take much capital to get started. You can spend as little or as much as you wish so long as you have a certain minimum, plus some reserve to carry you through the first two years. The minimum today should be $40,000 and should be unencumbered. Fifty thousand dollars would be better, in order to pay a decent living until the profits start coming into the business.

Before going into the retail florist business, it is essential that you have a thorough knowledge of the trade and all its branches, sufficient capital, and the incentive to work hard and long hours. Many people prefer to work for themselves rather than for someone else, even if it means sacrifices such as longer hours, possibly lower pay, harder work, and the worries of ownership.

There are two ways to open a business: (1) buy an existing retail florist shop or (2) build or rent a shop and start the florist shop from scratch.

BUYING A GOING BUSINESS

The advantages and disadvantages of buying an existing business were discussed in Chapter 4. However, neither the worth of the shop, nor the price to pay for one, was discussed.

DETERMINING WORTH OF A SHOP

In determining the worth of a shop, you must consider many important questions as follows:

1. What is the asset valuation? Assets are significant only as they enable a flower shop to sell its merchandise profitably.
2. What is the book value? This is the net worth and considered

a good evaluation, but it doesn't always hold up in the market place.

3. What is the reproductive value? This is the current cost of reproducing the assets of the flower shop. Owners who use this evaluation reason as follows: cost of duplicating the business may be higher than the balance sheet shows and inflation might have affected the price. The disadvantage is that the reproduction value has a tendency to be too high a price for the business. A new flower shop can be started for less.

4. What is the liquidation value? This is the amount that would be available to the owner if the store were liquidated.

5. What is the capitalization rate? This depends on the risks involved; the higher the risk of generating projected earnings, the lower the capitalization rate.

6. What is the store's earning history? By studying net earnings, you can get an indication of what can reasonably be expected in the future. This history is recorded in income statements dating back for five years or more.

7. What are the external influences? These include the national and local economy, location of the flower shop, competition, financial condition, and management of the store.

Determining the price to pay for an existing business is something like old-fashioned horse trading. It is hard to find a formula for automatically setting a fair price on a going business. Fundamentally, a price is set on the worth of the stock and fixtures plus the value of the future earnings to the seller. Price is also influenced by supply and demand, as well as the negotiating abilities of the buyer and the seller. A three-year survey conducted at The Pennsylvania State University of retail florist shops in the United States which were offered for sale in the trade papers, resulted in the following rule-of-thumb: Start with a base figure of 30 per cent of the annual gross volume of the sales. (A figure of five times the average annual earnings or net profit is cited by some florists as a reasonable figure for good will. This comes out to about the same amount.) To the 30 per cent figure is added the value of inventory and fixed equipment. If there is a building or greenhouse involved, the present market value of these structures is added. Thus, a $100,000 annual gross volume business with $5,000 in inventory and $10,000 in equipment (such as two refrigerators, truck, cash register, etc.) might be sold for $45,000. (The accounts receivable are included in the 30 per cent base.) This is a general method to use to get some idea of a base from which to start in pricing a business. However, location, type of customers, age of business, reputation, management, type of business, number of excessive accounts receivable, and the factor of supply and demand will all help to influence this figure either up or down. All of these factors must be considered.

STARTING INTO BUSINESS

Before signing any agreement to buy a business, ask yourself how long it would take before a similar business, which you started, yourself, would yield the same income. Opening a business at a new location offers a different set of circumstances than does buying an existing shop. It is an untried proposition and will require careful planning, management, and effective advertising to build up the business. We have already discussed the location and site of the shop, as well as the various types of flower shops.

If you rent a property, you may pay from 4 to 18 per cent of your gross volume of sales for rent. The value of a lease at a given location is in direct proportion to the dollar volume of sales transacted at that location. Various studies have shown that the average florist pays from 4 to 5 per cent of annual gross volume of sales for rent including utilities. It would be better for a new business to spend no more than 4 per cent of expected gross sales, if possible, and thus have more money to put into advertising, which must necessarily be higher for a new business than for one already established.

Leasing a business property today is more complicated than it may have been some years ago. To protect yourself, be sure you know all the provisions of the lease and have an attorney go over it. Be sure to read the *fine print*. Be sure also that the lease covers at least the following points:

1. The basis or amount of rent—either flat dollar amount or percentage of sales, or a combination of the two.
2. The date that payments are due.
3. The duration of the lease.
4. Definite provisions and terms for renewal of the lease.
5. Permissibility of signs for advertising.
6. Improvements which can be made, and who pays for them.
7. The responsibility for injuries to third parties on the premises.
8. What guarantee the owner makes.

9. Right to cancel on short notice by either party.

These are the important points which you should consider before signing a lease.

FINANCING A BUSINESS

Financing a business takes thought, planning, and capital. A healthy financial structure means having enough capital available at the proper time so that the business will run smoothly. A business needs capital for two main reasons: (1) to purchase necessary fixed assets and (2) to use as working capital. Necessary fixed assets mean only those which are absolutely essential to the business. Do not throw money down the drain on unnecessary items. Working capital is the money an operation needs for wages, supplies, inventory, overhead, and the financing of accounts receivable.

Essentially there are three ways to obtain capital for a new business:

1. By investing your own money.
2. By borrowing from banks or other sources.
3. By reinvesting the profits earned by the business.

The worst way is to borrow so much that every cent must go into paying off the loan, leaving no margin for changing conditions or increasing accounts receivable. Although a loan is the easiest way to obtain capital, it is also the most expensive. It is essential that you have some capital of your own—enough to purchase the fixed assets plus at least 50 per cent of the working capital needed by the business.

To obtain a loan from a bank, you will need the following:

1. A certified balance sheet and profit and loss statement.
2. Comparative balance sheets and profit and loss statements for the past five years.
3. An operating budget covering the next full year's operation.
4. A cash flow forecast for the period covered in the operating budget.

HOW MUCH?

We said earlier in this chapter that it would take a minimum of $40,000 to start in business. How is this figured? Let us assume you are starting a small business and expect to gross around $100,000 a

Figure 5-1. Nice display of inventory items. (Courtesy, Miller Florist, Warren, Ohio.)

year. The sales will take care of the cost of merchandise, and probably pay the rent, which, combined, will be about 52 per cent of the
gross volume. Do not expect to make any profit the first two years.
You will need money to pay salaries, taxes, advertising, and other
overhead expenses for the first year. This could amount to approximately $30,000 (30 per cent of gross sales—not including rent and
wire service membership). A delivery car or truck may cost $4,000 or
more, depending upon the type and age. Two refrigerators will cost
about $4,500 depending upon size and whether or not they are new.
A cash register will cost from $300 up. Allow $600 for baskets, ribbon, wire, and other supplies, plus $600 for pottery and refrigerator
vases. The total of these expenses comes to $40,000. Your own salary
is included in the overhead, but it will be low at first (10 per cent as
shown in Chapter 6), or $10,000. These expenses can be higher or
lower depending on the scale of the business you wish to establish
and whether the equipment is new or used. These are minimum
figures, and will increase as time goes on. A large amount of money
can be invested if the florst expects to have a larger gross voluem of
business. This is one reason it is important to plan the business carefully and try to determine the expected gross volume of sales. The
$40,000 should be in cash and unencumbered since you won't have

any profit the first two years. To determine if you can afford some gadget or piece of equipment, you will need to find out by a time study if the improved method will save time and how long it will take to pay it off. Loans from a bank will increase your starting capital, but also greatly increase your operating expenses to cover high interest rates.

Operating expenses and overhead compared to cost of merchandise and gross sales will be discussed in Chapter 6.

ALTERNATIVES

Before investing money in a retail florist shop, you might wish to consider the alternatives in the industry. With the increased specialization in our society, you have alternative opportunities for developing your skills and investing your capital. You can specialize in flower production, wholesale florist activities, retail flower store management, or combine production and retailing activities. In deciding upon which type of business to enter, consider personal preference, previous experience, and availability of capital. As an example, a florist shop with a greenhouse has many advantages, but it is much more costly to establish. A greenhouse may cost from $15 to $25 a square foot. Thus a 100' × 20' greenhouse might cost $25,000 in addition to the cost of the retail shop.

Floriculture is a very specialized business. Unless you are really interested in it, perhaps you should consider some other field. However, if you are really interested in flowers and plants, there is no better field. The opportunities for women are particularly good in the retail florist business.

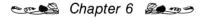

Chapter 6

OPERATING EXPENSES AND OVERHEAD

OPERATING EXPENSES

The costs of operation for the retail florist business are high and will fluctuate depending upon the gross volume of business. The total *operating expenses* will *increase* as the gross volume of sales *increases.* However, the *cost of merchandise* usually will *decrease* as the gross *increases.* The *net profit* percentage may *decrease* as the gross volume *increases.* Merchandise and labor are the two factors which change the most as the gross volume of business changes. These two figures when compared with gross sales will show the net profit for the business. All of these are tied together in the successful management of the shop.

The cost of merchandise is hard to check in many florist shop operations because many retail florists do not have separate figures for the perishable items and the inventory items such as containers, fillers, ribbon, and other materials which usually amount to from 3.5 to 6.5 per cent of the sale. The cost of merchandise is a major item of expense in the retail florist shop and offers a tremendous possibility for cutting costs. Another large item of expense is labor. The percentage of gross volume of sales utilized in labor (including the manager's or owner's salary) will vary from 15 to 30 per cent depending upon the gross dollar volume of business. A third large item of expense is that of overhead which includes rent, utilities, advertising, office expense, delivery, telephone, taxes, and depreciation. All of these items of operating expense, plus the cost of merchandise, must of course be less than 100 per cent of the gross sales if a profit is to be realized from the business. The net profit will vary from one to 10 per cent after taxes. A 10 per cent profit is the theoretical profit which most florists aim for, but few attain. Many retail florists who own their own shops do not include their own salaries in labor, but simply make periodic withdrawals, taking the profit out of the business. Many do not pay wages to their spouses who work regularly in the shop. Both of these practices lead to a false profit picture which shows the net profit to be higher than it is in reality. Pay a weekly salary to yourself as owner and to your spouse if working in your shop. In this way the net profit at the end of the year will give a truer picture of the business and the return on your investment.

Most figures published in recent years are *averages* and as such do not show the true picture of the florist industry. However, the only important figures are the ones from your own business, which show how profitably you are operating. If your profit is low, compare the percentage figures for your various operating expenses and cost of merchandise with the average given for shops in the same gross dollar volume category to see where the discrepancies occur. Then you will know where to try to change business management practices to obtain a larger profit. It may be in your cost of merchandise, payroll, advertising budget, bad debts, rent, or any other item of expense.

Let's look at some figures to see how operating expenses affect the profit picture. These, from a 1978 FTD survey, are shown in Tables 6-1, 6-2, and 6-3.

The survey showed that for the shops in this study, the gross profit ranged from 47.8 to 63.8 per cent. Total expenses ranged from 45.3 to 54.6 per cent of total sales. Principal items of expense for all groups of shops, classified by volume, were salaries and wages (ranging from 18.4 to 25.2 per cent), and operating expenses (ranging from 7.67 to 9.41 per cent).

The figures show very clearly that in retail florist shops, the cost of merchandise decreased as the gross volume of sales increased. This is due to better buying practices, as a florist can get a better price by purchasing in larger quantities and also is able to take advantage of discounts on inventory items. Expenses, on the other hand, increased as gross sales increased, due mainly to the need for more employees, resulting in a higher percentage of the gross going towards labor. Table 6-3, showing average figures for 787 FTD sample shops, indicates a variation from net profit of 17.7 to loss of 9.8.

Keep in mind that you as the owner or owner-manager do take a salary which is part of the percentage allotted to salaries and wages, besides receiving the net profit from the business. Also remember these figures are just *averages* of shops from all over the United States, and are useful for comparative purposes only. Many

Table 6-1. Profit and Expense Summary of
Limited Number of FTD Shops[1]

M=$1,000	Under $75M		$75M–$149M		$150M–$249M		$250M–$349M		$350M–$499M		$500M–$749M		Over $750M	
	1977	1978	1977	1978	1977	1978	1977	1978	1977	1978	1977	1978	1977	1978
1. Net sales	100%	100%	100%	100%	100%	100%	100%	100%	100%	100%	100%	100%	100%	100%
2. Cost of merchandise	46.6	52.2	44.1	46.7	42.7	43.2	42.1	43.0	39.9	39.4	38.8	39.4	37.4	37.2
3. GROSS PROFIT, includes other income	54.4	47.8	53.9	53.3	57.3	56.8	57.9	57.0	60.1	60.6	61.2	60.6	62.6	62.8

[1]Florists' Transworld Delivery Association, 1977–1978 survey.

Table 6-2. Operating Expenses by Ownerships Grouped as to Annual Dollar Volume[1]

As a Per Cent of Total Sales and Other Income

M=$1,000	Under $75M		$75M–$149M		$150M–$249M		$250M–349M		$350M–$499M		$500M–$749M		Over $750M	
	1977	1978	1977	1978	1977	1978	1977	1978	1977	1978	1977	1978	1977	1978
1. SALARIES AND WAGES														
Employees	18.0	18.4	18.0	18.8	22.2	22.2	19.91	20.27	23.1	25.2	18.5	19.6	21.1	20.9
2. OCCUPANCY														
Rent	3.7	3.6	3.5	3.1	3.36	3.42	3.92	3.37	1.85	1.83	2.6	1.8	2.2	2.5
Utilities (Telephone)	2.2	2.46	1.6	2.3	1.71	2.42	1.53	2.48	1.4	1.71	1.52	1.81	1.41	1.7
OCCUPANCY TOTALS	5.9	6.06	5.1	5.4	5.07	5.84	5.45	5.85	3.25	3.54	4.12	3.61	3.61	4.12
3. SELLING (other than wages)														
Advertising and promotion	0.82	1.01	1.2	1.4	2.0	2.4	2.28	2.41	2.2	2.0	3.3	3.8	4.0	4.0
Travel and entertainment	0.40	0.39	0.66	0.71	0.51	0.50	0.55	0.62	0.79	0.81	0.46	0.62	0.58	0.61
Commission—FTD "Incoming"		2.42		2.61		1.80		2.24		2.3		1.91		1.87
Clearing house charges		0.81		0.79		0.50		0.44		0.37		0.29		0.22
4. DELIVERY														
Delivery—(other than wages)	6.6	7.1	5.8	6.2	5.9	6.2	4.8	5.1	4.6	4.8	3.97	4.20	3.31	3.42
5. OPERATING EXPENSES														
(Overhead)	11.0	9.7	8.51	8.99	8.3	9.41	8.61	9.02	7.71	8.15	7.27	7.67	7.01	7.99
TOTALS[2]		45.89		44.9		48.85		45.95		47.17		41.7		43.21

[1]Florists' Transworld Delivery Association, 1977–78 survey.
[2]Does not include all expenses—does not total 100%.

Table 6-3. Expense Figures as Per Cent of Sales from a Selected Sample of 787 FTD Shops[1, 2]

	High	Low	Median
Cost of Goods	52.2	27.9	44.2
Other Income	13.2	7.7	11.2
Administrative expense	4.2	1.1	2.7
Occupancy cost	11.2	2.4	5.1
Design expenses (other than salaries)	4.4	.7	3.1
Delivery expenses	14.4	9.3	11.4
Marketing expenses (other than FTD)	9.1	.8	1.1
Operating expenses (bad debts, insurance, etc.)	6.6	3.4	4.4
Taxes	5.1	3.0	4.1
Other			
Total salaries (including officers/withdrawals)	35.5	26.1	25.7
Salaries—employees only: High—27.2; Low—17.1; Median—22.5			
Net profit	17.7	(9.8)	3.6

[1]Florists' Transworld Delivery Association, 1977–1978 survey of 787 member shops.
[2]Miscellaneous expenditures, such as utilities and other small expenses not included.

of our most successful shops are netting from 6 to 10 per cent of the gross sales as profit. Unfortunately, many retail florists are only realizing a net profit of from 1 to 3 per cent of the gross, which is less than they could get by investing their money.

Employees' wages vary considerably in various parts of the country, different cities, and in different gross volume shops. The federal laws regulating minimum wages and hours (including overtime, etc.) now cover all sizes of retail and service businesses. However, the amount you must pay varies according to your gross sales volume, assuming you are not engaged in interstate commerce. As the guidelines change frequently, write to the Regional Administrator, Wage & Hour Division, U.S. Department of Labor, for the most current information.

OVERHEAD

A retail florist shop can fail if the overhead costs get out of line. There are many items listed as overhead as seen in Table 6-2. Many retail florists also include rent, salaries, advertising, and delivery as overhead, while others count those as expenses. Some of these costs are fixed and cannot be controlled. However, others can be controlled, may be improved, and should be watched carefully. It is very

Figure 6-1. Unusual features and displays will add to the cost of overhead but are well worth it. (Courtesy, York Florist, Washington, D.C.)

easy for expenses to get out of line. Overhead costs should be watched by a suitably long-term overhead accounting system. Such items as *dumpage, overbuying,* and *bad debts* should be kept to a minimum. These are very important and often will result in a loss in profits. Excess buying with poor sales will result in too much dumpage of flowers. Bad debts will also reduce the profits. The advertising budget should be figured carefully so that you get the expected return from your expenditure. One of the most critical areas is in depreciation. It can give you a false profit picture if not figured realistically. This means figuring the loss in value of an item annually, due to wear and tear, based on the number of years you expect the item to last. There are three methods for depreciating items of equipment, and you must use the one best suited to your type of operation and expected profits. Check with an accountant as to which one to use for each item. It is important to depreciate the items carefully and truthfully so that they are exactly correct. If a 10-year depreciation is set up on an item that must be replaced in six years, a false picture is developed, and the florist is actually losing money, and may have trouble financing the new item.

The following message delivered in the 60's by a successful retail florist, Charles Hum, while he was president of Florists' Transworld Delivery Association, is something for all florists and potential florists to think about.

> While this past year has been a very good year for our industry, with business never better and sales at an all time high, we should not ignore the corresponding increases in wholesale prices, labor costs, delivery costs and in overhead.
>
> I am deeply concerned with keeping our industry's small retailers healthy, as our Association is only as vital as the retailers who comprise the membership. I am afraid that many retail florists have been so busy coping with sales, that they have not taken time to keep abreast of, and take account of, the rising costs that, if ignored, could turn these boom years into a period of serious financial difficulty for small businesses.
>
> Take time out during the summer months to look over the financial hard facts of your businesses. *Make sure you're getting paid properly for your flowers, your costs, and your services.* By being alert to costs as well as sales, you'll avoid the pitfalls that all too many small businessmen encounter.

BAD DEBTS

Bad debts occur in any business, and will not be a problem if kept to a minimum. In the retail florist business it is considered best to keep them at less than ½ of 1 per cent of the annual gross volume of sales. These can be easily checked from the records and if they exceed ½ of 1 per cent of the gross, then something should be done to correct it.

When a debt becomes bad or uncollectable, the deduction on the income tax form must be taken in the year in which it occurs. Many florists let their bad debts go much too long. You have actually loaned the customer the money, and if it is not paid, it is your money that is tied up. You cannot recover all of it, but you can get part of it by deducting it on your income tax return.

A bad debt is one which is uncollectable now and seems so in the future. This is after you have made every effort to collect it. Worthlessness is the test. It is not necessary for the entire debt to be uncollectable. You are permitted to claim a deduction for a partially worthless debt where it can be shown that the debt is recoverable only in part. A reserve for bad debts can be set up on the accounting procedure, usually based on past experience. For a new florist, it will be based on a *good guess* the first year.

If a bad debt is paid later after it has been deducted, you must report the payment on your income tax return as income, but only to the extent that the earlier charge-off helped reduce your taxes. The amount of tax saved has nothing to do with it. It is the amount of the bad debt that you were able to use advantageously as a deduction that is considered here. It is best to check with an accountant on this.

PERSONAL WITHDRAWALS

The amount of money you withdraw from your business for personal needs can have a tremendous effect on your shop, for good or evil. You can restrict your personal withdrawals and assure yourself of a solvent business, or you can withdraw more than is wise and lose the business. Determining the amount of cash you can take out of a business isn't as simple as it seems. Obviously you should not withdraw more than is represented by your net earnings. You must also hold back enough of the net earnings for expected repairs, new equipment, and other items.

Business survival dictates that you consistently withdraw less cash than your business earns. How much less will depend on your basic personal needs and your business needs.

Every year the business gets older so that eventually you will need to modernize. New equipment is needed periodically and even though you depreciate these items yearly, the total depreciation charges won't begin to pay for the replacements. You will be short, which means you are not staying even with today's higher prices.

To determine basic withdrawals, consult the previous year's income tax returns and estimate the net earnings. From this deduct the estimated income tax. Then determine the extra amount that will be needed for necessary replacements and set this aside. Figure the extra amount needed to increase the inventory and equity and deduct this. The resulting figure (which may be only ½ to ⅔ of the originally estimated earnings) is now divided by 12 to give some idea of the monthly withdrawal. You must stick to this and not be tempted to spend more on personal needs or you will be in financial trouble at the end of the year.

In a partnership it is no less important that there should be restraints and controls on personal withdrawals to keep the partnership from being strained.

Expenses and the costs of operation of a retail florist shop must be checked constantly so that the business will show a proper profit at the end of the year. Many florists check their income and expenses daily or weekly, while others do it monthly. Compare current figures with last year's figures to avoid any trouble at the end of the year. A successful retail florist should realize the expected profit, after taxes, if the business has been managed properly.

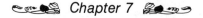

Chapter 7

STORE EXTERIOR AND WINDOW DISPLAY

STORE EXTERIOR

The exterior of the retail florist shop—including the appearance of the store and the display window—accounts for approximately 35 per cent of all sales according to several surveys. This figure is a little lower if most of the business is by phone, although many customers will still drive by and see the window displays. A customer's first impression of the store is very important, so the exterior must not be neglected. The design of the store should be in keeping with the rest of the shops in the neighborhood. There is no reason, however, that a shop in an older section of town cannot be modernized if it is not done to extremes. Don't make it too different!

There are essentially five things that make a store stand out, even at a distance:

1. The paint or building material of the front gives the first and best impression of the store.
2. Lighting at night helps to make the store stand out. Good lighting will include not only lighting inside the store but also the window display and the spotlights in the window and outside of the shop. People usually walk on the side of the street with the most lights, so this is a good means of advertising the shop.
3. The window is the most important part of the exterior of the shop and will be discussed in detail later in this chapter.
4. The sign should be prominently displayed so that people not only can read the name of the shop, but also can know the type of store. The sign should show up both day and night.
5. Plants and flowers always attract attention. If there is space in front of the store, and if the city ordinances will permit them, the use of window boxes and tubbed plants will more than pay for themselves.

Figure 7-1. Exterior stone carries into interior of the shop. (Courtesy, Penny Hill Flowers, Wilmington, Del.)

Figure 7-2. A very modern store front. (Courtesy, House of Flowers, El Paso, Tex.)

To find out how the store looks to others, try this simple test. Drive around aimlessly for awhile in your car and then turn around and drive slowly towards the shop. Use your imagination and pretend that you are an average citizen, not a florist. How good is the location? Are the parking facilities adequate? What is the first impression of the shop? How does the shop stack up with others in the neighborhood? Are the windows clean? Does the window display catch the eye and make one stop and look at it? How effective is the sign? Is it neat, clean, and freshly painted? If these impressions are good, and you like it, great! If not, then some changes must be made.

DISPLAY WINDOWS

The window display is one of the most powerful media of advertising in the world today. It is often referred to as point-of-sale advertising or visual merchandising. It leads all other forms of advertising in sales return for dollar expended. Window display as an art has reached its present high state of development as a direct result of competition. The primary purpose of a window display is to stimulate sales. One retail florist said, "Take something simple, display it properly and it will sell." The greatest advantage of window displays

Figure 7-3. Window display is attractive from both outside and inside the shop. (Courtesy, Fries Florists, Lancaster, Pa.)

over other forms of advertising is its low cost. Just ½ to 1 per cent of gross sales may be enough. The cost of flowers used in the display, which must be charged to advertising, will probably raise this by another ½ per cent.

Some florists say that "display is half the sale." A good window display will involve your creative imagination. The window is the biggest factor in accounting for up to 35 per cent of the sales in many shops. There are numerous types of windows from small, waist-high windows to those that stretch from sidewalk to roof and encompass the whole front of the store. The shop may have from 1 to 10 windows across the front. The majority of florists' shops in this country have from 1 to 3 windows of varying sizes. The modern trend in shops today is for the windows to extend from floor to ceiling with most of the front of the store in glass. These window walls lend themselves better to tall decorations, large displays, and help to open up the whole store to the customer on the street. They also provide more light inside the shop. Raised windows may be cheaper to decorate, but they are not as effective, nor do they give as much display area.

Fresh Material

Use flowers and plants in florist shop windows since they are the best form of advertising for a retail florist. Many other industries use flowers and plants to help sell their products, so why not the florist? Some pottery and novelties can be used, but there should always be some fresh plant material in the window. The windows should be changed quite often—at least every week—except when there is some very spectacular display for a holiday like Christmas or Easter. Then it can remain two weeks. The display should never be permitted to get dirty. A few large florists in the larger cities change their displays several times a week and one even changes them every day. The theme of the display should be appropriate for a holiday, local event, special occasion, or other idea. Simple designs are usually best, with just one main center of interest or focal point in each window. The window displays should not be crowded. Originality in display is necessary if the display is to be successful.

Eleven Seconds

A window display is a flashing picture to the average pedestrian. He / she approaches it, observes it, and responds to it, all in less than

Figure 7-4. Interior displays can be seen through the window from the outside. Co-author explains merchandise to employee. (Courtesy, Alexander's Flowers, Cleveland, Ohio.)

11 seconds. This picture must be attractive and interesting to bring customers into the store. Since the average pedestrian spends less than 11 seconds considering a window, the display has to "talk fast"—and even faster for passing motorists.

Every display window should do four things:

- **Attract attention.** The window display should attract the attention of people passing by. One way this can be accomplished is by motion in the window. Anything that moves will attract attention. Or it can be accomplished by color, illumination, or some unusual form or arrangement. The use of revolving colored disks in front of a spotlight will combine the two factors of light and motion very effectively.

- **Create interest.** After you have attracted the attention of the customer, you must create an interest in your display so the customer will stop and look at it. This can be accomplished by the timeliness of the display if it ties in with a holiday or occasion. It can also be accomplished by the use of a demonstration on how to use the merchandise, or by the use of novel or unusual flowers or merchandise items in the display.

 ✑ **Change the interest into desire.** The next step is to transform the interest in flowers to the desire for flowers or other merchandise on display. This is accomplished by stressing the use and need for flowers for a particular occasion. Try to sell the idea that flowers are the *best bet* and better than anything else. Display flowers and arrangements in such an attractive way that the customer just can't resist them. Turn browsers into customers.

 ✑ **Get the customer into the shop.** The final function of the window display is to get the customer to enter this store. This can be accomplished by the reputation of the store which has been built up through the years. It can also be accomplished by the physical layout of the shop to make the entry very easy. A wide level doorway and entrance is much better than steps or a narrow door. A light and pleasant store that looks inviting will also help to get customers into the shop, as will a shop that smells good.

The display is an information link between the consumer and the store. A display tells what is available, frequently at what price, and why it is available. The "why" factor (psychological motivation) is being emphasized in sales promotion today. Any florist can use it in displays because it is mainly appealing to people's emotions.

The following principles of a good window display must be kept in mind:

1. Each window should have a central theme or idea (and only one).
2. Avoid crowding because people will not stop and look at a cluttered window.
3. Design the window from the standpoint of the passerby. Remember the retailer has only 11 seconds to stop a pedestrian and get across the message.
4. Have a definite sales appeal to the display. The ultimate aim is to sell the merchandise.
5. Use simplicity of design if it is to be most effective.
6. Make sure the glass and floor are clean at all times.
7. Use the principles of good design and color harmony.
8. Replace the old and wilted flowers as soon as noticed. This should be checked at least once a day.
9. Use price tags that can be easily read on the merchandise. Whether or not the merchandise in the window is priced will depend on the type of shop and whether you think it is

Figure 7-5. Christmas window display. (Courtesy, Evans-King Floral Co., Forty Fort, Pa.)

worthwhile. Most florists and other retail merchants price all merchandise in their windows, and today's consumers like and appreciate it. Many florists price everything in the window and also in the store.

Do not give the windows a vacation in the summer; make them work for the business. Flowers are just a bit harder to sell during these months when home gardens are filled with blooms, and when some of the customers are away on vacation. Therefore, the window should be as good or better than usual. Fortunately, summer is also the time when a florist ordinarily has more time than usual to spend on the window display. Use this time to good advantage, set up some unusual displays, and keep it as clean as possible.

Window Backgrounds

The open versus closed background for windows has been debated for many years. There are advantages and disadvantages to both. Sometimes it depends entirely on the physical setup of the store. The open background is the more modern approach and of more advantage to most stores. It is less formal and lends itself to more casual shopping. It costs less to decorate since the owner can use the whole store for a background. Other advantages of the open background are as follows:

1. Displays can be viewed from both inside and outside the store.
2. Passersby can see inside displays as well as customers in the store. People seem to attract people, so use this as drawing power.
3. The store will be brighter, possibly requiring less electricity.

There are a few disadvantages to the open background, such as:

1. People are sometimes so interested in seeing what is going on in the store that they don't see the display in the window.
2. It is sometimes difficult to build a suitable background for a specific display.
3. More dirt and flies may accumulate in the store if not properly cleaned each day.

The fact that people passing by can see the florist working in the store is considered a disadvantage by some and an advantage by others. Some florists are even remodeling their shops so the customers can watch the designers practice their art. It seems apparent that the advantages of the open background outweigh the disadvantages in our retail florist shops of today.

Lighting

Window lighting is very important if you are to get the full value out of the window. Lighting works as a sales tool both for identification and attraction, but of first importance is identification. The first stress is on what is being sold; secondly, the trade name of the shop should be visible, with the accent on flowers. New colors have been developed to increase the effectiveness of lighted plastic signs. A new and sharper white enhances the brilliance of the reds. Incandescent lights are again being used for outdoor lighting. In many shops, the entire store front is a merchandising tool, using the wide glass fronts

CHECK YOUR DISPLAY

A check list can help you to evaluate your window display. Such a list should include:

1. Neatness and cleanliness. Sloppy housekeeping can reduce the effect of even an original display of quality merchandise.
2. Brightness. Colorful and appealing merchandise should be lighted so as to create the proper atmosphere. This increases the customer's ability to appraise the merchandise.
3. Selling message. Cards or props should clearly tell why the merchandise is desirable.
4. Focal point. Every display needs a central or dominant area to attract attention quickly. It should stop traffic so people will really look at what is in the window.

Evaluate your display by scoring each factor as follows: 0–no credit, 1–poor, 2–good, 3–excellent. Total possible points: 51.

ARRANGEMENT

1. Window not too empty _____   3. Main items stand out _____
2. Window not too full _____   4. No clashes in color _____

CLEANLINESS

1. Window clean _____   4. Props and fixtures clean _____
2. Floor clean _____   5. Merchandise (flowers) clean
3. Background clean _____   and not wilted _____

LIGHTING

1. Lights hidden _____   3. Some spotlights used _____
2. Lights clean _____

SELLING POWER

1. Background and props   4. Props do not overshadow
   seasonable _____   merchandise _____
2. Selling points stressed _____   5. Related merchandise
3. Show cards tell the story _____   used _____

TOTAL POINTS _____

as display cases which are invaluable when properly lighted. Size, brightness, contrast, and time are factors used in setting up eye-catching displays. Deluxe cool white fluorescent lighting outstrips all others for store use. However, as flower colors appear different under various fluorescent lights, this should be discussed with an expert from the power company so that the colors of the flowers will be enhanced. Some lights will give reds a bluish cast which can be disastrous—both red poinsettias and red roses must have a clear, bright color if they are to sell.

In the window displays, colored lights will attract attention and bring out the colors of the flowers. Use spotlights on the featured display items. For a more natural look, use spots the same color as the flowers, although white light can be used if you prefer. Recess the lights in ceiling of window area or wall; direct spots so they will not shine or glare into the eyes of the observer on the street or the customer in the store. To really show off the display to the best advantage, the light in the window should measure 150 to 200 foot-candles of light overall plus the spotlights.

One point frequently overlooked by store owners is the fact that as persons grow older they require more light with which to see. What may be adequate light for you may be entirely inadequate for older customers. Also, as women rarely stop at a dark, poorly lighted store—and almost two thirds of the florist's customers are women—the window must be adequately lighted to bring in the feminine customer. A test was made recently of 100 persons passing a store window with ordinary lighting. Only 17 stopped. When proper lighting was installed in the same window, 46 out of 100 persons stopped. This was 2½ times more than with ordinary lighting.

Periodically check the effectiveness of your window displays with the score card shown on page 63.

Chapter 8

INTERIOR SALES AND DESIGN AREAS:
FIXTURES AND EQUIPMENT

The interior of the shop with its physical features, equipment, and layout must be planned in advance. The layout of the shop is presented in Chapter 10, along with suggested model designs and remodeling ideas. This chapter will deal with the general interior for all shops with a discussion of the fixtures and equipment needed.

The interior of the store is very important because of the impression given people when they step into the shop. Will they be pleased or disappointed? The décor and style must tie in with the exterior and the windows. A customer does not want to step from an ultramodern front into a Victorian interior. The tie-in must be graceful and subtle with the interior a continuation of the exterior.

The color scheme of the interior is important and must be one that enhances flowers rather than detract from them. It must not offend the customer. It must be well planned and executed. The ceiling should be white or off-white to make the store as light as possible. White on the walls, however, is bright, and will not show off the flowers to the best advantage. Most florists have found that a soft grey, green, or grey-green will be best and the one that makes most flowers stand out to the fullest advantage. Black is an excellent background for many flowers, but is not the most practical. Who wants the whole wall of a shop black? However, a small section of black for a special display or feature would be excellent. Some florists prefer paneling on one or two walls rather than paint, and redwood or walnut is very pleasing and can be used for a good display of pottery and flowers other than red. For utility as well as appearance, some florists are using pegboard walls which are painted off-white, beige, or grey-green.

Good circulation is an essential feature of the interior. There must be ease of movement in the store for both the customers and the employees. In a large store this is necessary so that the store does not look crowded and cluttered with too many display tables, plants, and other items or fixtures. In a small shop the best method for good circulation is to have one open area in the center of the store with the display tables and shelves along the walls. Customers should have easy movement to see the displays and an open path to the display refrigerator. Customers should be able to move freely through the store without bumping into one another, except when the store may be crowded at holidays. Circulation should also be provided for the sales personnel so they can move around and show various items to customers without running into other customers. Employees should also be able to get to the wrapping counter and cash register very readily. Naturally the circulation will be curtailed or reduced at holiday time when the store will have more merchandise on display than during the other days of the year.

The interior of the store should be planned with ease of cleaning in mind. Everything on display must be dusted periodically, and

Figure 8-1. Designing is done in the sales area in some modern retail shops. (Courtesy, Fries Florists, Lancaster, Pa.)

this should be accomplished as easily as possible. The floor of the store must be cleaned frequently, and an interior planned carefully with this in mind will cut down on the hours of labor needed for this job.

Easy access to all supplies should be considered to cut down on the steps and time spent by employees both when waiting on customers and when making up design pieces.

There should be a systematic placement of articles of merchandise and supplies in the store. Items which are commonly used together should be displayed together. Displays should be grouped so that the customer can see all dish gardens in one spot, brass items in another, baby novelties in another, religious articles in another, and so on. There should be a systematic arrangement planned ahead of time to make the store as attractive as possible to the customer. This will help to make it easier for the customer to buy. Impulse items must be easily seen to be sold effectively.

Heating and air conditioning must be provided and should be a compromise of the preferences for the plants, customers, and employees. A cooler temperature is best for the plants and flowers, but not always for people. In the winter, heat must be provided, but the store should certainly be kept cooler than a person's home. Most retail florists are using air conditioning in the summer. It is beneficial to the plants, the customers, and the employees. Contrary to the belief of some retail florists, the air conditioning is not harmful to plants and flowers, and the cooler temperatures will make the cut flowers last longer. There is no evidence of injury to pot plants or foliage plants if the air conditioning is regulated properly.

RETAIL SHOP AREAS

The number of areas in the retail florist shop will depend on the size of the operation. There must be a sales area and a workroom or design area. The control center is very important and may be the office, a separate room, or just an area of its own which is convenient to both the sales and design areas. If the shop is large enough, a consultation room is very helpful for the discussions of funeral and wedding flowers. Sometimes this is a separate room, but often it is just one area in the salesroom, or the office itself. Storage rooms and restrooms must be provided.

The floor of the store should be a material which will not become slippery when wet, nor treacherous for walking. It should be a material that is easy to clean. Linoleum and rubber tile are better than wood. Asphalt tile is excellent but is more expensive. One of the best materials, found in some of the smarter shops, is carpeting. It is very attractive and easy to vacuum, but it is essential to get a good grade which will not spot with water. Outdoor carpeting is excellent for retail florist shops. Concrete floors are very hard on the feet, particularly for the employees. Flagstone, slate, and terrazzo are other materials which make attractive floors for retail florist shops.

Mirrors help to make a small shop look larger. However, don't use them on more than one wall or the effect will be destroyed.

Lighting

Good illumination is necessary inside the florist shop. Customers like to see a well-lighted store and want to see the merchandise easily. In the average retail shop, 150 to 200 foot-candles of light is desirable. In small shops the lighting will be about the same for the whole area. However, in larger shops the shop can be divided into different areas with various light intensities such as are recommended for most department stores. They use the 1-3-5-10 formula for foot-candles of light for lighting the store:

   1—Circulation area, 20 to 30 f.c. (no selling)
   3—Sales area, 3 times #1, 60 to 90 f.c.
   5—Showcase and counter display, 5 times #1, 100 to 150 f.c.
   10—Featured displays, 10 times #1, 200 to 300 f.c.

Retail florist shops do not have a separate circulation area as such, but they do have sales, displays, and featured displays to be lighted. Be sure there is adequate light in the shop. Light up the store, work area, and interior to the point where customers can see to make the right purchase of flowers, and employees can easily see to properly arrange the flowers.

Fluorescent lighting, like all other elements that go into a store or display area, contributes towards a psychological effect called atmosphere. All atmospheres are described as warm or cool. The warm white lamps help to produce a warm mellow atmosphere which is not too applicable to a retail flower shop. The cool white light helps to produce a cool, crisp atmosphere of modern interiors, and blends well with the natural daylight coming from the windows. Illuminating engineers recommend the deluxe cool white fluorescent light for most retail florist shops. It combines excellent color rendition with good efficiency, to produce an interior atmosphere

Figure 8-2. Acoustical tile ceiling and indirect lighting are used in remodeling a retail shop. (Courtesy, Fries Florists, Lancaster, Pa.)

which is similar to natural daylight. Thus, you can make your shop more attractive and enhance the appearance of the flowers, which will result in corresponding benefits to customers and you, yourself.

Incandescent lamps can be used very effectively in a retail florist shop. They will give the effect of sunlight on a foliage plant display. Featured displays can receive 200 foot-candles of light from the use of 150 watt R-40 floodlights.

Whatever type of light is planned for the shop, it must be adequate.

Equipment

In the sales area, *the display refrigerator is the most important piece of equipment.* (See Figure 8-3.) It should be located opposite the front door so that it will catch the eye and draw the customer to it. The

Figure 8-3. Display refrigerator with shelves and heated glass doors. (Courtesy, Frederick's Flowers, Souderton, Pa.)

display refrigerator is called the "silent salesperson." Keep a well-filled refrigerator on display at all times. It should contain not only cut flowers but made-up floral arrangements as well. Display refrigerators range in size from 3 to 36 feet long with custom-built ones of any size. The 8-foot refrigerator is the most common size although large shops will certainly need either a larger one or perhaps two of medium size. Many florists say that the proof of their profits comes from the excellent floral displays that they have daily in their display refrigerator. It is easier for the salesperson to sell from this display, as well as to upsell various purchases. Often customers will spend $20.00 rather than $15.00 for an arrangement when they see the difference in the display refrigerator. The manager should check the display refrigerator daily to make sure it is always well arranged and attractive. Frequently the display refrigerator is used for made-up arrangements, priced ready to go, while the stock of cut flowers is carried in another refrigerator called the storage refrigerator. The latter refrigerator is in the workroom.

The second most important piece of equipment in the store is the cash register. It is important to spend the money to purchase a good one. The government requires accurate figures from all businesses today, and many states have sales taxes which must be collected and accounted for on their records. The cash register can help to give a day-by-day accounting of your business, including cash and accounts receivable sales. Also you can keep track of your sales according to type of merchandise if you wish. The size and complexity of the machine will depend on the individual business. Fortunately, today's cash register not only keeps money but also can be a sales record keeper for the whole organization.

Florist shops differ greatly in the kind and amount of furniture and equipment in the store. Not all of the things discussed here will be found in all of the shops. The size of the store and the physical layout will, in a large part, determine how many of these things can be used. You will benefit from using the latest equipment to save time and work. Computers are being used by some florists today.

A wrapping table and counter should be an integral part of every salesroom whether large or small. It takes too much time and is a nuisance to have to go to the back workroom to wrap each order. Frequently the cash register will be placed on the wrapping counter. You can take advantage of the space under the counter for shelves to hold wrapping paper, tissue, plastic, ribbon, string, scissors, boxes, foil, stapler, and other items commonly used in wrapping orders for

Figure 8-4. A consultation corner for discussing wedding and funeral flowers. (Courtesy, Royer's Flowers, Lebanon, Pa.)

the customer. Good packaging is essential to the success of the business.

A writing desk, well stocked with a variety of small cards for all occasions as well as some plain ones, should be included in the salesroom. Most florists, but not all, consider it a courtesy to provide a place for the customers to sit down while writing their cards rather than to expect them to stand up and write while leaning on a desk or counter. Place the desk and chair out of circulation against a wall to assure privacy to the customer. The desk chair may also be used when holding consultations for wedding or funeral flowers or elaborate decorations in a small shop which does not have a separate room or area for this service.

Display tables and shelves are a necessary part of the sales area in a retail florist shop. The number and size will depend on the size of the shop. Provide as much display area in the salesroom as you can without giving the shop a cluttered look. There must be room to adequately display pottery, glassware, novelty containers, figurines, dish gardens, pot plants, permanent arrangements, and fresh flower arrangements. You may also handle other lines of merchandise such as brass, milk glass, candles, and many other items to be displayed for the customer. The display tables or stands should be of a mate-

Figure 8-5. A display area built into the wall. (Courtesy, Royer's Flowers, Lebanon, Pa.)

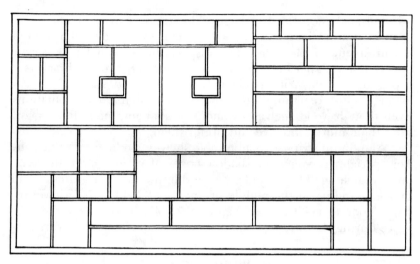

Figure 8-6. A 12-foot wall of wooden display shelves designed with various sized spaces for pottery and knickknacks.

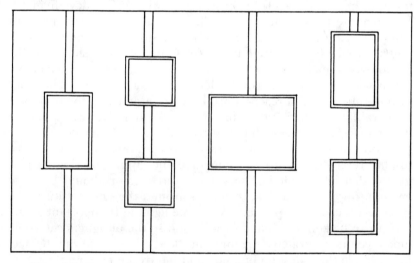

Figure 8-7. Free-standing shadow boxes on dowel rods along a 12-foot wall for feature displays.

rial which will fit in with the decor of the rest of the store. They may be wood, aluminum, wrought iron, or plastic and have glass, marble, formica, tile, or plywood tops. Some florists replace the glass with plywood at holiday times to display plants and other items with a minimum chance for breakage. The shape can be rectangular, round, square, triangular, dog-leg, or semicircular, and of a size that is convenient to the store. The display shelves can be of various materials and either built into the wall (Figure 8-6) or on brackets in a pegboard wall. With pegboard, brackets, and shelves you can arrange—and rearrange—the shelves in unlimited combinations. Even though wood shelves are more permanent, many florists consider them more attractive and prefer them.

Aluminum strips with adjustable shelves can be used effectively. For special arrangements, shadow boxes of various sizes and types are eyecatching. These can be recessed in the wall, set against a wall, or free-standing in the middle of the room, held with a dowel rod from floor to ceiling. (See Figure 8-7.) To increase your display space during the various holidays, add movable tables and carts.

WORKROOM

The workroom is another very important part of the shop and must be planned carefully in advance with efficiency in mind. Whether the area is large or small, you will need certain items of equipment for a successful operation. The storage refrigerator is essential. It may be a separate unit, as is found in many shops, or, for economy, in smaller shops one unit may be placed as a divider between sales and work areas with doors opening into each. The front section functions as a reach-in display refrigerator and the back part as a walk-in storage cooler for the workroom. However, a shop doing a larger volume of business will find it absolutely necessary to have one or more separate storage refrigerators, plus one or two display refrigerators, to accommodate the supply of flowers and greens that are needed. The storage refrigerator should be large enough to walk into and have shelves around the sides to utilize the space as efficiently as possible. Adequate lighting is important so the cooler can be kept clean and orderly and so the designers can coordinate colors accurately. Arrange the flowers systematically by age, for example the oldest on one side and the freshest on another. You might mark the cans the designers are to use first, or place them next to the door. Discard daily any material which is too old to use at all so that old, dead, smelly flowers do not accumulate. Assign one person to be responsible for rearranging the flowers in the refrigerator each day or for making sure that it is done.

The worktables should be of a convenient height for the comfort of the designers. You might prefer tables which are now avail-

Figure 8-8. Supplies conveniently located for each designer. (Courtesy, Bonnie Brae Flowers, Denver, Colo.)

able that are easily adjusted to the height of the designer. Ideally there should be a separate table for each designer. Five feet long by three feet wide is usually ample; a larger table takes too much space, and designers tend to spread out more than necessary. Many shops have several persons working at one large table; when they have been built in a U-shape, an S-shape, or an E-shape, these units will efficiently accommodate more than one designer. Each work station should be well lighted and have shelves and drawers for storing the materials most commonly used. (See Figure 8-8.)

Ribbon storage shelves or racks, another necessity, should be centrally located and easily accessible to all designers. In some shops the ribbons are stored on shelves along the wall next to the workta-bles; others provide an individual rack for each person, either at the end of the table or over it, suspended from the ceiling. (See Chapter 10 for more details.) A water supply must be located in a convenient spot for the use of the designers as well as for the unpacking of shipments. Many shops have two sinks for these purposes, but a more convenient method is to run a pipe along the ceiling over the entire area, with a hose and spray or mist nozzle suspended beside each designer's table. Thus the designer can easily fill the container and later mist the completed arrangement without leaving the table. A deep sink is desirable where the flowers are unpacked and put in water, so that tall cans can be filled easily. Hot water should be pro-vided here because the stems of all fresh flowers (except orchids) should be put in warm water (100° to 110°F.) to harden them when they arrive from the wholesale florist or greenhouse.

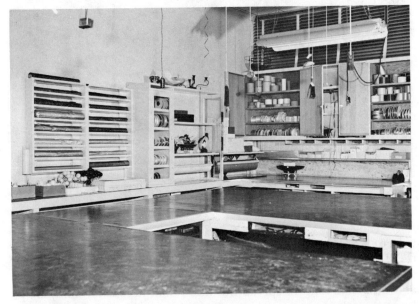

Figure 8-9. A design area with rolls of foil and ribbon neatly arranged. (Courtesy, Bonnie Brae Flowers, Denver, Colo.)

A separate corsage table or bar may be set up in one corner of the workroom where all the special materials necessary for corsage making can be kept readily at hand. (See Figure 9-11.)

Keep an order board in the control center or at the front of the workroom where it is convenient not only for the manager but also for the designers. There are many different ways to keep orders spearated and in order.

Most of the rest of the space in the workroom is devoted to storage and circulation areas so that the employees can move around freely without getting in each other's way. Provide as many shelves and cabinets for storage as possible. The more of the everyday materials that you can keep handy in the workroom, the better—it will save time and steps. If the workroom is small, keep just a few of such varied items as pottery, brass, novelties, baskets, papier-mâchés, frames, boxes, and other inventory items on the design room shelves. Store the rest of the stock in a storage room in the basement, attic, or garage. If all the containers are stored in another room or downstairs, a lot of valuable (and expensive) designer time will be lost.

Wherever your storage room is located, be sure the items are kept in good order and priced immediately upon arrival in the store. Be sure to include postage or shipping charges in your cost of merchandise before marking them up to retail price. Many florists arrange their stock systematically on the stock room shelves, with tags showing the date of arrival, supplier, stock number of the item, and the retail price. Some florists number their most frequently used stock items and enter them in a card file inventory system for reordering before the last one or two are used up; this system only works if an accurate count is kept as the merchandise is sold or used.

Retail florist shops differ greatly in size and arrangement. In addition to these essential items of equipment just discussed, many more can be used if the shop is large enough. There are also hundreds of inventory items listed in the florist supply catalogs—wire, ribbon, floratape, paper, containers, novelties, papier-mâchés, dried material, Christmas supplies, silk and polyethylene materials, etc.—from which you must determine your needs. It is doubtful if any one florist has every item that is available in the industry.

Chapter 9

EFFICIENCY THROUGH TIME AND MOTION

EFFICIENCY

Efficiency is a hard term to describe because it includes so many facets, but it is one which you must understand and apply to retail methods to be a modern business manager. Basically, an efficient retailing method is one which will produce the desired result with a minimum of effort, expense, and waste. Planning for efficiency must be applied to all work areas, all functions including delivery, and all employees. By boosting the efficiency of workers, you may solve many labor problems. Some tips to help prevent or solve labor problems are:

1. Break the job down.
2. Furnish the best tools.
3. Write down duties.
4. Train employees.

Improve efficiency through remodeling and rearranging the store. Chapter 10 discusses efficiency in both the sales and the design areas by showing examples of more efficient arrangements of equipment.

Sometimes efficiency requires innovative thinking rather than following your pre-conceived ideas. Consider some examples found in shops around the country. The Max Schling shop in New York City has incorporated the following in moving the shop after 39 years in one spot: Platforms in the display windows are on casters, and when they are pulled away from the window, they expose a continuous line of plant boxes which are filled with seasonal plants. The display refrigerator is so designed that the doors can be left wide open and the customers can walk in along with the sales staff to pick out their flowers. There is no sill to stumble over as the levels between the store and the inside of the box are the same. The designing space is out in the open in the store so that there is constant activity, which is of considerable interest to the customers. Heating, ventilation, and air conditioning are tied together in one thermostatically controlled system so that temperatures in the store are always cool and comfortable. Another example, Cauthorn's Flowers, San Antonio, Texas, has streamlined the bookkeeping system to increase efficiency in the office. It revolves around one simple statement form, designed to eliminate the accounts receivable ledger and speed up statement preparation. Frederick's Flowers in Souderton, Pennsylvania, has almost 5,000 square feet of sales area in which all of the displays are movable to give greater flexibility to the shop layout.

Many retail florists have redesigned their shops with efficiency in mind both in the sales/circulation area and in the workroom area. Some excellent examples are Royer's Flowers, Lebanon, Pennsylvania; Surf Florist, Miami Beach, Florida; Quality Flower Shop, New Orleans, Louisiana; and Tubbs of Flowers, Corpus Christi, Texas. All of these have installed design areas with top efficiency in mind.

These are just a few of the hundreds of ideas which contribute to efficiency in a retail florist shop.

TIME AND MOTION

Time is perhaps the most precious single commodity used in the retail flower shop. All florists are extremely conscious of time and its value—they are often faced with a lack of it causing loss of business, prestige, and money. Minor investigations in time-motion studies of retail flower shops have been carried on at Texas A&M University as an experimental problem at the undergraduate level, at Cornell University, and at The Pennsylvania State University. (See Figure 9-1.)

Time-motion studies have as their salient purposes the *saving of time* and the *economy of motion* in any work operation. The study of these two factors has evolved into the science of time-motion.

The procedure used in any study of a given operation or job may be divided into three general steps.

1. **Operation analysis.** The job is analyzed with the idea of eliminating every unnecessary movement and operation without affecting the quality of the end product. The best method of doing an operation is chosen by scientifically

Figure 9-1. A time-motion expert collecting data for The Pennsylvania State University studies.

measuring one method against another. This is ordinarily done by the close observation of a trained analyst, by precise stop-watch measurements of time, and by analysis of still or motion pictures.

2. **Work standardization.** A careful survey is made of existing facilities to find ways to improve the materials, tools, equipment, methods, and working conditions, so the employee can do the best work without being hindered or tired by inadequate facilities. It is here, perhaps, that the greatest contribution may be made to the florist's field by time-motion studies.

3. **Determination of "standard time."** After the first two steps are completed and time-motion principles are applied to the data obtained, the analyst calculates how long it should take an average worker, working under average conditions, to do the job. This "average" time is known as the *standard time.*

Application of time-motion study methods to the flower industry is relatively new. Observations indicate that *in most flower shops too little attention is given to convenience or the saving of labor in the arrangement of equipment or storage areas in workrooms.* Studies have shown that some designers make up floral pieces faster than others, an indication that improved work habits may be possible.

Labor costs of flower design are rising steadily; hence, any saving in labor which will increase output of salable floral arrangements with the same work force promises to improve the net income from the individual shop.

An increase in net returns is possible from two approaches: (1) greater output and more sales from the work of current employees and/or (2) the need for fewer employees in production of the present output.

Examples of Time-Motion Studies

For a clearer understanding of time-motion methods, consider a study conducted by The Pennsylvania State University Floriculture Division on time and motion in two different retail flower shops. You can use these same procedures to discover the efficiency of your own designers.

Designer Efficiency

Two types of retail flower shops—a family shop and a more

formal business—were observed in this study. Measurements were taken of both shops, and scale drawings were made.

To limit the scope of the study, only funeral vases and corsages were considered. Work on funeral floral pieces was observed on the day of the single two-hour viewing. Corsage designing will be considered later in this chapter.

A modified flow process chart as shown in Table 9-1 was used. This shows the observations reported for an average operation. Figures reported for "Price Range" were approximations.

During the preliminary observations when procedures were being established, the most common location for storage of various items was established in order to record usual distances traveled by designers in subsequent observations. For example, the papier-mâché funeral vases had no standard location in either shop. When arrangements were made immediately after flowers were delivered by the wholesaler, the fresh supplies often were used before the storage cans were placed in the refrigerator. When this occurred during an observation, the most commonly used vase location was noted and travel and time data to the proper flower storage area were included in the record.

Shop No. 1 was owned and operated by a married couple who shared the design duties; the man (Designer A) doing most of the work on funeral flowers and the woman (Designer B) doing most of the corsage assembly. Their son did the major portion of the delivery work.

The physical layout of the salesroom was near optimum in size and compactness for the average retail flower shop. The workroom (Figure 9-2) had many inconveniences and considerable waste space due to the lack of storage facilities.

The telephone was in a good position, easily accessible from both the sales and work areas. The only water source—a small, old-fashioned sink—was in a small closet behind the wrapping table in the salesroom. Additional storage space, located in the basement, was extremely cluttered, and much time was wasted looking for the desired items.

The workroom refrigerator was too small to hold an adequate supply of flowers. As a result, the designer often had to go to the salesroom refrigerator in the front of the shop for flowers.

Designer A took an average of 23.6 minutes and traveled 295.4 feet to complete a funeral vase. Designer B took 23.2 minutes and traveled 241.9 feet for a similar piece. (See Table 9-2.)

At this shop, the designer placed chicken wire in each vase to

Table 9-1. Flow Process Chart of Observations Reported for an Average Operation[1]

Item: Standard funeral vase

Florist shop: No. 1

Designer: B

Checker: H. W. Willits

Total distance: 235.8 feet

Total time: 18 minutes

Price range: $5 to $10

UNIT TIME (in minutes)	DISTANCE (in feet)	SYMBOL	EXPLANATION
	16.7	→	To vase storage
	16.7	←	Return with vase
		●	Cut, roll, and stuff wire into vase
	40.8	→	To front refrigerator
	40.8	←	Return with gladioli
		●	Place gladioli
	40.8	→	To front refrigerator
	40.8	←	Return with pompons
11:35		●	Place pompons and greens
11:35	39.2	→	To storage for delivery

[1]Standardized engineering symbols are used: → for initial travel, ← for return travel, and ● for operations.

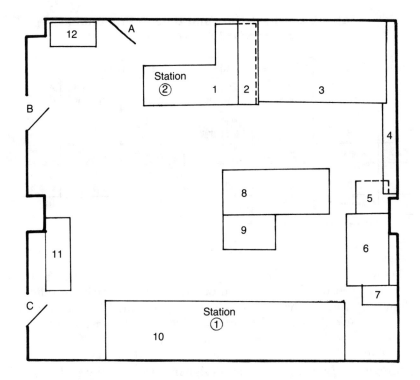

1-Secondary make-up table
2-Ribbon and netting supplies
3-Rear refrigerator
4-Miscellaneous shelves
5-Safe
6-Desk

7-File cabinet
8-Billing table
9-Auxiliary make-up table
10-Main make-up table
11-Storage shelves
12-Telephone table

Doors
A-To front of store
B-To cellar storage
C-To incinerator

Figure 9-2. The layout of a workroom in Shop No. 1 in a study conducted by The Pennsylvania State University.

hold the flowers, and only two types of greens were used: lemon leaf and a broadleaved fern. One of the most time-consuming operations was the trip to the sink to fill the vase.

The difference in the average distance traveled can be accounted for by two factors: Designer A always worked at Station 1 (Figure 9-2) and often made two trips for flowers, while Designer B,

Table 9-2. Travel Time and Data in Preparation
of Standard Funeral Vases

Shop	Designer	Distance (feet)		Time (minutes)		
		Mean	Standard Deviation	Mean	Standard Deviation	N[1]
1	A	295.4	68.1	23.6	12.8	13
	B	241.9	50.4	23.2	4.3	5
	Average	268.6		23.4		
2	C	92.1	20.0	11.0	1.2	6
	D	89.8	17.0	18.5	6.9	8
	Average	90.9		14.7		

[1]"N" stands for number of observations.

who worked at Station 2, frequently brought all of the flowers needed from the refrigerator in one trip. The similarity in time for design of funeral arrangements can be explained by the fact that Designer A did most of the funeral vases and thus made better use of his time while at the worktable.

Figure 9-3 shows average distance traveled for Designer A while arranging a funeral vase. The designer started at the order board (No. 6) and went to the design table (No. 1) with the order, then to the storage (No. 2) for a vase, and returned to the worktable. Then he went to the sink (No. 3) for water, to the front refrigerator (No. 4) twice for flowers, and then to the front of the store to the delivery table (No. 5). He then returned to the order board to start again. One trip to the refrigerator for flowers could have been eliminated.

Better use of the existing storage facilities could be made at Shop No. 1, and opportunities were ample for the addition of units that would increase capacity and efficiency.

The method of filling containers consisted of filling one small can several times and emptying it into the larger ones, which would not fit into the small sink. Facilities for filling containers with water could be vastly improved by the relocation, or expansion of those facilities now existing. With a slight change in present routine, a hose could be connected to the faucet for use in transferring water to vases, resulting in a marked increase in efficiency. A new sink could be installed in the workroom which would be much more satisfactory and more efficient.

At least one trip to the refrigerator by Designer A could be elim-

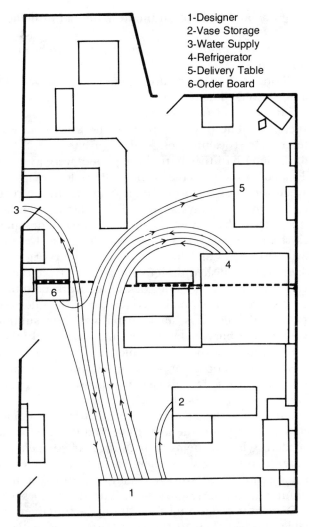

1-Designer
2-Vase Storage
3-Water Supply
4-Refrigerator
5-Delivery Table
6-Order Board

Figure 9-3. Travel pattern by Designer A in Shop No. 1 while designing a funeral vase. Area below dotted line enlarged in Figure 9-2.

inated by getting all necessary flowers for each arrangement the first time.

If the vase storage were located under the design table, 33.4 feet of travel also could be eliminated.

The use of new automatic boxes would considerably shorten the time required for packing cut flowers.

Desk work should be kept on the desk instead of being allowed to clutter a worktable.

Since this survey, many of these conditions have been improved in this shop.

Florist Shop No. 2 offered cards, pottery, and novelties for sale in addition to flowers. The owner (Designer C) had an assistant (Designer D), a driver, and two salesclerks, who served the customers entering the store. The physical space of the workroom was somewhat cluttered, but efficiently designed (Figure 9-4).

Due to the length of the shop, three phones were a convenience. One was located in the extreme front of the sales area, one in the office between the sales and work areas, and one in the rear of the workroom. Designer C always answered the phone when he was in the shop; the salesclerks answered only when the two designers were out. This system worked well, because the designers were the only ones familiar with the availability of flowers in the refrigerator. The driver picked up the finished designs for delivery from the refrigerated storage. The salesclerks came back to the workroom only when supplies were short in the display refrigerator in the salesroom.

Whenever business was slack, usually in the summer, the salesclerks were kept busy making bows, net puffs, and other storable items, and in dusting the shelved merchandise. The driver kept the windows washed, storage areas in order, and performed other similar tasks. All of these are efficiency improvement factors which will result in a more profitable business.

Immediately after the lunch hour on the days that funeral arrangements were on order, the driver checked the number and size of vases needed, selected them from storage, filled them with vermiculite, water, and some greens, then placed them on the designer's table. This job required an average distance of 29.4 feet and a time of four minutes per vase (Figure 9-5). The driver picked up the order (No. 1), went to the storage (No. 2) for the container, took it to the worktable (No. 3), then to the sink (No. 4) for water and returned to worktable, then went to the refrigerator (No. 5) for greens and returned to fill the container. This time could be reduced by filling the container with water on the way from the storage.

Even though the observed number of vases completed per designer was about equal (Table 9-2), Designer D usually did the majority of the funeral work, with Designer C inspecting. The two designers worked from opposite ends of the table (Figure 9-4), with Designer C at Station 1 and Designer D at Station 2. However, their overall travel for the average funeral vase arrangement was equal,

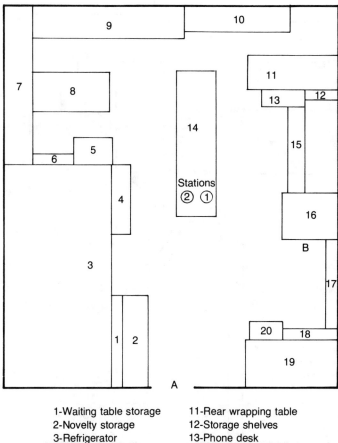

1-Waiting table storage 11-Rear wrapping table
2-Novelty storage 12-Storage shelves
3-Refrigerator 13-Phone desk
4-Ribbon storage 14-Main make-up table
5-Storage 15-Bow storage
6-Ribbon Storage 16-Can storage &
7-Storage   Order Rack
8-Table for storage 17-Vase storage
9-Storage 18-Vase storage
10-Potting table 19-Lavatory
20-Sink

Doors
A-To front of store
B-Down steps to cellar storage and outside

Figure 9-4. The layout of the workroom in Shop No. 2 in a study conducted by The Pennsylvania State University.

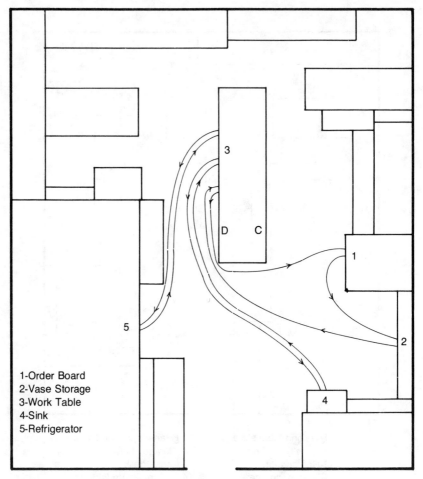

Figure 9-5. The movements of the driver in Shop No. 2 while filling containers for the designer.

thus accounting for the similar distances recorded on the flow charts.

The average distance traveled and time required for funeral vase assembly (Table 9-2) for Designer C was 92.1 feet and 11 minutes and for Designer D, 89.8 feet and 18.5 minutes. The experience of the designers probably accounts for the difference in time required for each arrangement.

Figure 9-6 shows the travel of Designer D for an average funeral vase arrangement. The designer started at the order board

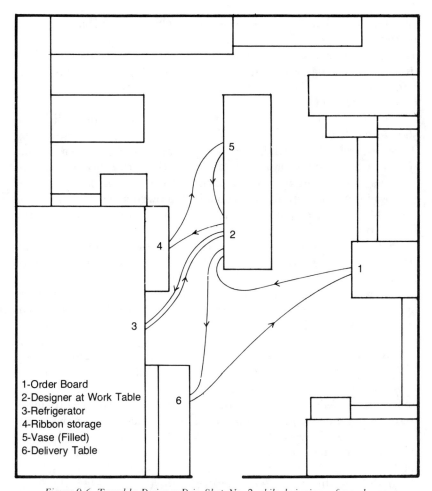

Figure 9-6. Travel by Designer D in Shop No. 2 while designing a funeral vase.

(No. 1), went to the design table (No. 2), then to the ribbon rack (No. 4), picked up the container the driver had filled (No. 5), moved to personal work station (No. 2), then went to the refrigerator (No. 3) and returned, then to the delivery table (No. 6), and finally returned to the order board to start again.

A double nozzle on the hose which could be used both to fill containers and for misting corsages, would eliminate the need for trips to the sink to fill funeral vases.

Rolls of ribbon would be more conveninet if placed nearer to the design table.

The two firms studied differed widely in organization and in methods of designing standard funeral vases and corsages. Shop No. 1, a family business, had many of the advantages and some of the disadvantages that are characteristic of this type of establishment. Shop No. 2 was a more formal business unit with the advantage of efficiency of operation.

Results of the respective travel and time observations of the two shops revealed a variation much in favor of the larger business firm. These figures also verified that individual designers differ in time required to make a design piece. Some of the differences are due to experience and pressure of the work load on a particular day.

The standard deviations (Table 9-2) showed a wide variation for each designer in distance traveled and time required between the several observations made in this study.

Changes in layout and location of supplies in Shop No. 1 could result in a much more efficient operation, with a resulting saving of labor.

Wages are constantly rising and the number of paid employees in the retail florist shop is increasing. Wages account for more than 50 per cent of the florists' total overhead. As one of the highest paid employees, it is important to have the designer work as efficiently as possible in order to keep overhead costs to a minimum. The first step is to arrange the workroom as efficiently as possible. Locate the design tables as centrally as possible between the sink, storage refrigerator, and storage cabinets. An excellent arrangement to improve efficiency is to locate the designer, container storage place, and storage refrigerator in a triangle with the water supply near by. This is the same triangular arrangement as is used in designing efficient, modern kitchens. Some shops have sinks built into the tables themselves. Since the path from the storage refrigerator to the design table is the one a florist keeps the hottest, it should be as short as possible.

Efficiency in Workrooms

A study was developed at The Pennsylvania State University to evaluate efficiency in the design areas of 15 retail florist shops which were visited to provide data to develop methods which would facilitate efficient production by the following methods: (1) to establish time standards for designing several selected pieces in retail floral shops and (2) to design efficient workroom layouts which could be used as standards for renovating, modernizing, or designing the workroom in a retail florist shop. (See Figure 9-1.)

Time studies were conducted by the university in 15 retail florist shops, whose size categories were as follows: $50,000 to $75,000; $75,000 to $100,000; and over $100,000 annual gross volume of sales.

Six set designs were timed in each shop. Three funeral baskets or papier mâchés and three artistic designs were timed.

The designers were timed with a stop watch, and the times were recorded on flow process charts. Elemental operation times, elemental transportation times, delays, and explanations for the times or delays were all recorded on the flow process charts. Flow diagrams were made by drawing lines of the designers' travel patterns on floor plans which were made prior to the actual timing of the indidivual. By measuring these lines, transportation or travel distances were determined.

After time studies were conducted in the 15 retail florist shops, four efficiently designed workrooms (Figures 9-7, 9-8, 9-9, and 9-10) were simulated in the retail floriculture laboratory at The Pennsylvania State University. Four floriculture students, trained in design, were timed in these workrooms as test shops. Each designer was timed making six set designs in a particular shop: three funeral pieces and three artistic designs. These designs were of the same quality and the same price ranges as those made in the 15 visited retail florist shops.

The results for the visited shops and the test shops were analyzed statistically and comparisons made. In most cases, *test shop times were significantly different from the visited shops.*

For artistic designs there was a 39.56 per cent decrease in total time when comparing the visited shop times to the test shop times. There was a 20.13 per cent decrease in operation time and an 89.10 per cent decrease in transportation time. Transportation distance decreased 76 per cent, showing the benefits of efficiently planned work areas.

For funeral baskets there was a 34.92 per cent decrease in total time, a 19.12 per cent decrease in operation time, a 91.85 per cent decrease in transportation time, and an 80 per cent decrease in transportation distance.

Time standards were computed for both the funeral baskets and the artistic designs. Separate time standards were developed for the visited shops and the test shops, since test shop times were significantly different than the visited shop times in most cases. Time standards were computed for the operation times as well as the total times, since total times varied more between shops than the opera-

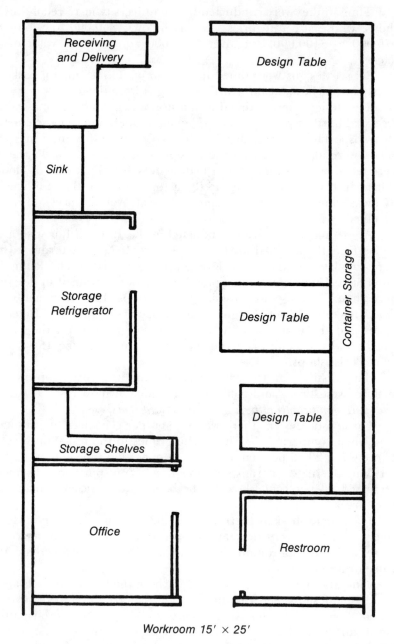

Workroom 15' × 25'

Figure 9-7. Simulated workroom for two to three designers, with the design table along the wall.

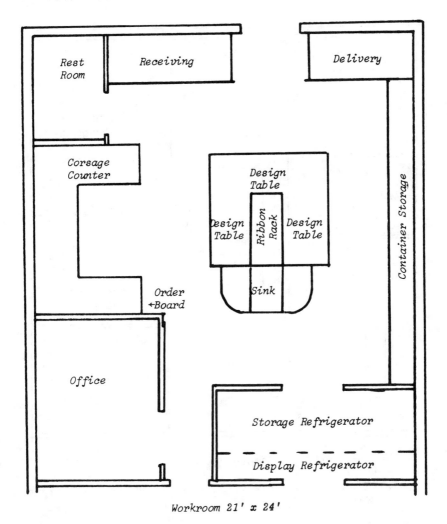

Figure 9-8. Simulated workroom for two to three designers, with the design table in the center of the room.

tion times. A valid time standard could not be developed if times varied too greatly between shops.

The computed time standards were as follows for the visited shops:

Funeral basket operation time, 16.79 ± 1.40 minutes;
Funeral basket total time, 21.45 ± 2.64 minutes;

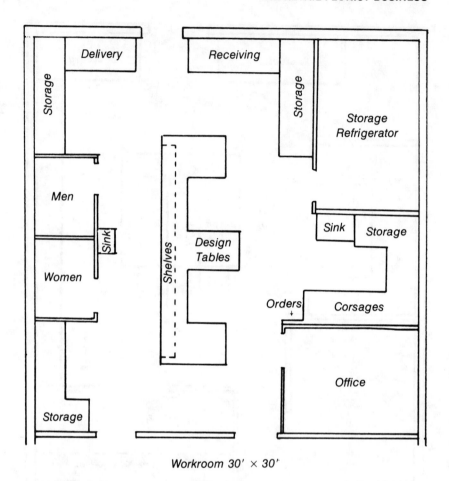

Workroom 30′ × 30′

Figure 9-9. Simulated workroom for three to five designers, with an E-shaped design table in the center of the room.

Artistic design operation time, 9.44 ± 1.16 minutes; and
Artistic design total time, 13.12 ± 1.72 minutes.

The time standards for the test shops were as follows:

Funeral basket operation time, 13.58 ± 0.48 minutes;
Funeral basket total time, 13.58 ± 0.53 minutes;
Artistic design operation time, 7.54 ± 0.54 minutes; and
Artistic design total time, 7.93 ± 0.51 minutes.

These are to be used for comparative purposes only with designers in a specific retail florist shop.

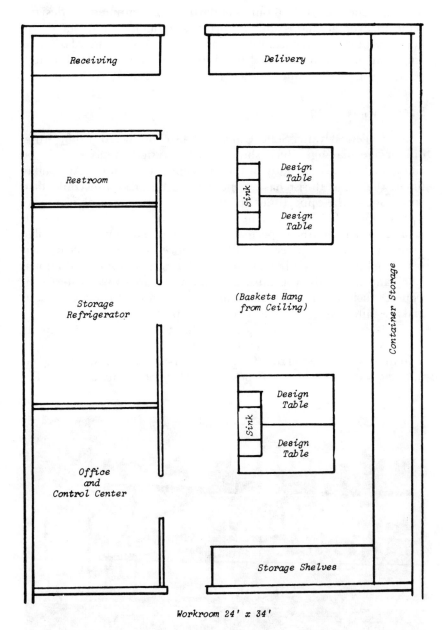

Figure 9-10. Simulated workroom for four to six designers, with paired design tables in the center of the room.

Since the visited shop time standards were computed for designs made in average shops under normal conditions, these standards would be of more practical value than the test shop standards. These time standards could be used for distributing the work load, determining cost, or detecting inefficiencies in the retail florist shop.

Efficiency in Corsage Making

The Pennsylvania State University also conducted a time study on corsage making, which showed many wasted motions could be eliminated by careful study of the problem and situation. At holiday times, the retail florist has an increase in business and could take advantage of the opportunity to run the operation at peak efficiency and economy. By reviewing the records of previous sales, you should be able to estimate the expected corsage sales. This makes it possible to order sufficient material well in advance and to contact trained personnel prior to the holiday season. To fully utilize the additional labor and materials, you must plan the work area for greatest efficiency. Much time is wasted in many shops hunting for materials and making unnecessary trips around the shop.

A corsage table was designed so that all materials were readily available and arranged so that corsages could be made in a minimum amount of time. (See Figure 9-11.) The corsage cabinet was designed in three sections, each 24 inches high, 24 inches wide, and 8 inches

Figure 9-11. A corsage cabinet designed for efficiency.

deep. They were arranged like an upside down U with the sides angled so that all materials were within 2 feet of the designer. The cabinet was set so that it was 3 inches lower than the designer's elbow for maximum ease and efficiency. The center unit contained seven compartments across the top to hold various sizes of wire. Under this was a styrofoam block to hold corsage pins and dowel rods holding ribbon and floratape. Under this were compartments for made-up ribbon bows. The left section was composed of compartments for various colors of chenille stems and flocked wire, dowel rods for rolls of net, and compartments of ready-made net puffs. The right section contained six 10-inch cans or vases to hold the flowers used in the corsages.

For this experiment 400 corsages were made using roses, carnations, and cymbidium orchids. Rose corsages were made by two methods: (1) the standard method using #22 and #26 wire, floratape, tied with corsage thread, artificial rose leaves, and a bow attached and (2) the flocked wire method using a ready-made frame of flocked wire, roses placed on the ends of flocked wire, and a bow.

Carnation corsages were made by two different methods: (1) the standard method using #22 and #26 wire, floratape, thread, and a bow of ribbon and (2) the chenille stem method using two chenille stems with a flower at each end, and a bow.

Cymbidiums were made by two methods: (1) the standard method using #20 and #26 wire, net puffs, floratape for wrapping and tying, and a bow of ribbon and (2) the water tube method using #20 and #26 wire, net, water tube, floratape, and a bow of ribbon.

All of these methods were divided into two assembly methods. Half the corsages in each group were made and timed on an individual basis, and the other half made and timed on an assembly line basis wherein all the frames, bows, and net puffs were made ahead of time, and enough flowers were wired and taped for six corsages. Then the corsages were assembled and timed as a unit to be divided by six for an average. This was repeated four times for a total of 24 corsages of each type under each method.

Average time required to make a six-looped bow was 20 seconds, to make a flocked wire frame was 45 seconds, with 7 seconds to wire a rose or carnation, and 6 seconds to tape a rose or carnation.

When the cymbidium orchids were made, the test showed little time difference between the standard wiring method and the tube method, as long as both were prepared by the same technique—both by assembly line or both by individual construction. The dramatic difference was the time saved using assembly line procedure compared to the individually made process. With the standard carnation corsage there was a reduction in time for total operations when made on the assembly line. Also there was a marked reduction in time with roses in the assembly line over the standard method.

Results showed that the time for making rose corsages with the standard method was cut in half on the assembly line and cut by three-fourths with the flocked wire method on the assembly line. The time for carnations in both cases was cut about one-quarter in time, and for cymbidiums the time was cut in half by use of the assembly line method.

Outstanding results were demonstrated when all the net, bows, and frames were made ahead of time and the corsages were made by the assembly line method in batches of at least six at a time. The time savings follow for various methods, prepared by assembly line method, compared to the time required to make the corsages on an individual basis, preparing net, bows, etc., as needed.

		Per Corsage	*Per 100 Corsages*
Roses:	Standard wiring	2 min., 10 sec.	3 hrs., 30 min.
	Flocked wire frames	1 min., 18 sec.	2 hrs.
Carnations:	Standard wiring	50 sec.	1 hr., 20 min.
	Chenille stems	20 sec.	½ hr.
Cymbidiums:	Standard wiring	1 min., 30 sec.	2 hrs., 30 min.
	Water tube	1 min., 23 sec.	2 hrs., 15 min.

Making bows, net, and frames ahead of time lowers the time involved in the actual assembly of the corsage materials. The assembly line method of making corsages in units of at least six will greatly reduce the time per corsage for roses and carnations. This will result in a saving of several hours for each 100 corsages made. For 10,000 corsages this could mean a saving of 200 to 300 hours. The greatest difference in this experiment occurred with rose corsages made in the standard method and one at a time, taking 4 minutes 45 seconds as compared to rose corsages made on an assembly line on ready-made frames, taking only 32 seconds. The figures shown were for one particular designer and should be compared with the time it takes each particular designer to make a corsage. These are not stated as averages for any and all designers, but are to be used for comparative purposes only.

MOTION ECONOMY

Many of Niebel's 10 major principles of motion economy can be applied to a retail flower shop. They are:

1. Motion of both hands simultaneously.
2. Tools and materials located close to and in front of the operator.
3. A fixed place for all tools and materials.
4. Gravity feed bins (not so useful to a florist).
5. The placement of tools and materials in a usable position.
6. Drop delivery (not applicable to a florist).
7. Let feet do the work of hands where possible—such as a pedal-operated sink.
8. Locate materials and tools for best sequence of motion.
9. Height of work space should be arranged to fit the operator (self-adjusting design tables).
10. Lighting comfort should be provided.

With these in mind, go through your shop analyzing each operation along the following lines: (1) Materials—Can cheaper materials be used? Is material uniform? Are materials of proper weight, size, and finish? (2) Handling of materials—Can material handling be reduced? Can distances be shortened? Are there delays in getting material? Can conveyors be used to move materials? (3) Tools and fixtures—Are they the best for the work? Are they in good condition? Are there enough on hand? Can both hands be used? (4) Operation—Can an operation be eliminated? Can the work be done in multiple? Can the sequence of operations be changed? Can two or more operations be combined? Would rearranging the work space help? (5) Operator—Is the operator qualified for the job? Can work conditions be changed? Can the operation be improved by further instruction?

TIMESAVER TIPS

ﻩ Keep the display refrigerator for display only. Offer arrangements as well as a selection of cut flowers and corsage flowers. Store flowers for use in the design room in the storage refrigerator. If you display, unrefrigerated, flowers which will be used by the designer during the day, consider them active storage. Place them in the sales area as close as possible to the design room.

- If your sales volume requires more than one designer, hire a sales clerk (at a lower wage) to wait on customers. The designer will accomplish more without interruptions, and the clerk can assist the designer during lulls between sales. (Some owners who are also designers prefer to wait on customers in order to establish personal contact with the customers. This factor must be weighed in relation to the time involved.)

- Have the salesclerk write enclosure cards and delivery tags, etc., at the time of selling to save the designer's time. Do, however, keep a small supply of these items and a pen at the design table for emergency use.

- Install a telephone extension near the design table.

- In addition to the wrapping counter in the sales area, set up a small wrapping table close to the design table to serve the designer when special wrapping is necessary.

- Insist that tools used infrequently by several people—heavy-duty shears or wire cutters, pliers, etc.—be returned promptly to a permanent place on the design table.

- If two designers work side by side or facing each other, provide a complete set of tools to each. Assign a work station to each designer on your staff; provide as much basic equipment and as many frequently used supplies as can conveniently be stored at that location.

- Prepare stock containers each morning before business gets started; stuff and fill them with water and flower preservative; store them near the design table. Put extras for a big day on the delivery table where they will gradually be replaced with completed arrangements.

- Employ a designer's assistant, at least for the busier days of the week, to prepare stock containers, unpack flowers, and keep active storage containers of flowers filled.

- Make every trip count; try to avoid going either way empty-handed—bring something back on the return trip. Better yet, load up both arms! Make up two arrangements before going to the delivery table or display refrigerator; by carrying one in each hand you cut your trips in half.

- If completed orders are stored in or near the refrigerator, collect the materials for your next order and bring them back to the worktable on your return trip.

- Select all flowers and foliages needed for an order in one trip to the cooler to avoid a second trip.

When many similar orders are to be filled consecutively, pull large refrigerator cans of the required flowers and foliage and place them near the design table.

During the day keep "hard" foliages, which will not wilt down if kept out of refrigeration, close to the design table.

TOP TIMEWASTERS

At a time-management seminar conducted by SAF, the following 15 items were reported to be the top *timewasters* of today's retail florist:

1. Telephone interruptions.
2. Drop-in visitors.
3. Meetings (both scheduled and unscheduled).
4. Crises.
5. Lack of objectives, priorities, and deadlines.
6. Cluttered desk and personal disorganization.
7. Ineffective delegation and involvement in routine or detail.
8. Attempting too much at once and unrealistic time estimates.
9. Confused responsibility and authority.
10. Inadequate, inaccurate and delayed information.
11. Indecision and procrastination.
12. Unclear communication and instructions.
13. Inability to say "no."
14. Leaving tasks unfinished.
15. Lack of self-discipline.

Chapter 10

STORE LAYOUT, REMODELING, AND MODERNIZATION

Store layout, remodeling, and modernization are the first steps to efficient retail operations as discussed in Chapter 9. Each shop, of course, is an individual case since there is no one average retail flower shop. However, efficiency is the keynote to the modern shop from the standpoint of management, operation of sales and design, and the customer. In an efficient retail florist shop, a full-time employee should produce approximately $50,000 in annual gross sales. This varies in shops all over the country from $45,000 to $60,000 per full-time employee. If your shop is not averaging $50,000 you need to develop more efficient methods of shop operation.

LAYOUT

Many retail businesses spend thousands of dollars studying store layout in order to have a more efficient operation. The general retail store is most concerned with square foot return, and how many actual dollar-sales can be realized from any given space. Too few retail florists give enough consideration to how their space is utilized.

In the general layout of the florist shop, an order must be sold, processed, made up, and delivered by the most efficient method with the least effort.

A good layout means putting the right equipment in the right places, so materials may be processed most effectively by the right method in the shortest time possible, and requiring movement and transportation of the shortest distance.

If possible, avoid locating in—or building—a long, narrow shop, because the areas are elongated, requiring extra traveling time between work stations. Large shops are not necessarily efficient. Small shops, being more concentrated, shorten distances, thus saving time, motion, and energy.

The selling area must provide ample area for circulation, display, and for taking an order. In most retail florist shops, this area is separated from the design area. However, some remodeled shops combine the design area with the sales area. (See Figure 8-1.)

Certain principles have been developed for doing work effectively at the design table: position the individual so most of the work is done within a convenient arm-reach; arrange the materials in an arc approximating the arrangement; conserve energy, avoid fatigue, and save time by using minimum body movements; rearrange the shop to permit the most convenient location of all items and the easiest handling of them; improve working routines; and locate tools and supplies conveniently.

REMODELING

The important and expensive step of remodeling is taken for

Figure 10-1. A remodeled office with windows into sales areas. Comfortable chairs for consultation. (Courtesy, York Florist, Washington, D.C.)

two reasons: first, to increase the efficiency of the shop; second, to attract new customers.

When you are going to remodel, put the greatest emphasis on the planning period. Take time to go into all of the physical needs of your shop, the most convenient placement of utilities, and your own personal taste. Take into consideration all of the following important factors: your overall goals, location, store size, equipment layout, lighting and electrical plan, water sources, heating and air conditioning, décor, and financing.

It is difficult to give specific details on the remodeling of a shop, because each one is an individual case. There is no one perfect plan. However, there are basic considerations which would apply to any shop.

Start with the front and exterior of the building—it has been estimated that 35 per cent of an average florist shop's sales result from the appearance of the store front. A good coat of paint may be all that is necessary to improve this.

Most modern retail florist shops today have an all-glass front, or at least as much glass as is practical. Whether the shop has one, two, three, or more display windows in the front does not matter. The main point is to extend them from the floor to the ceiling, so that most of the front of the store is glass. In this way, a passerby can see into the store and see customers in there. People attract people. The store itself will be lighter, be more inviting, and form a background for the window display.

You may need to change the exterior of the store to fit in with modern ideas. Choose from a wide variety of materials, including black granite, marble, wood siding, stone, brick, and concrete block. The main idea is to tie in with the other buildings in the neighborhood, particularly those recently modernized.

Include a new sign in the plans. Be sure that it is neat, large enough to be seen, lighted at night, and tells the customer that this is a flower shop, as well as giving the name.

The ideal entrance to a retail shop does not require a ramp or steps. For more visibility choose a glass door, single or double, but wide enough to allow easy access for large boxes and arrangements.

Select flooring that will be easy to keep clean and yet not too slippery when a little water is spilled. Either vinyl or indoor/outdoor carpeting are excellent. Choose a color and/or pattern that will not show every speck of dirt or muddy footprint.

The décor of the interior must tie in directly with the exterior. You may wish to consider paneling with redwood, walnut, etc., or you may prefer to simply repaint with a shade that will enhance the colors of your merchandise. Soft greens or neutrals are always good. For a special display, however, black would be a good choice to provide strong contrast to the flowers. For a simple, inexpensive remodeling job a fresh coat of paint may be all that is necessary for floor, walls, and ceiling.

As you think about solutions to your ceiling problems, be sure to consider adding light fixtures either in the window or the interior of the shop. Any changes must be made at the same time to avoid excessive costs. (See Chapter 7 for the advertising value of good lighting.)

Is your ceiling old-fashioned? Modernize with ceiling tile.

Is your shop too noisy? Install acoustical tile for beauty and quiet.

Is your ceiling too high? Suspend a dropped, false ceiling framework and complete with tile for an intimate, modern effect.

Want to conserve energy? Choose a light colored tile, whether patterned or plain.

When remodeling, determine the relative position of the sales and design areas by the fixed position of built-in refrigerators.

Place the cash register toward the rear of the sales area to induce customers to come further into the shop as well as to save steps for designers who may double as clerks.

The furniture and fixtures must tie in with the rest of the décor in the sales area. The size of your store and your volume of business will determine what units you will need. Probably the simplest setup would consist of one wall of display shelves, a writing desk, one or two movable display tables, a wrapping counter, and a display refrigerator. For a larger shop, add more display shelves, more tables—possibly tiered, a flower cart, writing desk with chair, and several chairs for customers. Only the size of the shop limits how many display tables you can use.

Although a whole wall may be utilized for varying-sized shelves and irregular spaces for pottery (see Figure 8-6), some areas may have shadow boxes to highlight particular displays. (See Figure 8-7.) For a modern look, paint the background of the shadow boxes black. The arrangement of display areas can be symmetrical or asymmetrical.

SALES AREA

The sales area is very important. Be sure it is attractive, inviting, not cluttered (except perhaps at holidays), and conducive to flower sales. Allow enough circulation area so that the customers can move around freely. In a small shop, the circulation area would simply be the open space in the middle. Provide enough room to handle customers on an average day without excessive crowding.

The most important piece of equipment in the sales area is the display refrigerator. Place it opposite the front door, so that it is easily seen by the customers entering the shop. This is the "silent salesperson" and should be so well lighted and attractive that it draws the customers to it.

Although some florists wrap all orders in the back room, an item to be taken by a customer should be wrapped in the front where the purchaser can see it being done. This will save time and steps for the salesperson. Make the wrapping counter easily accessible to employees, but not open to customers. Store wrapping supplies under the counter. To complete the sale efficiently, place the cash register here also.

Several possible floor plans have been designed for a workable sales area and are shown in Figures 10-2, 10-3, and 10-4.

Figure 10-2 shows the arrangement of a small sales area 20' × 28', with just one large window display and three display areas. There is good circulation in the shop even though it is small and has an open path back to the display refrigerator. A writing desk is located to the right of the refrigerator and the door to the workroom and office on the left. The wrapping counter is in the back left corner.

Figure 10-3 shows a larger store (30' × 40') with two display windows. Again there is circulation with an open path to the display refrigerator which is located in the far right corner. Besides the two window display areas, there are six display tables (including a flower cart) of various shapes and sizes to show the variety that might be found in the store. There is also a wrapping counter, desk, and three chairs for the customers.

Figure 10-4 shows the largest shop in this series (40' × 40') with plenty of circulation, and both an office and consultation room behind the display refrigerator which again is directly opposite the front door. There is a very symmetrical arrangement of the many display areas and tables. At holidays the glass shelves on the round tier tables can be replaced with plywood shelves to reduce the chance of breakage when you are displaying heavy blooming plants.

Study these floor plans to pick up ideas that you can adapt to your own store layout.

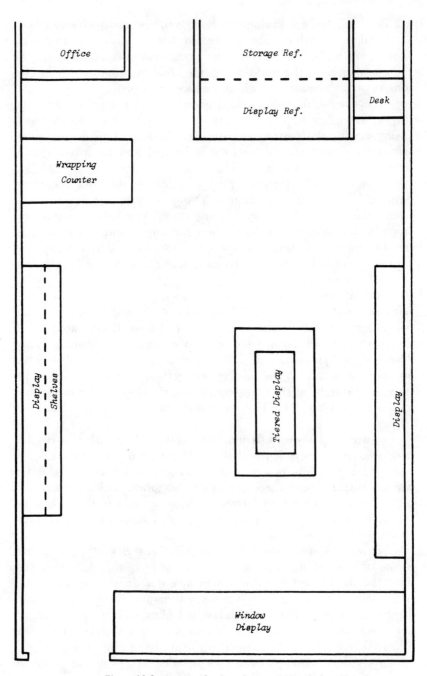

Figure 10-2. An example of a sales area 20' × 28'.

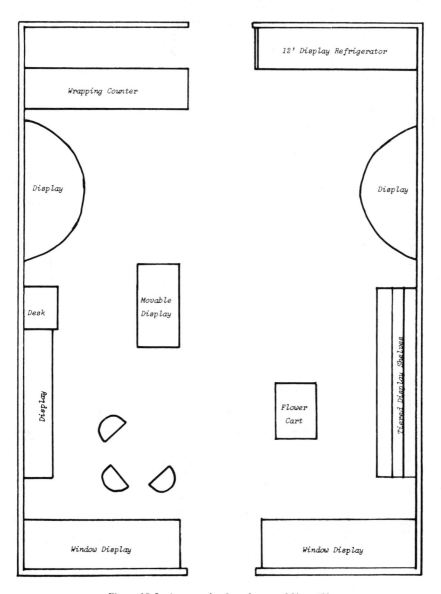

Figure 10-3. An example of a sales area 30' × 40'.

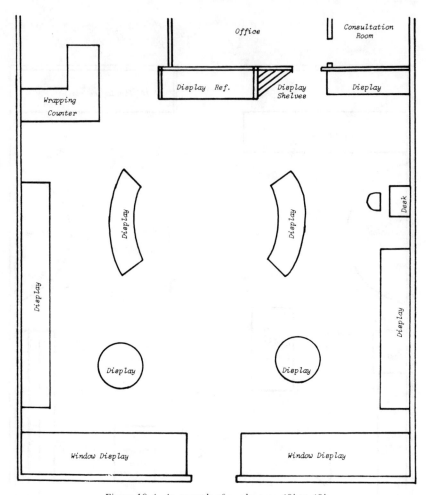

Figure 10-4. An example of a sales area 40′ × 40′.

WORKROOM

The design of your workroom can increase or lose your profit. In remodeling, plan and place each unit with the designers' efficiency in mind. Arrange the equipment to save both time and steps. More production from the same number of employees will increase your sales volume without an increase in overhead—which is another way to say "You increase your profit"! Therefore, an efficient workroom is well worth carefully detailed planning before remodeling.

The control center with order board should be easily accessible to the salesroom, workroom, and office.

Locate the design tables centrally between the storage refrigerator, sink, and storage cabinets. Allow each designer an area approximately 5 feet long by 3 feet wide, with drawers and shelves either above or below. Adjust the height of the table to the individual designer. Provide each designer with a clipboard or wall-mounted hooks to keep orders where they can be seen. Store bolts of ribbon and net on shelves or racks convenient to all the designers. For top efficiency have a separate table for corsage making where all materials and packing supplies can be kept within easy reach of the designer.

Whether to place the design tables in the middle of the workroom or against the wall is a long-standing controversy. Both arrangements have advantages and disadvantages. The ones along the wall have more drawers and shelves for materials used by the individual designer (Figure 10-5), but that space may be needed for storage of items used by everyone. Base your decision on the volume

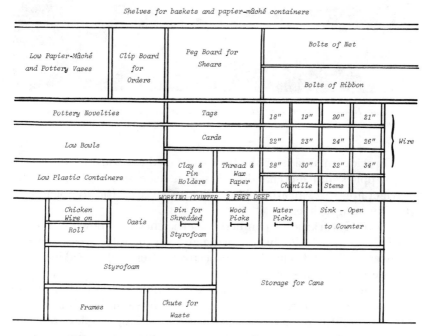

Figure 10-5. A sample work counter along the wall with all supplies conveniently located for designer efficiency.

of business and the physical layout of the present store. Whether you use separate tables for each designer (Figure 10-6) or U-, E-, or S-shaped worktables which accommodate several designers, be sure they are designed and located to give the greatest efficiency. You'll save money in the long run by installing an overhead water line with a nozzle above each designer's work station.

Figure 10-6. Individual worktables with sink for each designer. (Courtesy, Royer's Flowers, Lebanon, Pa.)

Provide an area near the back door of the workroom for receiving supplies and merchandise; install a deep sink and storage for refrigerator vases nearby. Also, allocate an area for completed orders awaiting delivery.

Several workrooms planned for efficiency are shown in Figures 10-7, 10-8, and 10-9 which coordinate with the sales areas shown in Figures 10-2, 10-3, and 10-4 respectively. Generally speaking, sales and design areas are about the same size.

Figure 10-7 shows a small workroom (20′ × 30′) with a storage refrigerator connected to the display refrigerator in front and an office beside the door to the sales area. Two design tables are in the center of the room. Beside them is located a U-shaped corsage counter with the order board mounted at one end and the water

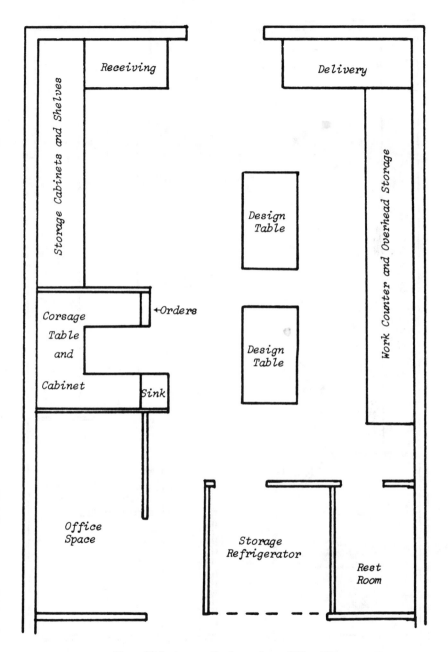

Figure 10-7. An example of a workroom 20' × 30'.

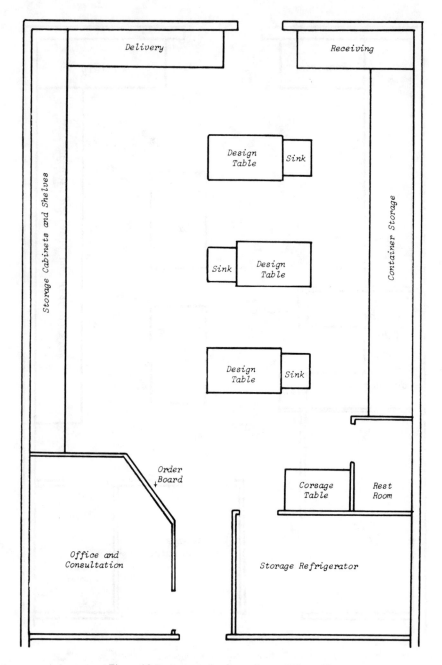

Figure 10-8. An example of a workroom 30' × 40'.

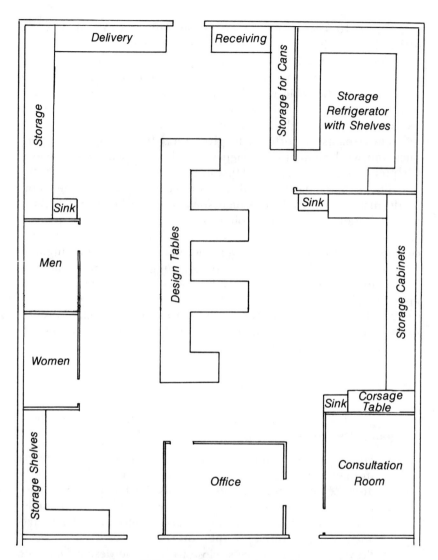

Figure 10-9. An example of a workroom 40' × 50'.

supply installed at the other end of the U. The other areas are storage and counter space.

Figure 10-8 has a larger workroom (30' × 40') with a separate storage refrigerator and a large office which also doubles as a consultation room. There are three design tables with individual water supplies.

Figure 10-9 is the largest workroom (40' × 50') and shows an office opening into both the sales and workroom, with a separate consultation room. The design tables are E-shaped with three sinks located adjacently. An overhead line with individual hoses spaced the length of the table would be more economical. Then one sink near the rear door would suffice. The large storage refrigerator is located in the rear right corner of the room.

These plans are offered to give you a few ideas on designing sales and workrooms for efficiency. Four other plans are shown in Chapter 9 (Figures 9-7, 9-8, 9-9, and 9-10).

The U.S. Department of Commerce has published a "Store Modernization Check List" which spells out the hows and whys of modernization to attain the following five goals: (1) better physical appearance, (2) better utilization of space, (3) up-to-date fixtures and equipment, (4) better heating, ventilation, and air conditioning, and (5) soundness and safety. The booklet suggests: "The retail shop owner should look at his office as if he were a competitor making an inspection."

Small Marketers Aid No. 54, prepared by the Small Business Administration, Washington, D.C., gives an excellent check list for retail store modernization.

TESTING YOUR LAYOUT

As you develop your own floor plan, quiz yourself on the following points. Did you—

- Position the design table, storage refrigerator, and container storage as the three points of your work triangle? Keep the distance between table and cooler as short as possible.?
- Locate all active storage at, or close to, the design table? Make room for critical materials by moving all less frequently used supplies to the storeroom?
- Provide a water source(s) close to both the design table and the receiving area where shipments are unpacked? Consider the possibilities of an overhead line to the design table? Make sure the sink in the receiving area is deep enough for tall refrigerator vases?
- Locate a delivery table convenient to the designers? Much time and energy is wasted in some shops by scattering completed arrangements around the sales and storage areas.
- Locate the design area as near the salesroom as possible, with

the cash register adjacent if a designer also functions as a salesclerk?

Be your own efficiency expert—mentally "make up" an arrangement step-by-step from picking up the order at the control center to placing the completed design on the delivery table; as you mentally make an arrangement, draw your traffic pattern on a copy of your proposed floor plan (see Figure 9-3), being careful to keep it legible! Analyze the results for any possible way to rearrange units for greater efficiency.

Chapter 11

MANAGEMENT

The management of a retail florist shop is a complicated procedure since it involves so many areas—from taking care of customer complaints to showing someone how to sweep the floor.

In most retail florist shops the owner is also the manager and must do many of the jobs personally. In larger shops the owner may hire a manager to oversee the many operations of the business. Either way, the management of a flower shop is a big responsibility.

To be a successful manager, you must know what you are doing, with very little guesswork involved. Your primary concern is to operate the business at a *reasonable profit.* Be ready to take on any job in the place and do it in a way that puts employees and customers in a good frame of mind. Establish a fair and profitable price for everything that you sell. It is up to you, the manager, to see that the price will take care of the overhead and all services which are performed. This is the basis for managing a successful operation. The price of an arrangement must include the cost of the flowers, cost of inventory items used, the cost of labor, the overhead, and a profit. The details of pricing are discussed in Chapter 14.

To manage properly, you must keep an accurate record of your sales volume, and know the sources of income including flowers or perishable merchandise, inventory merchandise, labor, wire orders, and transmittal charges. Every order filled can be divided into one or more of these five categories. You cannot manage successfully and know that you are operating with the proper markup if you do not know the amounts in each category. Herb Mitchell suggests that each florist have a rubber stamp made to itemize the sale. This should be stamped on the back of each order to be filled in by the designer and the salesperson. You can take all of the orders for one day and add up how much of the sales were in each category, and determine whether or not you are operating profitably. The figures for the wire orders must be figured on the net, not on the gross, since you do not retain the full amount from these orders (see Chapter 22); otherwise, your gross might look larger than it really is.

Perishable merchandise	$ _____
Inventory merchandise	$ _____
Labor charges	$ _____
Wire-order sales	$ _____
Transmittal charges	$ _____
Total sales	$ _____

The secret of a profitable operation is increasing volume without adding operational overhead. This calls for careful study by the manager so that this may be accomplished. There is a break-even point in any business where the income equals the expenses. Anything above this is profit, which can grow by increasing the volume without adding to the overhead. It depends on sound management.

You, the manager, must know all of the mechanical aspects as well as the financial manipulations of the business. You must be astute in the all-important phase of buying; whether it be cut flowers, plants, supplies, pottery, or gift items. Be a good judge of stock, and familiar with the price situation. Manage your inventory profitably so that you do not end up with too many nonsalable items. Plan how to move the merchandise before it is purchased and not vice versa. Be a disciplinarian with your time because *time is money.* Many retail florists, unfortunately, seem to feel that their time is worth nothing. Every person's time is worth something, and should be figured in the cost of doing business. It is important that you plan your own work as well as that of your employees. Particularly on slow days good planning is essential.

As the manager, you are responsible for the hiring of regular and extra help. You should be able to recognize the potential in applicants, and be able to explain the business to them. Make all new employees aware that they will have to work overtime at various times of the year. It is usually the job of the manager to train the new employees properly. You must also know how to handle your workers so they are satisfied with their jobs.

To see whether each employee is working to capacity, keep a record of the work done by each. As explained in a previous chapter, most florists can expect to gross from $45,000 to $60,000 per full-time employee, including themselves. The better florists try to attain a figure of at least $50,000 gross per employee. If a florist shop does not come up to the minimal $45,000 gross per employee, it is time to analyze the situation and make some changes. You may have too many employees for the volume of business; some of your employees may not be working as hard and producing like they should; your markup may not be high enough to provide a reasonable profit. Assign each employee a specific job and title.

In a well-managed shop every employee should be employed to become a specialist in some phase of the business, and you, as manager, must spend time tying the work of the specialists together. The salespersons must sell what is available, the greenhouse must grow the right crops for the designer, and out-of-town deliveries must be made up before the order that just goes across the street. The manager must control and coordinate the activities of all the employees. Inability to communicate effectively is one of the most prominent factors in *decaying* managerial skills.

The modern florist (and the successful manager) must know how to *merchandise*, whether through cash-and-carry specials or by other means. You must also be able to advertise profitably—which means knowing the basic principles of advertising as well as which media will bring in the expected return.

The manager must manage the shop, instead of just designing or doing odd jobs. The manager and owner must get along together and resolve differences of policy. The employees must be happy; a step in achieving this is keeping communication lines open between manager and employee. Compile a manual of procedures and policies for new employees to read. It is also your duty to supervise the deliveries, particularly at holiday times.

A good manager should keep the following 14 considerations in mind:

1. Never be "down." Be ready to take on any job in the place and do it in a way that puts employees and customers in a good frame of mind. A grumpy mood is catching.
2. Explain the markup to employees—how the percentages are figured and why merchandise is priced as it is.
3. Pay employees for attending sales meetings if they must be held after working hours. A good sales staff is worth the money.
4. Be honest with customers—they won't buy from a salesperson who's a fake.
5. Make a profit on all merchandise sold in the shop.
6. Keep up with the times—offer rental items. Your customers can rent everything from a car to rugs, furniture and original artwork.
7. Give a flower show. Cooperate with a bank, store, or other

commercial establishment. You can share the costs and the publicity.

8. Get out and look about you—the world's an interesting place. Don't let your creativity be limited by the boundaries of an order counter.
9. Remind customers that flowers are beautiful every day of the year, not just at holidays—encourage everyday use.
10. Set aside an area for self-service buying if your firm can't support a separate self-service shop for the customer who wants to brighten the day with a few daisies.
11. Try pricing flowers individually.
12. Maintain quality on self-service or take-home special flowers. The customers may be willing to accept imperfections, but two-day wilters won't bring them back.
13. Don't be concerned that a cash-and-carry operation will take business away from an "occasion," full-service shop. It seldom does—in fact, self-service encourages all kinds of flower buying.
14. Take advantage of the special appeal of faraway places in windows, commercial displays, or arrangements.

It is extremely important to cultivate ideas that will give your shop a guaranteed weekly income. These might be weekly bouquets of flowers in commercial places of business, weekly church bouquets, reminder services to regular customers, cash-and-carry weekly specials, or other ideas for a steady income. Be alert to new ideas and possibilities that can be expanded into such a guaranteed weekly income.

If you are both owner and manager, make the most of public relations and be active in civic affairs. Decide which public relations promotions will bring in the desired publicity and be worth the effort. These promotions should also be tied in with the advertising program.

As the owner-manager of a small business, you must determine the credit policy of the store and, in small shops, you may also be the bookkeeper, sending out the statements each month. As such, you must have a basic knowledge of simplified accounting and bookkeeping procedures followed by small retailers. (See Chapter 26.) Now in the 80's you must also know how to operate a computer, how to decide whether a computer is needed in your operation, and how to choose the one which is best for your particular shop.

Operating a retail flower shop is hard work for the most part. This fact alone makes planning imperative so that most operations in the shop can be done the easiest and most efficient way. There are several fundamental things that make any job hard. These include:

1. Lack of interest.
2. Lack of skill or knowledge.
3. Improper tools and equipment.
4. Makeshift equipment.
5. Crowded working space.
6. Poor working conditions.
7. Poor working methods.
8. Wasted motions.
9. Interruptions.

Any or all of these factors may occur in the average florist shop. To overcome these obstacles, you must give careful attention to these five considerations:

- Careful planning.
- Proper selection of personnel.
- Adequate training of employees.
- Proper work incentives for the employees.
- Appropriate equipment in a functional floor plan.

COMPLAINTS

Handling customer complaints is another big job for you, as the manager, and should be handled by you alone. The following eight recommendations are aimed to enable you to make adjustments and still retain the good will of the customer:

1. **Don't get excited.** The first job is to calm down a person who resents the inconvenience and loss of money believed (rightly or wrongly) to be your fault.
2. **Listen courteously and appear attentive.** Listening to the customer is to your advantage because the customer can talk, thus getting the problem out into the open, and become calmer. This may show both of you that the grievance is exaggerated.
3. **Assuage injured feelings.** Use soothing phrases if and when the customer pauses: "I know how you feel." "That's a good point."
4. **Get the important facts.** Now is the time to get the important facts by asking diplomatic questions without arousing the customer's ire again.

5. **If the customer is in the right,** and you are wrong, many florists simply admit this and make a settlement that's fair. You may have to do more than this to retain the customer's good will, but it will be worth it for the sake of future business.

6. **If the customer is wrong,** and you are right, don't show smugness. You should still make an adjustment even if it costs some money, in order to keep a *good* customer.

7. **Never underestimate the human element.** If you have only one complaint after selling 50 or 60 plants, it probably is not the fault of the plant, but just lack of care by the customer. You may revive the plant and save the sale. Explaining how to care for the plant or sending along one of the "care" tags will often forestall these complaints.

8. **Make the solution work to your advantage.** Don't say, "I think you're in the wrong, but I'll give you a new plant anyway." Instead, remark enthusiastically, "This is a wonderful plant for the living room, and because I know you agree, I'm going to give you a new one free of charge. It needs special care so let me tell you how to take care of it properly."

MANAGEMENT EFFICIENCY

Since poor work habits cost money, it is up to you, as the manager, to discover and correct them. This is particularly true today if you wish to compete successfully with other businesses and other florists in the area. With rising operating costs it is essential that every employee operate at top efficiency. Watch each employee and analyze the work habits of each. Herb Mitchell has several suggestions for increasing efficiency and fostering better work habits. He suggests the following: "(1) Watch the work pattern of each employee. There is a definite pattern for each job. (2) Always replace a bad habit with a good one. Don't just criticize without offering a solution. (3) Start the new employee out on the right foot. (4) Give a reason, and be sure it is a good one, for changing a work habit. (5) Be a good example himself. This may be the hardest one to follow. (6) Get participation from everyone. It takes only one person to upset the whole organization."

How much time should be spent by the owner-manager on managerial jobs and how much should be spent on small details? Since the majority of our florists are small businesses with the owner acting as manager, the following figures will give some idea as to the

Figure 11-1. Flower store owners and managers attending a retail florist conference.

amount of time that a small florist *might* expect to spend on various phases of the operation.

A survey from The Pennsylvania State University showed that the owner-manager of an *average small retail flower shop* spent 32 per cent of the work day doing miscellaneous odd jobs around the store. The survey was conducted over a 12-month period. Ten random observations were made each day during 14 working days each month for a total of 1,680 observations. Whatever the owner-manager was doing at the time of the observations, it was recorded. All observations were made at random between 8:00 a.m. and 5:00 p.m. on randomly chosen days. This included holidays as well as normal days.

The shop operations were divided into 25 categories and then condensed later into 12 groups. The percentage of time an owner-manager of a small average florist shop spent in each operation is shown in Table 11-1.

The survey showed that approximately 20 per cent of the owner's time was spent on waiting on customers, 16.5 per cent designing, 16 per cent working on the books, 12.5 per cent telephoning, and

Table 11-1. Per Cent of Time Spent on Specific Jobs by an Owner-Manager of a Retail Florist Shop

Job or Operation		Per Cent of Time Spent
1. Selling		20.0
2. Designing:		16.5
Corsages	2.0	
Funeral papier-mâché vases	8.0	
Funeral sprays and wreaths	3.0	
Home and hospital vases	2.0	
Weddings	1.0	
Novelties	0.5	
3. Business operations:		16.0
Accounting and bookkeeping	11.5	
Mail	1.0	
Pricing	0.5	
Writing orders	3.0	
4. Telephoning (sending and taking orders)		12.5
5. Employee and customer consultation		3.0
6. Unpacking flowers and merchandise		9.0
7. Packing orders		5.0
8. Personal delays (meals, haircuts, etc.)		5.0
9. Idle		4.0
10. Emergency delivery		1.0
11. Inventory		1.0
12. Miscellaneous		7.0
		100.0

3.0 per cent on consulting for a total of 68 per cent on the main operations involving the retail flower business.

Thirty-two per cent of the owner-manager's time was spent on miscellaneous items such as packing orders, unpacking merchandise, inventory, cleaning, personal delays, and meals. The personal delays are found in every shop as a part of the daily routine. They should be kept to a minimum.

The 4 per cent idle time could be spent more profitably in planning for specials, and other merchandising ideas to stimulate sales. This is too much time for a florist to be doing "nothing." Better planning would eliminate this.

The 7 per cent miscellaneous and 14 per cent packing and un-packing orders in many stores is done by employees which would leave 21 per cent more time for the owner-manager to spend on more important items of managership.

Successful management will mean more profits for the store. The following check list may show you areas for improvement to gain higher profits:

1. Is the merchandise priced to give the profit expected?
2. Is the buying being done carefully and economically?
3. Do you keep a careful check on all orders and merchandise and keep dumpage to a minimum?
4. Are all the sales personnel trained to upsell items and sell the merchandise which is in largest supply?
5. Do they try to sell related merchandise with each order?
6. Do you periodically check the inventory to be sure all items are selling?
7. Do you take advantage of good buys to increase the markup when possible?
8. Do you check all employees to see that they are really productive?
9. Do you keep a constant watch over all the various operations of the store?

Mismanagement caused over 90 per cent of the more than 12,000 small business failures in one year, according to Dun and Bradstreet as reported by Alvi Voigt, a few years ago. Forty-nine retail florists in the United States failed with a resultant loss of $900,000 to creditors. Many others failed without any loss to creditors, but with a loss of their own investment. Improved management organization and management development are, therefore, of great importance to the retail flower industry, which is primarily made up of small businesses. The report of Dun and Bradstreet stated that the most common factors in business failures were inadequate sales (50 per cent), heavy operating expenses (3 per cent), difficulties in collecting receivables (6 per cent), poor inventory (7 per cent), excessive fixed costs (4 per cent), poor location (5 per cent), competitive problems (21 per cent), and others (4 per cent). Management weaknesses were listed as plain incompetence (43 per cent), unbalanced management experience (18 per cent), inexperience (18 per cent), lack of knowhow in the particular field (13 per cent), and other reasons (8 per cent). (These two sets of figures are approximate figures only.) It is assumed that two out of five businesses failed because the *owners should never have been in business at all*. This shows very clearly the importance of management to the small retail business.

Why do customers leave a particular retail store? A survey in

Oregon gave the answer to some of the problems which occur in retail stores. These figures are for all retail shops, not only florists, but they are worth considering by retail florists. The figures show the percentage of people that gave each reason for leaving a retail shop and going somewhere else. (See Table 11-2.)

Table 11-2. Reasons Why Customers Leave a Retail Shop

	Per Cent
1. High prices	37.44
2. Poor quality of goods	11.87
3. Delay in store service	8.98
4. Indifferent salespersons	6.08
5. Errors	5.17
6. Substitutions of goods	5.02
7. Tricky methods	3.95
8. Store appearance	3.34
9. Misrepresentation of goods	3.04
10. Haughty salespersons	2.89
11. Overinsistent salespersons	2.73
12. Wrong management policies	2.73
13. Reluctance to exchange	2.13
14. Poor advertising	1.97
15. Ignorance of goods	1.90

"TEN COMMANDMENTS" FOR BUSINESS

1. Handle the hardest job first each day. Easy ones are pleasures.
2. Do not be afraid of criticism—criticize yourself often.
3. Be glad and rejoice in the other person's success, and study how it was achieved.
4. Do not be misled by personal dislikes. Both likes and dislikes may be used to advantage.
5. Be enthusiastic—it is contagious.
6. Do not have the notion that success means simply money-making.
7. Be fair, and do at least one good act every day.
8. Respect the chief. There must be a head to everything.
9. Have confidence in yourself. Believe you can do it.
10. Harmonize your work. Let sunshine radiate and perpetuate your relationships.

The manager's job in any small business is unique. Although you may be called upon to do many jobs if you are the owner too, your primary function is to see that all the work is done properly, smoothly, efficiently, and profitably. All of this takes planning, but more than that it also takes execution and evaluation. The job of the manager will vary in time from about 20 per cent doing, with 80 per cent planning and evaluating in a large shop; to 80 per cent doing, and 20 per cent planning and evaluating in a small shop. It's up to you, as the manager, to budget your time according to the operation of the retail florist shop.

Tie in all the aforementioned duties of the small shop owner and manager with the need to be concerned with delivery, general maintenance, and a host of other things, plus being a good designer—you'll see it takes quite an unusual person to be a successful retail florist.

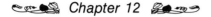

Chapter 12

HIRING AND TRAINING EMPLOYEES—
DESIGN SCHOOLS

JOB QUALIFICATIONS

A successful manager or owner of a retail florist shop will try to divide the employees into groups according to the job. In very small shops this may be difficult because one person may be selling, designing, and answering the phone. However, in most shops each person is assigned one main job. In the larger shops (over $500,000 annual gross volume of sales), each employee should have a specific job and title, as mentioned in Chapter 11.

In choosing the "right" applicant for an opening or evaluating progress in training, look for these characteristics, capabilities, and qualifications:

Designer Qualifications

1. Have good artistic sense and good designing ability, including knowledge of the fundamentals of the principles of design.
2. Have imagination, originality, and creativity.
3. Have some previous experience, including working in a retail florist shop during most of the nine major holidays.
4. Be quick and efficient in designing.
5. Have sufficient "business sense" to be economical in flower arranging to preserve the margin of profit. (See Table 14-2 for effect of one extra flower on profits.)

Salesperson Qualifications

1. Like people and show the initiative necessary for selling.

2. Be ambitious and a go-getter, not just an order-taker.
3. Be dependable and reliable.
4. Be efficient in serving the customer and in utilizing the time between customers.
5. Be in good health to be able to contact the public daily and to minimize absenteeism.
6. Know prices, types of designs, names of merchandise, delivery schedules, selling methods, and general store policies.
7. Have a pleasing personality and appearance to give the best possible impression to the customers.
8. Be diplomatic and courteous with all customers—a dissatisfied customer can spread ill will, and lead to more dissatisfied customers.
9. Be able to get along with other employees.

Buyer Qualifications

There should be just one person to do all the buying, preferably the manager or the owner-manager, who must impress the wholesalers that old or poorly grown merchandise will not be acceptable. This individual should:

1. Be familiar with the market and prices to be able to purchase economically.
2. Be familiar with the type and amount of merchandise which the shop's clientele will buy.
3. Know the potential for merchandising an item that is glutting the market.
4. Recognize a *good* buy.

Bookkeeper Qualifications

1. Be familiar with the fundamentals of accounting and bookkeeping.
2. Know how to file properly.
3. Know how to post entries and to keep the ledger sheets.
4. Know how to make out the periodic Profit and Loss statements.
5. Be dependable in completing work on time—statements must be sent out on time each and every month.
6. Be honest.
7. Know how to answer the telephone properly, either to take an order or to call a salesperson to the phone.

8. In some shops, know how to operate a computer. (See Chapter 11 on management.)

Delivery Person Qualifications

The delivery person, or driver, is more important than some florists realize. Many owner-managers will hire any high school student or unemployed person without realizing this individual's importance to the store. Often the delivery person is the main contact between the store and the customer or potential customer. This individual should:

1. Make a good impression.
2. Be neat and clean.
3. Be reliable. Handle flowers and drive truck carefully—if the designs do not reach the customer the same way they left the store, there will be complaints and many dissatisfied customers.
4. Be pleasant and courteous—help set a good image of the store.
5. Have a thorough knowledge of the streets and the numbering system in the town to avoid a lot of backtracking.
6. Be honest and trustworthy to collect C.O.D.'s and delinquent accounts.
7. Be a good, law-abiding, courteous driver.
8. Take pride in the truck and see that it is kept clean, greased, and filled with gas.
9. Be capable of helping out in the store between delivery runs.

Manager Qualifications

A manager who is employed by the owner to oversee all operations (see Chapter 11) must have all of the qualifications of a retail florist, including the abilities in the following list:

1. Be able to supervise the sales staff and designers and to set up the delivery schedules.
2. Be qualified to do the buying and to regulate the advertising program.
3. Be capable of operating a smoothly efficient and profitable shop.
4. Have knowledge of computers.

SELECTING EMPLOYEES

"Ninety per cent of your employee troubles can be eliminated at the time of hiring," according to one florist. Make certain to pick the right person in the first place. This is never easy for a small retail florist who must do a hundred things at once. The following are some of the things to look for in a new employee: (1) *productivity*—the ability of every employee to produce for the business; (2) *attitude* which will build good will—pride in the business and respect for the employer; (3) *carefulness with equipment*—the employee's pride in, and care of, the materials and tools; (4) *cooperation*—a necessity for an efficient and productive business; (5) *loyalty*—a must; (6) *honesty*—another "must" in every employee; (7) *ambition*—the desire to get ahead; and (8) *compliance with rules*—a vital point.

The following definite steps to be followed when interviewing an employee will result in a minimum of wasted time:

- Have the applicant fill out a simple application form for future use.
- Make sure the interview is relaxed.
- Get the applicant to talk about previous jobs and experiences. Don't get off on too many extraneous matters except to aid relaxation or to "fish" for information you can't legally ask for.
- Get the facts.
- Check the employment record of the applicant.
- Quickly check personality and skills by careful observation.
- Check appearance of the applicant.
- Find out the individual's attitude towards work and long hours. Explain the working hours and overtime at holidays.
- Explain in detail what the job involves and what is expected of the person hired.
- Get the applicant to ask questions.
- Keep control of the job interview to avoid wasting time.
- Analyze results and let the prospective employee know the decision as quickly as possible.
- Treat your employees in the same way they would be treated if they were represented by a union. This way you retain control of your business while they get the advantages of being organized, making it less likely they will want to vote in a union.

Most florists, as well as students, are not too knowledgeable about what is legally considered discriminatory on application blanks and as questions in employment interviews. As the interpretations may change from year to year, to avoid problems check with the U.S. Department of Labor and the Equal Employment Opportunity Commission for the current thinking.

LABOR MARKET

Where does the retail florist get new employees? Colleges, community colleges, high schools, trade schools, design schools, and neighbors are good sources of supply. Young people in high school and the early college years, young homemakers, and older women are probably the most readily available labor market in local areas. If you need more employees due to increased business, hire these people on a part-time basis first and train them before they become part of your regular staff. Some universities operate their own flower shops to give experience to the students, such as Mississippi State University, which trains over 275 students a year in the basics of floral design, and California Polytechnic State University at San Luis Obispo.

Besides high schools and colleges, there are now available other means of finding employees for the retail florist business. Several

Figure 12-1. Students learn floral designing at The Pennsylvania State University.

cities have set up schools with backing from Washington, D.C., under the Manpower Development and Training Act, and several florists have been paid to offer on-the-job training to future florists who want to learn the business. Many high schools are offering vocational horticulture courses with specialties in floriculture. The number is increasing every year, as are government-supported schools which train students to become retail florists.

TRAINING EMPLOYEES

When you hire employees, permanent or part-time, it is up to you as the owner-manager to train them properly. Regular help should be taught the value of a prompt and courteous approach to the customer, the manner in which to develop and close a sale, the proper way to answer the phone, the value of merchandise and how to handle it, and all the other essential areas of knowledge about the retail florist business. Extra help should be trained well in advance of the holiday.

Good, well-trained flower shop employees are hard to find. Consider the high cost of training an employee as an investment and the trained worker as a valuable asset to the business. It is in your best interest to do everything possible to keep your experienced personnel. Usually, an employee who stays in the business is attracted by something more than just wages and other benefits. However, the beauty of the merchandise, the fascinating work of creating an artistic design, and the importance of serving the customers can quickly be clouded by an employer who shouts instead of instructs, who bosses rather than leads, and who distracts rather than inspires the staff.

A wise employer recognizes that each new employee starts the first day with apprehension mixed with enthusiasm. Aloofness has no place in a flower shop, either with the employer or the employee. Everyone likes to be called by name, so be sure to apply this to each new employee from the very first day. Every employee is a human being and expects to be treated like one. Commands are given in the army, not in a flower shop. Once you have started an employee off on the right foot, you are well on the way to the all-important objective of keeping that person permanently employed.

Take time. Part of the fault with training employees seems to lie with the florist who either personally lacks confidence as a teacher for new employees (without reason in many cases) or else just doesn't take the time to do it. Why try to train a new employee for either full

Figure 12-2. Professor Pfahl gives personal attention to a future florist.

or part-time work the week before Christmas or Easter? This is the worst possible time, and yet this is exactly what some of the retail florists try to do—and then wonder why they fail. Every florist is much too busy for the few weeks prior to a major holiday to spend time to properly train a new employee. Some florists, however, do this year after year—and then complain that they can't get competent help and that the new employees aren't worth what they have to pay them. Often they wait until 10 days before Christmas and then try to get cheap help. "Forget the cheap help," says Bill Curtis of Phoebe Floral in Allentown, Pennsylvania. "There are many sources of good part-time help, such as school teachers, college students, retired clerks, and housewives."

Be systematic. Train new employees in a systematic businesslike manner, and do it at a time when you can concentrate on this and little else. Consider the training of new employees as a regular part of the business, and not something to be squeezed in on a hit-or-miss basis.

Training Procedure

1. Pay the employee a minimum wage while learning with a promise of higher pay when training or probationary period is completed and regular employment begins.

2. Arrange for the new employee to work in the shop every day for two weeks at least. This should be several weeks prior to a holiday. The summer is a good time to train and line up extra holiday help for later in the year. In fact, the summer is when you have the most time to train any new employee—yet florists seem reluctant to hire new employees in the summer.

3. Give the employee time to become acquainted with the merchandise, prices, charges, delivery, and other standard practices in the shop. A copy of procedures and practices should be given to the new staff members to read over and study at home. (It won't hurt to let the others read them once in a while, too.) Be patient until the new person learns the job. Don't be afraid to allow a little time for observing and absorbing the atmosphere of the shop. If not carried to excess, this is a vital part of the training process.

4. Personally introduce the new employee to the others, using first names to encourage the staff to be friendly and make the new person feel more at home.

5. Be definite with the new employee as to exactly who is the boss, and from whom to take orders (preferably just one individual).

6. Detail the new employee's duties, what will be expected of him/her, the fact that at times any person may be asked to do other jobs—even some quite menial tasks. Explain that at holidays *everyone* has more work to do and will have to work longer hours.

7. If the new employee is to do any designing, be sure to allow plenty of time at first to design several test arrangements. Stay with the new designer, giving help and guidance at the moment a problem starts, not later. Don't walk away, then come back and say, "It's terrible," or else just tear it up and start over, as some florists do. Help to build *confidence* in the individual.

8. Don't find fault with an employee (new or old) in front of other people.

9. Don't expect miracles the first week. Give the new person a chance.

10. Tell the new employee how to dress for the job. Some people will realize it just through observation, but others may not.

11. If the shop is large enough for separate designers, salespersons, packers, and drivers, have a set of procedures for each group to give to newcomers.

12. For part-time holiday help, go over the specific details for the holiday with all new employees several weeks before the holiday. Take a half-day and spend time explaining what you want done, the prices of various items, the merchandise that has been ordered which will be for sale, delivery schedules, and other procedures. If all the employees and part-time workers know these things, they won't be asking so many questions during the rush of the holiday. Many florists post several copies of prices of plants and cut flowers for the holiday around the shop so there will be no mistakes.

13. Stress to all new employees that they should be friendly, personable, and efficient when waiting on customers. Also, they should use common language. Employees should be salespersons, not order-takers.

14. Look to older and/or retired persons as an excellent source of part-time employees, as well as college students home on vacation for the holiday.

Most retail florists are well qualified to train new employees if they will just *take the time to do it*. They know their business better than anyone else—they know the merchandise and prices, they know how to design, and they should know how to sell. All that is required is to take a little time to systematically impart this knowledge to the new employees.

Training an Assistant

Many retail florists find themselves in a dilemma when it comes to vacations, attending meetings, and just taking some time off. They need an assistant, and yet feel that none of their regular employees can fit into that category. Thus, they go on for years without having a real vacation or attending florists' meetings which would benefit them and their business. Follow these suggestions when training an assistant:

1. Immediately after hiring, make your new assistant familiar

with the store in the simplest way—by sitting down and discussing the business. Describe its routine, problems, principles of management, present policies, and the plans for the future. Explain the responsibilities of the position and how and where it fits into the picture. Take plenty of time for this discussion.

2. Acquaint the principal co-workers with your new assistant; be sure they understand they will be taking orders from the new staff member. Personally introduce all employees.

3. Assign job responsibility with intelligence. Don't give too much at one time. Oversee progress in a general way, but don't check every move.

4. Expect the assistant to make mistakes—everyone does at one time or another, and your trainee doesn't have your experience. Errors can't be prevented, but make them *learning experiences*. Discuss them quietly and in private.

5. Always work in harmony with your assistant and share all your knowledge.

6. Encourage self-improvement by providing the various trade publications, as well as time to read them, and the opportunity to attend some of the conferences and conventions of retail florist organizations.

7. Give your assistant a salary commensurate with the responsibilities of the position.

Checking Top Salespersons

The importance of the sales staff cannot be overemphasized in today's business. The success of any retail florist shop is determined in large measure by the quality of its sales personnel. While they are being trained and going through a probationary period, there are at least 50 items which should be checked by the manager. These include items of sales ability, handling of customers, personal appearance, habits, honesty, willingness to do extra jobs when not waiting on customers, proper handling of merchandise, satisfaction with the job, and many other items which will result in better business for the store.

DESIGN SCHOOLS

After high school or college, it is usually advisable for you as a prospective retail florist to attend one of the many fine design

Figure 12-3. Students learn floral designing through experience.

schools located across the United States. Even if you have worked part time in a flower shop or have taken some design courses, the experience and practice at one of these schools will be worthwhile for the new ideas and techniques which help a person become above average as a designer. There are at least 25 such design schools in the country offering two- to six-week courses at several times during the year. Many of them are advertised in the trade papers such as *Florists' Review, Southern Florist and Nurseryman, and Flower News.* When you are looking for a job, you'll find it is well worth the investment to help get a good position. Some retailers will pay the way of a new employee to save the time required to teach design to the trainee, or of older employees to learn new techniques of design.

The hiring and training of employees is important to retail florists and should be given serious consideration. Too many retailers do not spend the time trying to find the right kind of employees for their shop or take time to train them properly once they have been found. The ultimate success and profits of the business rest with reliable, well-trained employees.

DISMISSAL

Today's laws are extremely complex in terms of employer-employee relationships. This means that mishandling an employee's dismissal may be costly to any business. Take precautions to avoid this by never dismissing an employee during a heated argument and being sure all terms of the original employment agreement have been complied with. It pays to have every agreement in writing. Be sure to check all records of payment to ascertain that nothing is due the person being terminated. Dismiss an employee only after carefully considering the case from all angles.

Chapter 13

BUYING

Buying is one of the most important functions of the manager or owner of a retail florist shop. Many florists have increased their net profit by buying carefully, and by knowing when and how to take advantage of gluts and discounts.

There are four areas of buying for the retail florist, each requiring a different set of skills and information. They are: (1) the purchase of perishable merchandise for resale, (2) the purchase of non-perishable merchandise for resale, (3) the purchase of expendable supplies (staples) for use with the perishables, and (4) the purchase of equipment and fixtures.

PERISHABLE MERCHANDISE

Buying perishable merchandise is one of the most important and most difficult practices involved in operating a retail florist shop. The skillful buying of flowers and plants requires a good deal of study, as well as considerable planning and experience. You may buy either in person or by phone. You must depend a great deal on the person on the other end of the line when you buy by phone. It is important to stay with one salesperson (when you find a reliable one) so you can teach that individual what quality of merchandise you want, the quantity and type of items which will sell in your particular shop, and your personal likes and dislikes. Telephone buying may cost about 10 per cent more in the long run unless you have a contact with a good, reliable salesperson. Because prices of cut flowers vary from hour to hour and day to day, timing is important.

In general, to be well informed about actual price conditions and the quality of merchandise available, you must personally visit the wholesale flower markets and greenhouses. Although a lot of valuable time can be wasted in the market, it is necessary to be well informed to operate at a profit.

Figure 13-1. Salesmen receiving orders from retail florists in a wholesale commission florist company. (Courtesy, Denver Wholesale Florists Co., Denver, Colo.)

Plan your buying ahead of time—it will be to your advantage. Keep accurate records on what portion of your business is funeral, wedding, hospital, gift, and cash-and-carry to help you plan what merchandise to buy. If you are located in a large city with several wholesalers, contact all of them to see what quality, quantity, and price of merchandise is available. At any time the sales personnel may alter the price, depending upon supply and demand for the product. Try to get the best buy possible. If ordering in advance for a wedding, see what each wholesaler can do and be sure to order ahead of time. The larger the order, the better the price should be. If you are ordering 50 roses, you will usually pay more per rose than if you are ordering 1,000.

Nothing is a bargain if it can't be used or sold. When there is a glut or an oversupply on the market, the wholesaler will try to sell in quantity. For this reason you must decide what you can sell and decide in advance what you are going to spend. By doing so, you will come out with less loss and more profit. This may not be true, however, if you are buying flowers with a long life. But ordering extra each time can lead to losses.

For sales promotions such as weekend cash-and-carry specials, plan ahead and buy in quantity at a price at which you can offer the merchandise at a suitably low price. Buy only what you will be able to sell in the special; if too much is left over, you may have to dump it. This type of merchandising is discussed in Chapter 16.

When buying in quantity, make an offer below the asking price. The wholesaler knows how low the price can go in order to make the sale, but may not volunteer a lower price—you must ask for it. During a glutted period, however, the salesperson will offer a good buy on a quantity in order to move the merchandise.

NON-PERISHABLE ITEMS

Every supply magazine and every trade fair for florists has hundreds of items which can be used and sold in the retail florist shop. The best advice on buying these items is to purchase wisely and well.

The actual job of buying is easier if enough time and effort have been devoted to planning, according to Herb Mitchell. He says: "The biggest job is selecting items which will move in a specific flower shop." Most of our successful florists do not buy what they like personally. They try to purchase what their customers like. You may ask the salesperson, who often will know which items are moving, what a comparable shop is selling. Some florists ask their spouses, sales staff, and a few good customers for their advice on some items to find out their likes and dislikes. However, no matter how hard you try, you will have a *lemon* now and then. Select merchandise for its sales appeal. Experience seems to be the best teacher for this.

One of the biggest problems in buying is deciding whether to buy a few items in depth, or to select many items and buy only one or two of each. It is usually wise to buy some each way. Be sure to buy enough of any item or group of similar items to make an attractive display. It is important to plan ahead and know how the merchandise is going to be sold. The sales potential of old stand-by items will be known, but new items are always a gamble.

Knowing *when* to buy is another important consideration. Planned buying demands that purchasing be accomplished on a definite schedule. If you place orders with every salesperson who comes into the store, it is practically impossible to keep an accurate inventory record. Certain items should be ordered each month, while other merchandise is only purchased once a year.

Prompt payment to take advantage of cash discounts will add to your margin of profit.

STAPLES

In the buying of non-perishable staple items such as wire, ribbon, papier-mâché containers, floratape, chicken wire, and other necessary items, there is usually a variation of price. The larger the quantity, the better will be the price. Many small florists buy these items one at a time as they need them, but this is the most expensive way to do it. If your credit with the company is good, you will get a better price for the items. Many florists will buy a year's supply of staple items if they have plenty of storage space. Sometimes it is possible to save up to 15 per cent in this way, which will often more than pay the shipping charges. Prompt payment also is an important buying procedure and one which will help with the profit picture. If you can get a discount by paying promptly (often within 10 days) this will increase profits. So, it is essential in your planning to have cash on hand to take advantage of discounts. Cash discounts are extremely important to business; take advantage of them. Even borrowing from a bank is well worthwhile. You may doubt this when you compare a cost of 15 per cent interest for borrowing money from the bank as opposed to 2 per cent saved if the invoice is paid on time. Even though the rate of interest from the bank looks greater, according to Jack Carman when speaking of cash discounts, 2 per cent for 10 days is equivalent to 36 per cent true interest per year. Compare 15 per cent per annum with 36 per cent, and in the course of a year, you can see that you will save considerable money by borrowing from your local financial institution in order to discount your payables. If you buy a year's supply of staples and save up to 15 per cent in addition as a quantity discount, you save even more.

EQUIPMENT AND FIXTURES

The purchase of equipment and fixtures will be determined by need. A good buyer knows when to replace equipment. If you have properly depreciated the items and set aside money to replace these items, then you should not have any trouble paying for the new equipment and fixtures. As mentioned in Chapter 6, you must set aside money for equipment and not take too much out in personal withdrawals. Whether you buy new or used equipment will depend on your needs, the cost of the item, and the amount of available capital. As in other buying, prompt payment may give a discount which is well worthwhile.

THE PURCHASING DECISION

For every purchase, you must make the following decisions: (1) what to buy: quantity, quality, color, and type; (2) when to buy: date or time of year to purchase material, or day of week; (3) when to receive: specify delivery dates for nonperishable items; (4) where to buy: contact several wholesalers and suppliers; (5) how to ship or deliver: the most economical way, but with proper handling; (6) how to pay: plan and budget ahead; (7) what to pay: price must be competitive. Try to get the best buy.

Buying is important; never hesitate to ask for a better price.

STOCK TURNOVER

Increasing the rate of stock turnover in a business is one of the keys to higher profits. You will make more profit per dollar invested in stock if you get a fast turnover of merchandise inventory.

To improve the stock turnover, you must know the current rate. In the retail florist business the rate of turnover, of course, for flowers and plants (perishable merchandise) is very rapid. However, on the non-perishable items it may be very slow. So, this discussion deals with the non-perishables or inventory items, termed "hard goods" by many florists.

There are several steps in determining your stock turnover rate: (1) Determine the dollar volume of the average inventory for the year. As an example, say $25,000. (2) Divide the average inventory into the cost of goods sold. For example, divide $25,000 into a theoretical $75,000 cost of goods sold. (3) The turnover rate is three, or three times a year you will have a turnover of stock.

The turnover rate can be increased by two methods: (1) increase the sales and keep the average inventory the same or (2) decrease the average inventory, and keep the sales the same. In this example, if the cost of goods sold increased to $150,000, the stock turnover rate would be six instead of three. Thus, the dollars invested in the business will *work harder for you* if you increase the rate of stock turnover in the business. If you control all other elements, and increase your stock turnover rate, then your profits will improve. Eliminate old stock and odds and ends to reduce the inventory. Too many florists keep lemons around longer than necessary, tying up their money in inventory. Get rid of the lemons periodically on a reduced sale table in the store, so you can invest in merchandise that will sell faster.

It should be obvious that the job of buying is one of the most important responsibilities of the manager or owner of the retail florist shop. Careful buying can greatly increase the net profit for the business.

Chapter 14

PRICING AND MARKUP FOR PROFIT

PRICING

Pricing is one of the most important functions, along with buying, of the owner or manager in the retail florist shop.

Price is determined by supply and demand. Generally, when the supply is greater than the demand, the price will decrease. Conversely, when the demand is greater than the supply, the price will increase. It is very important for you to be aware of all variables in determining supply and wholesale price. By increasing your awareness of all facets within the industry, you will then be better equipped to anticipate fluctuations and thus better control prices and profits.

Nearly 45 per cent of the retail florists in the United States charge the same price for arranged as for unarranged flowers according to a U. S. Department of Agriculture survey. This is not a good business practice. Every florist should have two sets of prices, one for arranged, and the other for cash-and-carry flowers.

Most prices in the retail florist business are figured on the cost of merchandise while profits are figured on sales. The majority of florists price their flowers on the basis of the wholesale price or cost of merchandise. However, the economists tell us that the price for flowers should be based on sales and the profit which the florists want from their business. Although pricing will not affect the actual cost of the merchandise to the florists, it does affect the cost of merchandise *percentage* as shown in the following example. A. Voigt has shown that with a business of $60,000 gross volume of sales, a 10 per cent increase in retail, or selling, prices will result in a 100 per cent increase in net income. Thus, the cost of merchandise changes from 55 to 50 per cent and the net-to-owner from 10 to 18.2 per cent. (Even a 5 per cent increase in prices will result in a 50 per cent net income increase.) Example:

A. Current situation:

Sales	$60,000	100%
Merchandise cost	$33,000	55%
Gross profit	$27,000	45%
Operation costs	$21,000	35%
Net-to-owner	$ 6,000	10%

B. New situation:

Sales	$66,000	100%
Merchandise cost	$33,000	50%
Gross profit	$33,000	50%
Operation costs	$21,000	31.8%
Net-to-owner	$12,000	18.2%

Thus, with an increase in sales due to the increase in price, the percentage of merchandise cost was decreased and the net profit was increased.

MARKUP

How do retail florists determine what they shall charge customers for their merchandise? Most of them have a definite policy, or think they do. Many florists claim to use a specific markup, but few of them actually follow it. There are several rules of thumb used by many florists which, unfortunately, do not lead to the desired profit. Surveys have shown that markup ranges from 50 to 200 per cent by various individual retail florists. The rule of thumb used by many florists for years has been 2 to 1, 2½ to 1, 3 to 1, or 4 to 1 markup. The average is 3 to 1. But the price should not be based on a simple markup. Most of them use a 2 to 1 on pottery and pot plants. This means they buy the item for $1 and sell it for $2. The markup is based on the cost of the item. The 2 or 3 to 1 markup started some 65 years ago at a florists meeting when a speaker mentioned that he used a 2 to 1 markup for pricing his flowers. Even though florists will tell you that they use a 3 to 1 markup, they don't do it all the time. They use it as a basis for pricing, and it is probably a legitimate markup *when the flower market is normal*. However, when they get a *good buy* and pay 5¢ for a flower which normally costs 12¢, they do not reduce the price to the customers, unless it is for a cash-and-carry special. Thus, if they sell the flowers for the same price per dozen all year, the markup at this time will be much greater than the 3 to 1. Likewise, when the market is tight or when there is a holiday, the wholesale price goes up; since they cannot raise the prices too far out of line, the resulting markup will be less than 3 to 1. Many florists try to hold the prices for the standard flowers at the same retail price all year, hoping that the markup will average at least 3 to 1 for the year. They hope, but many just don't know; this is a poor business practice.

Many florists, besides trying to start with a standard base, also determine the selling price for flowers by what they think their customers will pay. Many times they are wrong. Too many retail florists are order takers, not salespersons—they are afraid to upsell. Too many florist shops are charging the same price for arrangements that they did years ago, despite the fact that every other commodity in the United States has increased in price, most doubling or even tripling, causing operating expenses and overhead to go up tremendously.

Currently, the minimum range for funeral work through FTD shops is being quoted from $20.00 to $27.50, and the minimum for hospital arrangements is ranging from $15.00 to $25.00. Due to federal laws regarding price fixing, a minimum price for a type of arrangement cannot be set by the organization; the use of a price range is permissible legally and has the advantage of reflecting the variation in overhead and markup for different types of shops and locations.

At the end of the year, if you have not made the profit you anticipated, check the records to see if you have forgotten to make the price changes necessitated by your changing expenses and costs of merchandise. If this is true, now is the time to make the change and step up your markup. (Refer to Table 14-1.)

PROFIT

A selling price is a combination of four factors: cost of merchandise, overhead, labor (salaries and wages), and profit. *The price should not be based on a simple markup no matter how high it is.*

Remember that *keeping profits* is as important as *making profits*. One way is to reduce your tax cost wherever practical. A tax saving of $1,000 will net as much as sales of $19,200 if net profit before tax is 10 per cent.

Plan your profit. Profit comes from efficient control of overhead and labor, as well as the buying of quality merchandise at an economical price. Separate net profit from salary. A good businessperson, even if the sole owner, deserves to be paid a decent salary. Labor is the biggest expense item and must be included, along with profit, in determining the selling price of the item. An average

Table 14-1. Retailers' Markup Chart[1]

You Pay per Flower	100% Markup	150% Markup	200% Markup	250% Markup	300% Markup	350% Markup	400% Markup
0.02	0.48	0.60	0.72	0.84	0.96	1.08	1.20
0.03	0.72	0.90	1.08	1.26	1.44	1.62	1.80
0.04	0.96	1.20	1.50	1.80	2.10	2.40	2.70
0.05	1.20	1.50	1.80	2.10	2.40	2.70	3.00
0.06	1.44	1.80	2.16	2.52	2.88	3.24	3.60
0.07	1.68	2.10	2.52	2.94	3.36	3.78	4.20
0.08	1.92	2.40	2.88	3.36	3.84	4.32	4.80
0.09	2.16	2.70	3.64	3.78	4.32	4.86	5.40
0.10	2.40	3.00	3.60	4.20	4.80	5.40	6.00
0.11	2.64	3.30	3.96	4.62	5.28	5.94	6.60
0.12	2.88	3.60	4.32	5.04	5.76	6.48	7.20
0.13	3.12	3.90	4.68	5.46	6.24	7.02	7.80
0.14	3.36	4.20	5.04	5.88	6.72	7.56	8.40
0.15	3.60	4.50	5.40	6.30	7.20	8.10	9.00
0.16	3.84	4.80	5.76	6.72	7.68	8.64	9.60
0.17	4.08	5.10	6.12	7.14	8.16	9.18	10.20
0.18	4.32	5.40	6.48	7.56	8.64	9.72	10.80
0.19	4.56	5.70	6.84	7.98	9.12	10.26	11.40
0.20	4.80	6.00	7.20	8.40	9.60	10.80	12.00
0.21	5.04	6.30	7.56	8.82	10.08	11.34	12.60
0.22	5.28	6.60	7.92	9.24	10.56	11.88	13.20
0.23	5.52	6.90	8.28	9.66	11.04	12.42	13.80
0.24	5.76	7.20	8.64	10.08	11.52	12.96	14.40
0.25	6.00	7.50	9.00	10.50	12.00	13.50	15.00
0.26	6.24	7.80	9.36	10.92	12.48	14.04	15.60
0.27	6.48	8.10	9.72	11.34	12.96	14.58	16.20
0.28	6.72	8.40	10.08	11.76	13.44	15.12	16.80
0.29	6.96	8.70	10.44	12.18	13.92	15.66	17.40
0.30	7.20	9.00	10.80	12.60	14.40	16.20	18.00

You Pay per Bunch	100% Markup	150% Markup	200% Markup	250% Markup	300% Markup	350% Markup	400% Markup
0.50	1.00	1.25	1.50	1.75	2.00	2.25	2.50
0.75	1.50	1.88	2.25	2.63	3.00	3.38	3.75
1.00	2.00	2.50	3.00	3.50	4.00	4.50	5.00
1.25	2.50	3.13	3.75	4.38	5.00	5.63	6.25
1.50	3.00	3.75	4.50	5.25	6.00	6.75	7.50
1.75	3.50	4.38	5.25	6.13	7.00	7.88	8.75
2.00	4.00	5.00	6.00	7.00	8.00	9.00	10.00
2.25	4.50	5.63	6.75	7.88	9.00	10.13	11.25
2.50	5.00	6.25	7.50	8.75	10.00	11.25	12.50
2.75	5.50	6.88	8.25	9.63	11.00	12.38	13.75
3.00	6.00	7.50	9.00	10.50	12.00	13.50	15.00
4.00	8.00	10.00	12.00	14.00	16.00	18.00	20.00
5.00	10.00	12.50	15.00	17.50	20.00	22.50	25.00

[1]Determine the markup you want to charge, and this chart will give you the selling price per dozen (top chart) or per bunch (bottom chart).

florist shop will spend between 15 and 30 per cent of the gross volume of sales for the payroll, depending upon the size of the shop. Overhead is the cost of doing business, including rent, advertising, utilities, delivery, and minor items of expense. Overhead must also be considered in the pricing of items for sale. Although many florists figure the markup will take care of this, it often does not.

As an example, if you figure your profit at 10 per cent from the start, then you will have the following guide in determining the selling price: profit 10 per cent, labor 30 per cent, inventory 10 per cent, and overhead 27 per cent; leaving 23 per cent for the cost of merchandise. Since the markup on cash-and-carry items, and the markup on hard goods like pottery is a standard 2 or 2½ to 1, then the markup on the perishable items must be more than 3 to 1 in order to keep the total cost of merchandise at 33 per cent for the year. As the merchandise cost goes higher, the profit goes lower. Thus, a retail florist should start with the selling price and work backwards to find how much merchandise to use, rather than starting with the purchase price and trying to use a standard markup. Unfortunately, today the majority of retail florists use the old system of a 3 to 1 or 4 to 1 markup, hoping it will give them a profit. For some shops this works, but for others it doesn't. It is usually just a guess.

The pricing should be figured as shown in the following example. A $20.00 sale would be broken down into the following:

Profit (10%)	$ 2.00
Overhead (27%)	5.40
Labor (30%)	6.00
Inventory (supplies)	2.00
	$15.40
Cost of merchandise	4.60
	$20.00

This method leaves $4.60 to be spent on the cost of merchandise (flowers and greens). The total of the inventory merchandise plus the perishable merchandise equals the 33 per cent mentioned previously. *The perishable merchandise factor is the one that must be variable and reflect the proper markup to determine a decent profit.* Many florists figure their markup on a monthly basis rather than on an annual basis. This is good business because the percentage of overhead varies from month to month. According to a Michigan State University survey, it varied from 30.7 per cent to 50.9 per cent in one store during a 12-month period, as follows: January—41.8 per cent,

February—41.8 per cent, March—37.2 per cent (Easter), April—42.6 per cent, May—30.7 per cent, June—37.6 per cent, July—49.7 per cent, August—46.3 per cent, September—50.9 per cent, October—41.1 per cent, November—45.1 per cent, and December—35.6 per cent.

The hardest part for most retail florists is to charge for labor, delivery, and other expenses. They find it difficult to charge different prices for flowers if they are arranged, charged, and delivered. And yet, this is exactly what must be done—or at least it must be included in the selling price. As mentioned previously, a national survey showed that 40 per cent of the retail florists in the United States are charging the same price for arranged as for unarranged flowers. It is an unprofitable way to run a business.

Another hard job for florists is to figure the pricing of flowers for weddings. Instead of breaking it down into labor, cost of merchandise, overhead, and profit, they use a markup of maybe 5 to 1 or even 8 to 1, hoping this will cover everything. Some florists figure in the cost of setting up the wedding decorations, but forget about the time and labor involved in tearing them down and returning the materials to the store. All of this should be figured in the final price.

Another place where retail florists do not figure properly is in pricing pottery and other hard goods. The 2 or 2½ to 1 markup is fine, but many florists forget to include shipping charges. These must be added to the cost of the item before it is priced. Transportation charges can be quite high on some items and must be included in the sale price, otherwise the markup will be less than 2 to 1, which is the minimum. With increased costs in today's business world, a 3 to 1 markup is a better base for pottery and hard goods.

A 1975 survey of approximately 100 retail florists showed the following average markups:

Cost of flowers	Ratio
Boxed and wrapped	2.95 to 1
In corsages	4.24 to 1
In arrangements	3.28 to 1
In wedding work	4.57 to 1
In funeral wreaths and sprays	3.22 to 1
As flowering potted plants	2.47 to 1
As foliage potted plants	2.51 to 1

By comparing these figures with those in the preceding paragraph, it is easy to see why the average florist of today is not making a 10 per cent profit. (Chapter 6 shows 4.3 to 12.6 per cent, before taxes) The survey figures for markup are much too low. If you, as a retail florist, were to take the money which would be invested in the business and put it into a building and loan or other form of investment, you would receive at least 5 per cent return with no risk involved. Therefore, you are entitled to at least 7 per cent (net profit after taxes) plus a fair salary for yourself.

If the present markup is actually below that which is needed to insure a profit, it may be due to any of the following:

1. Setting prices too low.
2. Not buying properly.
3. Throwing in too many flowers.
4. Not coordinating buying and selling.
5. Dumping too many flowers.
6. Failing to ring up all sales.
7. Taking flowers without recording them.
8. Running too high an overhead.

Table 14-2, prepared by the late Professor Paul Krone, shows how the profits will suffer by throwing one extra flower into each floral design. The table and the following example are classics, showing that the way materials are selected for the design determines whether there will be a profit or a loss on the order. It is just as true today that two or three extra flowers (depending upon the price) will turn the profit into loss.

Example: Two $10.00 arrangements.

A		B	
12 glads	$ 1.00	10 glads	$0.80
9 asters	0.72	6 asters	0.48
1 bu. pomps	1.00	¾ bu. pomps	0.75
6 mums	1.80	3 mums	0.90
Container	1.00	Container	1.00
Greens	0.50	Greens	0.50
50% overhead	5.00	50% overhead	5.00
Total	$11.02	Total	$9.43
Loss	1.02	Profit	0.57

Profit should be figured on the selling price, not the cost of merchandise. Profit is not made until the sale is completed and paid. The figures for most other retail businesses are based on sales, so why not in the retail florist business?

Along with proper pricing to obtain a fair profit, go the subjects

Table 14-2. Money Lost with One Extra Flower Thrown In per Order

Yearly Volume	Average Order	# Orders Yearly	Average Cost per Flower					
			3¢	5¢	8¢	10¢	15¢	20¢
$ 25,000	$ 3.50	7,142	$214.26	$ 357.10	$ 571.36	$ 714.20	$1,071.30	$1,428.40
35,000	3.75	9,333	279.99	466.65	746.64	933.30	1,399.95	1,866.60
50,000	4.00	12,500	375.00	625.00	1,000.00	1,250.00	1,875.00	2,500.00
75,000	4.20	17,857	535.71	892.85	1,428.56	1,785.70	2,678.55	3,571.40
150,000	4.75	31,578	947.34	1,578.90	2,526.74	3,157.80	4,736.70	6,313.60

of selling and merchandising. All of these go together to give the retail florist a fair profit.

Profit is a legitimate element of the selling price, so be sure it is indexed with every article sold.

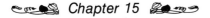 *Chapter 15*

ADVERTISING AND PUBLICITY

What is the difference between advertising and publicity? The end result is the same—to sell a product. In the case of the retail florist, it is to sell more flowers and related items to the consumer. The means by which this is done will differ. *Advertising means offering a product to the consumer which results directly in selling merchandise. Publicity,* on the other hand, *sells ideas* which eventually lead to selling merchandise. Advertising is done to get results *now*, which will make money for the business person. Consider advertising as an investment, not an expense.

Publicity is usually a means of promoting the idea of flowers and trying to build a favorable image of the retail flower shop. It is an indirect way of selling. Many merchants and industries use flowers in their ads to sell furniture, clothing, liquor, and other items, yet many florists are reluctant to use flowers for their own advertising and publicity. Fortunately for the industry, many of our more progressive florists realize the value of publicity and public relations. A retail florist a few years ago donated several hundred bulbs to beautify the grounds around city hall. The resulting publicity cannot be measured in dollars and cents to this florist, but there is no doubt as to the increase in business which resulted from this act. Another florist helped to landscape and beautify the area around a local bank which in turn improved the whole downtown area of his small town. Public relations, through publicity, is of great value in making the general public more flower conscious. Corsages have been donated to guest stars appearing on television shows by some of our retail florists. There are many ways to gain publicity for a retail florist shop.

ADVERTISING

Advertising is a more direct approach to induce people to buy flowers *now*. A good advertising campaign must be planned carefully in advance. Advertising should start readers thinking about the merchandise offered for sale. A good ad will attract attention, be brief enough to be easily read and quickly grasped, and bring results. A good ad should aim to leave the readers who cannot be sold at once with a favorable impression, so that sooner or later, as the need or occasion arises, they will remember *a particular ad and store*.

There are four key principles which form the basis of successful advertising. Good advertising—

- ◆§ Informs, helping the consumer buy more intelligently.
- ◆§ Tells the truth.
- ◆§ Conforms to the generally accepted standards of good taste.
- ◆§ Recognizes both its responsibility to help pay its own costs and its social responsibility to serve the public.

Considerations

There are several major points to consider when planning the advertising campaign for the year. They are as follows:

1. **The area to be covered with the ad.** What group of people are you trying to reach?
2. **The cost in relation to the expected return.** The decision here will be based partly on past experience, and partly on future expectations. What results do you expect?
3. **Size of expenditure.** The general average quoted by most successful florists is approximately 3 to 5 per cent of their annual gross dollar volume of sales. Include all types and forms of advertising, particularly the cost of window displays including the cost of flowers used and then dumped.
4. **The age and reputation of the store.** A new business should expect to spend more (4 to 6 per cent) than an older established shop (2 to 3 per cent).
5. **Location of the store.** This will be a big factor in determining which type of advertising to use.
6. **Time to advertise.** This seems to be the major question. Many florists and authorities will say to advertise *between the holidays*, many say only *at holidays*, and others will say to do both. Each florist must make this decision personally. Because each shop and location is different, you have very little concrete evidence to guide you. The authors believe, however, that you should have a planned advertising program all year, and advertise both at, and between, holidays.

7. **Long- and short-range objectives for the program.** Plan for the holiday as well as for the whole year.

Advertising must be well planned in advance. There are many factors to be considered when planning the advertising program for the year, including the following: (1) Compare the advertising expense with the gross volume of sales. What was the percentage spent last year? (2) Calculate the advertising expenses for each month during the year. (3) Determine what percentage of advertising expense will be used for each type of media. (4) Make sure you have the best space contract possible with the newspaper. (5) Be sure you are satisfied with the position assigned to your ad in the newspaper, or the spot on the radio. (6) Review and revise the direct mailing list to be sure it is reaching all the potential customers. (7) Be sure the mailing list is up-to-date. (8) Use the most effective postage rate on direct mail advertising. (9) Make a list of the non-productive advertising from last year. (10) Be sure the advertising job is as effective as that of your competitor.

Here are a few general advertising rules which you will be wise to keep in mind when planning the advertising campaign. (1) Try not to get tied up with any very long-term contracts. (2) Consider most advertising as an experiment and evaluate its effectiveness periodically. (3) Always advertise flowers and their uses.

Budget

In an issue dealing with advertising, the Bank of America's *Small Business Reporter* stated that retailers interviewed indicated an average advertising expenditure of 2.5 per cent, while service businesses reported average advertising expenditures of 3.5 per cent. Their total sample of small businesses indicated an average expenditure of 3.1 per cent of gross sales on advertising. The amount varied according to size of the business.

The Bank of America suggests than in addition to taking a percentage of gross sales, you should consider six factors in determining an advertising budget. These factors are:

1. **Size of business.** Consider gross sales.
2. **Type of business.** Stores depending on volume selling of highly promotional merchandise must spend more for advertising.
3. **Length of time in business.** The newer the store, the more advertising it needs to become established.

4. **Location.** Good advertising acts as leverage for a poor location, enticing customers to go out of their way for the promise of better merchandise, good customer services, bargain prices or some other advantage.
5. **Competition.** In order for a business to maintain its share of the market, advertising expenditures must bear some relationship to what competitors are spending. Aggressive advertising on the part of local competitors requires stores of the same nature to be equally aggressive.
6. **Size of market area.** Merchants operating in large communities usually must spend more for advertising than merchants in small communities. Media rates are based on circulation, and circulation tends to cover an entire community.

Media

There are 17 different types of media from which to choose. Consider the advisability of each for your particular shop and location. They are as follows:

1. **Window display**—one of the best for most shops if you are in the right location. Arrangements displayed in the store are considered in this category because they often are part of the window display.
2. **Newspaper ads**—very good in small towns, but may not be as good in the larger cities where you may be trying to reach only one section of the population. Use many small ads rather than just a few large ones.
3. **Direct mail**—the one advertising media which will work for all retail florists. You can aim the ad at a selected list of present and potential customers. You can very easily measure the return against the cost of the ad. Brautigam Florists of Chicago send out over 11,000 direct mail form color ads during the Christmas season.
4. **Radio**—good in small towns, but usually too expensive in large cities. Some florists allocate up to 75 per cent of their total advertising budget to radio advertising.
5. **Television**—good for Allieds, or large retailers who can afford it.
6. **Store front sign**—very good with little expense.
7. **Sign on truck**—good advertising with little cost.
8. **Yellow Pages in the phone book**—effectiveness depends on the size of the town and the type of store. There are pros

and cons on this type of advertising. Some florists feel it is a waste of money and claim people do not use the Yellow Pages for a florist. Others feel that new people in a community, particularly, will go there to find a florist, and feel it is well worth the money. However, the only people who turn to an ad of this sort are those who have already decided to buy. Remember that you must do $1,000 worth of business to pay for a $100 ad. The Yellow Page ad should tell why the customer will be better off by dealing with you in particular and inform about the merchandise and services offered.

9. **Bus ads**—prohibitive in cost to most florists but good for the Allieds.
10. **Outdoor billboards**—prohibitive in cost to most individual florists but good for Allieds and national advertising. They

Figure 15-1. An outdoor billboard tying in with SAF national advertising. (Courtesy, Miller Florist, Warren, Ohio.)

can be coordinated with television, and the Society of American Florists' campaign. The message must be brief, so the passerby can read it quickly.

11. **Magazines**—ads for high schools and local clubs. Consider these as a donation (not advertising) since they will be a waste of money in most cases.

12. **Motion picture houses**—success depends on the community.

13. **Organizational magazines**—an ad in *FTD News, Teleflora Spirit,* or *Florafacts* to increase the business from other member florists. Whether it pays depends on the size of the city and just how much of this business you wish to handle.

14. **Flowers**—The condition and artistic arrangement—an excellent means for advertising floral products and the store without any additional cost. Nothing can take the place of the reputation you build for yourself with your flowers. This is the foundation of the retail florist business, which determines its future success.

15. **Word-of-mouth**—spoken as friend to friend and attracts attention, arouses interest, creates conviction, and is very effective.

16. **Phone call reminders to regular customers**—an effective way to advertise. One possibility might be a call a year later to a man who bought flowers for an anniversary or birthday. Before making any calls, the florist should have all available facts about the customer and past orders close at hand.

17. **Cooperative advertising**—very effective through Allieds and other groups. The Society of American Florists and the Florists' Transworld Delivery Association both advertise nationally in a cooperative effort to help all segments of the florist industry. Colorado Carnation Growers and the Florida Gladiolus Growers Association advertise their particular flower nationally, aimed at the retail florist as well as the consumer.

   The SAF's Committee of AFMC does a tremendous job of advertising flowers nationally. Recently there is a trend for the producers (growers) to supply the funds for national advertising called "Floraboard," which is in its infancy.

How can you determine which type of media is best for your shop? Nearly three-fourths of the florists advertise in paid media one or more times a year according to a U.S. Department of Agriculture survey. Over one-third feature specific floral products in their advertisements. Nearly 40 per cent of the retail florists use newspapers, the most popular medium, to inform their customers of items featured. Other frequently used media are window signs, radio, and direct mail. To determine the proper media, consider the size of the city in which you are located, the type of the shop, the volume of business you expect, and the age of the store.

The results of various surveys indicate that the best advertising media for the florists in the smaller areas are: (1) newspaper, (2) direct mail, (3) window display, and (4) if the advertising budget allows it, radio. In most areas television is prohibitive in cost. A consistent newspaper advertising campaign, backed up by direct mail advertising seems to be the most effective for many florists. This is in addition to a good window display as discussed in Chapter 7.

Newspaper Advertising

There are certain specific advantages of newspaper advertising if you are a retailer in a small town, as follows:

1. You reach the largest number of potential customers. Probably no other single medium could deliver a message so completely and to so large an audience at one time.
2. You build good will and prestige as well as sales. The mere fact that you, as a small retail merchant, have your name in the newspaper lends a high degree of prestige value. The continued appearance of your name under an advertisement in the local newspaper, even if only a small insertion, places you and your wares in an acceptable position in the community, and thus builds good will.
3. You can tie your advertising message in with the news of the moment, thereby making it more effective. There are unique possibilities offered by the timeliness of the newspaper.
4. You can receive valuable aid in your advertising from the newspaper. Publishers have wide experience with preparing advertisements for insertion in their papers. The skill acquired from this experience is at the disposal of the advertiser, usually free of charge.
5. You can capitalize on the buying state of mind of the newspaper reader when inspecting the advertisements for bargains.
6. Your ad stays in print and can be seen whenever the newspaper is read.

Be sure to select the best ad mat. Professionally prepared advertisements in mat form will help to develop a strong selling ad at a minimum of work and expense, one which will increase sales for the flower business. Advertising mats that are distributed by suppliers are exceptionally good in a high percentage of cases. The advertising experts who prepare these mats devote their full time to the study of advertising problems to determine the best buying motives, to select the strongest selling appeals, and to create a good advertising message for local retailers. Tie in with national advertising when possible. A good example here is to tie in with the AFMC advertising program of the Society of American Florists, whose national advertising is expanding each year. Use timely or seasonal mats to tie in with the various holidays. Be sure to use a variety of appeals to be successful with different customers.

Many retail florists belong to an Allied in their own locality whose members—retailers, wholesalers, and growers—all contribute a percentage of their gross sales to the advertising of flowers. This benefits everyone in the industry. All retail florists should join their own Allied.

You can have a powerful, consistent advertising program with a limited advertising budget when you use small space newspaper ads for your flower business. Successful advertising is based on the three profit P's of success. Good ads are: **P**lanned, **P**ersuasive, and **P**ersistent. Remember that *repetition builds reputation*. Small ads will help to stretch the advertising dollars. Here are some good rules to follow:

1. Stick to one idea and one only in a small space ad.
2. Select the readers. Pinpoint the appeal to one group of customers; *i.e.*, an ad on the society page or the sports page.
3. Frame the ad so it will stand out.
4. Don't divide the ad into several parts—it is too small a space.
5. Don't crowd the ad.
6. Make sure it is easy to read. Establish a good reader "eye flow."
7. Include only the essentials.

The advertisement should appeal to the reader's self-interest, offer a product that is really wanted, be unique, picture the product or service, state the price, tell where to get it, and urge the customer to act *now*.

Direct Mail

Direct mail advertising is simply any sales message carried by mail to a regular or prospective customer. It is neither complicated nor difficult to use. It can sell, promote, introduce, or inform. Results depend on how well the program is planned and produced to do the job for which it is intended. The heart of any direct mail effort is the mailing list, which can be set up or obtained in many ways. Timing and cost are also important considerations.

Whatever form of direct mail advertising you use, to be sure the effort will be rewarded with increased business, remember the following key points: repetition, quality of the ad, the accuracy of the mailing list in reaching the people you want to reach, and choice of the best items to put across the message.

For direct mail advertising to be successful, do the following:

1. Mail to a select list of customers and prospects who can be given strong reasons for coming to your particular store.
2. Keep the list accurate and up-to-date. (Sending a mailer to someone who is deceased is irritating to the survivors.)
3. Tell them "what they want to hear"—benefits which they will gain from shopping in your store.
4. Make the sales message personal.
5. Tailor the mailing to fit the personality of the store, the merchandise and the services advertised, as well as the people to whom it is addressed.

Although direct mail is similar to other advertising, it has these distinctive characteristics which can be extremely valuable to you:

- It is a personal contact with a selected prospect.
- It can be sent to a limited number of especially qualified prospects.
- It can be concealed from competitors.
- It can be scheduled to reach the prospects on any given date.
- It can easily be measured for effectiveness in order to keep its cost in balance with sales and profits.

To set up the direct mailing list, start with your own customers, add people to whom you have delivered flowers from your customers, use lists of business executives, country club members, garden club members, new businesses in the area, and include members of various civic organizations. Screen these lists to make up your own list of special potential customers.

The Value of Advertising

Because many retail florists do not realize the value of advertis-

ing they do not spend enough money on advertising. Many successful florists and experts in the field of advertising have said that you
should spend from 3 to 5 per cent of your gross volume of sales on
advertising. Yet, the surveys show 1.01 to 4.0 per cent is usually
spent. (See Table 6-2). These figures, of course, may not include all
the expenditures which should be charged to advertising, such as
flower donations, cost of window displays, and flowers used in these
displays. When all expenses and monies are figured in that should
be charged to advertising, the figure should approach 3 to 5 per cent
of the gross volume of sales for the shop, including the planned
advertising campaign discussed previously. It is hard to develop an
advertising program around a percentage allotment, but it should be
used as a basis for comparison with other shops. To avoid spending
too much, plan in advance. Whether you figure monthly, quarterly,
or yearly, plan at least six months in advance and control by appro-
priations and budgets. Include all the costs for proposed advertising,
promotions, publicity, and public relations. The important thing is to
stimulate in the public mind an awareness of the pleasures to be
derived from the increased use of flowers in daily living.

PROMOTION AND PUBLICITY

Obtaining newspaper publicity for the shop will help business.
The best way is to make yourself known to more people by gaining
publicity for your shop. Most newspapers are glad to print items of
news—if they are news, and not just an attempt to get free advertising. Meet the editor of the newspaper and cultivate a nose for news.
Give stories a professional touch, and be sure to offer genuine news.
Publicity is indirect advertising in that it sells the idea of flowers, not
the flowers themselves. Even the large ads for mass market food
stores which offer flowers and plants help promote the concept of
using flowers in the home.

Open House

One of the best promotional ideas is to have an open house before Christmas and again before Easter. Planning is important here,
just as in any advertising campaign. Price everything that is on display. Show plenty of made-up items so customers can see how to use
the merchandise. Some florists, if the open house is held on Sunday,
do not sell any of the merchandise, but will take orders. Others set
up several cash registers and do a booming business. The newspaper

Figure 15-2. Christmas open house. (Courtesy, Buning The Florist, Inc., Fort Lauderdale, Fla.)

publicity will be tremendous. You might invite the local radio station to broadcast from the shop during the open house. It is impossible to measure the value of this in dollars and cents. Provide the opportunity for people to return to buy something they saw and liked but didn't get a chance to purchase. An open house can be an excellent traffic builder, but the event must be well planned, executed, and merchandised for maximum results.

Other Promotions

Promotions are used for several reasons: to create more business, to realize more profitable orders, to move over-supplies, and to eventually sell merchandise. Each promotion begins with an idea which is expanded by the florist. As an example, in the fall when automobile dealers are featuring new cars, approach the promotion manager and sell the idea that a window full of flowers shows activity and that something unusual is taking place. Sell dealers on mass display. Identify their sales and office personnel with boutonnieres and corsages. Some florists have talked automobile salespersons into giv-

Figure 15-3. A display of green plants, hanging baskets, and dish gardens. (Courtesy, Miller Florist, Warren, Ohio.)

ing the customer an orchid corsage or a pot plant each time a new car is delivered. Or sell them on the idea of giveaway items, such as individual roses or carnations, to each customer during their new model showing.

Another promotional idea to keep the volume steady is to sell a man on sending his wife 10 arrangements throughout the year. Tie in these arrangements with anniversaries, birthdays, and the major holidays—excellent for husbands who are forgetful!

Promote flowers in your window displays by tying in with a local event, movie, or news item of national importance.

Provide some free flowers or corsages for special programs on television. This can be done by an individual florist, by a group, or by an Allied.

Publicity and promotion can help sell flowers for any shop, but they must be planned in advance and correlated with the advertising program and expenditure of the shop.

Public Relations

Public relations is a form of publicity, and an indirect form of advertising. Basically, it is a method to interest people in a particular shop. It can be done by supplying bulbs as mentioned at the beginning of the chapter, by speaking to various groups, giving demonstrations, donating plants and flowers to public officials, or any of a hundred other ideas. Charge a fee for any talks and demonstrations that you give to cut down on the number of requests. These appearances cost time and money—weigh this against the advertising value gained.

Herb Mitchell says: "Public relations are activities performed in an attempt to create a favorable public opinion among customers and potential customers." He gives the following 16 examples:

1. Giving care information for cut flowers and pot plants.
2. Guaranteeing the merchandise.
3. Filling out the sympathy card on the reverse side with all pertinent information.
4. Providing adequate parking for your customers.
5. Advertising in local programs and yearbooks.
6. Using credit cards, which can be very advantageous to your business.
7. Acknowledging new accounts.
8. Following through to see that orders are satisfactory.

9. Servicing weddings.
10. Sending "thank you's" for business.
11. Contacting active accounts.
12. Using proper telephone atmosphere and techniques.
13. Checking driver contact with the customer.
14. Checking to see how your packages look.
15. Sending flowers from *you* to the customer on special occasions like birthday and anniversary.
16. Giving customer service.

Many of these are just good business practices as well as being good public relations.

In some shops, every customer who comes in to pay the bill is given a free flower. It is good public relations and gets customers to return to the shop.

Advertising boils down to the question of "Do you really want your business to grow?" If so, plan your campaign carefully. Decide *What* to sell, *When* to advertise, to *Whom* to advertise, *Where* to advertise, and *How* much to budget for advertising. It is up to you to plan your own advertising and do it carefully. Advertising, promotion, public relations, and publicity are all part of a well-organized successful florist business.

Chapter 16

MERCHANDISING—CASH-AND-CARRY

MERCHANDISING

Merchandising today is a far cry from the pushcart selling of flowers of our ancestors and yet they employed some of the same principles used today. Their success was based on letting the people see the flowers, having personal contact with the customers, and asking them to buy. Today you must do the same.

To merchandise flowers you must display them and use salesmanship to complete the sale. Merchandising means offering the right product to the right people, at the right time, in the right place, and at the right price. You already have the right product: flowers—a universally liked commodity. You do not have to sell people on flowers. You also can sell the merchandise at the right price. Many recent studies have shown the most popular range for merchandising flowers to be between $0.90 and $3.50. So, you can very easily meet two merchandising criteria. You must find the right people, the right time, and the right place. Mass market outlets are a part of the answer, but do not apply to the retail florist business except from the competitive angle. Advertising will help to find the people. A U.S. Department of Agriculture survey showed that 86 per cent of the florists contacted reported they used floral designs in their shop windows as a regular part of their merchandising program.

In shifting the emphasis from artistry to merchandising, you do not need to lessen your efforts in design. In order to direct and orient your business toward the requirements of the new market, you must become a merchant—not just in name, but in fact.

Effective merchandising depends on the establishment of a positive firm image in the public mind. To the person on the street, every retail establishment carries an image.

The tools of the merchandiser fall into four broad areas: price,

175

advertising, display, and salesmanship. Price is the most powerful merchandising tool of all and will be discussed later in detail. Advertising was discussed in Chapter 15. Display is an important part of merchandising, and no other product lends itself so well to display as flowers. Good merchandisers recognize that displays are the first step in getting the product into the customer's hands. Salesmanship must be developed to become a successful merchandiser of floral products.

The big sales expansion for flowers today lies not only with special occasion or holiday buying, but with the *everyday use of flowers in the home and place of business*. Promoting flowers for everyday use means publicizing flowers as a part of today's modern living.

In order to merchandise flowers and increase the use of flowers by the average consumer, you must endeavor to establish a buying habit for flowers. Merchandising is one way you can get people into the habit of buying flowers regularly. Concentrate your efforts toward selling flowers for the home. Between 80 and 90 per cent of the people interviewed in a survey indicated that they would buy flowers regularly if they were available at a low price—90¢ to a dollar per week. Most of these purchases would be for the home. Many florists are in danger of pricing themselves out of the market; roses are the best example of this problem.

Roses have been shown by several studies to be a good item for a special sale. Consumer preference studies have also shown that the number does not need to always be a dozen. Pompon chrysanthemums and gladioli have had wide acceptance. In pot plants we find that pot chrysanthemums, kalanchoes, and petunias are the best sellers in some shops.

Merchandising can be done all the time, not just to move surplus stock. To merchandise economically, you need flowers that are attractive, will last more than a few hours, are low priced, and are attractively displayed. They should be in constant supply, and sold in such a way that they are easy to buy.

Supermarkets place their products before 35 per cent of the consumers, while retail florists' shops attract only about 3 per cent of the consumers. This drawing power can be increased in the flower shops by following some of the ideas adopted by the supermarkets. Supermarkets are now reaching a hitherto florally untouched segment of the buying public. Surveys have shown that most people who buy flowers in supermarkets never patronize a retail flower shop.

MASS MARKET OUTLETS

Is mass marketing for the retail florist? The authors' answer to that is a qualified "yes." The mass market outlets offer a means of broadening the market. This can cause a significant increase in the sale of flowers for home use through impulse sales. This higher volume of sales will increase profits to the growers. It will ultimately increase profits to retail florists by increasing the consumer's awareness of flowers and by influencing buying habits to include flowers. If people are more flower conscious, they will purchase more flowers in retail flower shops for special occasions as well as for home use. Any promotion of flowers will eventually stimulate the sale of flowers through the regular conventional channels. The retail florist is the logical one to utilize mass market techniques. Some florists are operating supermarket flower stalls.

Flowers are being sold in convenience stores, drugstores, and supermarkets in the Denver area through two non-traditional firms.

Mass market outlets have been successful because they have created a demand for flowers through advertising and promotion. They depend on mass display, large store traffic, and a low markup. Their setup is entirely different from that of the retail florist.

The mass marketer has discovered that it pays to handle quality floral products in order to get good yet reasonable prices and make a profit. More than ever before, supermarkets are moving into both green and blooming pot plants. With quality and fair prices, the mass markets are making inroads into the retail florist business.

The supermarkets use advertising and promotion to the utmost. This integrated program of advertising and promotion can be used by retail florists on an industry level. The supermarkets recognize differences in people according to social class, religious groups, and regional groups. They isolate groups for their own business, and concentrate all their efforts on that group. Supermarket "competition" is not as real as one might think.

There are many ways of reaching the mass market. What will work for one individual will not always be best for another.

The authors believe that certain retail florists can embark in a mass market program. This is especially true if you wish to branch out into supermarkets and shopping malls. Kiosks in shopping malls have already been discussed. A kiosk or a branch shop in a mall is an excellent way to mass market flowers.

Another way to mass market flowers is through the managing

and operating of a flower section in a supermarket or department store.

The advertising and promotional program must stimulate the buyer to want the product or the satisfaction it provides. So far stimulation has not been provided successfully by floral promotion and packaging. This needs to be developed in the retail florist industry because packaging leads the goods to better merchandising, one of the avenues to increased sales.

A recent study at the University of Illinois showed that flowers competed favorably with other merchandise for net returns and gross profits per square foot of display space in both a variety store and a supermarket. Special sales of pot plants and small bunches of cut flowers were studied in these two stores and compared to sales in a retail flower shop. It was found that less expensive items sold better in the variety store, while more expensive items sold better in the supermarket and retail flower shop. Holidays, weekends, and special occasions had the largest influence on weekly sales. The quality of the merchandise was found to be of prime importance.

To encourage the everyday use of flowers and plants, maintain an adequate display of good quality merchandise at all times. This seems to be the area in which the mass markets fall down in most instances—and this is where the retail florist shop can have the advantage. Also offer an adequate selection of colors and varieties.

What about competition between retail flower shops and the big chain stores? In order to merchandise flowers you must concentrate on the reluctance of consumers to enter a retail flower shop. Recent studies have shown that the average person does not feel welcome, so will not enter a florist shop to browse. This condition has been brought about by the florists themselves. If florists are to merchandise flowers and increase sales in their shops, they must *make people feel welcome*. Successful merchandising depends on volume selling, which can only occur through increased store traffic.

If you have enough transient trade passing your shop to make it economically feasible, you can mass market cut flowers and pot plants. A lot depends on your location and how well the merchandise is advertised and displayed.

There are several advantages to the mass marketing of cut flowers and pot plants. One is that it increases the public's awareness of flowers and helps to get them into their homes. Second, it puts ready cash into your cash register, because so many of the flowers sold in mass markets are cash-and-carry. This ready cash allows you to take advantage of buying larger quantities at discount and saving 10 per cent by paying bills within the discount period.

You can increase total sales through cash-and-carry sales, as well as realizing profits by selling other items at the same time. If you can produce speed and ease in purchasing, as well as attractive displays, you will bring more people into your shop.

Find the approach to the mass market that will work best in your area. Don't be afraid of the mass merchandiser. If you run a clean, progressive operation and give quality and service, there's no way you can be hindered by the mass merchandiser.

A spectacular mobile merchandising innovation is called "Flowerama." It is designed for merchandising outdoor flowers in such areas as shopping centers, supermarkets, nurseries, and garden centers. The structure is pre-cut of translucent Filon panels and opens to a 24′ × 32′ selling area. It folds up to 8′ × 32′ and can be moved where the action is. Bachman's Bouquet Boutique is another merchandiser with accessible display. (See Chapter 3.)

CASH-AND-CARRY

Cash-and-carry, probably the most common form of merchandising practiced by florists, is applicable to almost all retail florist shops. You must decide for yourself what is best for you. A lot will depend on the type of store, location, and customers, but any florist, who wishes to, can merchandise through cash-and-carry specials. However, if you do decide to try cash-and-carry specials, give it a fair trial. Don't try it once and say it isn't any good. You must try *every weekend for at least six months* to be successful. The florists who are successfully offering cash-and-carry specials to their customers do it every weekend of the year including holiday weekends, with the possible exception of Easter and Mother's Day. Some offer a cash-and-carry special even on these weekends.

Why Cash-and-Carry?

Many florists wonder why they should try cash-and-carry weekend specials. There are several reasons. First, it will increase the total gross sales without additional overhead costs, which should increase the net profit. Second, it will get more people into the store which, in turn, will lead to more sales of related or impulse items if they are on display. Third, these sales will put actual cash in the cash register without any expense for bookkeeping. Fourth, these items do not need to be designed or delivered. Fifth, flowers can be purchased in larger quantity and at a lower price than usual. Sixth, the flowers not sold for cash-and-carry can be used the next day in funeral work. This means a higher profit because the material for these design pieces was purchased at a lower cost but sold in funeral work at the normal price, resulting in a greater markup. And, seventh and last, you will be helping more people buy flowers more often.

Saving the Customer Money

One of the best advertising gimmicks to use is to show how cash-and-carry is saving the customer money:

- No delivery. (Florists have reported delivery charges range from $1 to $5 per piece depending upon the city.)
- No bookkeeping or mailing of statements.
- No labor for designing.
- No container or box.
- Lower wholesale cost due to large quantity purchase.

All of these items reduce the cost of the merchandise to the consumer. Tell the customers that you are passing the savings on to them. They will understand and appreciate this.

The success of the program depends upon a good advertising policy, attractive display, and sticking strictly to the *cash-and-carry* restriction for everyone. If you explain the facts, the customer—even your best customer—will not insist on delivery and use of the charge account without an additional charge. If you start making exceptions, you will find yourself losing money instead of making it.

The success of tie-in promotions to take advantage of traffic drawn through cash-and-carry specials, depends upon the following:

1. Select an item which adds to the appeal of the special, or has a strong latent appeal of its own.
2. Price it and advertise it as a bargain.
3. Set up a mass display of the item.
4. Use personal salesmanship to the fullest. A good advertising program is necessary to tell the customer about the product, tell why it is a bargain, tell the customer which wants it will satisfy, and tell as much as possible about the retail operation which affects costs and the retail price.

How Much to Charge?

Offer cash-and-carry specials every weekend of the year at a price between $0.90 and $3.50. Studies at several universities have shown that when specials were offered at 35¢ and 50¢, the people felt it was too cheap for a retail florist shop and hesitated to buy them. When the price rose over $3.50 then the number of sales was curtailed. The success of cash-and-carry items lies in volume business. Most florists who offer cash-and-carry specials on a regular basis keep the price around $1.00. Some sell them for 95¢, which, if the sales tax is 5¢, brings it to an even dollar. Others sell at $1.00 plus the tax. Others use an uneven figure such as 97¢ or 99¢. You must determine your own price. Florists do not agree on whether to keep the price the same every week or vary it with market conditions. It is up to you to determine which policy you think will work best for you. Some florists try it each way for six months to see which is best. Pricing is based on the cost of merchandise. Most florists use a 2 or 3 to 1 markup. This should take care of all costs and expenses, since there is reduced overhead with this type of selling.

What to Merchandise?

This is a hard question to answer although there are some guidelines. The first of these is to work with the wholesaler and offer material that is in oversupply on the market. If there is no oversupply, then decide on some other flower. Flowers should be offered that are commonly known to the general public. Stay away from exotic flowers or flowers that are relatively unknown to most people. Roses have been shown by many studies to be one of the best year-round items for cash-and-carry specials. Pompons, gladioli, snaps, and carnations are also good items. You do not need to sell in dozen lots. If the wholesale price is such that you can offer only nine roses or one-half bunch of pompons, advertise it this way. If you can't merchandise at a markup of at least 2 to 1, it will not be profitable. However, always use quality merchandise (even if short-stemmed) or you will defeat the purpose of the program.

Will It Work?

Yes, for many florists, and not at the expense of normal sales. In a program in Pennsylvania a few years ago, all of the retail florists in a certain town offered cash-and-carry specials every weekend for a year. Aggregate dollar volume sales from all six shops increased 14.8 per cent over the preceding year. Net profits increased 19.3 per cent. Not all of this was due to the cash-and-carry specials themselves, but a good percentage was, according to the participating florists.

The potentialities of self-service in the flower industry are grossly underdeveloped. For instance, only a few florists among the many that offer specials today have the cash-and-carry items out where the customer can select the merchandise.

Successful Examples

Many florists all over the country have been trying cash-and-carry specials for years with great success. A florist in Nashville, Tennessee, sold 100,000 roses during the summer months and merchandised gladioli from November through May.

A particular retail florist was losing business to a supermarket across the street from his shop. He started offering flowers that were priced for home use through weekend cash-and-carry specials. He offers these every week of the year and furnishes no greens, designing, or delivery. He has educated his customers to the term "cash-and-carry." His total sales have increased by 15 per cent in a six-month period due to special sales. He says that people will return week after week to take flowers home. He also said that some of his summer weekends would be dull without these specials. He says these sales do not interfere with his usual flower sales. *He has competed so successfully with the supermarket, that the supermarket has discontinued the handling of cut flowers.* This florist is successfully merchandising flowers with advertising, display, lower prices, and quality merchandise.

Many florists have tried weekend cash-and-carry specials and are convinced of their success in helping to sell more flowers. The following are some typical remarks made by retail florists concerning special sales: "Specials have increased store traffic by 400 per cent." "Total sales have increased since I started cash-and-carry sales." "The sale of other items in the store has increased." "Advertising for special sales keeps my name before the public." "These specials create customer buying habits." "Specials do not cheapen the store name."

A few retailers have started to develop real techniques for merchandising, and others are following. Many retail shops, however, are not located in positions favorable for store traffic and merchandising. Some retail florists are not interested in low mark-up sales.

Separate your business into two types: service and cash-and-carry. You cannot live on special sales alone, but they can add to your gross income and profit. The success of this program rests not only with advertising, display, and pricing, but also the enthusiasm and initiative of the store personnel. Price alone is not sufficient for a successful merchandising program.

The study mentioned previously showed that gross income and net profits could be increased in every shop in one town and not at the expense of another. Each store showed an increase. This program also showed the importance of coordinated effort in purchasing, advertising, and an all-out promotion as a group.

The results of this year-long study of cash-and-carry specials showed the following: added gross income was accomplished with little additional capital and operating costs, merchandising helped to move the additional flowers on the market, a definite promotional appeal is needed to get people into the habit of buying flowers weekly, cooperative buying and advertising by a group of florists will greatly reduce the cost of the promotion, and the effectiveness of cash-and-carry specials depends upon the quality of merchandise offered at a retail price under $2.50, and for every weekend of the year.

SUPERMARKET COMPETITION

A study done by the Colorado State University showed that 90 per cent of chain supermarkets represented handle some type of floriculture products, although nearly half of them (48 per cent) don't handle cut flowers at all. Chains are starting to demand quality flowers and plants. The chains can no longer be looked upon as a place to dump extra flowers and plants. The majority of supermarket executives interviewed are in favor of retailing cut flowers and one-third plan to increase their involvement in this area.

Irwin A. Cochrun gives retailers the following 10 steps to increase sales if they wish to compete effectively with the supermarkets:

1. Make use of the power of pre-sold merchandising through the media of mass communications.
2. Speed the flow of goods to the selling shelves, and use bigger displays.

3. Use the power of lowered prices.
4. Make it easy for the customers to shop, and provide adequate parking.
5. Make it easy for customers to go through the store, and draw them past the merchandise items to the service counter.
6. Expose customers to the power of mass display.
7. Make the product salable by packaging cut flowers for ease in self-service.
8. Do not rush customers, but let them browse around.
9. Use alert, courteous, and helpful salesclerks.
10. Remove any bottlenecks in recording sales and the checking-out operations.

Many of these points can be used by retail florists.

INCREASED SALES

There are two distinct markets for flowers—necessity and luxury. The demand determines the prices of flowers for weddings, funerals, hospitals, and special occasions. The last U.S. Department of Agriculture study of distribution of sales of flowers indicated that 46 per cent of retail florist sales were for funerals; 19 per cent for hospitals; 9 per cent for weddings; 4 per cent for conventions and business openings; 5 per cent for church use; 10 per cent for home and office use; and 7 per cent for all others.

Ways to increase sales in existing retail flower shops are through the use of seasonal flowers, displaying arrangements of varying sizes to give a choice, separate pricing of flowers and services, and pricing all merchandise so the customer personally can make a selection.

Another way to increase the sale of flowers is by increasing the number of florists' holidays from the traditional 9 to 10 or 12. Why not promote flowers, as some florists are already doing, for other holidays and special occasions? Some suggestions would be St. Patrick's Day, Father's Day, Mother-in-Law's Day, Grandparents' Day, and National Flower Week.

Planning ahead to feature specials when the market is low in price and high in supply can be beneficial to the retailer, wholesaler, and grower, whether specials are a part of each florist's operation or not. Use these times to advertise real values to customers to get more of them to come into the shop. This is all part of a successful merchandising campaign.

Merchandising does not revolve only around cash-and-carry

specials at $1.00. Other quantities of merchandise can be successfully merchandised at $3.50, $5.00, $7.50, and higher if the florist has the kind of customers who will purchase these items. It all depends on how the merchandise is advertised, displayed, and offered for sale to the customer.

PHYSICAL LAYOUT

Another rule of merchandising is that a physical layout should draw the customer naturally and unconsciously into all parts of the store. Every possible item should be displayed so it is easily seen. Goods well displayed are half sold. The following list of important considerations is from Robert Ench, S. Klein Department Store:

A. An attractive and appealing interior:
1. Provide a convenient, symmetrical layout.
2. Have amply wide aisles.
3. Modern display fixtures and equipment are necessary.
4. Have low fixtures in the center, so that the whole area can be seen.
5. Most of the merchandise should be in plain sight and properly priced.
6. Attractive and orderly arrangement of displays and stock will increase sales.
7. Have an appropriate floor in good condition.
8. Use harmony of colors and forms so that the whole store makes a pleasant picture.
9. Have plenty of light so the merchandise is seen to best advantage.
10. Cleanliness of merchandise, fixtures, displays, and floors is essential.
11. The store should be properly ventilated or air conditioned.
12. The floor space must be large enough so that people do not feel crowded.
13. The store personnel shall be neatly and inconspicuously dressed, courteous, and eager to serve.

B. Traffic control:
1. Right or left hinging of entrance door.
2. Wide or narrow aisles.
3. Location of service counter and cash register at rear of store.
4. Locate staples or items most frequently asked for in out-of-the-way corners of store.
5. Change location of merchandise once or twice a year.

C. Eliminate blind fixtures and other hiding places for merchandise:

    1. Have 90 per cent of your merchandise on display.

D. Install open fixtures and make other provisions for display:

    1. Self-service fixtures.
    2. Low display tables.
    3. Island displays.
    4. Wall displays for tall merchandise.

E. Allot space to items in accordance with their sales volume and sales possibilities:

    1. Locate merchandise for convenience.
    2. Group related items together.
    3. Locate seasonal items in greatest traffic area.
    4. Locate specials in greatest traffic area.

F. Interior displays:

    1. Price mark every item displayed.
    2. Accompany merchandise with a sign telling what it is and its possible uses.

G. Window displays:

    1. Make the windows advertise the merchandise and the character of the store.
    2. Mark prices plainly.
    3. Display related items together.
    4. Tie in displays with local events.
    5. Tie in with national advertising.
    6. Put human interest into display.
    7. Do not crowd window.
    8. Make displays simple.
    9. Improve the window lighting.
    10. Change displays frequently.
    11. Keep everything clean.
    12. Motion attracts attention.
    13. Make the displays sell merchandise.

Merchandising means offering the right product to the right people, at the right place, at the right time, and at the right price. It can be done by retail florists as well as by mass market outlets. Successful merchandising depends on advertising, promotion, display, easy accesss, low prices, and quality merchandise.

Study your own situation to determine how you should best merchandise in your shop. Your employees must have the desire to merchandise flowers and use their salesmanship on these as well as other items.

Hundreds of regular retail florists are successfully merchandising flowers through cash-and-carry specials. Other methods will be developed in the future. Retail florists are proving every day that cut flowers and pot plants can be merchandised successfully with a minimum of effort and operating expense, even in the face of supermarket competition.

According to Alvi Voigt, the retail florists' share of total floral sales moved from 53.1 per cent in 1976 to 63.3 per cent in 1980, while the supermarkets' share only moved from 7.7 per cent in 1976 to 7.9 per cent in 1980.

Chapter 17

SALESMANSHIP

Salesmanship—the art of selling—is one of the weakest links in the present retail florist industry. Most retail florists are excellent designers, many are good business managers, but few are top-notch salespersons. It has been said by many people that most sales personnel in the retail florist business are *order-takers,* not salespersons. This is unfortunate, because the success of the business, and the profits realized, depend on the successful selling of the merchandise. Retail florists are caught between rising costs and shrinking profits; one solution is to increase sales. We have mentioned in Chapter 12 the qualities that you should look for in hiring your sales staff. To review: a salesperson should have the initiative for selling; must like people; be ambitious, dependable, and efficient; have good health; have a pleasing personality and appearance; be diplomatic and courteous; be able to get along well with others; and have a thorough knowledge of store merchandise, prices, and policies.

Salesmanship is actually one element of good merchandising. You cannot be a good salesperson unless you know what you are selling. Besides selling flowers, you are selling what flowers can do for people. It is your job to translate the characteristics of flowers themselves into the intangible messages they carry. This calls for selling skills far beyond that of an ordinary merchant. The better you know the product you are selling, the more successful you will be. You must tell people about your product and what it costs, and then get them to buy it. Eighty per cent of the retail florists in the United States, according to a recent survey, price mark all items displayed. Do not be afraid to price your merchandise so that the customer can easily see it. It will greatly help in the selling of both flowers and other merchandise.

To be a good salesperson, you must *want* to be a salesperson. You must like your product and believe in it, and you must like and trust people. Salesmanship is an art that takes practice. You must work at it to become a good salesperson. Many of the points of good salesmanship are just plain common sense.

It has been stated many times that a salesperson can sell anything by making it attractive and by showing a prospective customer how to use the item. Many florists have installed large, walk-in refrigerators for the customers. Allowing a customer to really see and handle the flowers fits in with today's philosophy of selling flowers. A florist should utilize the five senses as much as possible to succeed in selling.

The following highlights on selling are from Herb Mitchell. "There are three types of salesman: the order taker, the negotiation type, and the creative salesman. The order taker is just what the name implies. The negotiation type tries to bargain with the customer. The creative salesman, however, is the one who makes more sales for himself and the store, and is the one who upsells the merchandise and gets the customer to spend the most money for what he or she wants. Maximum satisfaction is the aim. Courage and confidence in himself and his product are two important factors in becoming a successful salesman. He should not be discouraged if he doesn't succeed at first. Throw out the attitude that 'this won't work' and say instead, 'it is worth a try.' "

To become a good salesperson, you should serve each customer in the best way possible. Develop a winning personality and constantly strive to improve it. As selling depends on communications, you must learn to communicate with your customers. They must know what you are saying, as well as what you mean. Communication is a two-way street between the salesperson and the customer.

First impressions are always important and the first 30 seconds that a customer spends in the shop may be the most important. There are four vital components of an approach to a customer which lead to a sale: (1) *The shop's name.* Use it in all discussions. (2) *The salesperson's name.* The customer likes to know the name of the person handling the order. (3) *The customer's name.* Find out what it is, use it, and remember it. (4) *The need.* Find out what the customer's need is and try to fill it.

You have a five-point selling job:

1. Sell yourself.
2. Sell the store.
3. Sell your ideas.
4. Sell the product.
5. Sell customer satisfaction.

To be successful, use various buying appeals to create a favorable impression for flowers and services. Convince customers that flowers are the best thing to buy for the occasion. Appeal to the aesthetic or utilitarian factor of flowers.

Selling is both an art and a science. It calls for careful planning. Keep in mind these three important steps to every successful sale: (1) *Interest* your customer in your merchandise and your ideas. (2) *Convince* the customer of the need for your products and services. (3) *Ask* for the sale—ask the customer to buy—*now*. This is where many sales are lost.

Because many sales training authorities say that 90 per cent of the sales are sold in the first 30 seconds, you must sell yourself and your store as well as impress the customer with your ability to serve and deliver the goods. Use the "you" approach to selling, and bring the customer into the discussion. Sell quality and not price. The six points for selling quality are as follows:

- Establish a quality atmosphere.
- Sell significant benefits of the merchandise.
- Point out the superior features of quality flowers.
- Always emphasize exceptional values.
- Sell the experience and reputation of the store.
- Sell friendly and reliable service.

Figure 17-1. An attractive and spacious area for selling. (Courtesy, Frederick's Flowers, Souderton, Pa.)

Many florists do not understand the value of their own time, their own ability, and their product and services. An understanding of their value and appreciation of their worth is essential if you are going to be a good salesperson. *You must believe in yourself first.*

UPSELLING

Upselling is the mark of a successful salesperson. This means selling a $15 arrangement to a customer who had expected to spend $10. Use the power of suggestion and use enthusiasm in selling. Give ideas and suggestions. Show the customer how beautiful the flowers are. It is always best to take the flowers out of the refrigerator, and let the customer see them and smell them. Don't just point to the flowers. Don't mention price unless forced to do so. When price is mentioned try to give the highest price to give the most customer satisfaction. Don't ask a question which gives the customer a chance to say "no." Close the sale by asking the customer "which one" he/she wants, not "if." Try to put the customer into the mood to say "yes," not "no." A demonstration will help to make the sale. This is very effective in store selling. Handle the merchandise with respect. Demonstrate a finished product whenever possible, not just the ingredients. Put the merchandise into the customer's hands as soon as possible. Sell the good features by telling the customer the benefits of the flowers and of this particular arrangement. Mention the features of the product, such as: fresh, long lasting, well designed, unusually arranged, colorful, newest variety, and other salient points which will help to complete the sale. Taking the customer into the delivery room to see the higher priced arrangements is also a part of successful selling. All of these practices will help you upsell your merchandise. This is also called *upgrading the sale.*

Men are easier to sell to than women, but over half of the customers in a flower shop are women. You need patience with all customers. Don't use high-pressure tactics as they are neither expected nor appreciated in a retail florist shop. A modern approach to selling is to encourage browsing and to make the customers feel welcome. Try to greet all regular customers by name. Remember their likes and dislikes in flowers. It is best to find out the occasion for the flowers and make two or three suggestions, letting the customer make the final decision. Always give a range of prices where possible. For example, a man went into a retail flower shop recently to get his wife some flowers for Valentine's Day. He asked the salesperson what was available. The salesclerk said, "We have roses for $20."

That was all the salesclerk said. The customer did not wish to spend $20 for Valentine's Day, and yet he did not want to be made to feel *cheap* by asking for something less expensive, so he said he would think about it. He left the store and bought his wife a $5 box of candy. The florist lost that sale and many more—the man is afraid to try flowers again.

Use the common names of flowers and plants, and not the scientific names unless specifically asked by the customer.

Color slide presentations of designs make impressive shop sales aids for all designs, not just wedding work.

Good manners are very important in successful selling. The following practices are considered *bad* manners and should be discouraged in the retail florist shop:

1. Being indifferent to a customer waiting for service.
2. Using a cold, impersonal manner with customers.
3. Arguing with or contradicting a customer.
4. Interrupting another employee when that person is waiting on a customer, without first asking permission from the customer.
5. Allowing friends to visit on the telephone.
6. Carrying on personal conversations within hearing of a customer.
7. Loud talking and laughing in the store.
8. Whistling or singing when there is a customer in the store.
9. Loud shouting or calling out instructions in the workroom or sales area.
10. Referring to customers or other employees as "honey," "dearie," "kiddo," or "my dear."
11. Chewing gum, smoking, or eating in the presence of a customer.
12. Men lounging around with their hands in their pockets.
13. Women powdering their faces or putting on lipstick on the sales floor.

PITFALLS IN SELLING

A survey of Michigan florists by a mystery shopper a few years ago brought out the following points on poor selling:

1. Many florists neglected the customer. She waited over 10 minutes for a clerk in one shop.

2. Florists were not careful enough about distractions and confusion in the store.
3. They didn't try to upgrade the sale. In most shops, she did not spend as much money as she had been prepared to for the items she purchased.
4. The florist did not try to sell related merchandise by suggesting other items to go with the flowers purchased.
5. Many florists did not know enough about their merchandise. Some salespersons did not even know the names of some of the common flowers in the shop.
6. They didn't suggest the uses to which flowers can be put.
7. They didn't attempt to close the sale in many cases. She walked out of nine shops without making a purchase.
8. They didn't show the merchandise to the customer, nor get it into the customer's hands.
9. In some shops, there was so much extraneous conversation that it took too long to make the sale. (At $5.00 an hour, it costs the florist $1.25 in labor time when the clerk takes 15 minutes to wait on a customer.)

ABC'S OF SELLING

Understanding the fundamentals of any science makes it possible to learn the more technical aspects. Here are some ABC's of selling more flowers to more people, suggested by J. Bedford:

Appreciate the opportunity you have to be engaged in the greatest business in the world—selling flowers.
Believe in what you are selling.
Compliment your customers honestly and sincerely every time you can.
Dedicate yourself to making a successful career of selling.
Enthusiasm is contagious and will help your sales.
Find the key reason why your customer wants to buy.
Give a little more attention and service to your customer, and you won't have to worry about competition.
Hesitate before you answer any question your customer asks. It will avoid arguments and give you time to think of the best answer.
Imagine your customer enjoying the benefits of what you are selling.
Justify every sales point you make so your customer is convinced of the truth of what you are saying.
Know all you can about your merchandise.
Listen for key words your customer uses when talking.
Memorize your customer's name when you first hear it.

Nail down each sales point in step-by-step strategy.

Obligate your customer to buy with an extra bit of service to him.

Persuade with all the enthusiasm you can generate.

Quote authorities who are well known to your customers so you can prove your sales points.

Refrain from knocking your competitor.

Say it with flowers.

Trade the benefits of what you are selling for your customer's dollar.

Use all the tricks of the trade in selling: enthusiasm, tact, confidence, and sincerity.

Visualize your customer owning and enjoying the benefits of your merchandise.

Work at selling.

X-ray your customer's buying mind to discover the real reason why your customer will or will not buy.

You are the key to more sales.

Zip up the sale quickly.

TELEPHONE SELLING

Real salesmanship counts more than ever today, and this applies especially to orders given over the phone. The telephone should never be answered by an inexperienced clerk who does not know what flowers are available and their prices, and who cannot make suggestions as to their use. Also, select a quiet location for the telephone, away from the cash register and other distracting noises.

There are many suggestions to follow when trying to sell by phone, including the following:

- Answer the telephone promptly.
- Speak clearly and distinctly so that you can be easily understood.
- Give the name of your shop and your name.
- Be cheerful and friendly, and speak with a smile in your voice. This is very hard for some people to do. A person should never sound annoyed at having to answer the phone.
- Be courteous even with wrong numbers.
- Avoid coughing into the mouthpiece.
- Never drop the receiver while the customer is on the line.
- Always let the customer hang up first. You may even get an extra sale that the customer thinks of at the last minute which you would lose by hanging up first.
- Know what merchandise is available and at what price, or post a price list by the phone.

- Be sure to spell names and addresses correctly and get the customer's name for billing. Repeat the order, so that there will be no mistake.
- Be sure the delivery date is correct.
- Be helpful, and treat the customer with as much consideration on the phone as if the person came in the store.
- Use the same good English as if face-to-face with the customer in the store.
- Help the customer to decide by making several suggestions.
- Acknowledge the customer's likes and dislikes.
- On funeral orders, it is not in good taste to say "Thank you." Rather say, "We will take good care of this order for you."
- Be sure to get the message for the card.
- Always ask if there is anything else the customer needs—any other way you can be of service.

Seven Faults

The Bell Telephone Company's research experts have found that there are seven common faults that are basic to poor telephone salesmanship. They are as follows:

1. Slow, indifferent, and incomplete answering of the telephone.
2. Failing to listen to what the customer wants.
3. Failing to use word pictures.
4. Failing to sell extra items, larger quantities, or better grades.
5. Failing to ask the customer to buy.
6. Winning the argument and losing the sale.
7. Failing to follow through.

Salesmanship in the retail florist shop, whether in person or by phone, is a very important part of the business. Some florists are order-takers rather than salespersons. They simply wait for a customer to come in and give them an order. More profits could be realized by many retail florists if they would increase their sales, even by as little as 5 per cent. With most customers, there is a chance to upsell if you really try to be a good salesperson. Sales techniques are published in many books. All it takes is for you or your employee to follow through, close the sale at the proper time, and *ask the people to buy*. You have the best product in the world to sell.

Chapter 18

CUSTOMERS AND CONSUMER PREFERENCES

The customer is the mainstay of the retail florist business—the one to whom the florist caters, and for whom the flowers and plants are produced, marketed, and sold. The retail customer is the ultimate consumer of the florists' products, and is the one who influences the whole operation and management of the retail florist business.

CUSTOMER IMPORTANCE

The purpose of every sale is to satisfy the customer, not only with the merchandise that you sell, but with the services that you provide, so that the customer will want to continue to come back to your store. *The store exists for the customer, not the customer for the store.* If the store, the merchandise, and the services do not please the customers, they will take their trade somewhere else. Customers say that they want salespersons to be interested, courteous, and intelligent. Each of these is important and can be developed by study and by noting how other successful sales personnel use their traits in pleasing their customers. (See Chapter 17.) Courtesy requires only the time of the employee while in contact with the customer. No other business-building technique costs so little or brings such good results.

IMAGE OF THE SHOP

The image created in the customer's mind by your shop is of utmost importance. What do people think of you and your shop? Try to find out. It has been said many times that the success of a sale rests with the first 30 seconds that the customer is in the shop. Do you greet all customers promptly, or at least acknowledge their presence if you are busy with another customer?

This is most important. Here is a true story that occurred recently to the senior author in a Florida retail flower shop.

The flower shop was one of the most attractive shops I had seen in a long time. Since it was in a shopping center mall, the front display windows were open. The display was simple in design, and very striking. The entrance was along a curved path through this attractive display, and into the retail flower shop itself. The whole picture was so inviting, it seemed to say "Welcome, come on in."

So, my wife, son, and I went down the path and into the shop to see this wonderful looking florist shop—and there the image changed. The shop itself was attractive enough, but being *ignored* by the store personnel ruined the entire effect. At the rear of the store was a latticed partition and we could see three people working in there. Through a glass partition we could see a man sitting in the office watching the people in the workroom. The three of us wandered around the shop looking at the flowers, plants, and gift items, and I spent considerable time looking at the fresh flowers in the display refrigerator. (I know that people like to browse around in a shop, but they do not like to be *ignored*.) We were in the shop between three and five minutes and still no one came out to greet us. If we could see them through the lattice, I'm sure they could see us. After five minutes (remember the first 30 seconds are the most important), we left the shop and no one even tried to stop us.

Once outside, I thought to myself that I have worked with retail florists for over 15 years so maybe I should try again. So I returned to the shop. As I came through the door, a man was standing behind the wrapping counter, and I thought "Fine, I'll talk to him about the shop." However, as I came through the door, he turned around and walked into the back room and joined the two who were still in the workroom. The man in the office still sat there. No one was busy on the phone or waiting on another customer as far as I could see. I wandered around for two minutes this time and decided to leave again.

Just as I was leaving, a woman came out and called to me to see if she could help me. There was no smile, nor any apology for keeping me waiting. I told her this was the second time I had been in and wondered why no one came out to wait on me, and she just said she was sorry. Her manner showed she didn't really mean it or care at all. She was quite unfriendly. I told her I was sorry because I worked with retail florists and liked to talk to them about their shops. She didn't reply to this at all. We both turned away, and I really felt bad about this experience.

I'm sure if I were an ordinary customer, not acquainted with many retail florists, my image of that shop, and florists in general, would be pretty poor. I probably wouldn't try to buy flowers again. There are many other gift items from which to choose, and I don't like to see people turn to these other items because of the unfriendly attitude of a florist or floral shop employees. Anyone could come out and greet a customer and say that someone will be with the person in a minute.

Americans resent the attitude of impersonal contact and are returning to more fundamental values, according to Chuck Johnston, past-president, TELEFLORA. Let the customers know you care about them and appreciate their business. Browsing is good for business and should be encouraged, but don't ignore your customers in the meantime.

Many retail florists do not realize the importance of greeting the customer immediately, nor do they realize the importance of the image they create. Unfortunately, the preceding related incident is not an isolated case. It happens much too often in our business and should *never happen at all*. People must be made to feel welcome in retail florist shops.

CONSUMER BEHAVIOR

During the 1970's, the consumer became an "economic animal" who, due to all the inflation and shortages, instinctively looked for bargains and sales. In the 1980's, people are even more cautious of how they spend their money and more concerned about getting their money's worth.

Motives for buying may be conscious or subconscious. Why do people act the way they do? Why do people buy certain products and not others? The answers to these questions lie in the area of social-psychological behavior according to our economists and psychologists. Flowers must be made more important in the customer's mind than other items, and it must become a habit to buy flowers often. Consumer behavior is related to habits based on various social ideas or values.

Values

Our society is governed by a set of social values which determine why people do things and why they buy things. Some of these values are as follows:

    ❧ Prestige—buying a luxury car as a status symbol.

- Conventional behavior—sending flowers or other items on certain occasions because it is expected.
- Function—buying things that perform a function in life.
- Self-esteem—choosing certain items for personal satisfaction.
- Remembrance—buying for sentimental reasons to recall past experience.
- Modernity—selecting up-to-date products to keep up with the modern world.
- Means of expression—expressing an emotion such as sympathy or grief at the time of a death.
- Aesthetics—buying to make the purchaser's environment more pleasing.

Status and prestige symbols have become so important in American life that you should appeal to them as motivations in your advertising and promotions. Flowers fit into some of these values more readily than others. Flowers do not perform a *function* as such—only in an indirect way—but they are a status symbol to some people. They are certainly used to express sympathy and other feelings. The sentimental value has been the greatest in the past, while the aesthetic is the value on which florists should be concentrating today. Flowers for gifts and home decorations should be pushed more and more; they can be used for many occasions. The following motivations make people choose to spend money on flowers rather than something else:

1. People like to live comfortably.
2. People like to possess things.
3. Flowers appeal to romance.
4. Flowers have always expressed love.
5. Flowers remember—they say, "I am thinking of you."
6. Flowers express sympathy and say things that most people find hard to put into words.
7. Flowers help in the desire to make money, as in commercial accounts. (See Chapter 37.)

Keep these ideas in mind when planning your advertising campaign.

APPROPRIATENESS OF FLOWERS

Flowers are very appropriate for any occasion. Florists should try to work on the value of *habit*. Habit is a great force in our present-day society. Try to get men into the habit of buying flowers for each holiday—then they won't be able to quit. Flowers are appropriate for men too, although not for as many occasions as for women. Factors which govern the appropriateness of flowers are: (1) groups of people—flowers are more appropriate for some groups than others; (2) type of occasion—flowers are appropriate for weddings, funerals, anniversaries, sicknesses, and birthdays; and (3) various circumstances—more flowers are sent from men to women; married and unmarried people differ in their desire for flowers and in the amount of money available to spend on flowers. Married men buy more plants because they last longer, while unmarried men buy more roses and cut flowers to express love. Emphasize *utility* to the married and *sentimentality* to both. Sick people and the aged are very receptive to flowers.

Another motivation for flower buying that you should utilize is the smell of flowers. People expect fragrance with flowers and expect to find it in a florist shop. It can serve as a good selling tool.

Figure 18-1. Attractive display of merchandise for the customers. (Courtesy, Miller Florist, Warren, Ohio.)

CONSUMER PREFERENCES

Several surveys have been conducted to indicate the preference of consumers towards flowers. Interviews with people who purchased flower specials have shown that only 12 per cent of the purchasers had planned to buy flowers before they saw them displayed. Between 80 and 90 per cent of the people indicated that they would buy flowers regularly if they were available at a low price. (Advantage of cash-and-carry specials, Chapter 16.) They indicated that they would be willing to spend $0.90 to $1.00 per week on flowers if they were available, and most of these purchases would be for the home.

In a study on consumer preferences for flowers, conducted by Dr. C. E. Trotter of The Pennsylvania State University, 1,152 individuals were asked to choose which of various gift items they would give for various occasions. The people did not know at first that it was a flower survey. The gifts listed were: personal clothing, candy, flowers, ornamental knickknacks, toilet articles, jewelry, and household items. The occasions were birthday, Easter, Valentine's Day, Mother's Day, Father's Day, wedding, anniversary, illness, expression of affection, and expression of appreciation. Of the 1,152 interviewed, 56 per cent had made one flower purchase in a year, and only 10 per cent had made three purchases of flowers in a year. They indicated flowers were appropriate, but they only purchased them half as often as they said they thought were appropriate. In most of the situations presented, less than half of the people indicated they would select and send a gift of any kind. For example, only 40 per cent said they would send a gift at all on Valentine's Day and only 10 per cent indicated it would be flowers.

The implication of this study is that there is a broad market to be developed. If consumers were educated to give flowers on more occasions, this would have a tremendous influence on flower sales. The following were three main reasons why flowers were given for a particular occasion as a gift: (1) the use of flowers for a particular reason, (2) the anticipated reaction of the person receiving flowers as a gift, and (3) the respondent's idea of the characteristics of flowers suited to the desired need. Flowers were considered highly acceptable gifts for women, but inappropriate for men, unless sick or old. To sell more flowers to more people more often, the flowers must be readily available in a broad range, of good quality, and offered at a reasonable price.

Flowers are the principal choice for certain holidays like Easter,

Christmas, Mother's Day, Valentine's Day, and Memorial Day. There is no substitute for flowers for weddings. Flowers are highly acceptable at funerals, but the "Please Omit" phase is reducing this market. The use of flowers for gifts for birthdays, anniversaries, and other occasions is the market which should be developed by the retail florist industry. The degree of competition between flowers and other items depends upon the social commitment associated with the event and the nature of the event. Education of the public to the proper use of flowers for various occasions is needed, along with a vigorous advertising campaign to sell more flowers to more people more often.

RETAIL FLORISTS' PREFERENCES

Consumer behavior and consumer preference studies have been conducted in many areas but not often in the florist industry. Retail florists are too often *apt to sell what they want to sell* rather than *what the customer wants to buy.* A study in Texas by L. J. Tolle on the purchasing habits of retail florists (not the florists' customers) showed that 32.4 per cent of the florists preferred carnations, 22.8 per cent preferred gladioli, 7.9 per cent preferred chrysanthemums, and 4.3 per cent preferred roses. Yet, from the standpoint of sales, we know that most people prefer pompons, carnations, and roses to all other flowers. The most important reasons for florists' flower preferences, aside from their personal likes, were versatility, keeping quality, ease of use, and the ability of flowers to make a "show." This same study showed the breakdown of florist sales by merchandise classes to be the following: funerals, 59.98 per cent; arrangements, 22.21 per cent; party decorations, 16.70 per cent; weddings, 8.75 per cent; corsages, 6.89 per cent; and bunches of cut flowers, 5 per cent. (These are estimates from the florists who responded to the questionnaire.) All of these areas (except funeral work) could be increased by finding out what consumers prefer for these occasions.

New and Tolle reported in 1964 that studies proved that the carnation was among the most popular and versatile flower sold by retail florists. Out of 36,024 orders, 5,863, or 16 per cent, used carnations. Forty per cent of all corsages contained carnations, and 34 per cent of all arrangements (including funeral) had some carnations in them. We don't know whether this is the preference of the customers or of the retail florists.

Consumers know and appreciate the value of flowers and want to enjoy them more often in their homes. Several surveys on consumer preferences for flowers and pot plants have been conducted. Mississippi research workers found that foliage plants were preferred over azaleas and pot mums, while red roses, yellow mums, red carnations, and pink gladioli were the favorites among cut flowers. Ninety-two per cent preferred a pot plant over an arrangement as a gift. A study in Memphis showed that roses were preferred over all other cut flowers; followed by pot plants, pompons, carnations, and gladioli, in that order. The Memphis study also showed that flowers were a favorite gift during an illness in any and all income groups of people. The retail flower shop was far preferred over supermarkets, five-and-tens, and variety stores for the purchase of plants and flowers. Most people in this survey preferred to receive a pot plant rather than cut flowers as a household gift, but preferred cut flowers for home decorations. Seventy-four per cent of the people surveyed had no desire to see their flowers arranged before buying them. (This seems to be opposite to the views on salesmanship that people like to see made-up arrangements.) Most people interviewed felt roses and snapdragons were the cut flowers that would last the shortest time, while chrysanthemums, gladioli, and carnations were expected to last longer. Although keeping quality was a factor in selecting some flowers, roses were still listed as a very popular flower. (Census figures for 1974 indicated all chrysanthemums first, carnations second, and roses third in sales.)

A study in Texas conducted by three panels of 25 members each found the following points of interest on consumer preferences and buying habits for flowers:

- The general public likes flowers, especially for the home, and will use them if they are readily available at a reasonable price.
- Customers want to know how to care for their plants. They prefer instruction cards which include scientific and common names, some history, and complete directions for plant care.
- Customer habits in using flowers can be changed or developed. Once the habit has been established, it should be cultivated continuously.
- In purchasing flowers, customers prefer a variety of choice, and *prefer the price to be plainly marked.*
- Consumers are concerned about the keeping quality of plants and flowers. This affects some of the purchasing selections.

A U.S. Department of Agriculture study consisting of 814 personal interviews with 426 women and 378 men showed the results in Table 18-1 regarding their preferences in business practices for florists. Customers like to have merchandise displayed and priced. With flowers, they like to make their own decision on what to order. Yet, a survey showed that less than 40 per cent of the florists displayed prepared arrangements in their shops for customers to see and buy when placing an order in person. However, over three-fourths of the florists who did display floral arrangements put a price on them for customers to see. We need more consumer studies to determine preferences in relation to variety, color, type of flower, length of stem, price, and other factors.

Table 18-1. What Consumers Want Improved

	Total	Most Important	Second Most Important	Third Most Important
	.... %			
Price tags prominently displayed	48	24	14	10
Tags on flowers explaining how to care for them	38	13	14	11
Fresher flowers	28	14	8	6
Flowers that last longer	25	6	9	10
More variety in flowers offered	25	7	11	7
Ability to select a variety of individual flowers to make up your own bunch	21	6	8	7
More helpful salespeople	19	6	6	7
Make better looking or more attractive arrangements	15	5	4	6
Smaller bunches of flowers	11	2	5	4
Longer store hours	9	2	3	4
More conveniently located	8	2	2	4
Honor credit cards	8	1	2	5
More comfortable atmosphere	5	1	2	2
Larger bunches of flowers	4	—	1	3

GARDEN CLUBS

Cultivate the members of garden clubs and handle the materials which they want to buy.

When friendly, inquisitive, probing garden club members wander into your shop, don't run and hide, rush around frantically covering up your supplies, close your eyes and hope they will go away, or hound them so closely they will leave. You would be turning your back on a wide-open source of additional sales. The National Council of State Garden Clubs, Inc., alone boasts a total membership in excess of 500,000, and there are thousands of others who do not belong to this national organization.

Take advantage of the volume sales potential they represent by attending their meetings and learning firsthand their problems and needs. They will not be a nuisance as some florists think if allowed to browse and pick out their own materials and supplies. They don't have to have extra services.

Stock salable supplies such as wire, tape, foams, chenille stems, water picks, preservatives, clay, pinholders, styrofoam, and other items that they want to buy. They will find them elsewhere if not in a florist shop. Let them browse and buy just one or two flowers at a time. This all helps to increase the volume of business, and will lead to *impulse* sales.

Be your own public relations representative. Offer your services as a guest speaker, which will afford a fine opportunity to publicize your own shop.

A successful florist will cultivate the garden club members, not fight them.

EDUCATION

All florists should embark on a consumer education program for the florist industry. This should be aimed to make the public more favorably disposed towards flower purchases. The retail florists should strive to change the image in the minds of the general public and make them feel *welcome* in their shops.

Understanding why consumers buy the way they do is important in any industry. We know people like flowers, so all the florist has to do is concentrate on increasing sales by encouraging them to buy more flowers for more occasions, more often.

William Cronin suggests that you find out what the town thinks of your shop and determine what you can do about capitalizing on your image. He suggests that each florist consider the following questions:

  ◆§ Is the shop an expensive-looking shop?
  ◆§ Is it a quality shop?

- Are the arrangements really artistic?
- Is it an old-fashioned shop?
- Is it considered a "late" shop with deliveries?
- Are you really merchandising flowers?

If you wonder if your answers are the same as your customers', try a little survey of your own to find out. Analyze the results and act on them. Set up a management program to improve the image of your store. Satisfying the desires of the consumers for accurate and timely information about floral products can help you to attract customers and expand your business. Encourage the use of flowers for home decorations and other special occasions.

Understanding why people buy as they do is an important aspect in any retail business, including the retail florist. Motivation research is a highly specialized part of market research being conducted in many areas. This affects all retail businesses. We need more of it in the florist industry so that we can effectively plan our selling and merchandising programs.

Chapter 19

TRADE PRACTICES AND
TRICKS OF THE TRADE

TRADE PRACTICES

There are several trade practices which should be considered by each florist. Just how they are handled depends on the location, type of shop, reputation, and desires of the owner.

1. **Sunday Hours**

    This policy will depend on the community and the type of store. Some shops in hotels, hospitals, and shopping centers may have to be open on Sundays. Most florists, however, should not have to be open on Sundays except at holiday times. Educate the public that you are closed on Sundays, and try to get other florists in the area to agree to the same procedure.

2. **Shop Hours**

    Some shops are open longer than others. You, yourself, must determine the store hours unless you are located in a shopping mall, in which case you will have to conform to the mall hours. Your type of business will influence your decision. If your hours are long, consider staggering your employees' starting-quitting times to avoid overtime. If you have a garden center in conjunction with the shop, you probably will have to pay overtime.

3. **Rental Funeral Containers**

    Many florists will rent baskets and vases for funeral designs, and pick up the containers later from the funeral home or cemetery. Some florists feel it is a waste of time and money because the containers get broken, lost, may leak, and are sometimes impossible to recover. Whether you charge full price or a rental is up to you.

4. **Other Rental Items**

Many items can be rented profitably, according to various florists. Phoebe Floral in Allentown, Pennsylvania, rents candelabras, aisle runners, skirts of satin, compotes, canopies, fountains, plants, turntables, heart-shaped wedding arches, apothecary jars, trees and tree stands (up to 50 pounds), and many other items. The secret of success in the renting of items lies in telling the customers and potential customers that these materials are available in your shop. Post a standard rental price so that there is no guessing and all employees charge the same price for each item. A rule-of-thumb for most non-perishable rental items at Phoebe Floral is to charge 20 per cent of the original cost, plus the cost of cleaning and polishing to get the items ready for the next rental. Bill Curtis, of Phoebe Floral, said that 25 per cent of one wedding order of over $800 was charged just for rental equipment. Most rental items are kept in a special room upstairs and are not open to public exposure until the special party or wedding. Few customers have their own elegant candelabras and special containers for a really large party. It's a natural for florists to rent these items and make a profit. Sometimes 20 to 25 per cent of a wedding order can be for rental items. Rentals make money.

Some florists have a large selection of containers and decorative pieces for rent for many decorations. M. Lange from Wilmette, Illinois, has been doing it profitably for over 35 years.

5. **"Loaning" of Palms**

It is a general practice for retail florists to "loan" palms, ferns, and cibotiums for weddings, funerals, and church or school decorations. However, it is hard on the fresh material, so the florist must make a charge and prorate it over a six-month period, which is the expected life of the plants. Many florists are now using permanent (artificial) palms and ferns because they do not have a greenhouse or suitable facilities for caring for the live plants. These are expensive, but can be used again many times.

6. **Floral Contributions**

As a retail florist, you will constantly be getting requests from various charity and local affairs for flowers or centerpieces. The advertising value from these is considered "nil," so you are usually just donating the flowers. This can eat into your profits. It would be better just to make a cash donation and deduct it on your income tax. Some florists have found the floral contribution form to be of help in eliminating these demands.

Printed Form to Be Used for Requests for Floral Contributions

REQUEST FOR FLORAL CONTRIBUTIONS

Organization _____ When Organized? _____

Address of Organization _____

President _____ Phone No. _____

Address _____

Secretary _____ Phone No. _____

Address _____

Type of Organization: CHARITABLE, NON-PROFIT, INCORPORATED, UNINCORPORATED, OTHER _____

Purpose of Organization _____

Event for Which Flowers Requested _____

Date _____ Time _____ Place _____

Type of Flowers Requested _____

Cost per Person Attending Event _____

Other Donations: Advertising Donated by _____

Printing Donated by _____

Entertainment Donated by _____

Dessert Donated by _____

Requested by _____ Title _____

Ask the person to fill this out and see what happens. Most people do not want to be bothered taking the time to fill out the form, and some are really embarrassed to put down that no one else is donating anything; they finally realize that there is no reason why flowers should be donated.

7. **Do-It-Yourself**

Some florists are providing a Garden Club Counter, Do-It-Yourself Table, or Knickknack Bar, which is stocked with ribbon, wire, floratape, chenille stems, pinholders, clay, spray paint, styrofoam, foam materials, and other items for the do-it-yourself flower arranger. Everything is priced, and most customers help themselves. A 2 to 1 markup is usually sufficient for these items.

8. **Slack Times**

What do you do with your employees who are not busy during the slack times which occur in every shop? Put them to work making bows, putting boxes together, inserting wax paper in the boxes, wiring and painting pine cones, making net puffs, checking supplies, and other small jobs that can be picked up at a moment's notice and put down when there is something else to do.

9. **Hospital Practices**

Find out what the rules are for receiving flowers at the hospital and abide by them. In general, hospitals appreciate florists observing the following conditions:

1. Check carefully the correct name, floor, and room number of the patient before making delivery.
2. Make sure all female patients are addressed by their own first name (not their husbands), such Mrs. Mary Smith, not Mrs. John Smith.
3. Arrange all cut flowers in containers that do not leak—no loose flowers.
4. Deliver all orders to the place or room designated by the hospital, or to the patient's room or floor if this is the hospital's policy.
5. Make all deliveries within the hours the hospital designates as acceptable.
6. Never send poisonous or irritating flowers or plants to the hospital.
7. Dethorn roses before delivery.
8. Make sure the patient is still in the hospital.
9. Check to be sure the patient can receive flowers—usually they are not permitted in the Intensive Care Unit.

These are just a few of the practices which differ from one shop to another, and which must be decided upon by the owner after careful consideration of each item.

TRADE PAPERS AND ORGANIZATIONS

To be a successful retail florist, you must keep up on new trends, developments, business suggestions, and other ideas which will help you keep up-to-date in the florist world of today. To do this, subscribe regularly to at least one of the weekly trade papers— and more than one if you can afford it. It is just like subscribing to your local newspaper. You wouldn't think of not receiving the daily paper in your own home town. At present there are three national weekly trade papers for retail florists, as follows: *Florists' Review, Southern Florist and Nurseryman,* and *Flower News.*

Three of the major telephone/wire organizations, Florists' Transworld Delivery Association, TELEFLORA, Inc., and Florafax International, Inc., publish a magazine for their own members, which you will automatically receive if you join. You can belong to more than one organization if you choose.

As a progressive florist, you should also join your local, state, and national trade associations. The local may be an Allied or a local group of florists such as the Allied Florists of Delaware Valley, Inc., New York Florist Club, Florists' Association of Greater Chicago, or any of hundreds like these. The state organizations may be one such as the Pennsylvania Florists Association, Michigan State Florists Association, Ohio Florists' Association, or any of the other state organizations. The Society of American Florists represents all segments of the florist industry on the national level. Its headquarters are in Alexandria, Virginia. Support of these organizations is an investment in the future of the florist industry in the United States.

TRICKS OF THE TRADE

1. **Styrofoam block for current day's orders.** Keep the daily orders in good shape in an orderly fashion for the designers by using a regular 36-inch piece of 2-inch styrofoam with nails about 4 inches long pushed through from the back of the styrofoam. Use them in pairs so that the orders can be placed on them, and grouped for delivery. In this way the orders can be filled by the designers according to time, and then by sections of the city. You, as owner-manager, can keep an eye on the orders and plan deliveries accordingly. Green styrofoam should be used for white order sheets, and white styrofoam for colored order sheets. The sheets will stand out much better that way. (See Figure 19-1.)

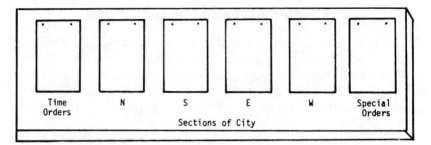

Figure 19-1. Styrofoam block with nails to keep orders separate at the control center.

2. **Designer's clip.** To make sure that the designer does not
   lose an order sheet, or that it doesn't blow off the table into
   the trash, hang a clip above the worktable to which is attached the order the designer is filling. A nail or hook can
   also be used.
3. **Preservatives.** Put some preservatives in every arrangement
   that goes out of the shop, including funeral vases and baskets. (If the funeral viewing is only one day, this won't be
   necessary.) Also, put a preservative in the water used to im-
   pregnate the various foams—Oasis, Quickee, Sno-Pak,
   Niagara, Fill Fast Foam, and others. As soon as the flowers
   come from the market, put preservative in each can or vase
   of flowers which will be placed in the storage or display refrigerator. The continued use of a preservative from
   grower to consumer has been proven beneficial. (See Chapter 24.)
4. **Plastic vases.** Check out the gold and silver plastic vases—
   they are quite inexpensive, very attractive, and will not tar-
   nish. Some are excellent for weddings and anniversaries.
5. **Pick-up notice.** Mimeograph a list of standard items as a
   quick and easy way to remind the driver to pick up items
   following various decorating jobs. Fill in the address and
   date, and check the items to be brought back to the shop.
   Have a place for the driver to initial it when the job is complete.
6. **Nozzles.** Install mist nozzles at each design table as a
   timesaver as well as added insurance that the flowers will
   last as long as possible. The initial expense of installation is
   well worth it. An overhead water line is installed along the
   ceiling for the full length of the workroom, with a hose and

a nozzle hanging down from the ceiling beside each designer. The designer can easily fill containers without having to go to the sink, and can also mist the arrangements when they are finished and ready for wrapping.

7. **Wire holders.** Use a six-pack of empty soda bottles as an inexpensive holder for floral wire. On one side put 16-, 18-, and 20-gauge wire for heavy work; put 24-, 30-, and 34-gauge wires on the other side for the lighter work.

8. **Styrofoam covers.** Cover the styrofoam base used for many floral designs with sponge rubber. It comes in many colors, is inexpensive, stretches tightly and neatly over the styrofoam, and is thin enough to be easily punctured by most flower stems.

9. **Backboards.** Achieve special effects very easily on designs for special occasions. Make up a series of styrofoam backboards with different items attached, such as a check book for a bank opening, a picture of the latest rock music group for teenagers, something from the kitchen for Mother's Day, and other items. When the order comes in, make up a neutral arrangement of flowers, attach the appropriate background, and it is all set to be delivered.

10. **Cymbidiums.** To increase the life span of cymbidiums, put one drop of water down each one's throat.

11. **Plastic rings.** Don't throw away the plastic rings from rolls of florists' tape. Trimmed with a flower or two, they become attractive napkin rings or can be used in anniversary designs.

12. **Underwater stem cutter.** Make flowers last longer by cutting the stems underwater. (See Figure 24-1.)

13. **Basic door swag.** Sell a basic door swag for Christmas with a set of reasonably priced trims that can be changed with the seasons. Try snowy branches and red ribbon and balls for Christmas, daisies for spring, strawflowers for summer, and Indian corn for fall.

14. **Novelties.** Incorporate a small, inexpensive novelty in each design piece that goes out from the shop, with the exception of funeral pieces. This helps to attract attention, and creates a favorable impression for the shop, since this added touch will be different from any competitor. The novelty can be artificial, dried, flower, fruit, or animal.

15. **Styrofoam fasteners.** Fasten styrofoam to the container and objects to the styrofoam with one of the materials that are

stickier than clay, called Sure-stick, Cling, and other trade names. These materials are excellent for anchoring driftwood in an arrangement. Medisco preservative is also an excellent glue for anchoring styrofoam in permanent arrangements.

16. **Bleach.** Thoroughly clean refrigerator containers to help make the cut flowers last longer. Some florists use a small amount of bleach in the water to keep the water, stems, and containers clean. It cuts down on the disagreeable odor which develops when flowers are in the water more than just a few days.

17. **Styrofoam protectors.** Attach a piece of flocked paper to the bottom of a piece of styrofoam used as the base for a floral design instead of pottery or some other container. It will adequately protect the furniture in the customer's home from getting scratched and give more customer satisfaction.

18. **Candle or spray for mums.** Use a candle or a can of mum spray wax to repair the damage of a shattered chrysanthemum. It is advisable for the truck driver to have one handy in the delivery truck at all times.

19. **Dish gardens.** Add a few flowers in water tubes to a dish garden to make it look much more attractive with very little cost. Just a few pompons will do it, and will help to give the store a better reputation because of this added touch.

20. **Plastic wrap for arrangements.** Wrap all artistic designs and floral arrangements in clear plastic. It protects them during delivery, but lets the arrangements be seen and admired by many people when they are delivered. It is a good way to advertise the product and helps to keep the flowers in a good fresh condition. It is essential in the north in winter.

21. **Time deliveries.** To be sure that time deliveries are delivered on time and not lost in the rush of doing business, place a bright red or orange sticker on the order. The manager and the truck driver will both be able to see it and can check the time of delivery very easily. This is particularly helpful during the rush at a holiday.

22. **Fast pot covers.** To cut aluminum foil fast and uniformly for use as a pot cover, make a board with a groove in it running the width of the foil roll. Attach a roller to the end of the board for the foil. Each time the foil is pulled across

the board, run a wallpaper cutter down the groove, thus cutting the foil neatly, evenly, and quickly.

23. **Tinted petal tips.** To color only the tips of carnation petals, spray a round spot of paint of the desired color onto a piece of aluminum foil. Roll the head of the carnation gently over the spot of paint to tint the petal tips.

24. **Portable tables.** Where space is at a premium, use portable design tables. They are set up for a holiday, then stored away the rest of the year or used for added display space when needed.

25. **Foliage.** Trim your foliage into unusual shapes to give the same old greens a new look.

26. **Wedding photos.** In addition to a book of pictures of wedding designs to show to a prospective customer, keep photos of the wedding work that you have done in the past. The photos may be in color or black and white. Some florists have two shots of each bouquet—one is a close-up of the wedding bouquet; the other is a photo showing how it looks when being carried by the bride or an attendant.

27. **Do-it-yourself counter or table.** Many people are interested in doing things themselves these days. It has become quite a fad. If there is space in the shop, consider installing a do-it-yourself table for your customers. It can be a serve-yourself counter. It is a good-will builder and will increase the gross sales if you do not let it get out of hand and interfere with the management and operation of the shop. Pinholders, clay, wire, floratape, ribbon, chicken wire, foam materials, and chenille stems are just a few of the items that can be sold here.

28. **Ribbon on boxes.** Tie the boxes of cut flowers and corsages with brightly colored corsage ribbon, rather than string or Scotch tape, to make the packages look more attractive and to attract attention. It is more expensive, but it may be worth it for its advertising value, depending on the customers and the type of shop.

29. **Stone chips.** An interesting and practical way to cover the floor of the display window or even the display beds in the middle of the store is with stone chips. They are attractive, require very little maintenance, and eliminate the worry and mess from spilled water. A watertight liner with a drain might be provided if you believe it is necessary.

Figure 19-2. Excellent display of foliage plants on tile floor in sales area. (Courtesy, Alexander's Flowers, Cleveland, Ohio.)

30. **Customer's special occasions.** Keep a record of birthdays, anniversaries, and other important dates for regular customers in order to bring in more business. Use a card file and keep it up-to-date. A note or phone call will remind the sender of the date and suggest a similar flower order this year. Be sure to remove the names of deceased people immediately from the file. This file can be operated by a handicapped person in the florist's neighborhood.

31. **Answering service.** Use a telephone answering service for evenings and Sundays if you feel it will benefit your business. It can even be used during the day at holidays with the arrangement that the service answers it only after the third or fourth ring. The service personnel must know how to receive telephone orders from the various wire service organization members. Some florists like this service and some do not. Some feel the answering service is too impersonal. If you use one of these services, it is a good idea to have the operators visit the shop periodically to see what is being sold and to learn about new ideas of operation.

32. **Pay phone.** Consider installation of a pay phone in a

shop—it can be an asset. It cuts down on the use of the business phone by employees and customers. It is excellent for sending out FTD, TELEFLORA, or Florafax orders without tying up the regular phone.

33. **Computers.** Assess the ways your shop could use a computer, determine the size of the unit and the programs you would need, then compare your projected savings to the investment required.

34. **Drive-in window.** Provide a drive-in window opening onto your parking lot if you have the space. This is very helpful and a timesaver both for the florist and the customers, particularly for will-call orders. For dances and holidays, educate the customers to call for their corsages at the drive-in window.

35. **Guarantee.** Consider following the example of a Des Moines, Iowa, florist who guarantees every flower order and asks customers to phone at once if the flowers do not come up to expectation. However, no complaint is honored after 24 hours.

36. **Colored cards.** Use colored cards for pricing arrangements in the display refrigerator to tell employees how old the design is.

37. **"Hot line."** Promote commercial accounts with an "Ice Breakers Hot Line." Advertise a special number for businesspersons to call for help in "breaking the ice" with their clients by sending plants or flowers.

38. **Protection.** Protect silver bowls from foam materials and chicken wire by buying old hand towels (very inexpensively) to protect the bottom of the bowls.

39. **Contact paper.** Try contact paper of various patterns to hide old cans and to use as a background for special displays.

40. **Bread loaves.** Use artificial loaves of bread for Thanksgiving and Christmas door swags and centerpieces.

You must determine whether or not the preceding tricks of the trade will be suited to your shop. However, it may be worthwhile trying most of them to see if they will improve the volume of business in the shop. There are hundreds of other tricks of the trade besides these few listed here.

Chapter 20

"PLEASE OMIT"

Many funeral notices today carry the words "Please Omit Flowers" or "In Lieu of Flowers, contributions may be made to. . . ." It is a practice which has caused a loss of business for florists in certain cities for 80 years or more. It is gaining popularity in many areas. The difficult part is that for many florists, funeral flowers make up from 50 to 80 per cent of their business. Thus, if people stop sending flowers to funerals, it can be a real hardship for these florists. It is also a practice which is very hard for the florist industry to combat. The Society of American Florists has a committee called the Florists Information Committee which helps florists in various cities talk to funeral directors, ministers, and newspaper publishers to try to discourage the use of these negative phrases. *The florist industry does not object to solicitations of money for contributions, as long as they do not mention flowers.* This way there is *no discrimination of an industry, and friends are free to send flowers, or make a contribution, whichever they choose.*

A funeral without flowers is very drab, dreary, and cold. Flowers add beauty to the casket setting and the funeral service. Flowers help to soften the grief caused by the death of a loved one. The funeral directors know this and are opposed to a funeral without flowers. Usually the family of the deceased realizes this also, and so there will almost always be family flowers and other pieces at a Please Omit funeral. This is embarrassing for friends who have not sent flowers.

There are people, of course, who do not want flowers at a funeral, and this is their prerogative. However, in many cases of "Please Omit," the family has been persuaded by some well-meaning friend or relative to ask that donations be given to some church, hospital, or charity in lieu of flowers. Various organizations such as the American Heart Fund, American Cancer Society, and others have told the Society of American Florists that they receive very few contributions in lieu of flowers from the funerals that make the suggestion. *These societies themselves do not solicit donations in place of flowers.* It has been proven that many people just don't bother sending either money or flowers to a Please Omit funeral.

Surveys show that the problem is greater in some cities than others, and worse now than 20 years ago in many, but not all, areas.

Many newspapers do not print the words "Please Omit Flowers" unless it is in a paid obituary.

THINKING BEHIND "PLEASE OMIT"

A survey by FTD in 1962 gave the following conclusions concerning "Please Omit":

1. It is fairly deep rooted in present-day society, and promises to grow in strength.
2. The chief proponents of "Please Omit" are members of the Protestant clergy, with excess floral usage as their main target.
3. Funeral directors were absolved from blame.
4. There is a changing attitude towards death.
5. There is a rise of religious influence at the time of death, and also an enhanced status of religious leaders.
6. It is closely tied in with our changing society.

These conclusions still apply today.

PUBLIC ACCEPTANCE

The public is accepting "Please Omit Flowers" because it is part of the changing pattern of today's living. There is a changing attitude towards funeral procedures as revealed in the following results of a recent survey: a growing desire for simplicity in funerals; the trend toward church funerals in preference to those in funeral homes; protests against the high cost of funerals (Jessica Mitford's book *The American Way of Death,* for example); feelings of waste associated with funeral flowers which are sometimes in excess, coupled with the post-funeral destruction of the pieces; a feeling that the money could have been put to better use; and the attitude that excessive floral tributes are symbols of conspicuous spending and thus in poor taste.

An indication of future Please Omit behavior is evident in the findings of a survey that 67 per cent of those who have inserted Please Omit notices in the paper indicated that they would do so again.

ROLE OF THE FLORIST

People have traditionally expressed their respect for the dead and sympathy for the bereaved by sending flowers. The custom is long standing, and though on the wane in some areas, will be with us for many years to come. There are three points to be kept in mind concerning funeral flowers. First, the role of the florist is that of merely serving the people who wish to send flowers to the funeral. It is the people who come to the florist. Second, the flowers represent sympathy extended to the bereaved. Third, it is not true that flowers are sent to the dead, who cannot see nor appreciate them. They are sent in memory of the dead and to help buoy up the spirits of the living as a token of respect for the deceased. They are an expression of friendship towards both the living and the dead. They show an understanding sympathy that is so hard for many people to express in words.

REASONS TO OMIT "PLEASE OMIT"

1. The obituary is a public announcement of the death, with the date and time of the funeral service. It is not considered good taste to openly anticipate an expression of sympathy.
2. A "Please Omit" or "In Lieu of" request causes embarrassment to friends. Some ignore the request and send flowers anyway. Thus, it is embarrassing to those who heeded the request and then find flowers at the funeral when they attend the service.
3. Capitalizing on the sympathy of friends to raise money for a special cause is distasteful to many people.
4. Most people do not contribute to the cause, which is generally not helped financially.
5. Many people resent being told how to express their sympathy and how to spend their money.

WAYS TO COMBAT "PLEASE OMIT"

There are many ways that retail florists can try to combat the Please Omit problem.

1. One of the most important ways is in the handling of floral designs by the retail florists themselves. This means you should:
   a. Use fresh flowers that conform to high standards of quality.
   b. Never use awkward, bulky, easily spilled floral arrangements.
   c. Be sure the arrangements have originality and good artistic design.
   d. Make sure they are properly wrapped and contain proper identification.
   e. Make sure the card is properly filled out.
   f. Use a previously used container *only* if it is in good condition.
   g. Deliver flowers on time. Many funeral directors are providing several small tables and stands in the funeral home for floral arrangements in attractive containers. Make sure that these arrangements are artistic and above average in design to help combat the criticism of flowers at funerals.
2. Talk to funeral directors, ministers, and the newspapers; request a member of the Florists Information Committee of the Society of American Florists to explain the situation to these local people. Most businesspersons are very understanding and will not deliberately try to ruin an industry.
3. Include funeral flowers in your advertising. The Society of American Florists has suggested many phrases to go with funeral flower ads which will not be offensive to the general public nor to your customers.
4. Adopt a positive sales approach, setting forth the purpose of funeral flowers, and the things that flowers do for the bereaved and for the relatives and friends.
5. Follow the recommendations of the Florists Information Committee.
6. Suggest sending a sympathy bouquet of flowers or a plant to the home after the funeral service. These should be artistic arrangements in good taste, which do not look like a funeral vase or basket. These flowers, and the message with it, are greatly appreciated by the family during the week following the funeral. This suggestion to the customer will reduce the loss of business due to "Please Omit," yet is very acceptable to the recipient and considered in good taste.

7. Work cooperatively with the funeral directors.
   a. The following are tips to florists on maintaining the good will of funeral directors from the Allied Florists of Greater Philadelphia, as reported by W. Camerisch:

   (1) Enclosure cards—print or type name of sender on front. Print or type name, address, relationship, if any, on the back of the card.
   (2) Sprays—wire the ends of styrofoam bars so they can be easily hung on easels or stands.
   (3) Casket sprays—they should be at least 2″ × 6″ × 36″ to allow for proper placing on the rack.
   (4) Papier-mâché containers—use a large size for large arrangements. However, be careful that such containers are not top-heavy. Do not put too much water in the container.
   (5) Preservatives—use no preservative or chemical in the water unless the manufacturer guarantees the material will not damage rugs.
   (6) Vermiculite—cover Vermiculite with a foam material.
   (7) Deliveries—weekdays before 5 P.M. Family work should be delivered before 3 P.M.; Sundays and holidays between 10 A.M. and 3 P.M. (These times are for the Philadelphia area.)
   (8) Baskets—don't use leaky baskets. If you do use a reclaimed basket that is still good, be absolutely certain the paint is dry. Also see that the baskets have a large enough base so as not to tip over easily.
   (9) Metal picks—please omit or carefully place in the sprays, any or all metal barbed picks used to secure flowers in floral pieces.
   (10) Spilled water—tell drivers before they carry baskets into the funeral homes to check to make sure that the base is dry, because water might have been spilled enroute.
   (11) Entrances—be sure drivers deliver flowers through the door designated for florists and flowers.
   (12) Hemlock—do not use it in sprays.

   b. Funeral directors are also trying to cooperate with retail florists. The following are tips to funeral directors on maintaining the good will of florists from the Funeral Directors' Association of Philadelphia reported by W. H. Carter:

   (1) Always handle flowers with love and care. Flow-

ers are symbols—the messengers of love—for
those who live on. Funeral home staffs should
always refrain from dumping, hauling, crushing,
and tightly packing flowers into flower wagons or
cars. People who witness this are sensitive about
the callous disregard for flowers. Improper handling can wreck the very beautiful service the funeral director strives so earnestly to achieve.

(2) Mark flower delivery entrances clearly. Signs at
some funeral homes are often washed out, beaten
up, and unsightly; and some even have direc-
tional arrows twisted or reversed.

(3) Consult your florist before you advise a family on
the price of any flowers, or request a certain type
or color of flower. Weather and season vary the
availability of some flowers during the year.

(4) If water level is not excessive, the arrangement
should not be emptied, since the water is used to
keep the flowers fresh, and to present the best
showing for you. It also adds to the stability of
the arrangement.

(5) Flowers should be placed so that the arrangement is in full view, and not half hidden by other
flowers.

(6) Flowers should be handled properly and promptly upon delivery.

(7) Special consideration should be given to the removal of flowers after the service, regardless of
whether the family or friends are present.

A mutual understanding on the use and handling of
flowers is necessary between retail florists and funeral directors.

8. Special phrase cards suggested for death announcements include the following:
   a. Memorials preferred.
   b. Masses preferred.
   c. Contributions may be made to (name of charity).
   d. Memorial donations may be sent to (name of charity).
   e. Memorials: (name of charity).
   f. Gifts to (name of charity or fund) appreciated.
   g. Should friends desire, contributions may be sent to (name
      of charity).
   h. Memorials may be made to the charity of your choice.
   i. Memorials established at (name of charity).
   j. Donations in (name of deceased) memory may be sent to
      (name of charity).

9. The final, and maybe the most important, point is for florists to recognize that "Please Omit" is here to stay and that they should concentrate on selling flowers for other occasions. Many florists are doing that now and report that funeral flowers are only 20 per cent of their gross sales rather than the 75 to 80 per cent that they were 20 years ago. *Let's sell flowers to the living!* Try to build up the sale of flowers for gifts, birthdays, anniversaries, and for home decorations. We should try to get the American people to use flowers in their homes every week of the year. *This is the business of the future,* and the place where the progressive florists of today are concentrating their best efforts, rather than spending time fighting "Please Omit"—except as noted in suggestion #1 under combatting "Please Omit." Efforts should be spent towards the following two lines of endeavor: combatting "Please Omit" and developing new areas for flower sales.

Chapter 21

DIVERSIFICATION

All florists today find that they must diversify in order to stay in business. Some will handle just the usual sidelines, while others are branching out in all directions and handling many items. It is important to round out the retail operation with giftware and containers to complement the flowers and plants. Diversification increases sales. Let's look at some of the logical as well as objectionable sidelines that might be considered by the average florist.

Diversification covers a multitude of areas, but for our purposes, diversification for a retail florist is defined as the renting or selling of items and services other than the traditional flowers and plants. Most florists are now diversified. A recent FTD member survey showed the following diversifications (in alphabetical order): airport shop, antiques, candles, candy, commercial accounts, department store branch, dried flowers, fruit, garden supplies, greenhouse growing, greeting cards, growth chambers, hospital shop, hotel branch, stamps, street vendors, and supermarket outlets.

The same survey showed that 40 per cent of the florists rented equipment or plants to their customers. The most frequently rented items are those for weddings.

A retail florist should have a perpetual inventory of all stock and accessories. Keep an up-to-date complete record on all items. There are many accessories which are used with flowers—they are almost too numerous to mention. However, there are a dozen or so logical sidelines which you may handle in your shop. It is up to you as an individual to decide which of these you should handle, and particularly which ones will make money for you. Several factors will help you decide on these sidelines, such as type of store, location, size of store, and type of customers patronizing your florist shop.

LOGICAL SIDELINES

Pottery

This is the best and most logical sideline for you to handle. You will use pottery containers every day in your designing, and you need a good supply for sale to customers. Hospital arrangements must be in containers as well as many funeral designs. Many customers will also purchase a container for flowers sent as a gift for a birthday, an anniversary, or other occasion. A good supply of plain, simple, and inexpensive containers is necessary. Don't buy too many fancy pieces, although a few for display and sale are good. Many novelty containers will be needed. Be sure to have a variety of colors, sizes, and styles, but only put one or two on display at a time unless they are to be merchandised. Keep the rest in storage. Compotes and other specialty items are good, if you have the type of customers who will buy them. Animals and grotesque figures will only have a limited sale, so don't stock too heavily on them. There are many pottery items which can be sold as a good sideline to the flowers in a retail florist shop.

Glassware

Glassware is another logical sideline for the florist. It is a "natural" because, like pottery, there are many glass containers and compotes suitable for holding flowers. The type of glass you handle will depend on your business. Have some inexpensive clear and opaque glass containers along with some milk glass. If you wish to handle expensive Venetian glass or crystal, make sure that your customers are the type who will buy them. Novelty and colored glass may be handled in limited quantities. Experience is the best teacher in deciding what types of glass items to handle, and how many to stock.

Candles

This is another item which you should have on hand for your own designing as well as for sale. Candles just naturally go with flowers and can easily be sold along with a centerpiece or flowers for a party. You are the logical one to supply them for weddings, parties, and many other social functions. If you have the space, set up a nice display of all colors, types, and sizes of candles. There is no loss

Figure 21-1. An excellent display of candles. (Courtesy, Frederick's Flowers, Souderton, Pa.)

with these as long as they are kept away from the heat. Christmas candles are handled by every retail florist. If space is limited the rest of the year, handle just enough for your own use. But, if you have the room, this is a good sideline to handle. There is no need for your customer to go to the five-and-ten or a hardware store to buy candles to go with the flowers when entertaining. This is another service you can advertise as being available to your customers. The candles will sell themselves if displayed properly. Along with candles, stock a supply of inexpensive holders to use for large parties. Usually these are rented, not sold. More expensive candle holders can be handled for sale to the customers. Candelabras are also sold in retail florist shops, besides being used for weddings and other decorations, and in the window display.

Brass and Copper

Whether you handle brass, copper, pewter, or other metal items will depend strictly on your customers and your own desires. These items are a logical sideline to the retail florist business, but only in a limited quantity. A florist can build up a good trade by handling these items. Buy cautiously at first to see how well they are going to sell.

Planters and Jardinieres

It is absolutely necessary to handle planters and some jardinieres. It makes sense to promote planters. The type and number will be determined by your clientele. Planters may be in pottery, brass, copper, plastic, or other materials. Jardinieres may be in pottery, wood, aluminum, or plastic. There are many different sizes, styles, and types, so it is up to you to decide how many and what types and kinds of materials you wish to handle. These are a necessary adjunct to today's increased sales of green plants.

Permanent Materials

Although many retail florists do not like the permanent (artificial, polyethylene, and silk) flowers and plants, they have been forced into handling them. It has proven to be a good sideline. Silk flowers have recently become very popular. Many florists just sell the loose flowers, while others sell the material made up in designs and arrangements. (It apparently has not interfered with the sale of fresh flowers, as feared by some florists.) The pros and cons of this sideline are discussed in Chapter 39.

Giftware

The most common form of diversification found in floral shops is that of giftware. According to a recent FTD survey, 75 per cent indicated they sold gift items in their shops. Gift business is best for florists who are located in high traffic areas and who have business accounts. Handling of giftware is one of the most natural sidelines for a retail florist. Flowers and giftware just go together. Giftware has become an established part of most retail florists' shops. Approximately $52,000,000 is spent yearly by retail florists for giftware items (including pottery and glassware). If handled properly, it represents a sizeable part of a florist's annual volume of sales. However, it requires intelligent buying, promotion, and salesmanship. Gift items should be sold as added sales, not as a substitute for flower sales. The extent to which you can invest in giftware depends upon the space and the money available for a profitable business. The items purchased should be different, in good taste, and be a good item to be merchandised and promoted.

One of the biggest problems for florists who go to a gift show is deciding what to buy. Some shows have 600 to 1,100 exhibitors of gift items. You must select relatively few of these items which will fit into your flower business. Make sure the item has a definite relationship with flowers. Speed-a-Gift is an excellent way to sell flowers and gifts. Many are accessories that can be used with flowers. The following tips may help you promote giftware:

1. Always look at a salesperson's line.
2. When placing orders try to obtain gift lines exclusively in your own area.
3. Frequently change the appearance of the giftware section by moving the merchandise around to different tables.
4. Have the buyer acquaint store personnel (designers and salespersons) with the new lines, giving them information usable in design work and in sales presentation.
5. When you buy a gift item in large quantity, have a promotional idea in mind to move the material.
6. Use window displays—they sell!
7. Display giftware filled with fresh flowers and/or plants.
8. Stage a clean-up sale to dispose of slow movers once or twice a year as necessary. When it comes to selling giftware, there is no better setting than a flower shop.

Driftwood

The handling of pieces of driftwood and manzanita branches is another logical sideline. You will need to have some on hand for your own designing, and it is a good sales item for customers who may want to use the material in their own arrangements, or in their own decorating at home.

Souvenirs and Novelties

If you are in a special area where there are many visitors to the town, you may want to handle local novelty items and souvenirs. Many florists do not handle these items, preferring to leave them to the five-and-tens and variety stores. Others, however, are handling them as a come-on to bring in more customers to the store where

Figure 21-2. Pennsylvania field stone walls and Vermont slate floor form background for display of gift items. (Courtesy, Penny Hill Flowers, Wilmington, Del.)

they may also sell them plants and flowers. Whether this is a logical sideline or not is debatable among retail florists. If you can make money at it *without losing your florist trade,* it might be worth a try. One word of caution—don't go overboard in handling these materials so that you lose your identity as a retail florist.

Greeting Cards

The small, plain enclosure cards are provided free by the florist. However, another sideline you might consider is a regular line of greeting cards, retailing from $0.25 to $2.00, for customers to purchase to send either alone or along with flowers or a plant as a gift. Whether you handle this sideline will probably be determined by the size of your shop and by your competition. To have a decent display, you will need to devote quite a bit of floor space to it. Another determining factor is the competition of stores nearby that are handling greeting cards. You may not sell enough cards to make it worth the effort and display space. However, if you have lots of foot traffic by the store, you might sell enough to increase your net profit. As with novelties, do not have so many cards on display that it looks like a card shop rather than a florist shop.

Christmas Supplies and Novelties

This is a very logical sideline which customers expect florists to handle. Ornaments, flocked and artificial trees, tinsel, figures and novelties, ribbon, pine cones, spray paint, styrofoam, candles, and Christmas tree stands are just a few of the items which you can sell at Christmas. Proper display and pricing is important. Many of the sales are cash-and-carry and impulse sales by people who came in to order flowers. It is best to have all Christmas items together in one spot or area. While some florists turn the whole store into a Christmas showcase, others feel these items should be separated from the main selling area. There are so many different novelty items that you must choose carefully and buy wisely, so you only stock what you can sell. When Christmas is over, you must either have a half-price sale to move the left-over material or else pack it away in storage for next year. Items held over for another year mean money tied up in inventory that you could use more profitably somewhere else. It is best to buy wisely and moderately and learn by experience. Many of the items will also be found in the five-and-tens, hardware, and discount stores, so it may or may not be a good sideline. However, many florists are competing very favorably with these stores for the same items. How deeply you want to go into Christmas novelty items is strictly up to you. Try a few at first and increase your stock as business increases.

Garden Supplies

This is a logical sideline for some retail florists but not for others. It requires a large amount of space and is especially good if you have a greenhouse. If you are in a small town where no one else handles these supplies, then stock them. The amount of stock will be determined by available space. Some florists have enough area and business that they have opened a Garden Center in connection with their florist shop.

Nursery Stock

For certain florists this is a good sideline which ties in with garden supplies. The main factors are space and competition. The sale of nursery stock is seasonal, usually only in the spring and early summer. This sideline, like garden supplies, may lead to the establishment of a Garden Center if you have the space and believe you will make a profit on this business.

Bedding Plants

Almost all retail florists handle bedding plants as a seasonal sideline. These include the annual flowers like petunias, marigolds, zinnias, snapdragons, pansies, and others as well as vegetable plants such as tomatoes, peppers, eggplants, etc. Geraniums are sold by all florists and are sometimes included in the group known as "bedding plants." Space is also a factor in deciding to handle bedding plants, although most florists will at least sell some of them. Bedding plants are sold from flats, pots, or market paks. The season for sale of these plants only lasts from four to six weeks, but the sales will increase the total volume of business for the year.

Florist Supplies

If you have the space, a good sideline is that of handling florist supplies, particularly for garden clubbers and others who like to try their hand at flower arranging. A separate bar or table should be set up with the materials properly displayed and priced for easy sale. This can be called a "Garden Club Corner," or "Do-It-Yourself Table." It can be self-service or not, whichever the florist desires. Make sure that everything is priced. The supplies handled here would be florist wire, chicken wire, pinholders, clay, styrofoam, foams, ribbon, aluminum foil, floratape, chenille stems, net, spray paint, and other materials for a do-it-yourself flower arranger. Many of these items, if well displayed, will lead to impulse buying and an increase in the total volume of sales with no extra labor.

New Products

Every month there are new products appearing on the market for retail florists to use in their designing, display, and for sale. It is impossible to list them all or to keep up with new trends unless you go to gift shows, trade fairs, see the salesperson's line, and read the weekly florist trade papers. The following are a few (out of hundreds) of the new items offered to florists in the past few years to give some idea of the type of merchandise being discussed: adapters for miniature candles, ashtrays, brass stands for plants, flower carts, flowers in glass, fountains and waterfalls, handy trowels, madonnas, paperweights, plant food, plant hangers, planter poles, plastic bird feeders, salad bowls and servers, snack table sets, sprayers, styrofoam, styrofoam adhesives, tiered plant stands, tints and dyes, trellises of aluminum or wood, television planters, wall candelabras, wall plaques, and watering cans.

Candy and Fruit

These were debatable items for many years for most retail florists. Now, however, many are finding candy and fruit to be very suitable for use in arrangements along with flowers. They make attractive gifts and should be considered as a good and profitable sideline, according to Alexander's Flowers, Cleveland, Ohio, to be used in conjunction with flowers, not as competition. Fruit baskets are sold in large quantity by many of the larger florists in the country. They are perishable, but all florists have refrigerators to use for their storage. Apples must be stored by themselves, not with flowers, because the ethylene they give off is injurious to flowers.

Figure 21-3. Giftware items on display. (Courtesy, Alexander's Flowers, Cleveland, Ohio.)

Wholesaling

A new way that some retail florists are diversifying is by branching out into the wholesaling of flowers and florist supplies.

Second Shop or Branches

Another way to diversify is by opening a second shop. There are problems with this procedure—it must be studied very carefully before you make your move. A Penn State survey of 100 selected shops in the United States showed that 38 had one or more branches and 4 even had 12 branches. This trend has become stronger over the past five years as it has been shown to be one of the best ways for a modern, progressive shop to increase business.

Figurines

Figurines are items that are used in and with many floral designs and seem to be quite suitable as well as profitable, according to many florists.

OBJECTIONABLE SIDELINES

So far we have discussed the logical or natural sidelines. Now let's look at some of the objectionable sidelines which some florists handle, but most stay away from.

1. **Clothing and neckties.** These items are not considered practical by most retail florists who find they take up too much space with very little monetary return.
2. **Garden books and magazines.** This is not a profitable sideline, as it takes up too much display area and attracts people into the store who do not buy flowers but who do spend too much time gossiping with friends and reading magazines. No Sale!
3. **Pets.** This is definitely an objectionable sideline for a retail florist. They create undesirable noise, odors, and atmosphere. Special facilities are needed as well as a large amount of space, with too much time having to be allotted to their care. (Yet, some florists handle canaries, parakeets, monkeys, rabbits, and dogs.)
4. **Antiques.** Although some antiques can be used for flowers, this is not considered a good sideline by many florists. The

items take up too much space and will attract too many browsers coming in to take up space and time without buying any flowers.

5. **Records.** This sideline is like some others, in that the florist will get too many people in the shop who do not purchase flowers. There is no tie-in with flowers.

6. **Television and appliances.** Very objectionable and ridiculous. No tie-in with flowers at all, and yet these have been seen in a retail florist shop.

7. **Wallpaper.** Another poor sideline with no tie-in with flowers.

8. **Linens and hats.** Another objectionable sideline with no tie-in. The shop will be filled with women not buying flowers.

9. **Cameras.** These will detract from flowers and take up too much of the retail florist's time.

10. **Wigs.** Wigs are sold by a florist in Florida who says they are profitable. This seems to be getting pretty far afield from the florist business.

Most of the preceding items discussed are objectionable; some are even ridiculous. They are listed here because they have been seen in various florist shops at one time or another.

Stay away from sidelines unless they tie in with flowers and will increase the sales and profits of the store—but not at the expense of flower sales.

This discussion does not include all of the logical nor all of the objectionable sidelines, but most of the important ones. There will be others as time goes on, and many changes will be made in the years to come. Some that are objectionable now may become logical in the next few years.

Chapter 22

TELEPHONING AND WIRING FLOWERS

The practice of sending flower orders by telephone or wire has grown into an industry of millions of dollars in the past 65 years. This is the practice whereby a customer can go into a retail flower shop in any city and have flowers delivered in another city by a second member florist. Flowers may be sent by this method anywhere in the world with the exception of the countries behind the Iron Curtain.

The procedure is quite simple in that the customer goes into a local retail florist shop, if that shop is a member, and places the order. The customer pays for the flowers, the phone call or telegram, a small service charge, and the tax if any. The service charge, which ranges from $0.50 to $1.00, is optional with the florist who takes the order, called the sending florist. For most of these wire or phone orders there is a minimum—$10.00, $12.50, or $15.00, depending on the sending florist and the particular organization to which that shop belongs. A discount of 10 to 20 percent (depending on the organization) is retained by the florist who takes the order, if it is $10 or over. This helps defray the costs of advertising and overhead. Most florists do not receive any discount for orders under $10, so it is optional whether the sending florist wishes to accept an order under $10 from a customer. Many florists do accept orders under this amount as a service to their customers. Other florists use $12.50 or $15.00 as their minimum wire order—each florist determines this minimum individually. However, the receiving florist must accept all orders over $10.00 from a member florist and must fill the order correctly and at full value. Most organizations handling wire or phone orders will retain 5 or 6 per cent of the order for advertising and clearinghouse operation expenses. Thus, the receiving florist receives approximately 75 per cent of the value of the order, but is obligated by membership in the organization to send out the order with a full 100 per cent value of the flowers. Although the profit is lower on this order than on others, the receiving florist will not lose money; however, the markup is lower than normal on the flowers. This same receiving florist will, of course, make up some of this deficit on orders transmitted as the sending florist, from the retained 20 per cent of all outgoing orders. The 20 per cent of outgoing orders which the sending florist retains will add to total gross sales, and if the shop sends out more than it receives, may, in fact, increase net profit. (See Chapter 6.) As an example: A customer orders a $10.00 arrangement and pays the florist $10.00 plus $0.50 service charge, plus $1.50 telephone charge, plus $0.30 tax. The florist taking the order keeps the $0.50 service charge and $2.00 (20 per cent discount). The $1.50 goes to the telephone company and the $0.30 to the government. $8.00 goes to the clearinghouse where $0.50 (5 per cent of $10.00) is retained. The receiving florist who fills the order receives $7.50 and sends out a $10.00 arrangement to the recipient. This varies slightly with the different organizations.

Obtain the following information from the customer for a phone or wire order:

1. Full name, address, and phone number of the customer sending the order, even if it is a cash order. You need this information to be able to refund the money if the order cannot be delivered, or to handle complaints.
2. Full name and complete address, (phone number if it is an R.D. or unusual address) of the recipient of the order in the other city.
3. The nature of the occasion for which the flowers are ordered.
4. The exact order of cut flowers, plant, or arrangement. Also be sure to get a second choice in case the first choice cannot be filled by the receiving florist.
5. The price of the order.
6. The message for the card. Be sure there is always a card even if the customer is sure the recipient will know who sent the flowers. The recipient *who does not know* who sent the order may be very annoyed and blame the florist because there is no card. So, for your own protection, be sure that there is a message and a signature. This is another reason for point #1, so that you can check back to see who sent the order if it is questioned by the recipient.
7. The exact date the order is to be delivered.

All of this information, except for the name and address of the customer (#1), is sent to the receiving florist. This florist must be a member of the same organization. The methods of sending this information between florists have gone through a number of changes over the years. At one time, the majority of orders were transmitted via telegraph or night letter if time permitted. Often the order was sent by mail if it was to be delivered 10 or 14 days from the date it was taken.

As time went on and the telephone grew in popularity and decreased in cost, the use of both telegraph and mail substantially decreased. Eventually, the telephone accounted for over 85 per cent of all floral wire orders transmitted.

But this too is changing. With the world now in the computer era, the floral industry has felt the need to keep up. Now a good percentage of floral orders are being relayed between florists across state and country by computer terminals which are owned and operated by the wire services.

The largest network of these terminals currently in use by the floral industry is the FTD Mercury Network. This system was developed especially for florists by Florists' Transworld Delivery Association in Southfield, Michigan.

Since its beginning in January, 1978, the Mercury Network has continued to grow in popularity until, at this writing, over 8,000 of FTD's retail members, as well as a number of industry non-retail affiliates, do approximately 45 to 50 per cent of their business over the Network.

To send an order over a Mercury console—operated much like a regular typewriter—order information is typed into the console and then transmitted through a central computer where it is checked for validity and then relayed on to the receiving florist. Hard copy for the order is logged in at both the sending and the receiving florists' terminals.

With the consoles, busy telephone lines and time zone changes are no longer a problem, making this method of transmitting floral orders especially efficient at busy holiday times.

In addition to increased speed and efficiency for orders, these new computer terminals have the ability to be more than wire transmitting devices. At present, they are also being used by members to communicate with FTD headquarters, other florists, and even many wholesalers and industry suppliers also on-line with the system. In the near future, the Mercury Network also will be able to handle a wide variety of bookkeeping tasks.

With the benefits of an in-shop computer, the ease of operation, verified copy for both sending and receiving florists' records, and costs that are comparable to telephone rates, it is easy to see why the Mercury Network is quickly gaining acceptance in the floral industry as the "modern" way to wire orders.

Most of the organizations concerned with the business of transmitting orders operate in a similar manner with just a few changes in procedure. Essentially the orders are transmitted as described previously. A report of the orders is usually sent weekly to a central office or clearinghouse where every order is processed on computers, and each florist is sent a monthly report tabulating all incoming and outgoing orders. Each florist then is sent either a check (if the net dollar volume of incoming order exceeds outgoing orders) or a bill (if the net dollar volume of outgoing orders exceeds incoming orders). These figures are based on the net amounts transacted, with all deductions figured on the transaction.

Each organization publishes a monthly or bi-monthly magazine for its own members. The magazine includes advertisements, articles of interest to retail florists, and a complete up-to-date list of all its members. The retail members are listed by state, city, and in alphabetical order by shop name. The names of the shops in each town or city are rotated each month so that the same florist is not at the top of the list every month, unless that shop is the only member florist in that city. Each shop has an individual organizational number (called a code number) for identification on all reports. Each order reported by each florist weekly must include the number of the sending florist and the receiving florist.

Some of the smaller retail florists in the United States do not belong to any transmittal organization, and thus transfer very few flower orders.

Retail florists may belong to one or more of the five principal flowers-by-wire or phone organizations operating in the United States today.

NATIONAL ORGANIZATIONS

Florists' Transworld Delivery Association (FTD)

Florists' Transworld Delivery Association is the oldest and largest of the organizations. It is a non-profit, member-owned cooperative and is the only such inter-city floral delivery service, according to William A. Maas, executive vice president and secretary.

The organization started locally in Milwaukee about 1892 and became nationwide in 1910, when it was known as Florists' Telegraph Delivery Association. The name was changed in 1965 after an earlier survey showed that the majority of its orders were transmitted by phone rather than by telegraph.

In 1980 an average 12.81 per cent of the total business by FTD retail flower shops came from FTD orders, for an average U.S. gross sales per shop of $184,000.

FTD membership includes, in addition to the United States, florists in Canada and others parts of North America, countries of South America, and Japan. FTD is part of an international organization with its clearinghouse and headquarters in Southfield, Michigan. It is composed of over 19,000 retail florists in the United States and Canada, teamed together with 29,000 other florists in approximately 150 different countries. FTD and two other organizations— Interflora British Unit and Fleurop—are affiliated in an international floral delivery network called Interflora, Inc. Total membership in Interflora is 48,000 retail florists.

FTD is a non-profit cooperative association of over 19,000 members, with the clearinghouse in Southfield processing all FTD orders monthly from the weekly reports from its members. The clearinghouse charges 6 per cent on the gross amount of all incoming orders for FTD operations. Of this amount, 4.25 per cent is used for FTD advertising and publicity.

The 20 per cent commission which is retained by the sending florist (the one who took the order) is only on orders of $7.50 and above. Any member may collect a service fee from a customer on each outgoing order. The two magazines published monthly by FTD are the *FTD News Membership List* and *Florist.*

Membership in FTD is by application to the organization by each individual florist, who is then investigated by an FTD committee. The florist applying for membership is accepted only after careful consideration, whereby a certain percentage of a long list of qualifications must be satisfied. The committee in charge of applications (the Membership Committee) is composed of member florists of the association who are responsible for enforcing the regulations that FTD members impose on themselves to safeguard the public. The organization is operated efficiently by an executive vice president/ secretary, group director of finance, group director of marketing, a president elected annually, and a board of directors also elected by FTD members. FTD is associated with American Express, Diners Club, and other credit card companies.

TELEFLORA, Inc.

The largest privately owned network of florists who transmit flower orders from one city to another or from one country to another is TELEFLORA, Inc. The company was started in Los Angeles in 1934, as a private corporation and was known as Telegraph Delivery Service, or TDS. In 1961, the company was identified as TELEFLORA, Inc. In 1979, TELEFLORA was purchased by Mr. and Mrs. Stewart Resnick, and today it is recognized as a strong, progressive clearinghouse with a marketing-oriented product and promotion division for keepsake floral containers that give added value of a gift item to floral purchases.

TELEFLORA is a family-owned corporation. As of 1982, over 16,000 retail florists are subscribers to the TELEFLORA clearinghouse service. Its owner/president is Stewart A. Resnick. His wife, Lynda Resnick, is TELEFLORA's executive vice president. Currently, TELEFLORA is headquartered at 2400 Compton Boulevard in Redondo Beach, California. TELEFLORA functions in the same manner as any florist clearinghouse network. The sending florist accepts an order from a flower customer for long distance delivery and refers to the TELEFLORA subscribers' directory to obtain the name of a retailer located in the city in which a delivery is to be made. Because this sending florist created the sale he earns a sales commission. If the order is $10.00 or over, he receives a 20 per cent commission.

TELEFLORA maintains its own comprehensive electronic data processing center, to keep accurate accounts of clearinghouse activity. Each month a TELEFLORA subscriber receives an accurate record of all orders exchanged. Only the delivering florist reports to the clearinghouse. Payment is guaranteed by TELEFLORA, regardless of the financial stability of the sending shop. Once a TELEFLORIST has accepted and delivered a flower order, he knows that TELEFLORA will reimburse him for that order.

Any retail florist who meets the following qualifications may apply to the TELEFLORA service:

- A shop must have a physical appearance which is acceptable within the local business community. The shop must be neat and well kept.
- A shop must have ample refrigeration to insure proper care of floral products.
- A shop must have a competent sales staff with properly

trained salespersons to meet the public and sell and take wire orders by phone.

- A shop must have a professionally qualified designer.
- A shop must carry an adequate supply of fresh cut flowers, flowering and green plants to meet the normal daily demands of its business.
- A shop must have an ample delivery capability to provide satisfactory daily delivery of all TELEFLORA orders.
- A shop must guarantee total consumer satisfaction with no exceptions.
- Authorized TELEFLORA representatives must be allowed access to all shops for inspection during reasonable business hours.

TELEFLORA promotes the services and promotions of its subscribers on network television and radio, in popular consumer magazines, business journals, and newspapers. This national and co-operative advertising reaches consumers in major and rural market areas. Additionally, a comprehensive selection of in-shop and local promotional materials is made available to all TELEFLORISTS for use in developing not only their flowers-by-wire sales, but their total product and service mix as well. Included are point of purchase displays; high quality counter display books for all-occasion sales and weddings; statement stuffers, greeting care cards, product care folders, radio and newspaper advertising production materials, and window, wall, and workroom posters.

With a professional retail service-oriented staff of over 30 field representatives, TELEFLORA also sponsors local TELEFLORA Units of florists which meet monthly for design programs, trade fairs, and business seminars. The wire service hosts informative annual conferences in various locations throughout the United States, has a low-rate credit card program, full-service insurance program tailored to individual florist's needs, and a monthly, full-color, award-winning magazine (*FLOWERS*) which circulates to over 22,000 subscribers in the floriculture industry.

TELEFLORISTS regain their clearinghouse fees by assessing the customer a service charge. Although this charge is optional, it is estimated that most TELEFLORISTS collect a service charge.

TELEFLORA, Inc. is international in scope, through its working affiliations with clearinghouses in the British Isles, Central and South America, Continental Europe, Australia, and New Zealand. In June, 1976, TELEFLORA, Inc., strengthened its international service through a working agreement with United Flowers-By-Wire Service Ltd., of Canada. This exclusive affiliation between the two corporately independent entities has resulted in the largest network of flowers-by-wire florists in North America, comprised of more than 18,000 retail flower shops in the United States and Canada.

TELEFLORA publishes a bi-monthly subscribers' directory (issued in February, April, June, August, October, and December) for its own subscribers. The directory includes a list of all TELEFLORA subscribers, associate members, and international affiliates, as well as advertisements and a newsletter with articles of interest to retail subscribers, employees, TELEFLORA Unit members, and TELEFLORA employees.

In TELEFLORA's subscribers' directory, the retail subscribers are listed by state, city, and in alphabetical order, by shop name. The names of the shops in each town or city are rotated each issue so that the same florist is not at the top of the list in every edition, unless he is the only subscriber florist in that city. Each shop is assigned an organizational number by which he is identified (called code numbers) on all reports. Each order reported by each florist weekly must include the number of the sending florist and the receiving florist. Associate TELEFLORA members, United Flowers by Canada members, and TELEFLORA Unit Officers are also listed, as well as TELEFLORA's International Affiliates. Once a year, in January, a special numerical subscribers' directory is sent to all TELEFLORA subscribers. This special edition of the subscribers' directory lists all retail members by *code number*. No advertisements are accepted for this special edition.

Florafax International, Inc.

The third wire service organization is Florafax International, Inc., located in Tulsa, Oklahoma. It was a privately owned organization. Kenneth F. Short began the company with only an idea in September of 1961 and watched it grow in five years to a membership of approximately 6,000 florists. Shortly after this, Florafax signed a reciprocal agreement, terminated in 1976, with the United Flowers-By-Wire Service Ltd., in Canada, thereby offering Florafax members the sending and receiving facilities of over 7,000 florists in the United States and Canada. In addition to this rapidly increasing North American membership, Florafax affiliates in scores of foreign countries are currently being added to the membership roster, making Florafax a truly worldwide organization.

Florafax is now a publicly owned company traded on the NAS-DAQ market with a symbol of "FIIF" and is quoted in *The Wall Street Journal* in "Additional Over-the-Counter Quotations." It is the only wire service in the country for which florists can buy stock in a total floral company. When TELEFLORA (now privately owned) was owned by Dun & Bradstreet Companies, Inc., florists could buy D & B Stock, but that was more than just a floral-related company.

Florafax signed a reciprocal agreement with United Flowers-By-Wire Service Ltd., in Canada; however, this agreement was terminated effective April, 1976. United Flowers-By-Wire Service, Ltd., in Canada was bought by John Bodette, former chief operating officer of FTD; he has now affiliated UFC with TELEFLORA. However, Florafax will continue to maintain outlets in Canada and will continue to maintain worldwide service.

In 1970, Florafax merged with Spotts International, Inc., in Minneapolis, Minnesota, to form the Spotts-Florafax Corporation with Richard H. Hughes as president and chief executive officer. In June of 1974, the corporation was sold back to the original owner, and the Spotts-Florafax Corporation became Florafax International, Inc.

Florafax's present membership is over 11,000 members. Florafax no longer offers the instant payment program. Florafax was the first major wire service in the United States to go to free sending, i.e., the sending florist keeps the full 20 per cent of the order with no clearinghouse commission taken from the sending florist. The receiving florist pays the entire clearinghouse commission of 5 per cent, hence receiving 75 per cent of the order, minus other fees and charges on the monthly statement. This system of free sending was instituted at the same time the reporting system was instituted, and it is identical to FTD and TELEFLORA.

Florafax is the only wire service which continues to publish 11 directories per year. TELEFLORA publishes only 6, and FTD publishes 8, with only 7 rotations. (Rotation is important since the florist at the top of the list in a city tends to receive more business in that month than anybody else, so for a publication coming out 11 times a year, the florist is rotated to the top of the list more times than with a 6-issue directory.) This directory is now called the *Florafax Directory*. In addition, Florafax publishes monthly the *Florafacts* magazine.

American Floral Services, Inc.

The newest and second largest major wire service is American

Floral Services, Inc., founded in December of 1970, and more commonly called A.F.S., with the headquarters in Oklahoma City, Oklahoma.

Since 1970, A.F.S. has grown to 15,000 subscribers and is commonly known as the most profitable wire service for the florists to use. When A.F.S. first came into existence, it introduced the concept of free sending. This meant that the sending florist was not charged a clearinghouse fee. This concept was later adopted by the other major wire services and by introducing free sending, A.F.S. was responsible for saving the floral industry over $2,000,000 by 1975.

In 1976, A.F.S. introduced the 2 per cent rebate program and by 1980, the florists of America had earned over $24,000,000 in extra profits from free sending and the 2 per cent rebate.

In September of 1980, A.F.S. introduced the "Unbeatable Extra Profit Rebate Program," and from this new program the florists earned another $1,000,000 by January of 1982.

With all of these new ideas, A.F.S. was responsible for the florists earning over $27,000,000 in extra profits, but this was not the only way A.F.S. helped the floral industry. In 1974, A.F.S. began a teletype communications system, linking florists throughout the continental United States for direct shop-to-shop transmission of wire orders, at a cost substantially lower than telephone charges. This network also connected retailers directly to growers and wholesalers.

The concept of having a communication system linking florists was later followed by Florafax in 1977 with System XXI and FTD in 1978 with Mercury.

Even though A.F.S. is the newest of the major wire services, this has never stopped it from constantly working for the florists, with the end result being that the florists have been able to operate their shops more profitably. In return, the florists have sent more and more of their orders A.F.S., which has made A.F.S. the second largest wire service in 11 short years.

Florists' Clearing Network, Inc.

Another organization is the Florists' Clearing Network, Inc., FCN, the newest and smallest of the wire-service-clearing networks, with offices in Fort Lauderdale, Florida. It is owned and operated by Stewart A. Resnick. It is not open to all retail florists, but it includes selected florists in each area of the country. The main factors of this new wire service for florists includes the following: total coverage, territory protection, national advertising, local advertising, cooperative buying, marketing studies, education and research, and new business concepts.

Flowers by Wire— Sears, Roebuck and Co.

A sixth organization to enter the field is not a florist organization, but is Flowers by Wire, operated by Sears, Roebuck and Co. Orders are usually delivered by a local retail florist.

In all of these organizations, payment is guaranteed to the receiving florist by the organization headquarters.

In figuring the profit picture, a retail florist who belongs to one or more of these organizations must list the wire order business as volume at *net* to avoid showing the wrong picture for total sales volume, and hence profit. Outgoing orders are listed at 20 per cent and incoming orders filled are reduced by 20 per cent, or whatever the percentage is for that organization. This is all part of the accounting procedure and also will affect the percentages of the gross volume that the florist lists for salaries, advertising, and other items of expense. They will not be accurate unless the net volume for wire orders is correct.

INTERNATIONAL ORGANIZATIONS

Three of the major organizations, FTD, TELEFLORA, and Florafax, are international in scope. The FTD international organization is known as Interflora, Inc. In order to bring all countries and all florists to a common understanding of the price of an order, they use the medium of exchange called a "fleurin." It is worth a certain number of U.S. dollars, British pounds, French francs, and so forth for each country. Thus, the orders are transmitted all over the world by fleurins, and each florist can translate this into national monetary value. It has helped to greatly relieve the confusion of the various monetary systems.

Another point of confusion has been cleared up by Interflora relative to terminology. Official definitions to be used in all countries have been described by Interflora for the following standard pieces:

"(1) Arrangement: Cut flowers arranged in a container (if plants required, this must be specified). (2) Bouquet: One or a variety of flowers on natural stems tied into an arranged bunch. (3) Corsage: Flowers arranged for a lady to wear. (4) Funeral Sheaf: Flowers and foliage with stems tied to form a fan-shaped arrangement. (5) Funeral Spray: An elongated flat assembly of flowers inserted into a foundation. (6) Wreath: Flowers and foliage arranged on a circular foundation. (7) Boutonniere: One flower for a gentleman's buttonhole."

The sending of flowers from one city to another is big business and increasing in volume every year. It is an important part of the retail florist's business and another important service to the customers. It is not a large money-maker, but it will help to increase volume and also net profit. For most florists, it is well worth the cost of membership.

In recent years one of the biggest boons to the retail florists in sending flowers-by-wire has been the use of computers. FTD has its own set up which gives instant transmittal of orders from one city to another between the florists using the FTD computer.

Chapter 23

PACKING, INSULATION, AND STORAGE—
GRADES AND STANDARDS

The packing, shipping, and storage of cut flowers is a wholesale as well as a retail operation, and important from the standpoint of making sure the flowers reach the consumer in the fastest, best, and freshest condition possible.

Most cut flowers are packed in cardboard boxes lined with newspaper and kept fresh with ice in the box. Even in winter ice is used around rose stems. A wooden slat is often fastened across the box to keep the flowers stable in shipment, and then the box is tied with heavy twine. The boxes are fastened on the outside with heavy twine, rope, or metal wire. In place of the wooden slats inside the box, some wholesalers tie down the flowers securely in the box with wide twine. Most of our wholesale florists use one of these methods today, although several special boxes, which have been on the market since 1958, will be discussed later in this chapter.

WINTER PACKING

Flowers freeze at different temperatures, so they must be protected in winter. The U.S. Department of Agriculture has given us the following temperatures at which freezing causes damage to the flowers: roses, 30°F.; carnations, 28°F.; chrysanthemums, 28°F.; gladioli, 28°F.; gardenias, 28°F.; orchids, 30°F.; poinsettias, 30°F.; irises, 30°F.; daffodils, 30°F.; violets, 28°F.; and Easter lilies, 27°F. Sheets of newspaper are used inside the box to keep the flowers from freezing. Research has shown the following lengths of time for which newspaper insulation will keep the flowers from freezing: 12 to 15 sheets of newspaper will hold the inside temperature above freezing for two hours if the outside temperature is 20°F.; 40 sheets of newspaper will hold it for one-half hour above freezing if the outside temperature is 15°F.

Most shipments of flowers are not out in zero weather too long. Often they are in boxcars, trucks, storage sheds, or planes.

In below freezing weather, it is advisable to spray the sheets of newspaper with water. As the water freezes, it gives off heat in what is called the "latent heat of water." Heat is absorbed from the water before it can freeze, and this helps to keep the flowers in the box from freezing.

Some wholesalers use an insulating paper called Kimpack in place of sheets of newspaper. One sheet of Kimpack is about equal to 15 sheets of newspaper. It is expensive, but requires less labor in lining the box.

SUMMER PACKING

In the summer it is best to try to keep the inside of the box below 65°F. The box is lined with 10 to 15 sheets of newspaper and should be set in the refrigerator for an hour before shipment. In hot weather it is necessary to use ice, dry ice, or a combination of the two in the box of cut flowers. After the box is packed with flowers, the ice is put in, either wrapped in newspaper or placed in a plastic bag, and tied to the box so it will not move around and injure the flowers. The amount of ice depends on the outside temperature and the method of shipment: 3 to 4 pounds of crushed ice in a 36" × 16" × 8" box (standard) will reduce the temperature 15 degrees for a period of 24 hours; the amount of ice is doubled when the temperature outside is above 90°F. One and one-half pounds of dry ice plus 2 pounds of ice can also be used in place of the 4 pounds of ice. This cuts down on the weight and bulk in the box. The dry ice must be kept in a plastic bag to keep the carbon dioxide from being given off too rapidly and causing damage to the flowers. Roses are packed with their stems in crushed ice most of the year to keep them fresh.

SPECIAL SHIPPING BOXES

Several special boxes for shipping cut flowers have been designed. In 1958, a new method for shipping carnations was developed by the Colorado Agricultural Experiment Station to improve the packaging and shipping of carnations. The box eliminated newspaper, ice, and wooden boards. It saved up to 40 per cent of the shipping costs. The new containers are 36 and 48 inches long, and come in widths of 12, 16, and 20 inches. They are lined with a 6-foot square piece of polyethylene film which makes an airtight seal that retains the moisture. Two cardboard inserts in the top and bottom of the box help to keep the flowers secure while in transit.

In 1963, Davis Brothers in Denver announced a new semi-automatic machine that eliminates twine. It uses pressure-sensitive filament tape and a semi-automatic taping machine to accomplish a neat, trim, and economical box reinforcing.

In 1964, Kenco of Dayton, Ohio, manufacturers of permanent flower arrangements, announced they could ship permanent arrangements to any retail florist in the United States. This was made possible by using a carton package designed by the Packaging Division of Olin Mathieson Chemical Corp. An inner pack in the carton made of a scored sheet of corrugated board holds the floral arrangements firmly in place.

Other methods of packing and shipping are being tested in various parts of the country.

Figure 23-1. Packaged carnations ready for shipment. (Courtesy, Denver Wholesale Florist. Co., Denver, Colo.)

COLD STORAGE

Cut flowers are stored in refrigerators to make them last longer. The lower the temperature, the better, down to 35°F. The effects of temperature on the keeping quality of cut flowers are discussed in Chapter 24. Most cut flowers are stored with their stems in water in a refrigerator that is kept between 35° and 40°F. Orchids and gladioli should be stored above 40°F. The closer to 35°F. that the wholesaler and retailer can keep the other flowers, the better they will be. Reducing the storage temperature from 50°F. to 35°F. will almost double the keeping life of the flower.

Flowers should be moved as quickly as possible from the grower to the consumer. Some wholesalers and retailers keep the flowers too long in the 35°F. storage and then, when the consumer receives them, they go bad and do not last as long as they should. This procedure of keeping cut flowers in water in a refrigerator too long is called pickling, and should be avoided. Pickled flowers do not help the image of the florist industry, nor do they help retail-wholesale relationships.

Do not store fruits such as apples, bananas, or avocados in the same refrigerator with flowers, as the ethylene gas given off by the fruits will shorten the life of the flowers.

DRY STORAGE

A process developed at Cornell University can be used by the grower to hold cut flowers for a week or more without harming their keeping quality or length of life. This method can be used only by growers who have the facilities to hold flowers during a glut (a period of oversupply on the market), so they can sell them later at a better price. Or they may hold them for a holiday in case the flowers bloom a little too early. Again, they will get a better price. However, the procedure for dry storage requires special equipment and precise directions. The growers must follow directions and not try to keep the flowers beyond the specified time or they will end up with poor quality material. In this method, flowers are not put in water, but are stored dry. As soon as the flowers are cut and graded, they are packed in airtight cans, boxes, or Leverpak drums. The containers are lined with polyethylene or wax paper but not newspaper. The boxes or drums are sealed so they are airtight and placed in a special storage refrigerator held at 31°F. with no more than one degree fluctuation in the refrigerator. A good circulating fan must be used. In this way, the flowers packed in the boxes or drums will be kept at a constant 31°F. temperature in a dry condition. When the flowers are removed from storage, the stems are cut and put in tall cans of hot water (100° to 110°F.). They are then placed in a 35°F. refrigerator and hardened for six to eight hours before shipping. If these directions are followed exactly, cut flowers will have as good quality and be as fresh as if they had just been cut from the plant, provided they are not kept in dry storage longer than the recommended times, which are as follows: roses, up to 18 days; carnations, 3 weeks; chrysanthemums, 4 weeks; snapdragons, 2 weeks; gardenias, 2 weeks; irises, 3 weeks; and tulips, 4 weeks. Orchids and gladioli cannot be held in dry storage. This process should be used only by growers with special facilities to hold the storage refrigerator at exactly 31°F.

BUD CUT FLOWERS

The packaging and shipping of bud cut carnations is becoming more common every day. More flowers can be shipped per day, and the retailer gets them before they are fully open. Recently, standard mums were being bud cut and shipped. The retailer must use an opening solution to open the buds when they arrive.

TUBE PACKAGING

Prepackaging tulips in polyethylene tubes is a relatively new form of packaging used more extensively in Europe. The cut flowers are bunched, put into a clean plastic bag, and fed into a machine which extracts all the air from the bag. A burst of nitrogen gas is injected, and the bag is heat sealed. The inflated bag cushions the flowers and protects them against bruising during shipment and handling. These flowers will last at least one week; the nitrogen helps stop flower spoilage. This process has been used in the United States by a Florida company, which markets carnations, gerberas, asters, tulips, daffodils, irises, and freesia.

RETAIL PACKING

Packing of flowers in the retail shop is important to insure delivery of flowers that look neat and are undamaged. There are at least a dozen different sizes of boxes available from the supplier. Select one which is just large enough to hold all of the flowers in the order without crowding, and not so large that the flowers look lost and the box of flowers looks skimpy. Line the box with wax or tissue paper, which should extend over at least two sides so it can be folded over the flowers. Place the flowers very neatly in rows with each row moved slightly down in the box so that most of the flowers can be seen.

The stems of roses are often inserted in a small block of foam to keep them fresh. Greens may be placed in the box first, or put in last on top of the stems. Insert the card inside the box on top of the stems and greens. Close the box and wrap with paper, or tie with string or ribbon. Florists differ in their handling of boxed cut flowers. If the boxes themselves are attractive and have the name of the shop on them, the string or ribbon is all that is necessary. If the box is plain, it may be wrapped in paper before being tied with string or ribbon.

POT PLANT WRAPPING

Pot plants are almost always wrapped with foil or crepe paper around the clay pot to make it more attractive to the customer. By dressing up the pot plants, you can improve the image of your shop. Some pot wraps are already cut to size to fit various pots, while others are on a long roll to be cut by the florist. There are several different pot wrap materials on the market from which to choose. If a jardiniere is sold with the plant, no pot wrap is needed. Some florists use a pot wrap around a foliage plant, while others do not. However, all of them use a pot cover of some sort around flowering pot plants. Plastic pots usually do not need a cover.

Some florists wrap the plants for delivery in plastic, cellophane, or their own wrapping paper, which they either tie with string or staple.

The art of putting on a pot wrap and then wrapping the plant for delivery can easily be learned with a little practice.

Many florists use paper sleeves which are drawn up around the plant to make wrapping very easy. Since poinsettia flowers are so fragile, each individual bloom is usually wrapped separately in wax paper with a rubber band around it to hold it in place, before the whole plant is wrapped.

Many florists today are using clear plastic bags to package both arrangements and pot plants. This type of "bagging" is neat and easily done. It is usually suggested that a supporting stick be inserted to hold the plastic away from the flowers and foliage.

GRADES AND STANDARDS

The grading of flowers is a process which should be done by the grower before the flowers are shipped to the market. Grades and standards are almost non-existent in the florist industry, except for some gladioli, carnations, bulbs, and roses. The meaning of "grades" and "standards" is to set up a system of standards or media by which a commodity can be separated into various grades or classifications. It sets up a common language so that the grower, wholesaler, and retailer all know what the others are talking about. Roses have been graded for many years according to stem length, and pompons have been sold according to the weight of the bunch. But there is no one standardization for all the florists all over the country. It will be of tremendous value to retail florists when they can ask for a certain grade of cut flower, and know for sure the number of flowers, size of bloom, length of stem, and *quality* of the flowers they are getting.

The florist industry is the only industry selling perishable products that is not subject to some grade standard. Grades and standards will be set up by the U.S. Department of Agriculture *only* upon request of the industry. The Society of American Florists is studying grades and standards for the florist industry. They have the following six objectives:

- To devise and promote a system of grading for cut flowers which will adequately classify the material of the industry.
- To choose a method for the evaluation of flower qualities which is positive, based on universally accepted scales of measurement (ounces, inches, numbers); can be reduced to writing, and will remain inflexible from season to season.
- To choose a nomenclature which shall not depreciate the merchandise in the eyes of the consumer.
- To establish grade limits for the various cut flower crops.
- To offer such a system to the trade for voluntary acceptance.
- To establish a continuing re-examination of the use of standard grades.

The Society of American Florists has already established the following points: (1) Four standard grades are sufficient for most crops. (2) The weight of a flower correlates very closely with quality, and this coupled with stem length and diameter of the flower, serves to sort flowers into different grades. (3) The SAF Committee on Grades and Standards has adopted the following grade classifications with corresponding colors to be used to designate the proper grade: Blue, top quality; Red, second; Green, third; Yellow, fourth; and White. The committee is proposing the use of colors rather than names, which seem to differ in various parts of the country. Only minor defects are tolerable in the Blue, Red, Green, and Yellow grades. Any flowers which exceed the minimum tolerance are removed as not worthy of recognition by the Standard Grade "stamp of approval." Those not qualifying are relegated to the White grade, as in the case of split carnations and bullhead roses.

The producer of cut flowers who qualifies and uses the SAF Standard Grades is obligated to pledge adherence to the grade definitions to the best of his/her ability. The degree of compliance will be judged by others in the industry. No enforcement agency is to be used, but economic attrition will separate those who persist in substandard procedures.

When grades and standards for cut flowers are adopted for the whole industry, it will be of benefit to growers, wholesalers, and retailers, and will tend to eliminate a lot of poor quality material from the market.

Proper handling of cut flowers from the producer to the consumer is essential to the success of the retail florist industry. With a highly perishable commodity like flowers, everyone in the industry must work together to make sure the flowers, which may have been growing in the greenhouse for 4 to 12 months, will reach the consumer in the best possible condition. High quality merchandise will help to promote flowers to the general public.

Chapter 24

KEEPING QUALITY OF CUT FLOWERS:
CARE PRACTICES AND USE OF FOAMS

Approximately 20 per cent of all floral crops harvested are never utilized by the ultimate consumer; they're damaged in the marketing channel. In economic terms, it costs the average retail florist about 90¢ for every fresh flower arrangement sold. This 90¢ is passed on to the consumer and absorbed out of the retailer's profits. The improper care of floral crops represents the most significant factor contributing to this 90¢ loss. The question arises: What can retail florists do to maintain the quality of floral crops when purchased, and thus reduce this loss?

To answer this question, you must first understand and be able to judge the quality of floral crops. Quality at the time of purchase is assessed from the relative values of several characteristics that together determine the acceptability of the product. Specific qualitative guidelines that you can use at the time of purchase are more valuable.

With improvement of your ability to select higher quality crops, probability of shrinkage is reduced, as are losses expected from improper care and handling techniques. After all, floral crops of higher quality are probably better able to withstand adverse conditions longer.

The life of a cut flower is extremely important to both you and the customer. Flowers are a luxury item with a relatively short life, and are considered carefully before being purchased. While all customers are aware that flowers will only last a relatively short time, most do not know how to make them last longer. It is up to you to educate them.

The short vase life of cut flowers could be one of the most important reasons for the inability of florists to develop an appreciable home use market in the United States. Consumer surveys have often reported that one reason people do not buy fresh flowers for home decorations more frequently is "They last such a short time." Many people are buying the permanent flowers for the home, not because they are cheap, because any florist knows that the cost of a good silk or polyethylene flower is not low, but because they last longer.

KEEPING QUALITY

The keeping quality of cut flowers is affected by the proper handling of the product from the grower to the customer. The way the cut flowers are grown in the greenhouse, along with various environmental and cultural conditions, will affect the life of the cut flower. The treatment and time involved in getting the cut flower to the consumer will affect its life. It must be moved quickly and handled properly. There are many factors which affect the keeping quality of cut flowers, but the discussion will center on the main ones of concern to you, the retail florist, and the customer.

The most important factor determining cut flower life in the home is the ability of the flower to maintain its turgidity, so it must be put in water as soon as possible.

The quality of the flower is important to you as well as to the consumer. There are various factors which you look for in flower quality. These include: (1) freshness or keeping life of the flower; (2) flower color, intensity, fragrance, shape of the bud, petals, size, and individual flower area; (3) number of florets, spacing, and floret drop in the flower spike; (4) stem length, stiffness, brittleness, and straightness; and (5) perfection and glossiness of the foliage.

There are certain practices which should be followed by all florists and all segments of the industry if you are to sell flowers that will last, according to Dr. Marlin Rogers.

The newest program to improve the keeping life of cut flowers for the consumer is the "Chain of Life Concept," according to Dr. George Staby of The Ohio State University. This is a basic concept that will benefit every segment of the floral industry and increase consumer demand for flowers. It is based on information on postharvest physiology concerned with lengthening the consumer life of fresh flowers by the care they are given throughout the distribution channels—grower to shipper to wholesaler to retailer to consumer. All who handle the product (flowers) must use every means within their power to move the flowers to the next person in the chain in the shortest possible time. The grower strives to give the best possible product with the longest shelf life to the wholesaler, who in turn does the same to the retailer. The retailer's obligation is to the ultimate consumer. Each "link" in the chain must use a floral preservative and the optimum temperature and humidity to insure the consumer a product with the longest shelf life known for that flower.

Practices for All Segments of the Industry

1. Move flowers as quickly as possible from the greenhouse to the living room.
2. Use lower refrigerator temperatures. Most cut flowers should be stored at temperatures between 35° and 40°F. Orchids and gladioli, however, should not be stored below 40°F. There is a lot of deterioration of flowers in storage; this can be kept to a minimum if they are stored as close to 35°F. as possible. Deterioration consists of the following: opening of the flower which reduces its quality, loss of food during respiration which reduces the keeping life of the flower, development of mold which clogs the water-conducting cells, ethylene injury to certain flowers, and fading of the color of certain flowers.
3. Use floral preservatives. They should be used universally by the grower, wholesaler, retailer, and consumer. There are several commercial preparations on the market today including Floralife, Petalife, Morlife, Roselife, Burpees Everbloom, Oasis Preservative, and others. Dr. John Mastalerz, The Pennsylvania State University, has shown that the life of some cut flowers can be increased up to 200 per cent by the continuous use of preservatives in the water from the cutting bench to the consumer. Research at The Ohio State University has shown that cut carnations will last up to 18 days in a certain preservative solution, as compared to 6 or 7 days in plain water. This was accomplished by using the preservative constantly from the time the flower was cut until it died. Chemicals such as QC, CCC, B-Nine, ethylene oxide, nitrogen, sugar plus hydrazene sulfate, benzidine, and maleic acid have been studied for their effects on the keeping life of cut flowers. Not all of these materials are effective on all flowers. Some of these are still in the experimental stage. Controlled atmospheres for storing flowers have also been conducted with decreased oxygen and increased carbon dioxide to make cut flowers last longer, but the dosages are so critical that no practical application can be given at this time.

4. Wash flower vases after each use. Careful cleaning of the vases gets rid of the micro-organisms that plug the ends of flower stems and result in premature wilting and collapse of the cut flower. Nonmetallic containers are best for flower storage. Metal containers can partially inactivate certain preservative solutions, thereby decreasing the vase life of the flower.
5. Handle flowers carefully to avoid bruising. Flowers should not be jammed into storage vases or shipping boxes.
6. Watch for ethylene injury from gas leaks, fruits (apples, bananas, avocados, lemons) stored in the refrigerator, or close packing with flowers like callas and peonies which emit ethylene. Roses will turn blue and lose their petals, carnations go to sleep, snapdragons lose their florets, and tulips lose their petals if too much ethylene is present.
7. Throw out diseased material quickly, and keep the refrigerator clean. Botrytis fungus (gray mold) on carnation and rose petals can spread rapidly at low storage temperatures and high humidity.
8. Use hot water or a hot floral preservative solution to revive badly wilted flowers. Water at 100° to 110°F. is best.
9. Maintain 90 to 92 per cent relative humidity. Humidities lower than 80 per cent can greatly reduce lasting qualities; humidities over 92 per cent can result in environments too conducive to pathogen growth.

Practices for Retailers

1. In the final step before selling flowers, take a good look at the way you and your employees handle flowers. Every time someone handles flowers roughly and bruises them, it reduces their potential keeping quality.
2. Cut the stem end of all flowers as they arrive in the shop and place immediately in hot water to which has been added a preservative.
3. Instruct your customers in the best ways to care for their flowers to give long-lasting satisfaction. Recommend the following steps to the customer to make cut flowers last as long as possible:
    a. Cut ½ inch from the bottom end of the stem. Make a slanting cut with a sharp knife. This will avoid crushing

the water-conducting cells and will quicken the intake of water.

   b. Remove all leaves and thorns which will be under water in the container.

   c. Use a clean vase or container.

   d. Harden the flowers by placing the cut stems in hot water (100° to 110°F.) and placing the container of flowers in a cool place for two hours.

   e. Use a chemical preservative in the water which may be obtained from a local florist.

   f. Add water daily to the arrangement.

   g. Do not place the flowers in the direct sunlight, in a draft, or near a radiator.

   h. Put the vase of flowers in a cool place overnight. Even down on the floor will help.

   i. Consult a local retail florist for information on the best way to make specific varieties of cut flowers last longer.

4. Be careful in the use of foam products for flower support. Be sure there is room in the container to add water after the flower arrangement arrives at the consumer's home. Include with each foam arrangement an "Add Water Daily" tag.

5. Use floral preservatives for all flowers sent out of the shop. The material should be in all vases, baskets, papier-mâché, and foams in containers. Even loose cut flowers in a box should have a small package of preservative included.

6. Use flower wax on those flowers most subject to early wilting, particularly those flowers in make-up work which are not in water.

7. Sear or singe the stem end of latex-exuding flowers before arranging them.

8. Move the flowers as rapidly as possible from the florist shop into the hands of the customer through the concept of the "Chain of Life" as mentioned previously.

9. Cut the flower stems under water by use of an underwater cutter such as the Felly Flower Cutter. (See Figure 24-1.) This cutter has all stainless steel and nylon parts so nothing will wear out, plus it is very easy to operate.

Rose Research

Research at Michigan State University has indicated that rose

Figure 24-1. Felly Flower Cutter. (Courtesy, Al Felly, Madison, Wisc.)

vase life can be considerably extended, and that virtually all premature wilting of cut roses can be eliminated, according to the late Professor Paul Krone.

Best results are dependent on proper care and handling from
the time the rose is cut until it dies of old age in the customer's
home. Professor Krone offered the following specific recommendations for handling roses at the retail store:

(1) Upon receipt of the roses, cut the stems with a sharp knife.
(2) Remove the lower leaves and place roses in warm water
(100°F.) to which a good preservative has been added. (3) Condition all roses in the refrigerator for 4 to 6 hours at 35° to
45°F. (4) Do not cut through the bark when removing thorns
or leaves. A quick, safe, and easy way of removing leaves and
thorns is to use a glove or cloth on the hand for protection and
simply pull it down over the stem. (5) Do not scrape the bark.

This procedure will not increase the water up-take and may cause damage by cutting through the water-conducting cells. (6) Do not crush the ends of the stems. This practice can reduce the vase life of the flowers in water by as much as 2.9 days. (7) Use a good preservative in the water both in the refrigerator cans and particularly in vases in which roses are arranged. (8) If foam materials are used be sure the foam is thoroughly soaked, has a preservative, and be sure there is room for the customer to add water every day to the arrangement.

AIR PURIFIERS

There are several air purifiers and ozone machines on the market today for retail florists to use in their storage and display refrigerators. These help to keep down the fungus growth and gray mold in the refrigerator cans. The cans stay cleaner for a much longer period of time, and some florists have reported a longer life to their flowers. Some damage has occurred, especially to carnations, so you must experiment with the proper amount of material to be injected into your size refrigerator. Some wholesalers are also using these machines and reporting that the air is fresher and that the flowers seem to stay fresher, last longer, and look brighter.

FOAM MATERIALS

There are many foam materials on the market today being used by retail florists to make designing easier and faster. Some of these materials seem to reduce the keeping life of some of the cut flowers. Improvements have been made in the past few years so that this condition has changed for the better. Foams with preservatives added will now increase the keeping life of cut flowers over foams without a preservative. Recent research at The Pennsylvania State University and Michigan State University has shown that cut flowers last almost as long in *certain* foams with preservatives as in water. However, flowers still last the longest in water plus a preservative. Some of the newer foams have a preservative in them and are very good. Tests have been conducted on materials such as Oasis, Jiffy, Quickee, Fill Fast Foam, Camelet, Niagara, and Sno-Pak.

In general, the following recommendations can be made when cut flowers are used in the foam materials, according to the late Professor Krone:

&3 Be sure that the block of foam is thoroughly saturated.

- Change the water frequently in the container in which the foam is soaked.
- Submerge the block in water containing a preservative or be sure there is a reservoir of preservative water in the container.
- Keep the cut ends of the flower stems below the water level.
- Provide a reservoir of water in the container.
- Insert the foam so that water can be easily added to the reservoir. Do not completely fill the container nor jam it in tightly, unless you provide a V-notch along the side where water can be added.
- Do not push the cut ends of the stems through the block of foam.
- Do not move the stems after inserting. If the stems are pulled back an inch, the cut end of the stem is not in contact with the water that is necessary for the survival of the flower.
- Soak the block of foam in a preservative before using.
- Instruct all customers to keep the reservoir filled with water at all times.

PACKAGING

The proper packaging, wrapping, and delivery of plants and flowers are closely related to the keeping quality of cut flowers and pot plants. Make sure that the flowers leaving your shop are wrapped and packaged so that bruising does not occur. Cut flowers, floral designs, and plants should all be wrapped properly so that damage from temperature and handling is kept to a minimum. They should be delivered in the same excellent condition as when they left the shop. All of these things will insure the keeping quality of the flowers and result in greater customer satisfaction.

The repeat business in the florist industry is based on quality flowers and materials. The real criterion for quality is how the flowers look to the customers and how well they last in the hands of the customer. There are other qualities that are important to the retailer such as color, flower spacing, number of florets, and length and strength of stem, but freshness and the ability to last as long as possible are the most vital. It is up to everyone in the florist industry to handle the flowers properly and quickly from the greenhouse to the home. It is the obligation of the retail florist to use only fresh flowers and to tell customers how to take care of them to make them last longer. This is essential if we are to develop the home market for flowers as mentioned in Chapter 20 to help offset the drop in funeral flower orders.

DELIVERY

Services in many shapes and forms are a positive asset in the independent retailer's continuous battle with discounts and chain stores. In today's mass market economy, service is just about the only thing which you, the independent retailer, have to distinguish yourself from the mass market crowd.

Of course, service costs money, and this expense must be passed on to the consumer in one form or another. Therefore, you cannot afford to be overly generous on service without charging for it if you want to remain reasonably competitive with your non-florist competitors. However, retail florists have a tradition of service, one of the most important of which is *delivery*.

Here are some good reasons for offering delivery as a service to your customers:

1. If an order is phoned in, it usually must be delivered; be ready to suggest additional items which can be delivered with no extra cost to you or to the customer.
2. Delivery encourages additional purchases that the customer might otherwise hesitate to carry home.
3. Good will created by delivering even small orders can lead the customer to give the store substantial business on other occasions and may build up a sizeable account later on.
4. Delivery is something that customers just naturally expect and take for granted, as they do the extension of credit.

Since service is the very backbone of the retail florist business today and will be even more important to the industry in the future, you must consider the expenses involved in a service such as delivery. This is one phase of the process of selling flowers where most of the competition fades out of the picture, and the florist automatically sits in the driver's seat, according to Bill Curtis, Allentown, Pennsylvania. We have to think of deliveries from two angles: the provider of the service—the florist; and the receiver of the service—the customer.

It is a common procedure in all retail florist shops to concentrate on getting the order made up and out on delivery; at this point many florists consider their job finished. However, you have the responsibility to see that each piece of merchandise reaches the recipient properly. Several factors should be considered by the florist, including the following:

    ⋑ Has the product been designed properly so that it will travel without being disarranged? Before the introduction of tape, clips, springs, and forms, we found that bouquets and arrangements would often lean or tip over; but now, with all the new gadgets on the market, there is no excuse for this.

    ⋑ Is the merchandise wrapped properly to withstand either heat or cold? Keep in mind that half the thrill of receiving a gift is in the unwrapping. Wrap not only for appearance's sake but also for protection from becoming bruised or broken as well as from being damaged by the elements.

    ⋑ Is the package addressed properly and can the customer read the card that is attached? Proper addressing will save the driver time in making deliveries. A sloppy procedure could be very costly in time and money. Do delivery equipment and the driver properly represent you as being a first class service business? The truck and the driver are often the

Delivery Area	Rush Orders	DESIGNERS					Finished Orders
		A	B	C	D	E	
North							
East							
South							
West							
Will Call							

Figure 25-1. Wall construction with pigeon holes to keep orders separate for systematic designing and delivery of all orders.

only contact a customer or potential customer may have with the shop.

✎ Is the delivery being made at the proper time? While timed deliveries should not be encouraged, more and more businesses that are closely related to the florist business are becoming conscious of the time that flowers are delivered. Hospitals and funeral homes usually have set hours for flower deliveries which should be observed by all florists and their delivery staff.

Have a delivery cut-off time in your shop beyond which no order should be taken for that day's delivery. Always explain this so the customer will know the order will be delivered tomorrow, and why it is impossible to deliver it today. This is a good and economical business practice.

CUSTOMER VIEWPOINT

Consider deliveries from the standpoint of the customer. A poll of some of the better floral customers in one town showed the following complaints:

1. The driver delivers a floral arrangement either filled with water or with no water at all. In the one case the recipient ends up with a wet floor, and in the other, a wilted arrangement. In either case, a vase half filled with water plus a simple "Add Water" tag would have prevented an irate customer.

2. In another case, as an arrangement of chrysanthemums is handed to the customer, one of the flowers hits the door and shatters. A smart driver will have a candle or can of spray wax in the truck to repair the damage on the spot. (See Chapter 19.)

3. Another complaint is about leaving flowers at the front door when no one is home. If the family does not use the front door, they may not find the flowers for several days. Either place a tag on the back door, or leave a tag on the front door and return the arrangement to the shop. Call before delivering a second time. Some drivers hang a tag on the door, and leave the flowers at a neighbor's house. It often depends on how far the customer is from the shop. In any case, a follow-up phone call is important to make sure the proper person receives the flowers.

Flowers should always be delivered to the front door, even in an apartment house. They are in a category of their own and not to be classed with general deliveries. It is the one commodity which is an exception to the rule of "deliveries are to be made only in the rear." A good rule is to deliver flowers to the door that has the mailbox.

DELIVERY PROBLEMS

Downtown stores in medium-sized communities usually face more formidable delivery problems than other florists. The more widespread the customers are in an area, the greater the cost factor and more unwieldy this service may become. Many shops rely on cash-and-carry business. The neighborhood flower shop almost always runs its own delivery service. It must accomplish several objectives at the same time: get the merchandise to the customer in the shortest possible time, do this with the greatest possible efficiency and accuracy, be able to handle the largest possible volume at the lowest possible cost, and eliminate mistakes and delays in delivery.

DELIVERY COSTS

Full-time delivery personnel are an expensive part of the business, justified only by high volume. Part-time drivers, who also do other jobs for the store, help to keep the costs down. You must decide for yourself whether to own vehicles outright or to lease them. Both systems are expensive, and the pros and cons for each situation must be considered. There are advantages and disadvantages to both, which relate directly to the size of the shop, volume, and size of the community.

Cooperative delivery is practiced by various groups of retail florists, particularly in the very large cities such as Philadelphia, Los Angeles, Chicago, and New York, where it is uneconomical for each retail florist to try to deliver to all parts of the city. There are also delivery companies who will pick up floral orders in one central spot and deliver anywhere in the city for a certain price per piece. All of these systems must be weighed against each other as far as costs are concerned. In small towns, however, the cheapest way is probably to own your own truck and hire your own delivery person. Most retail florists in the United States use this system.

According to recent surveys, florists estimate that deliveries cost them anywhere from $1 to $3 per piece. However, a few florists have reported costs as high as $5 per delivery. The size of the city has a direct relationship to the cost, as does the volume of business. The best way to reduce delivery costs is to encourage will-calls. Some florists lease all their vehicles because it is cheaper for them, but this requires a study of all delivery costs. Others lease because they don't have the time to worry about operation and maintenance.

FREE DELIVERY

A 1965 statistical report (the most recent available) from a U.S. Department of Agriculture survey of 2,000 retail florists from all parts of the country showed that 97 per cent of the florists surveyed offered free delivery to their customers. (This is not true today.) It showed that 77 per cent of the sales were delivered free and that the delivery costs to all the florists averaged 76¢ per item. (At present, a range of $1 to $3 is reported.) This is considered an average expense for an average florist and, of course, must be absorbed somewhere in operating costs which help determine the price of the flowers, as discussed in Chapter 14.

In the same survey, many florists, regardless of size, offered free delivery. However, 72 per cent of these florists did have some restrictions on order size and/or distances for free delivery. Set a minimum price for free delivery, whether it is $6.00, $7.50, or $10.00. Below this minimum add a delivery charge.

It was noted that nearly 85 per cent of the larger florists invoked delivery restrictions as compared to only 66 per cent of the smaller florists.

Only about 16 per cent of the florists used commercial delivery service for all, or part, of their deliveries. Those florists most often using this service were the larger florists (over $500,000 sales).

At the time of the survey, air-conditioned vehicles were scarce among the florists. Only 13 per cent of those surveyed used them. However, an additional 18 per cent, particularly the larger florists, favored their use and felt that it would help to have them.

Of the surveyed florists, 63 per cent said that they never pool deliveries, 31 per cent said that they pool deliveries occasionally, and 6 per cent said that they pool deliveries often. This is one place where many florists in both large and small communities could cut down on their delivery expenses.

DELIVERY POOLS

Retail florists use more than 100 million gallons of gasoline each year. Nearly all of this is used on deliveries. Looking to the future, florists must start to conserve. One authority on the subject is strongly in favor of delivery pools. Florists in the same area can band together and send all deliveries out in one truck with each florist paying a share of the expenses. Some delivery pools are more complex than others. One example of an elaborate system is a Washington, D.C., pool of 26 florists. This pool operates as a cooperative, charges a $100 entry fee, and follows a strict set of written rules. Complaints are handled by a committee which reports to a board of directors. The board meets four times each year and issues dividends annually. More and more florists are beginning to realize how delivery costs can severely cut into today's profits. No matter what the size of the pool, it cannot work without mutual respect and cooperation among its members.

EQUIPMENT

The equipment varies with the individual shop. Some retail florists find that a station wagon is adequate. Others use a small van or a regular florist's truck. Some florists, who do a lot of decorating, need a larger special truck which will be high enough inside to haul trellises, ferns, palms, cibotiums, and other items. Some florists need only one vehicle, while others need several. Almost all florists hire other drivers with station wagons or trucks for the holidays.

An insulated truck is best in all areas. The northern trucks must be equipped with good heaters. Many florists would benefit by using an air-conditioned truck.

Install racks and braces in the truck to hold vases, baskets, and sprays in place during delivery. There are many ideas for holding containers in the truck, from the use of sand bags to an iron stand with two or three springs that clip over the lip of the container and hold it steady. Each florist has favorite methods and gadgets to use.

The truck can be plain black, colored, multicolored, or even polka-dotted, depending upon how much attention you wish to attract. No matter what color or style you use, take advantage of the advertising value of the truck. For very little cost you can have your name, address, and phone number painted on it. The lettering should be small and neatly done. Many florists also include the emblem of their wire organization. A flower design is sometimes added to call attention to the fact that it is a florist's truck.

Adequate insurance on the truck is absolutely essential.

Consider using uniformed delivery personnel. However, be sure the outfit you choose is something very snappy, not sloppy!

Delivery is one of the most important services and the most costly service you render to customers. Your responsibility does not stop with the sale and the designing, but goes on until the item is delivered in a fresh and good condition. It is up to you, as the manager or owner, to select the orders according to delivery areas and give them to the proper designers at the proper times. Coordinate the designing with the delivery schedules. Delivery costs money so it must be figured into the sale price of the item. The delivery person is as important an employee as the salesperson and the designer. Often your driver is the major link between the store and the customer. Your reputation frequently hinges upon the delivery person, who is often responsible for the image of the store in the eyes of the consumer.

Chapter 26

ACCOUNTING AND BOOKKEEPING—
KEEPING RECORDS

ACCOUNTING

Accounting practices of retail florists vary a great deal. A variety of methods have developed within individual shops, and, no doubt, have been improved from time to time as the business has grown or as it has been acquired by one generation from another. New shops have adopted a number of the basic rules, thus building up their own accounting procedure around the traditional markup policy discussed in Chapter 14.

In every flower shop, regardless of the size, bookkeeping is the main artery of the business, according to Herb Mitchell. You cannot manage a flower shop successfully without advanced planning, and when you don't know what's going on when it's happening, it is impossible to look ahead and plan intelligently. Many florists say that it is foolish to worry about bookkeeping and accounting. They feel they can hire trained accountants to do this work for them. However, unless you understand what the accounting figures really mean, you are not in a position to manage intelligently. No one but you, yourself, is in a position to understand and interpret the accounting figures of the business. The accountant can tell you how much you have made or lost, but you, personally, must understand the figures to be able to improve your operation.

Many small retail florists do the bookkeeping themselves, so they should know the fundamentals involved in accounting and bookkeeping—keeping records.

SIMPLE SALES ANALYSIS

An intelligent manager should make a sales report and sales

analysis daily. In small operations especially, it is easy to let all the bookkeeping go until the end of the month. This is a mistake, as the accounting operation should be done on a daily basis. In the average florist's shop, a sales report and a sales analysis can be prepared in less than an hour; it is well worth the time it takes. There are only two records you need to keep in order to have a satisfactory sales record, according to Herb Mitchell. The first is a daily sales journal and the second is a monthly summary or re-cap sheet. (See Table 26-1.)

The purpose of a daily sales report is to give you a form on which to make a simple sales analysis, as well as to give a report of net sales for the day. The purpose of a monthly summary sheet is to keep account of net sales on a daily, weekly, and monthly basis. These can be easily compared with last year's figures to see how this year's sales compare. The two illustrations presented here show how these forms accomplish the job. The incoming and outgoing wire sales order plus telephone charges must be considered and adjusted so that the florist will get a true picture of net sales.

The main goal in all retail florist shops is to make money. Keeping books and studying records is sometimes dry and difficult work, but it must be done in all businesses. The retail florist business deals with a perishable commodity. Flowers cost money, and the markup has to cover the loss of flowers if you do not buy according to your daily sales. The most important accounting practice is the budget record of purchases related to daily sales. The secret of making a comparison of these two factors is doing it by percentages. Following this method, you can control your gross profit and see almost daily your possible net profit for the month; you can thus allocate average monthly overhead expenses on a daily basis.

RECORD KEEPING

Record keeping is one of the most necessary phases of business management, yet too few retail florists place the proper emphasis on it. Without records, a business operates with no organized direction. Records should be kept for legal reasons as well, and to get the business back in operation following a disaster.

The three reasons why you need records are as follows: (1) for determining your true income, (2) for reducing your tax liability and avoiding penalties, and (3) for managing your business better. Keep the following check points in mind if you wish to be successful:

1. Consider the basic points on keeping effective books.

Table 26-1. Sales Records for June 1[1]

Daily Sales Journal

Amount of Reg. Sales	Amount of Incoming Wire Sales	Perishable Merchandise	Inventory Merchandise	Outgoing Wire Orders	Phone Charges	Labor
$ 5.00		$ 3.75	$ 1.00			$0.25
7.50				$ 6.00	$1.00	0.50
10.00			1.50			0.50
4.00		8.00				
		4.00				
	$15.00	12.25	2.00			0.75
25.00		19.00	5.00			1.00
3.00			3.00			
20.00		17.00	2.00			1.00
	10.00	8.00	1.50			0.50
12.50				10.00	2.00	0.50
$87.00	$25.00	$72.00	$16.00	$16.00	$3.00	$5.00

Adjustment for outgoing wire orders (80%) is $12.80.
Adjustment for incoming wire orders (20%) is $5.00 and phone, $3.00.
Adjusted daily rates: $72.00, $16.00, $-1.80, $3.00, $5.00
Daily sales report: TOTAL NET SALES: $91.20 ($87.00 + $25.00 − $17.80 − $3.00 = $91.20)

(The total of the first two columns should always equal the total of the last five righthand columns.)

Monthly Summary of Net Sales

Date	Total Net Sales	Perishable Items	Inventory Sales	Wire Order Sales	Phone Charges	Labor
June 1	$91.20	$72.00	$16.00	$−1.80	$3.00	$5.00
June 2						
June 3						
June 4						

[1]Courtesy of Herb Mitchell.

2. Check to see if the records are really useful.
3. Make sure you understand the statute of limitations.
4. Have proper storage for your records.
5. Keep your accounting practices up-to-date.
6. Always report pre-paid income under the proper circumstances.
7. Handle depreciation properly.
8. Keep accurate tax-withholding records.
9. Watch out for unusual expenses, such as entertainment, personal bills, and business losses.

Profit and Loss Statement

The system of keeping records, whether manual or computer, should be so designed that it gives you the results of operations as clearly and as quickly as possible. These records should provide two financial statements every month, a profit and loss (P&L) statement (Table 26-2) and a balance sheet (Table 26-3). A P&L statement shows very quickly for any time period, covering any operation, the position of the business at that time. The P&L statement in Table 26-2 is a sample which shows how much money the business earned or lost in that month. The real management dimension comes into effect, however, when you take this statement and compare it to what your business accomplished in comparison to what it should have done—that is, what was planned and budgeted for that month.

A look at Table 26-2 shows that profits were down in the current year even though sales exceeded the previous year and anticipated sales budgeted for the current year. This shows that something was wrong and, therefore, the rest of the figures should be analyzed. The figures show that the cost of merchandise was up and out of line, and that delivery, payroll, and other expenses were higher than budgeted. Something was wrong with the management; either the figures were not budgeted properly or the operation was not managed properly. If expenses could not be cut, the only solution would be to increase prices, and to be more careful in buying to reduce the cost of merchandise. If the prices were in line, then the expenses should be checked. This illustration shows the importance of the P&L statement for the successful management of the retail flower shop.

There are seven basic parts to your profit and loss statement (also called your operating statement).

≼§ **Sales**—your total sales for the period covered by statement.

Table 26-2. Profit and Loss Statement for January

Item	Current Year Budget	Current Year Actual	Previous Year Actual	% Increase or Decrease	% of Total		
					Budget	Current Year	Previous Year
Net sales	12,000	12,300	11,500	+7.0	100.0	100.0	100.0
Cost of goods sold	4,400	4,900	4,150	+6.5	36.6	39.9	36.1
Gross profit	7,600	7,400	7,350	+0.5	63.4	60.1	63.9
EXPENSES							
Delivery	720	750	710	+0.4	6.0	6.1	6.2
Payroll (adm.)	1,200	1,200	1,200		10.0	9.8	10.4
Other payroll	1,800	1,900	1,600	+2.6	15.0	15.4	13.9
Expenses	3,000	3,150	2,750	+3.5	25.0	25.6	23.9
Financial	200	200	200		1.7	1.6	1.7
Totals	6,920	7,200	6,460	+6.5	57.7	58.5	56.1
Net operating profit	680	200	890	−7.0	5.7	1.6	7.8

Table 26-3. Balance Sheet for 1981 for John Smith, Florist

Balance Sheet, December 31, 1981

Assets

Current Assets:

Cash		$ 5,000
Accounts Receivable	$ 3,500	
Less: Allowance for Bad Debts	500	
		3,000
Merchandise Inventory		7,000
Total Current Assets		$15,000

Fixed Assets:

Furniture and Fixtures	$ 2,500	
Less: Allowance for Depreciation	1,100	
		1,400
Building	$40,000	
Less: Allowance for Depreciation	10,000	
		30,000
Land		20,000
Total Fixed Assets		$51,400

Deferred Charges:

Prepaid Insurance	$ 250	
Office Supplies Inventory	150	
Total Deferred Charges		$ 400
		$66,800

Liabilities and Proprietorship

Current Liabilities:

Accounts Payable	$ 3,500	
Wages Payable	200	
Interest Payable	400	
Property Taxes Payable	350	
Accrued Liabilities	300	
Total Current Liabilities		$ 4,750

Fixed Liabilities:

Mortgage Payable		$13,500
Deferred Credits to Income:		
Advance Rentals		50
Total Liabilities		$18,300

Proprietorship:

John Smith—Capital, December 31, 1980		$45,000
Add: Net Income for 1981		6,500
		$51,500
Deduct: Withdrawals in 1981		3,000
John Smith—Capital, December 31, 1981		$48,500
		$66,800

- **Cost of goods sold**—what you paid for things you sold during the accounting period plus freight charges.
- **Gross profit**—sales minus cost of goods sold.
- **Operating expenses**—the money you spent that was necessary to operate your shop during the accounting period. Includes the salaries or wages paid to your designer, truck drivers, salespersons, and if you are incorporated, it includes your officers' salaries. It also includes many other expenses such as rent or payments on your building, selling and advertising expenses, delivery vehicle expenses, packaging expenses.
- **Net profit before taxes.**
- **Taxes.**
- **Net profit after taxes**—the money left for: reinvestment in your business, withdrawals by owner, debt repayment, dividends to stockholders, additions to accounts receivable needed as your business grows.

The two most frequently used financial statements are the profit and loss statement and the balance sheet. They should be used together to give a true picture of the business. However, the P&L statement is probably read and studied more often than the balance sheet. The accuracy of one depends on the accuracy of the other, and time must be taken in making them out. As mentioned previously, the P&L statement serves to tell how well (or poorly) the firm and its management have performed in the past. Since the time involved and the actions recorded are fixed and unchangeable, the information derived is of use only with respect to plans for the future. The usefulness and applicability of any financial statement is dependent upon its accuracy. The accuracy must be thought of in terms of reasonableness of judgment as well as in an arithmetic sense. Two important things to keep in mind concerning P&L are: (1) If you don't know where you have been, it's hard to tell where you are going. Having comparable percentages on your P&L is a fast, easy step for you to take to position yourself to make more money. (2) Financial management is comparison. If you don't have your P&L in a form that gives you good basis for comparison, you can't to a good job of managing your shop finances.

Balance Sheet

The balance sheet (Table 26-3) must give an accurate account of the present value of the property owned by the firm. It must show the assets and liabilities, and often indicates the net worth of the business. The biggest errors in the preparation of the balance sheets occur in connection with the inventories and the major fixed assets. In order for the balance sheet to be of maximum benefit in making management decisions, these items should be accurately reported. The balance sheet must balance, hence the need for accuracy. If the inventory increases during the year, this must be reported. Don't assume that it is always the same. If the building increases in value over the years, this must be included. If the assets are wrong, the balance sheet will give a false picture of the business.

Cost Analysis

Many florists use a simple cost analysis system so that each month they can easily check on all the items of cost and expense. This can be compared very easily with the last month or the same month last year. Often florists do not realize their expected profit, and this monthly statement may show them why. Each column on a single ledger sheet should be used for the same items each month so that comparison will be easy. If one expense is out of line, it should be corrected for the following month. Table 26-4 is a sample cost analysis sheet.

Double Entry Bookkeeping

The simplified accounting system recommended for most retail florists is called a double-entry system of bookkeeping. With this system, the records show property received and exchanged, cost of conducting the business, and the profits of the business. It is based upon the principle that each transaction involves an exchange of equal value, and the record must show the value of property or services received and exchanged in each transaction. The double-entry method requires a record of both property and services.

The following explanation of terms refers to the double-entry method only:

- **Bookkeeping**—the record of business transactions in the proper sequence and properly arranged in a blank book.
- **Business transactions**—exchanges of goods or services by which the business is affected.
- **An account**—a record of all transactions with any one person or with any particular kind of property, services, revenue, or expense.

Table 26-4. Cost Analysis for May

Flowers and Greens	Supplies, Boxes, Wire, Pins, Ribbon, etc.	Advertising, Printing, Postage	Delivery, Garage, Gas, etc.	Salaries	Rent, Utilities, Taxes	Miscellaneous Expenditures
$ 82.00	$11.60	$38.80	$13.75	$110.00	$220.00	$ 1.93
122.00	7.20	23.10	3.80	82.00	5.50	2.80
50.25	12.30	16.50	5.10	137.00	4.90	5.50
86.50	10.15	1.50	28.00	55.00	—	0.55
$340.75	$41.25	$79.90	$50.65	$384.00	$230.40	$10.78

◆§ **Debits and credits**—all accounts are affected in two ways: one opposite to the other; plus and minus.

◆§ **Classification of accounts**—all accounts must be properly classified, and this is the most important feature of accounting and bookeeping.

◆§ **Asset accounts**—accounts showing the value of property belonging to the business. Current assets are property bought for resale. Fixed assets are value of property bought to be used in the business, but not for resale.

◆§ **Liabilities**—obligations owed by the business are in three classes: (1) verbal promises (trade creditors), (2) written promises (notes and mortgages payable), and (3) money owed to stockholders.

◆§ **Current liabilities**—these include accounts payable, notes payable, installment purchases, taxes, etc.

◆§ **Fixed liabilities**—these represent the value of long-time obligations such as real estate mortgages.

◆§ **Accrued expenses**—outstanding obligations at the end of the year; earned payroll, rent due, taxes, etc.

◆§ **Income accounts**—accounts showing profit derived from sale of merchandise or services: sales, income from rent, commissions, and miscellaneous income.

◆§ **Operating accounts**—expense accounts which may be selling or administrative.

Daily Summary of Business

Figure 26-1 shows a copy of the Florists' Transworld Delivery Association Daily Summary of Business from its Uniform Accounting System. This form should be filled in daily so that the manager can tell at a glance the amount of sales, cash received, accounts receivable, and expenses for the day. It gives a good picture of the business for the day, to help the manager figure out how well the shop is doing on a day-to-day basis.

OTHER BOOKKEEPING SYSTEMS

National Cash Register System

Some florists are using other methods for their records. Many florists are using their cash register for their bookkeeping, such as Brill's in Ardmore, Pennsylvania. They use the National Cash Regis-

DAILY SUMMARY OF BUSINESS

FTDA UNIFORM ACCOUNTING SYSTEM

DEBIT OR CREDIT ACCT. NO.	CASH RECEIVED		DEBIT OR CREDIT ACCT. NO.	CASH DISBURSED	
CR 301	Sales, Taxable		DR 102	Deposited in Bank	
CR 302	Sales, Exempt		DR 121	Purchases of Merchandise	
CR 216	F.T.D. Outgoing (Gross)		DR 261	Owners Withdrawal	
CR 221	Sales Tax		DR 23	Maintenance & Repairs	
CR 306	Relay or Service Charges		DR 31	Advertising	
CR 52	Telephone & Telegraph		DR 41	Delivery	
CR 111	Received on Account See Other Side For Names & Amounts		DR 51	Postage, Office Supplies	
CR			DR		
CR			DR		
CR			DR		
CR 63	Cash Over		DR 63	Cash Short	
DR 101	Total Cash Received		CR 101	Total Cash Disbursed	
	Add Cash At Beginning of Day			Add Cash At Close of Day	
	These Totals Must Balance			◄─────────────────►	
	CHARGE SALES			ACCOUNTS RECEIVABLE CONTROL	
CR 301	Sales, Taxable			Due From Accounts At Start of Day	
CR 302	Sales, Exempt			Add: Total Charges Today	
CR 216	F.T.D. Outgoing (Gross)				
CR 221	Sales Tax			Less: Received on Account Today	
CR 306	Relay or Service Charges			Due From Accounts At Close of Day	
CR 52	Telephone & Telegraph				
DR 111	Total Charges			CASH IN BANK CONTROL	
				Balance in Bank At Start of Day	
CR 303	F.T.D. Incoming (Gross)			Add: Deposit Today (As Above)	
DR 106	F.T.D. Receivable				
				Less: Checks Issued Today (See Record)	
				Balance in Bank At Close of Day	
				Other Credits (Add)	
				Other Charges (Deduct)	
				Total Cash in Bank At Close of Day	

Form 321

PREPARED BY_____ DATE _____ _ _____

Figure 26-1. Daily summary of Business Form 321 from FTD Uniform Accounting System.

ter system which does a total bookkeeping job for them. It not only keeps track of cash receipts, but handles the charge sales as well, and produces reports that give a shop picture of the state of the business. The tape in the register is printed in a special optical type font, legible to both human and electronic eyes. Every detail of each sales transaction, as well as other bookkeeping entries, is recorded on the cash register's internal audit tape. Each month the register tape is sent to an NCR data processing center. With this system, the shop gets daily analyses as well as monthly ones. Daily summaries come directly from the cash register tape, and show such things as total of cash and charge sales for the day, the amount of sales tax collected, how much the shop took in from promotional specials, the value of incoming and outgoing wire service orders, and the total service charges collected. The following are the reports which the NCR data processing center prepares at the end of the month:

1. Cost inventory management report.
2. Sales summary analysis.
3. Sales and tax report.
4. Income statement.
5. Balance sheet.
6. Accounts receivable aging analysis.
7. Statements for each customer. The shop simply mails the statements to the customers without having to type them each month.

Mellon Bank System

Another system offered to retail florists by certain banks is the Mellon Bank System.

The Mellon Bank Billing System has been developed to emphasize simplicity, and to impose only minimum demands on the retail shop itself. When the service is installed, the florist receives an IBM 1001 Data Transmission Terminal and a complete file of prepunched cards, one for each customer. The transmitting unit is linked directly to the Datacenter over existing telephone lines. The florist has no more typing of statements, copying ledgers, and no stuffing, sealing, or stamping of statements. The customers receive professional-looking itemized statements promptly, and the florist receives a prompt payment which is opened by Mellon Bank employees who automatically credit payment to the customer's account and deposit the money in the florist's free Mellon Bank checking account. Each day the florist's office employee dials the telephone number of the receiving key punch unit in the Mellon Datacenter and, when ready, inserts the customer's cards into the IBM transmission unit. The florist's account number and customer identifying number are automatically transmitted. The employee transmits the amount of the charge or payment, and the designation of purchased items by prearranged code. The florist receives the following reports daily:

1. Transaction journal.
2. Trial balance journal.
3. A summary of all daily activity including charges, payments, adjustments, month-to-date and year-to-date receipts.
4. Deposit tickets for money automatically credited to florist's account.
5. IBM cards for new customers.

The florist receives the following accumulative reports monthly:

1. An aged trial balance report showing delinquencies in 30-, 60-, and 90-day categories.
2. A listing of all new customers and closed accounts.
3. A recap of sales to include number and dollar amounts in each category.

Mellon Bank prepares and mails a detailed statement to each customer with a duplicate copy sent to the florist. Banks in other areas of the country are offering the same type of system to florists.

FTD Complete Billing Service

Florists' Transworld Delivery Association has set up a billing system for its members, which includes many advantages to the individual retail florist. An FTD representative shows the florist how to assemble the names of all active accounts, and FTD prepares a small plastic customer card for each name. The florist receives two machines: an encoder and a visible index file. FTD also sends the plastic customer cards, a master customer list, master customer list binder, four- or five-part sales slips, three-part payment slips, and additional new customer forms. The FTD representative shows the florist how the system works.

The advantages of the FTD Complete Billing Service to the florist are as follows:

1. It does the entire job including stamping and mailing the statements.

2. It does away with ledgers and ledger-keeping routine.
3. It provides the florist with a regular monthly list of all accounts 30, 60, or 90 days overdue.
4. It provides the florist with a monthly statement of who the active accounts are, and how much they buy.
5. It gives the total charge sales month by month.
6. It makes it unnecessary for the florist to prepare and submit an FTD Report on Orders Filled.
7. It gives the florist an automatic way to follow up with direct mail in the statements. The system handles all facets of the business, not just FTD orders alone.

Computers

With the advent of computers into the florist industry, you are now able to use them to take care of many of the bookkeeping procedures previously done by hand. This includes the accounts receivables, overdue bills, costs of various functions, previous purchases and amounts, lists of customers' preferences, inventorying, birth dates, anniversary dates; and many other functions which are now performed by computers. However, to be economically feasible to own one, you must utilize the computer to its fullest advantage.

The keeping of records and a system of accurate accounting and bookkeeping is one of the most important aspects of the retail florist business. You, as the manager, must have accurate reports to use in keeping track of the business and its profits to be able to accurately plan for future business.

Whether or not you use one of the record keeping or billing services offered to retail florists depends on you and your type of business. Figure your costs and time involved in keeping books, sending statements, and other transactions, then compare this to the cost of one of the newer systems. Accountants have told retail florists that if they send out less than 400 statements monthly, then it is more economical to do it themselves.

The bookkeeping and accounting can be done by the manager, a bookkeeper and accountant, by a machine through any of several processing outfits, or by computer. Whatever method is used, accuracy is the keynote, along with a constant analysis of the records. The size of the shop and total volume of business will help to determine which system you should use.

Chapter 27

CREDIT AND COLLECTIONS

CREDIT

Credit is the name usually given to money borrowed for business purposes. Credit, like any other tool or resource used by an owner of a business, has a cost, must be managed to be effective, and has disadvantages as well as advantages. There is probably no business tool that can cause economic or personal problems faster than misused credit, but well-managed credit can provide convenience, a positive cash flow, and a profitable business. The old saying "Credit properly extended is half collected" still holds true.

No sale is complete until the money has been collected. It is essential for you, a retail florist, to develop a good credit and collection policy and stick to it. The accounts receivable can make or break you. Remember that you are loaning money at no interest, and even banks don't do that!

The most important reason for the extension of consumer credit is that it affords retailers a fairly constant volume of business that could not be obtained if they were operating on a strictly cash basis. There are very few cash florists; 95 per cent of the retail florists surveyed recently indicated that they offer credit to their customers. Their losses for bad debts are only 1 per cent of their gross sales.

Here are some of the principal advantages of credit selling:

- It creates more store traffic.
- It brings in more sales.
- It increases unit sales.
- It results in greater customer loyalty.
- It improves your competitive position.
- It raises your income.
- It increases your profits.

You can't develop a successful credit policy overnight, however. It must be well planned and promoted.

Credit Cards

An increasing number of consumers are turning to the use of the credit card in exercising more efficient debt management. By doing this, they make use of the credit card issuer's money for 30 to 60 days. From your point of view, you have the advantage of offering no-risk credit—you know you'll collect from the credit-card company—for which you pay a percentage on each transaction, plus an annual fee. Accepting credit cards is a customer convenience which makes selling easier and encourages multiple sales. Many customers are even charging weddings on credit cards. You can expect an increase in business when you begin accepting credit cards, but be sure that the increase covers your additional costs.

Charge Accounts

The charge account is customary in the credit field today, and you must go along with it. In simple language, a charge account presupposes that statements are sent by the merchant every month for the purchases made during the previous 30 days with payment of the entire amount expected within 10 to 30 days after receipt of the bill. Many statements contain a note to this effect.

There are many reasons for you to extend credit, including the following:

1. It is a builder of sales volume.
2. The charge customer generally buys quality goods because the price is not as great a factor when the article is charged as when cash is paid.
3. It develops confidence between the customer and the store personnel.
4. The use of credit apparently develops closer relationships between the management and the customer.

There are also reasons why the public uses credit, particularly regular charge accounts. For instance, expansion in the use of the telephone has made it simple to order by telephone, and such orders must be charged to the customer ordering; the customer uses the retailer's money, interest-free, for 30 days; and more permanent records are kept of charge transactions than cash transactions, in case an adjustment is necessary.

A U.S. Department of Agriculture survey showed that florists' credit policies are probably the most liberal of all the businesses in the United States. Moreover, only 12 per cent of the florists add a service charge to accounts considered past due.

However, it is very difficult, under the many federal regulations pertaining to credit and credit-reporting, to get information on which to base a decision whether to grant credit. For instance, if a woman applies for credit in her own name, you cannot ask about her marital status, let alone her husband's name and/or occupation. Neither can you ask a person's income. About all you can ask is the customer's full name, address, and occupation, plus credit references (get two), and a bank reference. You may find businesses and even banks are very cautious about giving information due to the many credit-reporting regulations.

Keep in mind that a person who is refused credit has the right to demand, in a personal interview, the reason credit was denied. This is a tough subject! The reason cannot be considered discriminatory—such as where the applicant lives, or what his/her marital status is. If you based your decision on a report from a credit reference, you must tell who gave the report; the applicant can then go through the same process with that firm, possibly implicating it under the credit-reporting laws. It is little wonder that businesses and banks are reluctant to furnish such information to another firm. They can, however, give information to a credit bureau without fear of repercussions. The bureau has the responsibility to determine a rating on the basis of factual information and defend that decision to the applicant, if challenged. Therefore, you can get accurate information without the possibility of unpleasantness and/or legal ramifications from a credit bureau report—for a fee, of course.

For fuller information, write directly to the Federal Trade Commission in Washington for the regulations and current interpretations of the laws.

One florist has instituted a system which gets many customers to pay in one week. The billing system uses a three-copy order pad. The original is white, and the copies are yellow and pink. On the day the order is filled, the pink copy is mailed to the customer as an acknowledgment of the order. The other two copies are filed. Many customers pay within a week of receiving the pink copy, thus providing cash coming in every week. If a customer does not pay by the first of the following month, the yellow copy is mailed. This saves the time of making out a separate statement. When only the white copy is left and payment has not been received, the florist telephones the customer. This is just one system—many florists have adopted variations of this procedure.

Some florists use a system called "cyclic billing," which means sending statements according to the letters of the alphabet. It spreads the billing out over the 30-day period easing the end-of-the-month workload. It also brings cash into the store every week. Some customers do not like this system, so it must be explained to them. Accountants tell us that a retailer should have at least 10,000 accounts for it to be worthwhile. By this criterion, it would not be applicable to the majority of the retail florists in this country.

Centralized billing and several other billing systems used by many retail florists were discussed in Chapter 26.

DELINQUENT ACCOUNTS

In the collection of delinquent accounts, there is a basic formula: **Remind—Request—Insist—Act.**

- Don't be afraid to ask for the money. Remember, it belongs to you—you just loaned it to the customer, interest-free.
- Don't allow accounts to grow cold.
- Do set up a definite policy and stick to it.
- Don't write unpleasant or libelous letters.
- Do make personal visits—they are often more effective than telephone calls or letters.
- Do try to get slow accounts caught up—people who are delinquent will avoid your shop.
- Don't let up on your efforts—if your customers do not pay, you may have to borrow money at very high interest rates to pay your own bills.
- Do handle the overdue account the best way—avoid it. The next best way is to have an efficient billing and collection process.

COLLECTION POLICY

Set up a definite collection policy similar to the following:

1. Mail the statements promptly on the same date each month, preferably before the first. Many florists close their accounts

on the 25th so the statement arrives before all the first-of-the-month bills.

2. Mail the second statements prior to the first of the following month. Some florists send it on the 15th.

3. Add a 1 per cent service charge monthly after 30 days. Be sure this information is printed on all statements to comply with credit laws.

4. Send a follow-up letter on the 15th of the next month. Don't give the customer time to forget it.

5. Mail a second follow-up letter on the 1st of the next month.

6. Make a telephone call on the 15th. This is important. Be courteous, and find out why the bill hasn't been paid. Suggest the customer stop in and pay at least part of it.

7. Send a final letter stating that drastic action will be taken.

8. Turn it over to a collection agency after it is six months overdue.

9. Write it off as a bad debt after one year.

One florist has adopted a policy of sending three notices for past due accounts receivable. The first notice reads as follows: "PLEASE AND THANK YOU are brief and to the point. So won't you PLEASE send us your remittance for $. THANK YOU!" The second notice is as follows: "NOTICE. We are most willing to extend favors as far as possible, but your indebtedness is past due. In sending you this reminder for payment, we are asking nothing more of you than our creditors demand of us. Please give this your immediate attention. $ past due." The third notice reads: "FINAL APPEAL. Repeated statements and courteous treatment have failed to bring in your remittance of $, long overdue. Settlement must be made within 10 days from the above date to avoid claim being placed with our attorney."

Some florists use a drastic looking Final Notice, printing it so it looks like an official legal document. It does bring results for some florists.

To be sure that collection letters will collect, the following advice is given from the American Collectors Association, Inc.:

1. Send at least two statements to the customer before a letter.

2. Mail the first collection letter not more than 10 days after the last statement has gone unanswered.

3. Do not use more than one collection letter in urban areas, and not more than two in rural areas. If the customer has not

DEMAND FOR PAYMENT OF DEBT

_____

_____   Creditor

_____

_____   vs.

_____   Debtor

_____

TO THE DEBTOR

NOTICE! The above named CREDITOR makes demand on you for payment of the sum of $ _____ with interest at the rate of _____ per cent per annum.

NOW THEREFORE, unless said amount is paid to the creditor at the creditor's place of business in the city of _____, County of _____, State of _____, within _____ days from the date hereof; or you make provision for satisfactory adjustment thereof, legal action will be necessary, incurring COSTS and EXPENSES in addition to amount of said claim, as well as the embarrassment of this action.

Dated at _____, this _____ day of _____ A. D. 19____

FINAL NOTICE

paid the bill, there is a reason for it. A telephone call may help you find this out.

4. Write the letters to appeal to the customer.
5. Use the "you" approach rather than the "we" approach.
6. Use motivating factors. Appeal to the customer's sense of honesty, security, etc.
7. Write complete letters, including the date of purchase, amount of the bill, what the order was, and where to send the money.

8. Meet the standards of the four C's to be effective at collecting: Courteous, Clear, Concise, and Correct.

Colored Stationery

Since color is an attention-getter, use it in the envelopes and second statements to attract attention. Many florists will use a plain envelope or a window envelope so that people might think it is a check and will not know whom it is from—at least they won't throw it away before opening it.

If a person complains about poor flowers and refuses to pay, try to straighten it out and get a satisfied customer. Let a chronic complainer go elsewhere for credit and merchandise. You will be further ahead in the long run.

BAD DEBTS

Bad debts should be less than ½ of 1 per cent of the volume of sales. They should be written off annually. Remember, unless a bad debt is written off in the year it is ascertained to be worthless, it may be turned down by the federal income tax office. The statute of limitations differs in each state. Don't let an account go too long, or legally the customer doesn't have to pay, although morally obligated. The U.S. Department of Commerce tells us that $1.00 is worth $0.90 after two months, $0.67 after six months, $0.45 after a year, $0.23 after two years, and $0.01 after five years. Therefore, it hardly pays to try to collect it after one year.

BLACK LISTS AND COLLECTIONS AGENCIES

In the past, black lists have been effective in small communities, but under the present credit-reporting regulations, they cannot be used.

Collection agencies are used by some florists and abhorred by others. Many florists are reluctant to turn over their bad accounts to an agency. However, some florists will send out an "official looking" demand for payment of debt. You will have to decide how drastic your action must be to keep bad debts at a minimum. Bear in mind that you lose money, not make money, on a sale for which you haven't collected within six months; you have nothing to lose by making such a customer angry and losing that type of future business. Anything the collection agency brings in is better than nothing!

Also, if you are too patient, the debtor may "skip town" before you get tough.

Check the following factors to determine whether you are granting credit efficiently and to discover any weaknesses in your system. Are you:

- Selecting new customers carefully and through a definite credit investigation?
- Making sure that each applicant and present customer clearly understands the credit terms?
- Setting and controlling credit limits for your various customers?
- Sending statements promptly?
- Following a well-organized and efficient collection procedure?

SCREENING PHONE ORDERS

The problem of screening phone orders from strangers is one which you must solve for yourself. The policies adopted by retail florists across the country are many and varied. They go all the way from a retail florist in Portland, Oregon, who, a few years ago, advertised: "If you've got a phone, you've got a charge account at . . . florists," to a florist in New York City who says over the phone: "It is not our policy to accept orders from unknown persons." These are the two extremes—many florists are in-between. Podesta-Baldocchi in San Francisco reported several years ago that they would accept all phone orders up to $15.00. Then they would check the address immediately. If there seemed to be any doubt, they would bill the sender right away. In fact, many florists always bill a new account immediately as a means of establishing a credit rating for the customer. Most florists will ask for the person's home address, business address, phone number, and credit references. Some florists will ask who recommended the shop to the customer; and often this is sufficient. Some florists use the system requiring the new customer to stop in and pay cash for the first order before it is sent out. Undoubtedly the size of the city will have a lot to do with the policy you adopt.

If you do accept orders from unknowns over the phone, be sure to check them if they sound phoney. One of the authors was in a florist shop recently in a large city when a phone order·was received from a new account for a basket to be sent to another individual at the same address. The manager was suspicious, called the address, and found it was an automobile agency with no one there by either name mentioned on the order. Obviously, it was a prank which could have been costly to the florist in materials, time, and delivery. Often a phoney will hang up when asked to give a bank reference, how the shop was recommended, or why credit is requested. A legitimate customer will have the answers to these questions and be willing to tell you.

No matter what system you follow, be sure to explain the policy to each new customer.

REDUCE THE NUMBER OF CHARGES

One retail florist has been able to reduce the number of charges by using a simple plain pad for orders from people who are not regular charge customers. When these people are told the amount of the order, most of them pay cash. This reduces billing expenses and gives more cash for operating the business. Of course, the regular charge order pads are used for regular customers.

ABC'S OF CREDIT AND COLLECTION

A. Set up a definite credit policy and stick to it—probably from 25 per cent of sales for new shops, up to 70 per cent for established shops will be charged.

B. Obtain general information such as name, address, phone number, and one or two references.

C. Screen phone orders from strangers.

D. Join your local retail merchants' credit association.

E. Send statements to new phone order accounts immediately.

F. Close accounts on the same date each month. The 25th is considered best by many retail florists.

G. Send statements promptly each month. Most customers appreciate prompt billing.

H. Follow up unpaid accounts quickly and at regular intervals.

I. Send the second statement before the 1st of the following month.

J. Send a follow-up letter on the 15th.

K. Send the next letter on the 1st of the next month.

L. Make a telephone call on the 15th.

M. Send a final letter or notice on the 1st of the next month.

N. Add 1 per cent service charge after 30 days.

O. Check collection letters with your attorneys. Don't be liable for a lawsuit. Good collection letters should make friends, not enemies.

P. Since color is an attention-getter, choose a different color from the regular statement for the reminder statements.

Q. As a last resort, turn the account over to a collection bureau.

R. Write off all bad debts annually. Don't let them accumulate.

S. Keep the bad debts below ½ of 1 per cent of the gross volume of sales.

T. Be methodical to keep the business healthy.

CREDIT STANDING OF THE BUSINESS

How about your own credit rating? This is also a very important part of the subject of credit. Many florists get into real trouble by not keeping their own credit rating in good order. It is good business because it will help the profits if you can get discounts in your buying as was discussed in Chapter 13. Always take advantage of cash discounts if you can. In addition, if you need a special favor or something in a hurry from a wholesaler or supplier, your chances are much better if you have a good credit rating.

There are also times when you may want to borrow money from the bank. It may be to start in business, to buy another business, to buy more equipment, to remodel and modernize, or to expand your present business. A bank will rate your credit standing according to five C's:

1. Character—dependability and reputation.
2. Capacity—achievement as a businessperson.
3. Capital—your ability to provide 50 per cent of your needs yourself.
4. Collateral—security to guarantee a loan.
5. Conditions—the influence of business trends in general, and the tightness or easiness of credit at the moment.

Remember that a banker analyzes your financial statement to determine the loan, assessing your economic health by the following ratios:

- **Current ratio.** Current assets divided by current liabilities. It should be at least 2 to 1.
- **Quick assets to current debt.** Cash, receivables, and other ready cash items divided by current debt; 1 to 1 is the best rule-of-thumb.

- ✑ **Debt to capital.** Money owed to creditors compared to owner's money in the business. The lower the ratio the better.
- ✑ **Fixed assets to capital.** Real estate, buildings, and fixtures divided by net assets. The ratio should be kept as low as possible.
- ✑ **Inventory to working capital.** Per cent of working capital tied up in inventory. An abnormally high ratio will result in a shortage of cash to meet other expenses.

Not only will these factors help you determine your chances of a bank loan, but they will give you a good picture of your business as a whole.

Credit, which is commonly known as "man's confidence in man," is a vital and necessary part of the entire business world, including the retail florist business. Handled properly, it can help to enlarge the gross volume of business with the end result of a better profit for your investment.

 *PART TWO*

FLORAL DESIGN

Chapter 28

HISTORY AND PRINCIPLES OF
FLOWER ARRANGEMENT

The reputation of the retail florist and the backbone of the industry rests with the floral designs produced by each florist. Anyone can put a bunch of flowers in a Mason jar, but it takes a trained artist to arrange those flowers in an appropriate container so that they form an attractive design.

Flower arrangement is the art of arranging flowers and/or plant material in a container in a pleasing manner. It is a picture in which living lines and colors are the artist's medium. The purpose of flower arrangement is to create something that is pleasing to the eye.

Floral design by the florist is something more than just the art of flower arrangement. It also includes the science of putting together materials which, when used with flowers, create an artistic design far beyond an ordinary flower arrangement. Thus, you, as a retail florist, build your reputation on artistic designs, wedding designs, and funeral arrangements. Floral design requires imagination and originality to make one florist's artistic designs different from those of competitors.

HISTORY

The history of flower arrangement goes back many centuries to the two different civilizations of the Orient and Europe.

The Oriental history of flower arrangements comes to us from the Chinese and the Japanese. It was the Japanese who refined it into a special art which is uniquely based on religion. It was primarily a worship, or prayer, to the gods and goddesses. The emphasis of Japanese flower arrangement is on line design using mainly twigs and branches with few flowers. Each bud, branch, and flower should be seen. The line designs are primarily based on a three-line arrangement consisting of heaven, man, and earth. Heaven is the tallest and most vertical line, earth is the lowest and is horizontal, and man is in between, usually 20 to 30 degrees from the vertical line of heaven. Heaven is always the longest line.

There are many variations to the Japanese arrangements which represent different types of prayers and messages, but all conform to the three lines or planes, no matter how many pieces of plant material are used. The materials may number 3, 5, 7, 9, or 11 branches, all in just three planes. The stems are usually held together for 2 to 4 inches above the rim of the container to give the effect that it is one piece of plant material growing out of the container. Some of the arrangements are formal or classical while others are informal, free-style, or naturalistic. They all, however, are line designs based on heaven, man, and earth, and stressing twigs and branches with just a few flowers.

European flower arrangements date back many centuries, and have always been based on mass and color. The arrangements have changed during the centuries and have come to be called Period Arrangements. These include the Greek Classical, Medieval, Renaissance, Flemish, Italian, French, Colonial, Georgian, and Victorian, and refer to various eras in Western or European history. Arrangements from those eras differed in types of containers, types of flowers, use of accessories, use of fruit, and the type and size of the design. However, even though they changed as civilization changed and were appropriate to each era, still they were mainly arrangements based on large quantities of flowers with many colors.

MODERN

Modern American flower arrangements are a combination of the Japanese and the European. They have the characteristics of both types; so today we call them line-mass arrangements, stressing color. They are characterized further by originality, simplicity, and depth, which make them different from other arrangements around the world. The mass is often quite small like a focal point, and not the enormous mass of the European.

A modern American flower arrangement is a planned composition; whereas a bunch of flowers is not.

Figure 28-1. A vertical flower arrangement of gladioli for the home.

PRINCIPLES

Flower arrangements are based on the following nine specific principles.

Design

Design is the overall shape or form of the composition. It is the planned relationship between flowers, foliage, container, and the surroundings. It is influenced by various elements and rules.

The elements of good design include line, form, pattern, texture, and color.

- *Line* means that under every good design there is a skeleton or framework which is the underlying linear pattern that holds the whole composition together. All arrangements start with a linear piece of plant material such as a leaf, twig, flower, or branch.
- *Form* refers to the geometric form or line design which is the outline of the flower arrangement. Today there are 13 forms or line designs which any flower arrangement may possess. These are the basic line designs which you achieve when you practice your artistry. Select the line design that you are going to use before starting to work. These 13 will be discussed and illustrated later in the chapter.
- *Pattern* is a silhouette against a space, and may be linear or mass, or a combination of the two. It is made up of voids and solids. Voids are just as important as solids. A void is open to the space around the arrangement and not to be confused with holes within the outline of the arrangement, which are very poor in floral design. A void is used in an L-shaped arrangement to change the design of a normal asymmetrical triangle, and to use fewer flowers. The void or space adds to the design.
- *Texture* is the structural quality or feel of the materials used. They may be fine or coarse. Texture is a characteristic of flowers, foliages, and the container. It is always best to combine materials which have a similar texture. Never put orchids in Mexican pottery, or zinnias in fine Venetian crystal.
- *Color* is such an important item it will be discussed in detail later on in this chapter.

There are certain rules of design which must be followed if the designer is to make an artistic arrangement which has good design and composition. These are:

◆ Proper height and width of a flower arrangement are necessary. The general rule to use on most designs (except horizontal) is that a flower arrangement should be 1½ to 2 times the height of the vase or the length of a bowl or tray. This height is measured from the rim of the container to the top of the tallest flower. The tallest flower should also be the longest. The width of the arrangement is less than twice the height, except in a horizontal arrangement. This becomes obvious when we consider that the tallest flower is also the longest flower in the arrangement. The width can be just slightly less than twice the height or it can be a great deal less, depending upon how wide or narrow the arrangement is to be. A low horizontal arrangement such as a centerpiece is the exception to these two rules.

◆ Good design usually includes only one, two, or three colors. Four different colors, not counting green, is the absolute maximum unless you are making an old-fashioned bouquet, or period arrangement.

◆ Two or three different types of flowers are the optimum. Four would be the maximum for most designs.

◆ Buds and small flowers should be at the top and outer edges of the arrangement with larger flowers at the bottom and towards the center.

◆ Light colors are usually at the top of the arrangement with darker colors at the base. This helps to give the arrangement better balance.

◆ There should be a ratio of approximately three light flowers to every dark one if they are the same size.

◆ When less than 12 flowers are used, it is best to use an uneven number.

These rules will help you to achieve good design in your floral arrangements.

Balance

Balance is stability. It is the relationship of the component parts so that they create the impression of being stable. The arrangement should not look like it will fall over to the right, left, front, or back.

Balance gives a visual weight to the arrangement, and makes it more pleasing to the eye. Visual weight is determined by the size of the plant material, distance from the axis, and tonal value of the plant material. There are two types of balance: symmetrical and asymmetrical. Symmetrical balance is formal balance where each side of the center line is the same and equal in visual weight. An equilateral triangle (with all sides equal) is a good example. Asymmetrical balance is informal and one in which the two sides of the center axis are entirely different, but equal in visual weight so they will appear stable. This is illustrated by a seesaw where the heavier person is in close, and the thin one is out at the end. And so it is with flowers. The type of balance must be decided upon before the designer begins an arrangement, since it determines exactly where the first flower is to be placed. (See Figure 28-2.)

Symmetrical   Asymmetrical

Figure 28-2. Two types of balance: symmetrical and asymmetrical.

Scale

Scale is the size relationship of the component parts of an arrangement. The size of the flowers should be reasonably related to each other, although they all don't need to be exactly the same size. That would lead to monotony. For instance, Easter lilies with violets would be out of scale; whereas roses and snapdragons would be acceptable. Scale is also important in the relationship of the floral design to the table or to the space where it is to be used. Proportion is the relation of overall size to the space it is to fill and is important so that the whole picture will be complete.

Harmony

Harmony is achieved if all of the component parts of the arrangement are in tune with each other. This applies to color as well as to the textures of the materials used—they must all blend together.

Focal Point

Most flower arrangements (like a painting) have a focal point or center of interest. This is needed to keep the eye from wandering aimlessly all over the arrangement. The focal point is just above the rim of the container, and at the base of the tallest flower, leaf, or candle. It is usually the largest flower, darkest flower, or a cluster of many dark flowers. It usually extends out a little in front to give depth to the arrangement, and is on line with the rim of the container.

Accent

Accent is accomplished through contrast and is used for emphasis. The focal point is the greatest accent point, but there can be several other subordinate accent areas in an arrangement. Sharp contrasts may occur through color, size, form, or texture of materials used.

Rhythm

The feeling of motion or swing in an arrangement is called rhythm. It is achieved by the placement of various parts so that the eye is carried through the arrangement with a feeling of smooth motion. It leads the eye to the focal point. It is an easy path along which the eye may travel through the arrangement of lines, forms, colors, and light or dark areas.

Repetition

Repetition is achieved by using one or more elements several times in the arrangement to add more interest to the design. It may mean repeating a flower such as a rose, a color like red, an object like a pine cone, a large ti leaf, or other items several times throughout the arrangement. Not all arrangements have repetition as the term is used here. One dozen red roses in a bowl has no separate repetition unless we think of it as 100 per cent repetition of red roses. Repetition is mainly used to add interest and provide contrast.

Figure 28-3. Laboratory where students learn the principles of flower arranging.

Unity

Unity means a oneness of the parts of the design. The whole composition must be a complete unit, and not look like several groups of flowers put together without relation to each other. All white snapdragons at the top and all red roses at the bottom would look like two unrelated parts of the arrangement and lack unity, unless there was an integration and repetition of each flower in the arrangement. An arrangement must have unity to be a whole composition with good design.

COLOR

Color is the most important characteristic of flowers. Everyone is conscious of color and is affected by it emotionally. When customers exclaim over a floral arrangement, it is often due to the color or colors used. Red is the favorite color of women, while men favor blue. Violet is the next most popular color. Then come green and orange, with yellow the least liked of all colors, even though it is bright and cheerful. In this text the term "color" will be used to refer to the primary, secondary, and tertiary colors of the spectrum as well as the tints, tones, and shades of various hues. Color is translucent in flowers, while color in pigment is opaque, so we have two different color mediums with which to work when arranging flowers in a container. Often a true red flower will not match the true red in the container. *Hue*, the pure color itself found in the spectrum, is seldom found in flowers. More often in flowers we find the tertiary colors as well as tints, tones, and shades of one hue. The three primary colors are red, yellow, and blue. The three secondary colors are orange, green, and violet. The tertiary colors are combinations of primary and secondary colors such as red-violet, yellow-green, and green-blue. A *tint* is a hue plus white, and is lighter than the true hue. It gives a psychological effect of being uplifting. A *tone* is a hue plus grey, is duller than the pure hue, and gives a soothing effect. A *shade* is a hue plus black. It is darker than the true color, and gives a depressing effect. Other psychological effects from colors are spiritual from violets and purples, coldness from blue and green, and warmth from red, orange, and yellow.

Color harmony is the characteristic that we are looking for in a flower arrangement because this is a combination of colors which is pleasing to the eye. There are six main color harmonies of interest to floral designers. They are understood more easily through the use of a color wheel, which makes color harmony more understandable than a straight line spectrum of colors.

1. *Monochromatic* harmony is a harmony using tints, tones, and shades of the same hue. There is a whole scale of just one hue from light to dark and from bright to dull which gives interest to any arrangement. It can be a combination of two, three, or four colors.

2. *Analogous harmony* refers to two or three colors that are adjacent to each other on the color wheel. They may include primary, secondary, or tertiary colors; such as yellow, yellow-orange, and orange.

3. *Direct complement* is the first and foremost of the four types of *complementary* harmony, which use colors opposite to each other on the wheel. This harmony includes just two colors that are directly opposite to each other on the wheel, such as yellow and purple, or red and green. This combination is the most popular one used in flower arranging today and gives the greatest contrast. The colors must be used in unequal amounts to be effective.

4. *Split complement* is a harmony made up of exactly three colors. It includes one color plus the two colors (one on each side) adjacent to its direct complement. An example would be orange with blue-green and blue-violet.

5. *Triad* is a color harmony which is also made up of three colors only, such as red, blue, and yellow, that are equidistant from each other on the color wheel. A red and yellow combination is not pleasing to most people unless tempered with some blue or blue-green.

6. *Tetrad* is often called a *double or paired complement*. It includes four colors that are equidistant from each other on the color wheel and is made up of two direct complements that are at right angles to each other. It is not often used in flower arrangements because four is considered too many colors for most designs. Orange, yellow-green, blue, and red-violet would be an example.

Color is a definite part of the design but must not be spotty. Group the flowers of one color together in one or two different areas in working out the design. There must be contrast and repetition, as well as a blending of colors to achieve the best design and to avoid a spotty effect.

Many colors, such as blues and violets, are lost under artificial light, particularly if seen from a distance. Artificial light usually casts shadows which change the intensity of some colors. Fluorescent lights have a different effect on color than do incandescent lamps and must be considered in display and decoration. This is particularly true in churches, clubs, halls, and meeting rooms.

We have discussed briefly the history of flower arrangement and the principles of good design. The rules and principles should be used as guidelines only, and not considered unbreakable under any circumstances. An artist who has learned how to design may break some of the rules and still have a perfect design. The arrangement may be much higher than twice the height of the container, but if it still has balance and scale it is acceptable. All of the principles are not applicable to all flower arrangements, as has been pointed out. The best way for a person to learn floral design is to go by the rules and principles at first and then get lots of practice. That is why we recommend that a future florist attend a design school and work for a florist to get the experience that is necessary to become a good designer. The reputation and success of the florist shop rests upon the artistry of the design work, including originality and imagination which will make the arrangements different from those of competitors.

Chapter 29

CONTAINERS AND ACCESSORIES—
STEPS IN CONSTRUCTION

CONTAINERS

The primary purpose of the container is to hold flowers, foliage, and water. You have a wide selection of containers for resale and for use with your designs. Experience and practice, as well as the occasion, will usually dictate the type of container to use. The price of the arrangement is also an important factor. We are not going into specifics in this text on the variety of shapes, sizes, and styles because there are too many and they change every year. However, there are a few general rules to follow in selecting the proper container for a flower arrangement. The main criterion for selecting the proper container is *suitability*—that is, suitable from several standpoints, including:

- Correct size to hold the flowers.
- Proper scale to the flowers used.
- Appropriate cost for price of order.
- Proper design for the occasion.
- Compatible texture to blend with the flowers.
- Appropriate color. This consideration is very important. It may duplicate the color of the flowers, or it may be the direct complement of the color of the flowers. Green and black containers are excellent for almost any design. White is very good, but the arrangement should include some white flowers to cut down on the contrast.

The container should enhance the flowers, not dominate the arrangement. Plain and simple containers are best for most arrangements. However, an ornate container may be used if the customer picks it out or brings it into the store to be used. Know your customer's likes and dislikes before sending out an arrangement in something other than a plain and simple container. Sturdy containers should be used for heavy flowers like gladioli, chrysanthemums, and stock, while fragile containers should be used for delicate flowers. Silver bowls are very effective for anniversaries and formal decorations. Pewter, copper, and brass are all good for certain flowers and special occasions, but they are not used in the same quantity as are pottery and glass. Plastic containers and papier-mâchés are very inexpensive and are used for many arrangements when the customer does not want to spend much money on a container.

If a base or stand is used under the container, it is considered as part of the container. Thus, when the designer measures the container to get the correct height of the arrangement, the base is measured also. Not too many of these are used in the retail flower shop except in special arrangements.

ACCESSORIES

An accessory is any object included in the composition but detached from the plant material in the container and supplemental to the theme. It may be a candle, pine cone, book, picture, fruit, or any of a number of figures and figurines. It can be a flower if it is a complete flower like a rose. However, a rose petal or a snapdragon floret is not an accessory. These do not add to the composition and give the illusion that the flowers are old and falling. Styrofoam novelties are used as accessories for many special occasions and party decorations. An accessory must be appropriate and fit the arrangement in scale and color harmony. If an arrangement is complete without an accessory, leave it out. If the arrangement is symmetrical, then the accessories must be too, such as two candles, one at each end of a symmetrical centerpiece. If the arrangement is asymmetrical, then the accessory or accessories must be arranged in an asymmetrical design. The symmetry of the accessories must conform to the symmetry of the floral design in order to have proper design for the whole composition. The accessory or accessories for an asymmetrical arrangement will usually be just on one side of the arrangement. The three tests for adding an accessory are: (1) Does it contribute to the design? (2) Does it supplement the theme? (3) Does it harmonize in color, size, and texture?

MECHANICAL AIDS

There are many different holding devices for florists to use to make the flowers stay in place in the containers. These are often called mechanical aids and are absolutely necessary for good designing. The type used will depend on the container, type of arrangement, and the personal preference of the designer. We will briefly list the main ones used by retail florists today.

1. Chicken wire or wire mesh is one of the most common materials used in tall pottery containers, papier-mâchés, and baskets.
2. Pinholders are used in the low bowl and tray type containers, securely attached with floral clay.
3. Foam materials (Figure 29-1) which absorb water, such as Oasis, Jiffy, Quickee, Fill Fast Foam, Niagara, and others are used in tray containers, tall containers, and sometimes on the top of baskets, pottery, and papier-mâché containers. They can be used also as the foundation for wreaths and sprays.
4. Shredded styrofoam (Tufflite) is a good holding device in any type of a tall container. It does not absorb water, but holds the flowers in place very well while allowing plenty of room for water in the container.
5. Regular styrofoam is used as a base and holder for many arrangements which do not need water. Or, if moisture is

Figure 29-1. Foam material taped into a black tray container.

needed for a few flowers, a piece of foam material can be
used in a small plastic cup or wrapped in foil, and placed in a
small hole dug out of the styrofoam.
6. Regular greens such as laurel, cedar, hemlock, and others
which are slow to decompose are used by florists in papier-
mâchés and baskets as a mechanical aid to hold the flowers in
place.
7. Sahara is an excellent dry foam for dried arrangements. The
aid will be determined by the individual florist and the type
of container used.

STYROFOAM

The use of styrofoam has increased the artistry and attractiveness of many designs. Florists with imagination and originality have
been able to upsell their merchandise and make a good reputation
for themselves. Most florists have a styrofoam cutter to use for small
designs, and a regular saw for larger pieces. Novelty items of any
size and shape can be cut out, painted, and used in a number of
designs. For a musician, a design can include a styrofoam sheet of
music, a musical note, or some appropriate instrument. For any special occasion, an article appropriate to the theme can be cut out of
styrofoam: cake, parasol, shoe, Santa Claus, reindeer, tree, flower,
instrument, figurine, number, etc. There is no limit to the articles
that can be shaped out of styrofoam. Styrofoam items are often used
in window displays—from a small cone up to an organ entirely made
out of styrofoam. Many bases for arrangements are made out of
styrofoam. One word of caution on using a hot wire styrofoam
cutter—do not inhale the fumes! Cut the styrofoam in a well-
ventilated room.

PAINT

Spray paint in every color imaginable is available. These paints
spray on very easily and can be used on flowers, foliage, styrofoam,
pottery, and other items like pine cones. There are advantages to
spray painting materials for an occasion like a silver or golden anniversary or for an arrangement to fit the décor in the customer's
home, particularly when you do not have the correct colors of flowers and accessories. Foliages are often spray painted at Christmas for
more festive effects. A word of caution—do not use spray paint on
every arrangement which leaves the shop—it can be overdone. Used

correctly and in moderation, spray paint can be a great help in making designs and arrangements more interesting and pleasing to the eye. Spray paint only in a well-ventilated area.

STEPS IN CONSTRUCTION

Before you start to construct an arrangement, there are three things to decide. These will be determined by the type of arrangement, placement, occasion, and your ideas as the designer. First, you must know if the arrangement is to be one-sided or an all-around arrangement (one which is attractive from all sides). If this is not specified, then you must make the decision. Second, you decide if it is to be symmetrical or asymmetrical so that you will know how and where to place the first flower. Third, decide what type of line design or geometric form to follow. (There are 13 line designs discussed in Chapter 30.) Those three things must be decided before you can begin because it is impossible to start with an asymmetrical design and end up with one which is symmetrical—unless you start over.

There are seven main steps to follow in constructing an arrangement, whether it be in pottery, glass, metal, papier-mâché, or a basket. (See Figures 29-2, 30-11, and 34-26.) The exception to this procedure, low horizontal arrangements, will be discussed separately.

1. After selecting the proper container and seeing that it is clean, put in whichever mechanical aid is going to be used and add water. Never start a flower arrangement without water in the container.
2. Establish the main line of the arrangement by putting in the tallest flower first. It should be 1½ to 2 times the height of the vase or width of a bowl or tray, as measured from the rim of the container to the top of the tallest flower.
3. Add the secondary lines for the width. Two flowers will be used for a one-sided arrangement, and four flowers for an all-around arrangement. In the one-sided arrangement, the two flowers will be horizontal if the arrangement is symmetrical; while one will be vertical and one horizontal if the arrangement is asymmetrical. In an all-around arrangement the four flowers will all be horizontal (one to each point of the compass) if the arrangement is symmetrical; while one flower will be vertical and three horizontal if the arrangement is asymmetrical.

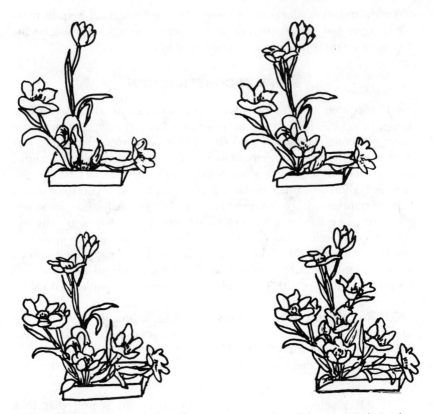

Figure 29-2. Steps in constructing a flower arrangement: One-sided, asymmetrical triangle.

4. If a focal point or center of interest is to be used, add it now or after step 5. One large flower, a dark flower, or a cluster of flowers is placed at the base of the tallest flower and in line with the rim of the container. There is just one focal point in a one-sided arrangement, while there will be two or three in an all-around arrangement, if any are used at all. Many all-around arrangements do not have a focal point.

5. Fill in the arrangement with flowers of various stem lengths for interest, with some towards the front and some towards the back for depth. Don't crowd in too many flowers. None of the flowers should extend beyond the imaginary border formed by the height and width flowers. This step may be interchanged with step 4 depending upon the habit of the designer.

6. Look it over and add or take away flowers and/or foliage. Either add another flower to complete the design or else remove one. Remember not to exceed the number needed to make a profit on the design. Snip out excess foliage or add more if needed.

7. The final step is to let it alone! Once you are finished with it, do not change it. A good designer will be satisfied with it when it is first completed—so let it alone.

There are always exceptions to the rules and steps in construction, and a low horizontal arrangement such as a centerpiece is constructed in a different manner. Place the two longest flowers to give the proper length of the arrangement. (See Figure 29-3.) These two flowers will be horizontal and resting on the rim of the container. Add two more horizontal flowers to give the width of the arrangement. Put in the vertical center flower to give the height, which usually will not exceed 12 to 15 inches for a table centerpiece. Place four slightly horizontal flowers in the four corners. Add the rest of the flowers making sure that they do not extend out beyond the lines of the framework formed by the length, width, and center flowers. The horizontal arrangement will be roughly a long, low pyramidal form. (See Figure 29-4.)

Figure 29-3. Three flowers form the length and height of a horizontal arrangement.

Figure 29-4. A completed horizontal flower arrangement frequently used for a table centerpiece.

FAULTS

There are certain faults that you should recognize and avoid to achieve a perfect design. They are the following: (1) straight line—flowers forming a straight line, (2) cross stemming—stems of flowers crossing each other above the rim of the container, (3) sandwiching—two or three flowers sandwiched, or crowded, one on top of another, (4) flower stepping—flowers arranged in equal steps along the margin of the design, (5) equal ranging—all flowers mathematically equidistant from each other, (6) parallelism—all flowers facing in exactly the same direction, (7) massing—two many flowers jammed in the container, (8) combining too many colors, (9) combining too many flower types, (10) lacking depth or third dimension, (11) hiding flowers, (12) not finishing base. The arrangement should always be finished around the base with flowers, greens, or ribbon.

These faults should all be avoided in good design.

If the principles, rules, and steps in constructing an arrangement are followed, the design should be above average in attractiveness. Experience is the best teacher in achieving the ultimate goal—a perfect composition. Each florist will develop individual methods for design, and will rely on personal experience. The better the designs are, the better the reputation of the shop.

Knowing these principles and procedures is what makes the florist a professional; prices should reflect this knowledge, just as in fees set by other professionals.

Chapter 30

LINE DESIGNS

There are essentially 13 line designs or geometric forms which flower arrangements may take. However, most of our retail floral designs fall into one of eight line designs so we will discuss these first. The vast majority of designs from a retail florist shop are in the form of some sort of triangular design. These are the most popular, pleasing, and easy to accomplish.

FLORISTS' DESIGNS

1. **Symmetrical triangle or pyramid.** This is the most popular design for vase arrangements as well as many funeral vases, papier-mâchés, and baskets. The three sides are equal, or else the two sides are equal with a different length base, and the triangle is completely filled in with flowers and greens. (See Figure 30-1.)
2. **Asymmetrical triangle.** This is an off-sided triangle in which the two sides of the center axis are entirely different. The one side is short and more vertical, while the other is longer and more horizontal. The line of the design can extend either to the right or left. It is completely filled in. (See Figure 30-2.)
3. **Right-angled triangle.** This is an asymmetrical triangle that is L-shaped. It employs a void as part of the design. It is an asymmetrical triangle not filled in. It is pleasing in design and uses fewer flowers, thus is more economical from a cost standpoint. (See Figure 30-3.)
4. **Open triangle or inverted T.** This is one of the newer forms of triangles which is an American interpretation of the Japanese Moribana. This can be either symmetrical or asymmetrical with the triangle not filled in, and the two sides

Figure 30-1. A symmetrical triangle or pyramid.

Figure 30-2. An asymmetrical triangle.

Figure 30-3. An L-shaped, or right-angled, triangle.

Figure 30-4. An open triangle.

of the triangle angled slightly toward the front rather than in a straight line as is found in the conventional triangle. It also uses less flowers and is of economic importance to the florist. (See Figure 30-4.)

5. **Horizontal.** The horizontal arrangement is typified by the regular centerpiece for the dining room table. It is symmetrical and an all-around design. It is long and low in the shape of a very low triangle or pyramid, or possibly an upside-down crescent. It can be used in a low container for a centerpiece, or designed in a wide container on a pedestal or stand. It may be either round or oval in shape. (See Figure 30-5.)

6. **Vertical.** This is a tall vertical arrangement that is quite narrow and has tall, slender lines to the design. It is very effective in a narrow wall space. If it gets too wide at the base, it will become a pyramid. (See Figure 30-6.)

7. **Hogarth.** The Hogarth or S-curve is one of the most attractive of all the types of flower arrangements. It is very popular with garden club members, but not as much with retail florists. The flowers must all be wired to get the lower part of the S, making it take longer to make this type of design. Many designers like to try it and use it when they have the time to work on it. (See Figure 30-7.)

8. **Crescent.** The crescent-shaped flower arrangement is a half-moon type of design. It is an asymmetric arrangement with one side higher than the other. It must be a wide crescent, and not a U or V shape. It is very useful for coffee table arrangements where the viewer is looking down on the arrangement. (See Figure 30-8.)

Secondary Designs *(less used by retail florists)*

1. **Round.** This is a mass type of flower arrangement in which the flowers are all put together with an outline that is a full circle. (See Figure 30-9.)

2. **Oval.** This mass type arrangement is similar to the round design except some flowers hang over the rim of the container in front to form an oval rather than a circle. (See Figure 30-10.)

3. **Spiral.** The spiral, or figure-9, arrangement is formed by parts of two crescents forming the figure-9, but with an opening in the top of the arrangement. It is hardly ever seen in flower arranging today.

Figure 30-5. A horizontal arrange-ment.

Figure 30-6. A vertical arrangement.

Figure 30-7. A Hogarth or S-curve.

Figure 30-8. A crescent arrangement.

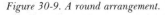

Figure 30-9. A round arrangement.

Figure 30-10. An oval arrangement.

4. **Zigzag.** The use of plain branches and twigs may lead to a zigzag pattern of design. It is an asymmetric type of arrangement and only used on certain occasions. Hawthorne branches often give this effect. Some florists use this type of design to make a gumdrop tree or life-saver tree for a child.

5. **Diagonal.** This type of design is an asymmetric form with the flowers and foliage placed in the container to form a diagonal line across the container. It usually reaches from twice the height of the container down to the table top. It is not often used because the straight line is not too pleasing to the eye. With two slight curves it becomes a Hogarth which is more pleasing. Or by bending the straight line at the rim of the container it becomes a shallow right angle, or L-shape.

These then are the 13 line designs or geometric forms from which you can choose. Two geometric forms which are displeasing to the eye and are to be avoided are the square and the rectangle. Almost all good designs come out to points rather than straight lines or sides. This is true of the eye level pattern as well as the outline of a centerpiece or horizontal arrangement. Squared sides are not pleasing.

The majority of retail florists use the triangle, vertical, and horizontal designs for most of their work.

When planning the design to be used in flower arrangements, keep in mind the various flowers which will be useful to achieve dif-

Figure 30-11. An asymmetrical triangle arrangement of snapdragons and irises in a pedestal container.

ferent forms and which are typical of the various elements of design. *Line flowers* that are useful for height and width, and give the proper line to the arrangement are gladioli, snapdragons, stock, standard chrysanthemums, and delphiniums. *Mass flowers* which are used for focal point, contrast, and interest are roses, carnations, chrysanthemums, daisies, and asters. *Form flowers* which are useful because of their unusual form or shape are orchids, calla lilies, gloriosa lilies, anthuriums, bird-of-paradise, red hot poker, poinsettias, and Easter lilies. *Filler flowers* which are useful to fill in between the other flowers in place of greens are baby's breath (gypsophila), feverfew, statice, sweet peas, small pompon chrysanthemums, and cornflowers. These are just a few of the many flowers available in each group.

Anyone can learn to arrange flowers in a container. To be a successful florist, however, you must be the one who makes more eye appealing artistic designs so that people will come to your shop because of superior designs rather than going to some other shop. This helps to build your reputation and helps to get more customers into your shop. It ties in very closely with the successful management of a retail florist shop along with pleasant, courteous service. When you develop this ability you are giving something extra, and you can charge accordingly for this professional service. Originality is the key word.

Chapter 31

HOME DECORATIONS AND
TABLE ARRANGEMENTS

HOME DECORATIONS

Flowers for home decorations are becoming more and more popular all of the time, but florists have only started to develop this market. As mentioned in a previous chapter, people will buy more flowers for the home more often, if the flowers are readily available at the right price. This is the type of business which you should be cultivating: not only the cash-and-carry for the home, but also your designs for decorating the home for special occasions.

Advertise and promote flowers for home decorations, particularly for parties, dinner guests, and special occasions. Follow this with good salesmanship when the customer comes into the shop. Find out what the occasion is, where the flowers are to be used, the color scheme of the home, and the décor for the party, then make suggestions for really beautifying the home with flowers. It is essential for you to obtain as much information as you can concerning the decorations for the home. The possibilities are unlimited as far as you, the florist, is concerned. The main limiting factor may be the amount of money the customer wishes to spend. A good florist, however, should know how to do a good job with the funds available, or else how to persuade the customer to spend more so that it will be a good decorating job—one which will please the customer and guests.

Uses in the Home

There are many places where flowers can be used in the home; it is up to you to suggest these to the customer. Most people are aware of the beauty of flowers in a centerpiece on the table, but

Figure 31-1. A symmetrical buffet table arrangement plus two candle accessories which tie in with the candle in the painting.

don't realize that flowers can be used elsewhere to brighten the home. The following are some of the places where flowers and plants can be used effectively in the home:

- A dining room table centerpiece is the most common place for flowers in the home.
- The buffet table can be used for special occasions. The

placement of the table will determine the type of arrangement to be used.

~§ The coffee or cocktail table is an excellent place for a flower arrangement in the living room.

~§ End tables can be used for matching arrangements.

~§ The luncheon table is a good place for using just a few flowers. (These table-type arrangements will be discussed in detail later in this chapter.)

~§ The television set can be used for a small arrangement of flowers, which may not last too long due to the heat given off from the set. You might suggest a permanent arrangement for this spot to be replaced by fresh flowers on special occasions. Be careful of water on the T.V.

~§ The hallway is a good place for flowers to greet people as they enter the home. They can be placed on a table or stand if available, or even on the floor. This is an excellent place for a large foliage plant, the size to be determined by the space available.

~§ People often place flowers on the mantel over the fireplace, or on the hearth. Several suggestions are in order for the hearth, such as an arrangement of large flowers like gladioli, a vase of greens such as laurel, rhododendron, or pine, a flowering pot plant, or an attractive foliage plant such as a philodendron, ficus, or schefflera.

~§ The bathroom is another place where a small flower arrangement can be used to brighten the room, both for the family and for friends.

~§ A small fresh flower arrangement in the bedroom is an added touch for overnight guests which tells them that the host and hostess are glad to have them in their home.

~§ A landing on the stairway is a good place for a foliage plant.

~§ Flowers or a plant can also be used to brighten a dark corner of the living room. You can make many suggestions for flowers and plants in the home if you are aggressive and make extra sales if you are a good salesperson.

Find out from the customer just where the flowers are going to be used and for what occasion. Flower arrangements for a party, a birthday, or an anniversary can be quite different from flowers for the everyday decoration of the home. If the customer is sending flowers to someone else, try to find out the occasion and where the flowers are most likely to be used. It is also helpful if you can find

Figure 31-2. An artistic design for the home.

out something about the color scheme and décor of the home to which the flowers are going. An arrangement with coordinating colors will enhance not only the room but also the arrangement itself.

Flowers can be sent to men and children as well as to women. Men appreciate an arrangement for the den or office if it is not dainty. Make it masculine, using strong, bright colors such as bright red gladioli, red and white carnations, or red roses in a bold design. Including some men's accessories such as a pipe, cigars, sports magazine, card, fishing equipment, or other items will add interest to the arrangement and make it more appreciated. These arrangements are also acceptable to men on Father's Day, on their birthdays, or during illnesses. Children enjoy receiving a flower arrangement if it includes some accessories that they can use while they are sick or confined to the home. Have things available to use in these arrangements such as candy, crayons, comic books, cards, games, puzzles, books, magazines, and small toys, or else be able to get them quickly and easily for the design. Use bright, bold colors for boys and pastels for the girls. The colors should tie in with the accessories. The container can even be a tiny wagon or some other item which the child can play with when the flowers are gone. An imitation flower soda is a big hit with many sick children. Teenage girls also appreciate flowers, either in an arrangement or in a corsage for the school dance. Cultivate the teenagers and college students to get them into the habit of purchasing flowers, so they will continue to do so the rest of their lives.

Home Table Arrangements

There are essentially five types of table arrangements for the home and each of them has different characteristics and must be designed differently to fit the proper table. You really need to know where the arrangement will be placed to be able to design it properly. (See Figure 31-3.) If the customer does not know where it will be placed, many florists will send out a centerpiece for most of the average home orders. There are many important points to keep in mind for various table decorations.

1. **Dining room table centerpiece.** The centerpiece should be an all-around arrangement attractive from all four sides. Usually, it is a symmetrical arrangement placed right in the middle of the table. However, in special cases it may be an asymmetrical design placed off-center on the table. It must,

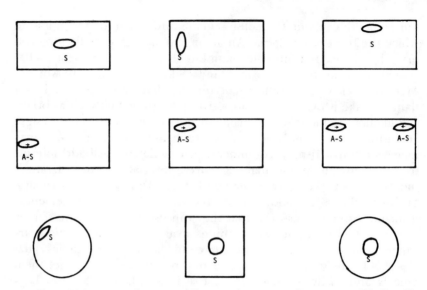

Figure 31-3. Various placements of flower arrangements on dining room and buffet tables for different occasions. (S: symmetrical; A-S: asymmetrical; → direction of the line of the design.)

in general, take the shape of the table: round for a round or square table and oblong for an oval or rectangular table. Keep the size in scale with the table. Make it low enough to see over (12 to 15 inches) or thin enough to see through, so that it does not interfere with the diners. The colors and textures must fit with the appointments of the table. (Marigolds are not used with crystal or the best china and silver.) The arrangement should not interfere with the diners while they are eating—it should not hang over the water glass or into the salad. There will probably not be a focal point, but if any is used there must be two—one for each side.

2. **Buffet table.** There are several choices for a flower arrangement for a buffet table. If the table is along the wall, the arrangement should be one-sided. It can be as large as the table, room, and price will permit and any height and width. It will be symmetrical if placed in the center of the table and asymmetrical if placed at one end. In placing the asymmetrical arrangement, be sure the line of the design flows to the center of the table, which means the high side of the asymmetrical arrangement will be the side closest to the edge of the table.

If the table is in the center of the room, the arrangement must be all-around and attractive from all sides. A symmetrical arrangement can be placed in the center of the table or at one end if turned sideways on the table. An asymmetrical arrangement is placed at one end of the table with the line of the design flowing towards the center of the table.

3. **Coffee table.** Scale is the most important point for a coffee table arrangement. The size must be in scale with the size of the table. The arrangement is usually low to fit the table and should be attractive from all angles since 90 per cent of the coffee tables in our homes today are out in the center of the room. It may be symmetrical or asymmetrical, depending upon the placement on the table, and should, in general, take the shape of the table.

4. **End tables.** Here is an excellent place for two matching arrangements if there are paired end tables. The flower arrangements should be small so they are in scale with the table and will not interfere with a lamp or other object used on the

Figure 31-4. A symmetrical arrangement for the center of a coffee table.

table. They are usually one-sided arrangements but may be all-around depending upon the setup of the furniture. They can be symmetrical and identical, or they can be asymmetrical, with one the mirror image of the other. The line of the design of both will flow towards the furniture between the two tables. If there is only one end table, the arrangement can be either symmetrical or asymmetrical to fit in with the arrangement of the furniture in the room.

5. **Luncheon table.** If the customer is having a formal luncheon or bridge luncheon, suggest some flowers. If several bridge tables will be used, provide a small arrangement for each one. It may be just one or three flowers, or a few pompons in a tiny container for each table. If it is a large formal luncheon, the arrangement will be larger and similar to a buffet table arrangement or a table centerpiece. You might also suggest a single flower for each woman to wear at the luncheon. These always look festive on the table when the guests arrive.

These are general suggestions for various table arrangements, but not the only ones. The customer may accept your suggestions, or have definite personal ideas for various table decorations. Unusual artistic designs are often used, showing real originality and the imagination of the designer. Home decorations are a good place for you to portray your designing ability.

Planters

Indoor planters are now an integral part of home decorations and should be planned and filled by the retail florist, rather than by someone less familiar with plants and their proper growing conditions. These contain mostly foliage plants although seasonal flowering pot plants can be added. Foliage plants and their uses and growth are discussed in Chapter 36.

Mantel Arrangements

Flower arrangements for the mantel can be used to decorate the home not only at Christmas, but also for any special occasion when the customer is entertaining or decorating. The arrangement can be any width or height if it fits the scale of the fireplace and the room. It is one-sided and can be symmetrical or asymmetrical, depending

upon where it is placed. In designing the arrangement, remember
that the arrangement should be held in the air to see how it looks.
Mantel arrangements are always seen either at eye-level or from
below eye-level. A flower arrangement may be beautiful when seen
from above, but lose much of its artistic design when placed up on a
mantel. If two arrangements are used on the mantel, they should be
asymmetrical mirror images of each other. You should know how to
place them properly. The high sides of the arrangements will be
towards the outer edge of the chimney with the low sides towards
the center if the focal point on the mantel is low like a clock, bowl,
figurine, or mantel scene such as is often found at Christmas. However, if the focal point is a large picture, mirror, or statue, the two
arrangements will be reversed with the low sides to the outside and
the high sides framing and pointing towards the focal point. (See
Figure 31-5.)

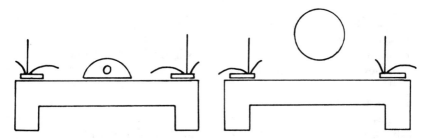

*Figure 31-5. Two different settings for mirror image flower arrangements on the mantel
based on the size and type of the center of interest.*

Banquets

Table arrangements for banquets require skill in designing because of the limited facilities usually found at clubs, halls, and
churches. You need a good deal of advance information from the
customer to do a good job. Find out the number of people attending, as well as the number and size of the tables. The arrangement of
the tables is essential, because the tables can be individual, requiring
an arrangement on each one, or they may be set up in some geomet-
ric pattern such as T, U, E, H, L, or |≡. If there is a speaker's
table, it should have the largest arrangement. The number of centerpieces is determined by the number of people, size of the tables,
and how much money is available for the job. If people are sitting on
only one side of the tables, the arrangements can be wider than

normal. Most clubs and churches use very narrow tables, with people sitting on both sides of them, which does not leave much room for the flowers. Be sure to find out the width of the tables—if the centerpieces can only be 6 inches in width, it takes a clever designer with just the right flowers to stay within bounds. If you know the number of people but not the exact length of the tables, you roughly estimate 1½ feet per person if they will be sitting close together or 2 feet per person if they are sitting more comfortably. When deciding on the number of centerpieces for the banquet, take into consideration that three smaller pieces may be better than one large one on a very long table. If there are many individual tables, and the money available will not pay for a centerpiece on each one, suggest a bud vase for each table with one flower and some greens, plus extra greens around the base of the vase.

CONTAINERS

In decorating for the home or for banquets, you may use the customer's containers or your own. Keep a supply of inexpensive containers of pottery, glass, and plastic on hand for sale or rental, whichever the case may be. Often you can rent the containers and pick them up later. Inexpensive glass or plastic containers can be figured in the price of the decorations, and then the arrangements left with the hostess. Be sure the containers do not leak. Do not use wire around papier-mâché to hold in the chicken wire—it may get wet and rust, leaving a spot on the tablecloth. If you use a pin holder in a silver bowl, be sure to use a guaranteed non-tarnishing clay to anchor the holder.

The use of a few greens around the base of the flower arrangement trailing over the edge will help to partially hide the container and give it a finished appearance. This is particularly needed for papier-mâché, plastic, and other inexpensive containers which do not add anything to the beauty of the design. A silver bowl would not require anything to hide or detract from its beauty.

SUITABLE FLOWERS AND FOLIAGE

The promotion of flowers can be further enhanced by knowing what flowers and foliages are available for sale and to be used in floral designs. (See Tables 31-1 and 31-2.) This list includes a number of garden flowers which some retailers handle. Common foliage plants available for use in the home are listed in Table 36-1.

Table 31-1. A Selected List of Various Common Flowers Useful in Floral Designs

Scientific Name (Genus)	Common Name
Achillea	yarrow
Agapanthus	agapanthus
Ageratum	ageratum
Anthurium	anthurium
Antirrhinum	snapdragon
Aquilegia	columbine
Arabis	rockcress
Arctostaphylos	manzanita (branch)
Aster	China aster
Astilbe	astilbe
Aubrieta (Bougainvillea)	bougainvilla
Bellis	English daisy
Calluna	heather
Camellia	camellia
Campanula	bellflower
Celosia	cockscomb
Centaurea	cornflower, bachelor's button
Cheiranthus	wallflower
Chrysanthemum	many types and varieties of chrysanthemums—pompons, standards, disbuds
Cleome	spiderflower
Delphinium	larkspur, delphinium
Dianthus	carnation—regular, miniature
Digitalis	foxglove
Euphorbia	poinsettia
Freesia	freesia
Gardenia	gardenia
Gladiolus	gladiolus
Gomphrena	globe amaranth
Gypsophila	baby's breath
Hedychium	ginger—red or torch
Helichrysum	strawflower
Hyacinthus	hyacinth
Iberis	candytuft
Ilex	holly
Iris	iris
Kalmia	mountain laurel
Lathrus	sweet pea
Liatris	liatris
Lilium	lily
Limonium (Armoria)	statice

(Continued)

Table 31-1 (Continued)

Scientific Name (Genus)	Common Name
Lupinus	lupine
Mathiola	stock
Matricaria	feverfew (var. of chrysanthemum)
Mimosa	mimosa
Narcissus	narcissus, daffodil
Nicotiana	nicotiana, tobacco
Orchid—many genera and species (Cattleya, Cypripedium, Dendrobium, Laelia, Odontoglossum, Oncidium)	orchid
Paeonia	peony
Papaver	poppy
Phlox	phlox
Protea	protea
Pyrethrum	painted daisy (var. of chrysanthemum)
Ranunculus	ranunculus
Rosa	rose—standard hybrid tea, miniature, multiflora
Rudbeckia	black-eyed susan
Salvia	salvia, sage
Stephanotis	stephanotis
Strelitzia	bird-of-paradise
Tagetes	marigold
Tulipa	tulip
Viola	violet
Zinnia	zinnia

Table 31-2. A Partial List of Foliages Useful in Floral Designs

Scientific Name (Genus-Species)	Common Name
Asparagus densiflorus Sprengeri	Sprenger fern
Asparagus retrofactus	ming fern
Asparagus setaceus	plumosa fern
Dryopteris erythrosora	leatherleaf (Baker) fern
Cordyline terminalis	ti leaf
Eucalyptus pulverventa	spiral eucalyptus
Pittosporum mayi	pittosporum
Podocarpus macrophyllus	podocarpus
Gaultheria shallon	salal
Kalmia latifolia	mountain laurel
Laurocerasus caroliniana	cherry laurel
Buxus sempervirens	boxwood
Thuja occidentalis	western red cedar
Vaccinium ovatum	huckleberry

Flowers for home decorations, gifts, special occasions, and banquets are the ones florists should be promoting today. It takes advertising, promotion, salesmanship, and good design to accomplish this, along with all the ideas of merchandising. This is the market that many florists are concentrating on to help combat the loss in funeral flowers taking place in our present-day society, as discussed in Chapter 20, "Please Omit."

The preceding discussion shows how important it is for you to do a real selling job. By asking a few questions, you can ascertain the type of party the hostess is going to have and then sell accordingly. The availability of rental items like candelabras, bud vases, or punch bowls can be stressed at this time and will result in extra profit. Promoting flowers for home decorations is developing into big business today.

Chapter 32

CHURCH AND HOSPITAL FLOWERS

CHURCHES

Flower arrangements for churches offer you many opportunities to publicize flowers and to improve your own reputation. There are several points that you must keep in mind when arranging flowers for churches.

- Special rules and regulations of the particular church must be followed.
- The arrangement should be large enough to be seen from the back of the church.
- It should be bold and distinct, not feathery; however, it should not be so large and outstanding that it detracts from the church service.
- It should serve to enhance the service, not dominate it.
- The flower arrangement must not impede the church service in any way.
- No part of the flower arrangement (including the greens) should stick out in front of the cross.
- The flower arrangement should be provided with a background of greens so that the flowers will show off to the best advantage. Often the natural background for the flowers in the church is not the most desirable. Yellow flowers are lost in front of the gold pipes of the organ.
- The arrangement should have a definite design to it that ties in with the décor of the church.
- When the arrangement is placed, take care to avoid spilling water, which may damage the carpet or furniture.
- Flowers should be placed so they can be seen by all, but will not obstruct the view of any of the members of the congregation.

Style of Churches

There are various architectural styles of churches in this country, and there are many which conform to no real period or style. Along the East Coast most of the church architecture has been influenced by Sir Christopher Wren, the great English builder, whose architecture is typical of the Georgian period. Farther south the churches are influenced by the Greek temple revival style. These two types of churches have much white in them with columns, pillars, paneling, and many windows. Many of these are not too large for the flower arrangements to be in graceful vases with many types of flowers which can easily be seen by the small congregation. There will be plenty of light and an absence of shadow, so the colors will show up well. In the Southwest the adobe, stone, or crude masonry churches prevail. They are neutral in color with small windows and dim interiors. Bright, strong colors in pottery containers are appropriate. Many Midwest churches follow the Gothic style of architecture from Western Europe with tall, slender windows and peaked arches topped with a high spire. The light is soft and diffused through stained glass windows which adds to the beauty of the flowers used. Strong colors are better than pastels, but blues and purples should not be used. The arrangement must be large and bold to stand out in these churches. A type of church found all over the United States is based on the old Roman Forum with an auditorium-like interior. It is almost square with the distance from the pulpit to the rear of the church, the same as from one side to the other. It is the hardest of all in which to achieve a pleasing effect with flowers, and the one most in need of it. Many churches have special stands for the flowers, while others place their flowers on the platform or altar. The placement of the flowers so as not to impede the service or obstruct the view of the people in the congregation may not always be the best from the standpoint of the design of the arrangement. Nevertheless, do your best to make the arrangement as artistic and pleasing as possible.

Containers

The containers in churches are an important part of the design and often the greatest drawback to the designer. For some reason or other, the vast majority of vases in our churches today are tall, narrow, upright containers with very little flare at the top. Often made of brass, they are very beautiful, but the most difficult of any container in which to design flowers. Some have a tall, narrow cylindrical insert only 2 or 3 inches in diameter. Many of these creations really tax the ingenuity of the designer. Often in Protestant churches they are used in pairs, and it is difficult to design two matching arrangements to be placed side by side. The style of the vase should conform to the style of architecture of the church. It should have a firm base and should be suitable in size to the size of the church. The vase should be wide-mouthed with a flaring lip. This gives the designer more chance to provide the best artistic design possible. If you use your own container, choose brass or pottery; papier-mâché is too "cheap" looking. It is hard to discuss vases of very modern design because so few churches can use them. However, vases can be contemporary in design, very attractive, and still be practical to arrange. Brass, aluminum, stainless steel, chromium, and opaque glass can all be used if they are designed with a wide or flared opening and a sturdy base. If you are in a congregation that is building a new church, it would be wise to consult with the architect and the minister to discuss the type of containers and their placement as contemplated for the new church. You will avoid headaches later on. Your experience and knowledge is of value, and will be appreciated by most architects and clergy.

Figure 32-1. A student is given pointers on her flower arrangement by Professor Pfahl while another student observes.

Designs

The design of the flower arrangement should be the one most suitable for the church. The one used more often than any other in our churches today is that of the symmetrical triangle or pyramid. Depending on the placement, an asymmetrical triangle can be used. Both of these are mass arrangements and show up well in most of our churches. In modern churches, florists should try using the open triangle, right-angled triangle, vertical, and Hogarth curve. If they are well designed, they will be appropriate and will not look out of place. It's time that retail florists put some new designs into our churches, and get away from the old type massed pyramidal arrangements every Sunday.

The colors which are suitable for the church will depend on the type of church, color of the interior, and amount of light present. If the church is painted white inside and there is plenty of light, any color will do. However, blues and purples do not show up at night, in subdued light, nor in a very large church. Blues and greens are good to use in summer, while reds, oranges, and yellows are best in the winter because of their psychological effects on people.

The final analysis of flowers used by the retail florists for churches will depend on the flowers available to the florist and the amount of money allocated for the arrangement. Many churches budget a certain amount to be spent each Sunday. Others vary this from week to week. Many times individual customers will pay for the flowers on a particular Sunday, and the florist should charge what is necessary to make the best showing to make the customer satisfied with the flowers.

Special Holidays

Florists must plan ahead to have flowers and plants available for churches for special occasions and holidays. (1) *Easter* is the holiday when Easter lilies and palms are used in most churches. These are traditional, although some churches are changing to pot plants of spring flowers like hyacinths, tulips, and narcissi. (2) *Christmas* is typified by poinsettias, cyclamen, and red and white flowers, plus Christmas greens and candles. Christmas wreaths and swags are also used in some churches, including an Advent wreath. (3) *Mother's Day* is another holiday when flowers are used in the church. Red and white, pink and white, or all white flower arrangements are appropriate. Pot plants that are acceptable would include lilies, cyclamen, azaleas, and hydrangeas. (4) *Palm Sunday* is typified by using palms and palm branches. (5) Many churches have services on *Thanksgiving*, and the flower arrangements should emphasize the bountiful harvest and horn-of-plenty. Fall-colored leaves are appropriate as are pompon chrysanthemums, sheaves of grain, seed pods, and bunches of grapes. Bittersweet is often used to add color to the arrangement.

Religious Symbolism

Flowers have come to play an important part in the religious life of America. The use of flowers in church-connected activities has long been established. Most florists have a repertoire of suitable arrangements for each of these occasions: wedding, baptism, confirmation, and funeral. The use of flowers in worship services, though perhaps equally well established, had until a few years ago no comparable collection of designs. Professor L. J. Tolle, formerly of Michigan State University, studied the liturgical days of the church calendar, and has designed a symbolically correct arrangement for every season of the Latin church year. The Christian symbolism of flowers is of two types. First, there are individual species of flowers which have become associated with Christian ideas or events such as: the rose as the symbol of messianic promise, the lily of the Resurrection, the iris of the Trinity, the almond as symbolic of a miracle, etc. Second, flowers and plant life have a general significance which is relevant to the churchly arts. St. Paul saw the seed or bulb as an allegory of the Resurrection. Christ used the lilies of the field to teach His Disciples to trust in God. There are many other examples. Mr. Tolle has designed 17 arrangements for the following church calendar: Advent, Christmas, Epiphany, Ash Wednesday, Lent, Palm Sunday, Maundy Thursday, Good Friday, Easter, Ascension Day, Pentecost, Trinity Season, Feast of the Assumption, Reformation Day, All Saints Day, Thanksgiving, and Sabbath Day. The details are in articles written by Professor Tolle. The articles are available through the Society of American Florists, and titled as follows: "Flowers for the Sabbath," "Flowers in Presbyterian Worship," "Flowers in Catholic Worship," and "Flowers in Methodist Worship."

Sales Opportunity

Churches offer a wide opportunity for sales and service, as more and more enterprising florists are discovering. Irving Allen, former chairperson, Florists Information Committee of the Society of American Florists, points out that the uses of flowers and plants in churches are many and varied. They provide an excellent source of sales, particularly when a church contracts with a florist to handle all its floral work. Since the floral pieces are seen by the entire congregation, they are an important means through which florists can attract new customers.

An extra bonus from church work is improved relations with the clergy. The florists who are on good terms with the clergy they serve are in an excellent position to know about and head off any "in lieu of" threats.

Consider this list to see which of these services could be introduced into your local churches:

1. Altar flowers. Most churches have flowers on the altar each Sunday. Many maintain a Flower Calendar, and members sign up for a Sunday on which they furnish the memorial flowers or flowers marking an anniversary.
2. Flowers or plants for shut-ins and hospitalized people. Often the altar flowers are delivered to these people following the Sunday service. In addition, some churches order special arrangements for members who are ill.
3. Wedding flowers.
4. Funeral flowers.
5. Flowers for bereaved members and their families are often included in the church budget. Flowers are sometimes wired to parents of deceased members.
6. Special arrangements for church holidays, such as Christmas, Lent, and Easter.
7. Boutonnieres for ushers.
8. A single flower to identify each new member on the Sunday the members join.
9. Floral arrangements for church suppers, teas, and other social events.
10. Plants and flowers are often used throughout the church building to decorate corridors, console tables, and the sanctuary foyer. Flowers and plants add warmth and a note of welcome.
11. Arrangements or corsages for new mothers.
12. A single flower on the altar to commemorate each new birth in the congregation.
13. A planter or screen of foliage in front of the choir loft.

14. A single flower presented to parents who present a child for baptism.
15. A plant or flowers may be sent to each new member. One church accompanies each order with a card saying, "Water this plant regularly and it will grow. Attend church regularly and both you and the church will grow."
16. A plant or cut flowers presented to each participant of every-member canvass.
17. Decoration of the platform is being used by more and more Christian Science churches. Planters on the platform and steps leading to it afford florists an opportunity to design and maintain the plants. This idea has been used extensively in the South and has spread to many other areas.
18. Some florists welcome new ministers to the community with plants or flowers.

The church field is tremendous for the retail florist. Educate yourself on the customs of individual denominations as well as the church calendars. Acquire several books on the subject to become more knowledgable. One florist reported in 1966 that he added four new churches in the fall, making the total 24 every Saturday. The weekly service ranged from $4 to $35. His overall church volume in 1972 was over $28,000 including holiday work.

The sales opportunities for church flowers is without limit, and is another market to be developed in the retail florist business in the face of the decreasing funeral flower business.

HOSPITAL FLOWERS

The hospital flower business is one of the mainstays of many retail flower shops. This is particularly true in the summer and fall and during the long winter months after the Christmas holidays.

Many hospitals throughout the country regard floral arrangements as a nuisance, although doctors and nurses alike realize the benefit of flowers to the morale of the patients. When the floral arrangements are huge space-consuming baskets of flowers, they are a nuisance. It is up to the retail florists to put more thought and effort into hospital flower arrangements. Sell the customer on the use of prestige flowers in an expensive arrangement in order to build up the order but hold down the size. Few hospital rooms have sufficient space for large bouquets, and even when they have, most hospitals lack the personnel to care for flowers properly. As a result, the blooms quickly droop and fade, and patients, visitors, and hospital personnel are all left with a poor impression of florists and their hospital arrangements.

To prevent hospitals from joining the ranks of those who would omit flowers altogether, it is up to the individual florist to improve the image of flowers by sending only compact, minimum-maintenance flower arrangements to the hospital. Some of this will require education of the customers. You may be acquainted with the situation in the hospitals, but it will not do much good if you do not convey this information to the customer who is ordering hospital flowers. The customer who learns the situation and the facts concerning the problems with hospital arrangements will often agree to a small, minimum-maintenance flower arrangement, dish garden, or pot plant.

You can also help the relationship with hospital personnel by observing the regulations concerning flowers. Some of these rules were given in Chapter 19. If every florist would find out these rules from the local hospitals and abide by them, it would strengthen the position of all florists.

Many florists, to take advantage of the demand for hospital arrangements, are displaying floral arrangements in the lobbies of

Figure 32-2. A well-planned workroom for making all types of designs, including the hospital arrangements shown. (Courtesy, Frederick's Flowers, Souderton, Pa.)

hospitals as second shops. If only a display box is used, the personnel from the gift shop may handle the sales.

Effects of Flowers on Oxygen Supply

A florist trade journal reported in 1965 an article about the bad effects of flowers in a hospital room. It was written by a doctor and hinted that the oxygen-consuming floral arrangements had a damaging effect on the hospital patients. Drs. Boodley and Fox at Cornell University conducted a study in a small room with 10 dozen roses and found that the roses only used up 1¼ per cent of the oxygen in the room space in one day, and the total carbon dioxide consumed was less than ½ of the oxygen consumed. This was in an airtight room, which is not typical of our hospitals. The door is opened many times during the day. Their conclusions showed that *flowers do not endanger the oxygen supply of a hospital patient.* This so-called damaging effect is only a myth.

Florist Designs

Turn over a new leaf when it comes to hospital designs. Since rooms are small and display space is limited, large flower arrangements are a nuisance, besides being in poor taste and inappropriate to the situation. Small arrangements not only fit better but are more appropriate. Florists may raise the objection that small arrangements will mean selling down their product. Certainly this is not the case. Instead of a large, spreading mixed bouquet, try using two or three cymbidiums or cypripedium orchids with a few sprays of Baker fern and a branch of manzanita in a good quality small container that the recipient can keep as a remembrance or a few choice chrysanthemums in a slender cylinder vase with a figurine to add interest, and all fastened to a piece of styrofoam.

You have unlimited possibilities to use styrofoam novelties cut out and designed to fit each patient. Children's toys, books, crayons, and many other items can be used to add interest to the arrangement. A man will appreciate an arrangement which includes some masculine object as has been mentioned previously in Chapter 31. Flower arrangements for men should give the impression of strength and masculinity through use of strong colors and sturdy accessories, which get across the message of cheer without being coy or flimsy. A dish garden or pot plant is very acceptable to most patients, and will last much longer than a flower arrangement. Some florists insert a few flowers in a plastic water tube and add it to the dish garden. Others add a few flowers to the water-holding center of a bromeliad (pitcher) plant. A few flowers in a water tube with a little ribbon can even be placed on the tray or night stand so that the patient can see the flowers more easily. These can be replenished every few days if the patient is bed-ridden for a long period of time. A pot plant should be accompanied with a care tag to tell the patient and friends how to take care of it, and when to water it. Most nurses will not have time to care for it. If the flower arrangement is in one of the foams, an "Add Water Daily" tag should be included with the arrangement.

Also, avoid sending poisonous plants like primroses or flowers with lots of pollen or a strong fragrance. Many people love hyacinths, but would find them overpowering in a hospital room. If fruit is added to the arrangement, consider the harmful effects to flowers of ethylene gas given off from ripening fruits such as apples, pears, and bananas. Carnations will close up, snapdragons will drop their florets, and roses will turn blue and lose their petals if the concentration of ethylene gas is too heavy.

The director of the hospital and the volunteer staff can be "worth their weight in gold" to you. Their help and understanding should be cultivated. At all costs you must have them on your side, so that the greatest benefit possible will be obtained for your flowers.

Always remember that you, as a florist, are not only a designer and salesperson, but also an educator. Inform your customers about the best selection of flowers and plants to send to the hospital and tell them how you can best serve them. Your customers will appreciate this consideration and return it with increased business.

Chapter 33

FUNERAL FLOWERS

The sending of flowers to funerals to express sympathy has been practiced for many decades in this country. While the use of flowers has been curtailed in some areas due to "Please Omit" (Chapter 20), it will undoubtedly continue to play a large part in the retail florist business for many years to come. It ranges from 80 per cent of the business for some florists down to 20 per cent of the business for other florists.

The handling of flowers for funerals and advising the relatives of the deceased is another opportunity to offer valuable service to the customer. You are a consultant as to what flowers are available, what types of arrangements are most appropriate, and how they should be handled.

You must be able to handle the order for flowers in a sympathetic manner. Show an interest and understanding of the situation as well as have patience with the person ordering the flowers.

FAMILY FLOWERS

When the relatives of the deceased come into the shop to discuss the family flowers for the funeral, this discussion should be in private if possible. Often a florist uses the office or consultation room for this, so the customers may sit down. You must tactfully get information on the deceased before making suggestions. The age and sex of the deceased are necessary, as well as the relationship of the survivors. Talk to the relatives and find out what they have in mind, then make suggestions of what would be most appropriate and suitable. You must know if the casket is to be open, closed, or a half-casket. If the deceased is female, the color of her dress may be important. There are several types of designs recommended for the family flowers. They may be a double spray, single spray, blanket, scarf, garland, or sheaf for the top of the casket. It may be a floral rosary in the casket lid, or a cross. It may be one large vase of flowers at one end of the casket, or a pair of vases of flowers, with one at each end of the casket. Some customers will request a floral pillow or other emblem. Sometimes a corsage is placed inside the casket on the pillow or in the hand. There are many possibilities for family flowers, often dictated by the deceased, the relatives, or the customs of the community. The flowers may be ordered by phone, and the same sympathetic understanding and patience must be practiced by the florist. If a spray is used on the casket, it should be on a rubber-footed frame to protect the casket. Nothing must be used which will mar the casket itself.

Flowers are sometimes ordered by the family through the funeral director; usually it is a specific order. This is one reason why it is advisable to work cooperatively with funeral directors so that they will not take orders for flowers which are unavailable nor take orders whose prices are too low to make a presentable showing. *The funeral director should let the family and florist decide on the flowers,* but many of them do it themselves as a part of their service. Some florists give a percentage to the funeral director for all flower orders sent them. This is unethical and a *very poor business practice*—besides being one that can be financially disastrous. Some florists give a 10 to 20 per cent discount when their own net profit for the year is only 6 per cent. It doesn't make good business sense. *Funeral directors are not florists and have no legitimate reason for taking flower orders,* or expecting a commission on them. Florists must work with funeral directors and vice versa. (See Chapter 20 on tips to florists and tips to funeral directors.)

OTHER FUNERAL ORDERS

Treat anyone coming in to order funeral flowers with the same interest and understanding as you would the relatives of the deceased. Handle the orders properly and recommend something that is appropriate. Find out the sex and age of the deceased and the relationship of the customer. The cost of funeral flowers usually comes up early in the conversation. Most florists have a minimum which is only mentioned when specifically asked for by the customers. Many retail florists will quote a range of three prices so the customer can choose without asking for something cheaper. A good salesperson, however, can upsell the order. If you know or can find out something about the customer, you can estimate what that person is in the habit of spending. Often you can get $30 instead of $20 for the order by upselling and telling the customer how much better the $30 piece will be. Don't just say it's bigger, but use descriptive adjectives to describe it. An executive from a large company who calls or comes in and is quoted $15 will be insulted and may go elsewhere. A person in this position may have $50 to $75 in mind. Ask questions and listen to the customer to determine the price to quote. If a person is representing a group of neighbors or associates who may have collected a definite amount of money, you will then be limited to that figure. If the group doesn't have a set figure, again don't quote such a low price that it will produce an arrangement that is too small to represent a group of people.

Be sure to get all of the information accurately, particularly the time and place of the funeral. This, plus the name and sex of the individual, is most important for telephone orders to a funeral in another city. Don't depend on the other member florist to know the details of the funeral unless the customer does not have the information and asks the other florist to find out. A phone call should produce the desired results.

There are also many types of designs which may be chosen for funeral flowers from friends, relatives, or associates. The majority of funeral pieces in the country today are either sprays, vases, or baskets (including papier-mâché containers). However, many funeral homes have small tables and stands so that artistic home-type vase arrangements can be used. There are many emblems and designs which are popular in certain sections of the country. These include crosses, pillows, gates ajar, broken column, broken wheel, vacant chair, harps, wreaths, and many others. Some florists haven't made one of these in a year, while others make them every week. Many areas of the country are getting away from some of the more elaborate emblems. If the deceased was a member of a club, lodge, or trade association, a floral emblem may be sent by that organization. These are still used in most sections of the country by Eastern Star, Odd Fellows Lodge, Masons, Knights of Columbus, and many others. You must keep these styrofoam frames on hand if you are in an area where they may be used. The techniques of some of these designs will be discussed in Chapter 34.

Funeral flowers should be delivered in good condition and on time. The tag must be accurately written with all of the correct information. Often the signature card is kept by the family. Many florists put a brief description of the flower arrangement on the back of the card. This is just another little service offered by the florist to enable the family to write a more personal thank-you to the sender of the flowers. It is nice to be able to mention a spray of yellow roses, a basket of white and lavender chrysanthemums, or a vase of pink carnations rather than just thanking someone for the flowers sent. The card is usually placed in an envelope or cellophane bag, and should be securely fastened to the floral piece. If there is a bow of ribbon on the arrangement, the card may be pinned or paper clipped to it. Don't use a staple as it is too hard to remove. If there is no ribbon, the florist may use a paper clip and attach it to the leaves, or use a wire, ribbon, or string to fasten it to a piece of the foliage or one of the stronger stemmed flowers. The funeral directors in your community may have established a common procedure regarding where and how to attach it. Each florist has a particular method, but the main thing is to have the card securely fastened. Either the card should be legibly written, or it may be typed—possibly in script, which is attractive, appropriate, and easy to read. There should be no mistakes on the card, and the family must be able to read the person's name easily and accurately. It is embarrassing for the family to thank the wrong person for the flowers, or to not thank anyone at all for some flowers. Usually the florist is blamed if an error occurs.

You can do a lot to curtail the growing problem of "Please Omit" and "In Lieu of Flowers" by using good judgment in your handling of funeral flower orders. More artistic designs of attractive floral pieces rather than large massed arrangements in too lavish a display will help to avert criticism of funeral flowers. Also suggest artistic arrangements of flowers to send to the home.

Be sympathetic, interested, and understanding in handling people who are ordering flowers for funerals, as well as able to make suggestions and execute designs which will be best suited and most appropriate for that particular funeral. A florist with a good imagination and originality can send out many pieces to the same funeral without having them all look the same. The customers will appreciate it, and so will the family of the deceased. All florists should do their best to make funeral designs more attractive and more appropriate, and to handle all funeral orders properly. It is not in good taste for a florist to say "thank you" for a funeral order.

 *Chapter 34*

DESIGN TECHNIQUES: CORSAGES
AND FUNERAL FLOWERS

Design techniques are primarily learned at design schools, design courses in our colleges and universities, and by experience in retail florist shops. Here are some basic ideas that will be helpful to the person interested in becoming a retail florist.

WIRING

The wires which most retail florists have on hand run from #18 (heaviest) to #32 (thinnest), in the following gauges: 18, 19, 20, 21, 22, 23, 24, 26, 28, 30, and 32. The length which most florists use is 18 inches, although some florists prefer wire cut in 12-inch lengths for certain design work. Wire also comes in spools for use in making wreaths and sprays. The wire is used to strengthen the stems of many flowers so they will not bend or break and will help to hold the flower head in the proper position. In corsages, wire replaces the natural stem. Every flower and most foliage in a wedding bouquet is wired. Wires are used on most flowers in funeral work to give added support to the stem. Wires are used on flowers in vase arrangements for the home only when it is absolutely necessary. Wires are unsightly and considered objectionable in the home. Sometimes the flower has a very weak stem and requires a wire for support if it is to be used in a vase arrangement. By using good quality flowers you can keep the usage of wire to a minimum. The wires used in funeral vases, baskets, sprays, and wreaths are used at the discretion of the designer to make sure the pieces arrive at the funeral in the best possible shape and design. Some florists wire all flowers in funeral work to give the best protection. Other florists wire very little. It is mainly a question of habit. Most florists wire the flower stems which

need additional strength to arrange satisfactorily or to keep breakage to a minimum during delivery.

There are many ways to wire flowers, depending on the flower
type and the use of the flower. A rose is wired one way for a corsage
and a different way for a funeral spray or in a vase arrangement.
Various methods are shown in Figures 34-1, 34-2, 34-3, 34-4, and
34-5. The piercing method is used on roses and carnations for corsages, wedding bouquets, and funeral sprays. The clutchwire
method is used on individual gladioli florets and funnel-shaped
flowers for corsages and wedding bouquets. The hookwire is used
on any daisy-, aster-, or pompon-type flowers for corsages, wedding
bouquets, funeral work, or vase arrangements. The flower heads are
removed for corsages and wedding bouquets, but the stems are left
on for other designs with the wire twisted around the stem to give it
needed support. The hairpin method is used on lilies, daylilies,
funnel-shaped flowers, or any daisy-type flowers for any of the designs. The straight wire is used when the stem remains attached to
the flower for funeral work and for vase arrangements. This is used
on roses, carnations, chrysanthemums, daffodils, irises, gladioli, and
many other flowers. Spike flowers are usually wired with the hook-
straight wire, with a small hook either pushed into the stem or
twisted around the lowest floret of snapdragons and stock. Some

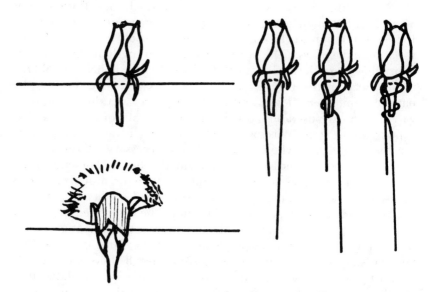

Figure 34-1. Piercing method for wiring flowers such as roses and carnations.

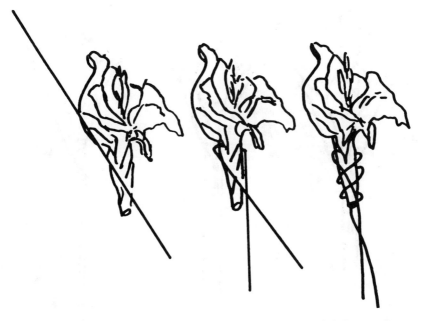

Figure 34-2. The clutchwire method for wiring flowers such as gladioli florets or for putting an extra wire on a flower.

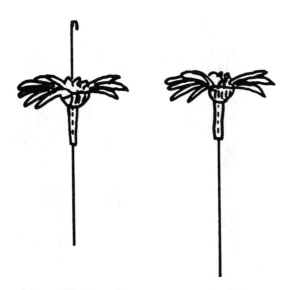

Figure 34-3. The hookwire method for wiring any daisy-type flowers.

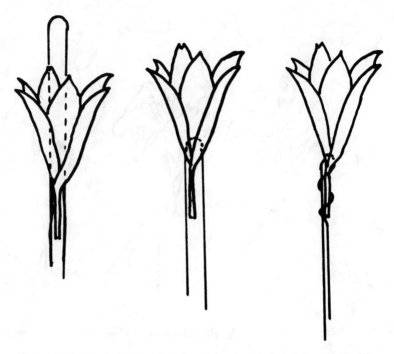

Figure 34-4. The hairpin method for wiring funnel-shaped flowers like lilies and stephanotis.

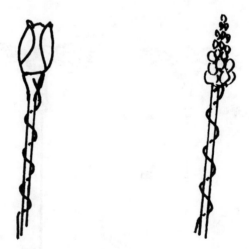

Figure 34-5. The straight wire method for wiring flowers like roses and snapdragons which still have their stems attached to the flower.

flower stems are hollow inside so the wire can be pushed up inside, giving good support, although invisible. Unfortunately, this method can only be used on relatively few flowers such as calla lilies, daffodils, thick-stemmed snapdragons, majestic daisies, short pompons, and several others. The size or number of wire used for flowers cannot be given here because it depends on the use of the flower, size of the flower, size of the stem, and thickness of the stem. It must be learned by feel and experience. Some flowers like lilies-of-the-valley, pansies, stock florets, and hyacinths are quite difficult to wire. Patience and practice are necessary to learn how to wire these.

RIBBON

Ribbon comes in different colors, styles, materials, and widths. Most of the corsage ribbon is narrow and comes in sizes 2, 3, 5, and 9. Funeral and Christmas ribbon comes mainly in two standard widths: #40 (approximately 2¾ inches wide) and #120 (approximately 4½ inches wide). There are other sizes, but these are the ones commonly used by florists today. There are several ways to tie a bow of ribbon. The method which is shown in the following sketches can be used on corsages, wedding bouquets, funeral sprays, funeral wreaths, Christmas wreaths, and Christmas door swags. With a little practice, it is very easy to learn to make an attractive bow. The size of the bow will depend on the amount of ribbon used. One and one-half yards of material will make an average-size bow. The procedure for tying a bow is as follows:

1. Hang the ribbon over your left thumb with the long side in front, and about 2 inches behind the thumb as shown in Figure 34-6.
2. With your right hand take the long side of the ribbon and loop it under and around the left thumb squeezing the ribbon between the left thumb and forefinger as in Figure 34-7. When using satin ribbon, it is necessary to fold the ribbon over each time you pass the ribbon under your thumb, to keep the satiny side out. Otherwise, all loops on one side of the bow would be shiny and all loops on the other side dull.
3. Grasp the ribbon with the right hand about 3 inches from the crushed part and make a loop in the air, bringing the ribbon to the spot between the left thumb and forefinger, and crushing it between the two as in Figure 34-8. The ribbon must always be looped under so that the ribbon will fit between the

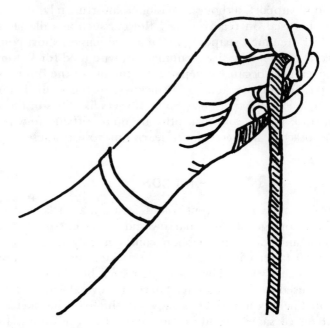

Figure 34-6. The first step in tying a bow of ribbon.

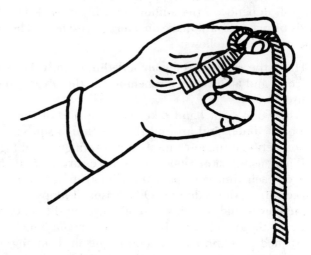

Figure 34-7. The second step in tying a bow of ribbon.

Figure 34-8. Forming the first loop in the bow.

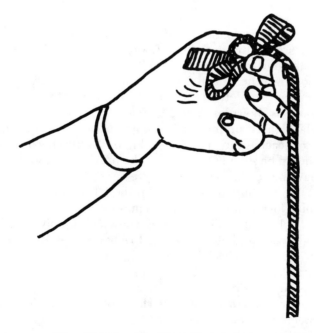

Figure 34-9. Forming additional loops in the bow.

Figure 34-10. A completed bow of ribbon.

left thumb and forefinger. Never leave the ribbon flat, but
squeeze it after each loop. Looping over instead of under will
make bow tying more difficult.

4. Go down the ribbon 3 inches and loop it under, squeezing it
   between the left thumb and forefinger. Thus, the first two
   loops as shown in Figure 34-9 are formed.

5. Make three or four more loops in each direction until the
   bow reaches the proper size (Figure 34-10). Each set of loops
   should be slightly larger than the previous set, so the bow will
   have more character to it.

6. While holding all the loops in the left hand, take a piece of
   thin florists' wire, chenille stem, piece of Curly-Q, or a piece
   of ribbon and insert it over your left thumb. Pull it down
   tightly around all the crushed ribbon pieces and twist firmly
   in the rear. This will hold it tightly together, and it can be
   attached to the floral design piece.

7. Fasten the ribbon bow securely right up under the bottom
   flower in a corsage and as close to it as possible—a gap between flowers and ribbon is poor design. The excess wire
   that remains after securing it to the corsage or funeral piece

is either cut off or else pushed into the flower stems so that no one will run the wires into his/her fingers.

WRAPPING WIRE STEMS

As the artificial wire stems on flowers for corsages and wedding bouquets are not attractive, they must be covered, generally with floratape or parafilm. These come in many different colors, but most florists use green, white, orchid, and brown. White flowers should have their stems wrapped with white material, while the orchid is used on regular cattleya orchids and the brown on cymbidium orchids. Green is used for most other stems and in larger amounts by the florist than any other color. Both tapes come in rolls of ½ inch and 1-inch widths. The method of wrapping the tape is to place the material behind the stem as close to the flower head as possible. The flower is held in the left hand and the tape in the right. As the left hand slowly turns the flower, the right hand guides the tape around the wire and stretches it tight. In a few seconds the wire stem is as attractive as the natural one.

CORSAGES

In making corsages, remove the flower heads from their stems and attach an artificial wire stem, as discussed previously under "Wiring." Flowers with artificial stems are wired for several reasons: to reduce bulk by removing the natural stem, to reduce the weight of the corsage, for ease in making the flowers face the right way, and to keep them in place even if they start to wilt a little.

The flowers should be properly hardened before being used in corsages. After this, most of the stem is removed from the flower, leaving about a quarter of an inch of stem. The number of wire to use will depend on the size and weight of the flower head. Usually the florist uses #20 or 22 on roses because the head is heavy. The method of wiring will depend on the type of flower in the corsage, as shown in the previous sketches. The piercing method is usually used on roses and carnations; the clutchwire on gladioli florets; the hairpin on stephanotis, individual hyacinth florets, and daylilies; and the hookwire method on daisy-type flowers. The main factor is to provide a good artificial stem without adding weight.

The wire is next wrapped with floratape or parafilm of the appropriate color.

Find out from the customer just where the flowers are to be

Figure 34-11. A corsage of two cymbidium orchids.

worn, and the color of the dress, if possible. Each of the four places where corsages are usually worn requires a special type. A shoulder corsage is normally triangular or shield-shaped with the ribbon at the bottom, as in Figure 34-11. Sometimes a double corsage is made for the shoulder with the ribbon approximately in the center of the corsage. The waist and wrist corsages are double corsages made by constructing two small triangular corsages and tying them together with the bow of ribbon in the center. A wrist corsage is fastened to a frame (several are on the market) that will easily fit onto the wrist. A hair corsage is made without the use of greens or a ribbon and may be made in one of several shapes. In any corsage the buds and small flowers are used at the top or outer edges with the larger, open flowers at the base, just as in vase arrangements.

Construct the corsage by putting the buds, flowers, foliage, and bow of ribbon together in a pleasing design. Start with a leaf and bud at the tip, followed by two small flowers as shown in Figure 34-12. Add foliage at each step in the construction, not at the last. Tie the first three flowers together firmly by using corsage thread, wire, chenille stem, or Curly-Q, or by twisting one of the wire stems around the others—any method is satisfactory. Turn the flowers to the front or to the side to fit into the design. Add foliage and one flower at a time, making sure to tie or wire them firmly to the others.

Figure 34-12. The first three flowers put together one at a time in a corsage.

Figure 34-13. A shoulder corsage complete with ribbon.

Figure 34-14. A rose corsage with Baker fern backing.

Cut off all long stems and add a bow of ribbon at the base. The completed shoulder corsage should resemble that shown in Figure 34-13. Always tell customers to wear the corsage with the flowers upright—the way they grow in nature.

Florists use either fresh foliage or artificial leaves in corsages. Rose foliage should not be used as it will not hold up. Many florists use Baker fern, asparagus plumosus (called grass), evergreen foliage, huckleberry, magnolia, laural, or salal. (See Figure 34-14.) Greens belonging to the flower such as gladiolus, iris, camellia or gardenia, or fancy foliage like croton, may be used.

FUNERAL FLOWERS

Mossing

Mossing is a procedure considered old-fashioned by some florists, but still used by many others in certain areas of the country. The material used is sphagnum moss, which has been well soaked overnight in plenty of water. Moss is used in wreath frames, emblem frames, and sometimes as a base for funeral sprays. The frame is lined with foil to hold in the moss and improve its appearance. The moss is squeezed so that all excess water is removed from it. Then it is packed tightly into the frame and tied with spool wire or wreath thread. It is then ready for the insertion of flowers, which may be wired with a short heavy wire to hold into the moss or attached to a metal pick with a Pix machine and then stuck in the moss. The moss helps to make the flowers last longer. Some florists are using one of the various foam materials or strips of styrofoam in place of the moss. It depends on the preferences of the florist and the customs of the locality.

Figure 34-15. A styrofoam bar for making a funeral spray.

Sprays

There are many ways to make funeral sprays. Some are tied loosely, while others are inserted into a foundation base. The primary foundations on the market that can be used are Oasis, Jiffy,

Figure 34-16. A background of salal foliage inserted into a styrofoam bar.

Figure 34-17. The first three flowers are placed to outline the triangular design of the funeral spray.

Quickee, Sno-Pak, Aquatainer, styrofoam, moss and Wet-a-pack. (See Chapter 24.) The flowers are wired in different lengths and inserted into the base to form the desired shape of the spray. Foliage is used as background, edging, and filler for the sprays. Sprays are usually triangular, oval, round, or crescent in shape. They must be made so that they can be easily hung on an easel. If styrofoam is used as a base, the flowers are wired and then inserted into a water pick before being inserted into the styrofoam. This is not necessary with the other foundation materials, all of which retain moisture in the media. There are many different sizes of styrofoam spray bars

Figure 34-18. Funeral spray is filled with flowers and greens.

Figure 34-19. Small flowers (pompons) used as a filler to give a full effect to the spray.

for the base of various sized sprays. Each retail florist has a preference in methods of making sprays and wreaths. There are several good books of funeral designs on the market.

The steps in making a funeral spray on a styrofoam spray bar are shown in Figures 34-15 through 34-20.

Figure 34-20. A completed funeral spray with bow of ribbon.

Figure 34-21. Papier-mâché container with chicken wire.

Containers and Baskets

Many materials are used as fillers in containers to make the flowers stay in place. Some florists use greens such as cedar or hemlock, chicken wire, shredded styrofoam, vermiculite, or one of the foam materials. Other florists use a combination of two or more. If you are using a basket, you may wire the first (tallest) flower to the handle and may do the same with several others to keep them in place during delivery and handling. Bows of ribbon are often used in baskets—on the handle, down front, or attached to a bamboo stake in the middle of the arrangement. Although many florists don't use any bow of ribbon at all, or just one, some will use two small ones and fasten them together with a piece of ribbon. Often this adds color and interest to the arrangement. A bow will also fill in a hole, and may be cheaper than adding two more flowers. Steps in making an arrangement in a papier-mâché container are shown in Figures 34-21 through 34-26.

Figure 34-22. Salal as a background for a funeral arrangement.

Figure 34-23. First three flowers form the triangular design for this funeral container.

Figure 34-24. More flowers added to the arrangement.

Figure 34-25. Pompons added as a filler flower to the funeral arrangement.

Figure 34-26. A funeral arrangement complete with a bow of ribbon for a focal point.

Foams

The use of the various water-holding foam materials has been a boon to the retail florist. They make designing much easier and more varied. They have many uses, and the details of their uses and directions for handling are discussed in Chapter 24.

There are many more design techniques employed by various retail florists than can be discussed here. The best ways to learn are by attending a design school or college, by observing other florists and designers at work, and by getting plenty of practice.

There are several excellent retail floral design books on the market today to fire your imagination.

Keep in mind that "time is money" and in any design or arrangement that takes time, you must charge the customer for it.

Chapter 35

WEDDINGS: DESIGNS, SERVICE, AND BACKGROUNDS

"Open marriage, trial marriage, swinging marriage . . . the fads come and go. A few linger on. But there is growing evidence that traditional marriage (with some changes) is very much alive and well," states Joan Barthel in an article on marriages in the *Ladies' Home Journal.* According to Herb Mitchell, "Today once again young people are placing great value on the traditional wedding ceremony." Everywhere you look, old-fashioned marriage is back in style. And that's good news for the flower industry. Weddings represent anywhere from 5 to 30 per cent of a florist's business.

The tradition of the June wedding is declining in popularity. The National Office of Vital Statistics reveals that only 12.5 per cent of marriages take place in June. August accounts for 10.9 per cent, September for 9.4 per cent, December for 9.1 per cent, and July for 9.0 per cent. January has the lowest figure—only 5.8 per cent.

Weddings are a time for flowers, and a good part of the total business of many retail florists. The attitude of florists on weddings varies all over the country. Many florists handle hundreds of weddings in a year, while others only have one or two or none at all. Some florists say they don't want weddings and can't make any money from them, while others really cultivate the wedding business, like Frances Jones Poetker who has handled over 12,500 weddings. Weddings can run from $10 to $10,000. Wedding bouquets usually cost from $15 up. Selling wedding flowers can often be a tedious and frustrating task, but also a very rewarding one.

Florists in general have the job of introducing the soon-to-be-married customer to the beauties of a wedding that is properly planned with flowers, while you have the task of selling the potential customer on your particular shop. The extent to which you wish to compete for your share of this profitable business is your own choice. Florists throughout the country agree that courtesy and confidence are main factors in wedding work. Another big factor in wedding business is your shop's reputation. Florists who are really trying for this market will set up special wedding window displays in the spring of the year, and use direct mail advertising to bring this business into their shop. Many florists provide the flowers for fashion shows or bridal shows put on in department stores. A tie-in with a wedding fashion show is invaluable from the advertising standpoint of an individual florist.

Today's bride seems to prefer the natural look in her wedding flowers, with lots of color. Many are using permanent bouquets, particularly silk flowers, which give the bridal party a memento of the occasion. The great majority, however, still prefer fresh flowers. A trend is also toward more simple church decorations and more lavish flowers and decorations for the reception.

CONSULTATION AREA

When a prospective bride comes into the florist shop to discuss her flowers, you should have a special place for the discussion. Many florists have a separate bridal consultation corner, while others use the office. A separate room is not necessary, but some special spot should be used, even in a small shop. A bridal consultation corner should do two things: make the bride comfortable and give her a sense of privacy. Some retail florists simply stand behind the counter and describe the wedding flowers. This is a poor way to conduct wedding business. The minimum requirements for comfort are two chairs (with a third available nearby, to be pulled up when the bride's mother sits in on the consultation), plus a desk or table on which to spread pictures, fabric samples, writing materials, order blanks, and a book of wedding pictures. Some florists have a small projector or viewer set up so the bride can see colored slides of bouquets designed by their shop.

A sense of privacy is important during the bridal consultation. It makes the bride feel that she has your undivided attention, and that she is free to discuss costs without being overheard by others. She feels you are really interested in her and her wedding.

Even in a tiny shop, the illusion of privacy can be given by the use of a temporary screen or some tall foliage plants that help to screen off one corner of the shop. Larger shops may have a special consultation room containing a sofa, coffee table, chairs, and lamps

Figure 35-1. Wedding consultation room with fabric on the walls. (Courtesy, Frederick's Flowers, Souderton, Pa.)

to provide the greatest comfort possible. Some florists who service large expensive weddings may need room to show the water color paintings that are made to show the bride exactly how the wedding and decorations will look. It all depends on the space available in the shop, the number, and the size of weddings anticipated.

A good consultation corner is worth the effort it takes to achieve. Many florists have found that their average wedding order increased by several dollars after they provided a place where the florist and the bride could confer in privacy and comfort.

COSTS

A problem which often confronts a florist is that of a mother and daughter who come into the shop and the mother says, "My daughter is getting married next month, and I would like some flowers for her—something very nice and very pretty, but I don't want it to cost too much." Both the florist and the customer will have prices and costs in mind, but it is a fatal mistake to get caught in the problem of price discussion without adequate information.

Figure 35-2. A bridal bouquet of roses, tiger lilies, and variegated ivy. (Courtesy, Alexander's Flowers, Cleveland, Ohio.)

Figure 35-3. A bridal bouquet of carnations, baby's breath (Bristol Fairy), and Baker fern. (Courtesy, Alexander's Flowers, Cleveland, Ohio.)

The florist should assume the lead by asking questions such as: Where will the ceremony be held? What time of day is it to take place? How many bridesmaids and ushers are in the party? Is it to be formal or informal? What is the name and address of the groom? It is advantageous to get this information in writing. This gives the florist some idea of the size and cost of the wedding itself. Certainly $50 for the flowers will not suffice for a church wedding with a reception afterwards which in itself may run into thousands of dollars. The flowers must be appropriate and adequate for what the customer has in mind.

Some florists express the opinion that the flowers used in a wedding must carry at least a 5 to 1 or 7 to 1 markup in order to compensate them for the time involved. "It is impossible to say that this markup is correct for every shop," says Herb Mitchell. He believes you should make it your business to know exactly what it costs to do a wedding. Find out how much time is spent by each employee involved, and the cost of the materials. From these costs you should be able to determine the margin of profit you will make. Time is the most expensive item in the retail flower shop and must be considered—not only the time to make the bouquets, but also consultation time, time to set up the decorations, and time to take them down and return the props and materials to the shop. Many florists, unfortunately, forget to figure in time to remove the decorations after the wedding is over. You cannot afford to give away your time.

Be sure to price the wedding for profit. Alan Preuss, a florist in Wauwatosa, Wisconsin, uses a formula to estimate the correct price for bouquets. He has worked out a chart showing the exact retail price required to make a profit for each flower used. Representative 1970 prices were: roses, $1.00 each; carnations, $1.00 each; pompons, $0.50 each; stephanotis, $0.50 to $0.75 each; etc. These prices hold true except for the major holidays. Another florist in Tampa, Florida, J. W. Wilson, uses as his formula the basic retail price times 20 per cent for design materials, times 20 per cent of that figure for labor.

TYPES OF SERVICE

Many florists are offering successfully two types of bridal services. There are some brides who are interested in the absolute minimum flower requirements and want no service whatsoever. There are many weddings in this category. It is important to realize this, for you might price yourself out of the market if you think that every bride is interested in your complete service.

Florists who offer complete bridal service often class their services as *package service* and *custom service*. Flower shops that successfully and profitably promote a complete wedding service handle the smallest as well as the largest weddings, and have their services well defined. The package service is the least expensive and usually only two or three styles of bouquets are offered with definite prices suggested. Simple bouquets are planned and sold. The bride pays for the wedding before the ceremony and the flowers are delivered to the church without service.

Most florists require a down payment from the bride's family at the time the wedding is booked. The remainder will be paid before the wedding ceremony in the case of a package deal or to a stranger; the family will be billed later if they are one of the florist's regular good customers.

The custom wedding service permits the florist to become an important part of the wedding. Some florists will arrange everything, including invitations, complete reception including the catering of food and drink, and all details of the wedding. There are many weddings that offer the florist the opportunity to sell this complete service. This will be determined at the first interview. There are two definite opinions about selling this service. Some florists feel that the markup they use for wedding flowers should be great enough to offset all the costs and labor involved in completely servicing any wedding. Other florists feel that they should itemize the service and the extra labor items. Either method is satisfactory, as long as you make sure you are getting a profit for each operation.

If you are servicing the complete wedding, provide the aisle cloth and see that it is placed at the correct time. If the bride wishes to prevent guests leaving the church before the wedding party has left, provide the ushers with the bolts of ribbon or cording to be strung across the backs of the pews. See that the groom has his boutonniere, and that the attendants are carrying their bouquets properly. Often the florist will supervise the wedding party and start each one properly down the aisle.

BRIDAL CONSULTATION

One of the most important areas in developing wedding business is conducting the wedding consultation. This is when the bride

Figure 35-4. A bridal bouquet of gardenias, lilies-of-the-valley, stephanotis, and Sprengeri. (Courtesy, Yorktowne Studio, Inc.)

Figure 35-5. A bridal bouquet of gardenias, stephanotis, and ivy.

will make her decision concerning the type and amount of wedding flowers she will use, and whether or not you will get the business. It is preferable to handle the wedding interview on an appointment basis. This conveys the impression that weddings are important.

Because the average bride and her family are none too familiar with the responsibilities for a wedding, you, as a bridal consultant, should be prepared to answer their questions. It helps to know the full list of their responsibilities in connection with the wedding, including opinions about the bride's gown and trousseau, wedding announcements and invitations, music for the wedding and the reception, flowers for the wedding and reception, bouquets and gifts for the bridal attendants, reception expenses, wedding cake, wedding photographs, and transportation. In other words, you should be a professional authority on weddings.

Frequently, the customers (brides or mothers) will have preconceived ideas which are not practical. Deal with them tactfully and firmly—do not leave a customer with the impression that you will try to get certain flowers when you know it is impossible at that season of the year. Or, if a customer just wants a background of greens, it is up to the florist to point out the beauty of the pageant, and that the decorations should be a complete design as well as serving as an appropriate background for the wedding party. Flowers should enhance the appearance of the bride. Colors of bridal flowers, gowns, and decoration must all blend together in perfect harmony. There is no one best design for a bouquet, but loose, round bouquets and cascades are particularly popular now. Also, the carrying of one rose with greens is gaining in popularity. Here are some mini-ideas for today's weddings: (1) Bouquets with a light, feathery look have a greater appeal than structured formal designs; (2) Bridal gowns with a touch of color are becoming more popular. The creative florist will know how to pick out the pastel pink or blue in such a gown and tastefully incorporate it into a beautiful bouquet; (3) When spraying candles in a wedding arrangement, use a floral tint rather than darker tones; (4) If the tulle tufts ordered from the wholesaler do not match the bridal gowns, spray white ones to match; (5) Check with the bride on Monday or Tuesday of the week of the wedding. It really pays off.

"PLUS" SERVICE

A retail florist who wants wedding business must be able to give "plus" service. Be aware that foresight, careful planning, patience, tact, and sound business practices are required to enhance your reputation in this field and realize a respectable profit for your efforts. The following steps are used by Frances Jones Poetker in her shop, which has serviced over 12,500 weddings:

1. During the first appointment with the bride, adopt a reporter's tactics and get answers to the ancient questions: who, what, when, where, why, and how, as they apply to the decorations. Determine whether the bride and her mother like things to be frilly or tailored, exotic or traditional, stark or sentimental. Ask where the gowns are being bought, what refreshments will be served, how many guests will be invited, and other questions. Costs should not be discussed at the first meeting but get some idea of what the family is planning to spend.

2. The second step is often overlooked by the florist. He should check the credit rating of the customer.

3. Next discuss costs and availability of anticipated merchandise requirements with the wholesaler.

4. If the size of the job warrants it, look at models of dresses chosen. Go and see the church, club, or home, particularly if unknown, before committing yourself to the specific price and ideas.

5. Send the customer a detailed estimate with a breakdown of costs involved. Indicate how much is allowed for each item. Each item includes a price range of about 30 per cent from maximum and minimum figures. Always include an "if available" clause in the estimate. Be as specific as possible about flowers and colors. *Be sure to include a price for your own time.*

6. Schedule a second appointment to get a firm commitment.

7. When all arrangements have been concluded with the mother, try to leave open the bride's bouquet to be decided upon by her alone, or by the bride and bridegroom.

8. Talk to the bridegroom's mother concerning her corsage.

9. Several days before the wedding, check all details with the bride and her mother.

10. Have a final consultation with a representative of the church, club, or hotel to see that no other activity is scheduled just preceding or immediately following the wedding. This could present a problem in setting up and removing the decorations.

11. The precise place and time of delivery of bouquets, corsages, boutonnieres, headbands, etc., must be ascertained.

12. The decorating crew is briefed on any expected trouble or problems, and given a diagram for decorations, and an exact schedule for each activity. You need experienced help to set up and take down the wedding decorations quickly. Just before the wedding, check to be sure the place is clean. Lastly, be certain the candles are straight.

Figure 35-6. Attendants' bouquets including arm bouquet and flower girl basket. (Courtesy, Alexander's Flowers, Cleveland, Ohio.)

No smudges or finger marks must be on the candles.
These things are vital to future relationships with everyone
concerned.

The preceding steps are an excellent guide if you wish to specialize in custom service of your customers.

RELIGIOUS ASPECTS

It is important to know the customs of the various religions and
also the specific rules and regulations of the churches or synagogues.
Many priests, ministers, and rabbis have definite regulations as to
the placement of flowers and decorations in their places of worship.
If you are wise, you will consult these individuals prior to weddings.
The following suggestions are given as general guidelines, but keep
in mind that individual churches will have more specific regulations:

1. It is not considered good taste to plan a large wedding during Lent or Holy Week in Protestant churches.
2. Some ministers prefer that weddings not be held on Sundays.
3. The use of altar flowers and other decorations is customary
   in Protestant churches.
4. The Episcopal wedding ceremony is taken from the Church
   of England ceremony and often has a nuptial mass for the
   bride and groom immediately following the wedding ceremony.
5. The use of flowers on the altar and as decorations is customary in the Roman Catholic Church. In cases of a mixed marriage, the couple will sometimes stand outside the altar rail,
   which may affect the floral decorations. Each diocese has its
   own wedding regulations.
6. Jewish tradition undoubtedly calls for a more extensive use
   of flowers than any other religious faith. The wedding ceremony is considered the most important point in a person's
   life and is extremely sacred as a family occasion. The ceremony is different because of the requirements of the canopy,
   or chuppah. The two prime musts for the Jewish wedding
   are the canopy and the table or stand that holds the goblet of
   sacramental wine. In present times the canopy is stationary
   and stretches approximately 7 feet by 7 feet. It can be made
   of silk, satin, plastic, greens, or canvas. The supporting posts
   can be of wood, wrought iron, steel, aluminum, plastic, or
   styrofoam. Often the canopy and the background trellis of

greens must be supplied and designed by the florist. Normally the canopy is decorated with flowers and garlands, which are more popularly used because of their clear and ethereal lines. It is impossible to describe all the ways to decorate the canopy. Other decorations are necessary depending upon where the wedding is to be held.

EXTRA FLOWERS FOR EXTRA SALES

Basic Items

The flowers normally used include the bride's bouquet, attendants' bouquets, corsages, boutonnieres, and floral decorations in the church plus reception decorations. Often bouquets from the church are moved to the reception. There is no limit to the places where flowers can be used. Palms, ferns, cibotiums, and foliage plants can create a background. Ribbon bows are often placed on the ends of the pews, and candles in candelabras are used in most weddings. Include in your planning such rental items as the aisle runner, candelabra, candles, standards, and baskets.

Extra Items

Besides these most basic flowers for the wedding, suggest the following extras to the bride:

1. Flowers surrounding the cake and perhaps a few for the top of the cake.
2. A ribbon bow with a few stems of lilies-of-the-valley or other tiny flowers tied to the handle of the serving knife.
3. Aisle or pew decorations.
4. An arrangement atop the piano or in some other strategic place.
5. Flowers for the table at the wedding rehearsal dinner.
6. Flowers for the table for the bridal party at the wedding reception.
7. Corsages for the grandmothers.
8. Corsages for those who gave special assistance during the reception.
9. The going-away corsage for the bride, which the groom may forget.

Many florists have found the rental of other items like the cake knife, tea service, and punch bowl and cups to be very popular.

Figure 35-7. Wedding cake decorated with flowers. (Courtesy, Yorktowne Studio, Inc.)

WHO PAYS?

The costs of the wedding flowers and decorations are borne by the bride's parents and the bridegroom according to custom. Traditionally, the bride's parents will pay for all the bouquets of the bridesmaids, matron of honor, and attendants. They usually do not pay for the bride's bouquet. They will pay for all the flowers and decorations in the church, home, club, or wherever the service and the reception are held. The groom will pay for the bride's bouquet, bride's going-away corsage, corsages for the two mothers, and all boutonnieres for himself, best man, ushers, and the fathers. It is optional if he wishes to pay for the bouquets for the bridesmaids. The cost of the rehearsal dinner and its decorations are also the responsibility of the groom or his parents.

However, along with many other customs of the traditional wedding ceremony, many young people today are discarding the customary way of dividing expenses. Many times it is the parents of either bride or groom who "foot the bill" for most of the wedding, but this all depends on the economic status of the two families involved. With or without the financial help of their parents, the couple divide the bill to suit their budgets.

DECORATIONS

Wedding decorations can be very simple or very elaborate. They can range from one vase of flowers up to floral displays which cost thousands of dollars. It is impossible here to attempt to discuss all of the floral decorations which you might use for a wedding. There are many factors involved as well as unlimited possibilities of what you can do to decorate for a wedding. Several design books are available with excellent pictures of decorations for all types and sizes of weddings.

The following wedding decorations were planned and executed by a student who had worked only part time in two retail flower shops before he did these decorations:

> Two 18-foot blue spruce were sprayed white and placed on either side of the altar. Next came two Hogarth arrangements of chartreuse spider mums, green gladioli, light green Scotch broom, and 4 pounds of green grapes in each one. They stood 8 feet high on mahogany pedestals, with smilax around the base. Farther down were two smaller trees (6-foot) also sprayed white. On the altar rail and on every third pew were white holders with two dozen Seventeen roses and a cross

of Scotch broom sprayed white. White satin bows marked the remaining pews. The aisle was draped with 115 feet of rope made from trailing pine and covered with white cloth.

The bridal bouquet was four dozen white roses and three dozen stephanotis accented by pearl hearts and green velvet leaves. The matron of honor carried green cymbidiums and the two attendants carried white roses in silver bowls. The flower girl carried a basket of white roses and daisies.

For the reception, the tables were draped with white linen. The bridal table was on a 24-foot stage which was draped with white and hung with smilax. Natural blue spruce trees lined the stage. In the center of the bridal table was an arrangement of pink roses, white snapdragons, and two large pink satin hearts joined to two doves with ribbons to their beaks. On each end of the table were fancy cupid candelabra which were 5½ feet high and 4 feet wide which contained two dozen white snapdragons, three dozen pink Sensation roses, and white Scotch broom. The cake table was draped in white and hung with smilax. At each peak of the smilax (25 peaks) were clusters of pink roses and bows. The tops of the bridal and cake tables were decorated with emerald foliage and pink roses.

BACKGROUNDS

Backgrounds are very important to weddings and for any kind of decorations. Sometimes you use the church background itself. Often, however, you will provide a background of greens, candles, and flowers. If the wedding is not held in a church, you may provide a trellis or lattice of greens, garlands, and flowers. Or you may decorate one end of the living room for the wedding. Whatever is used must enhance the flowers and the wedding party, but should not dominate the service. Greens and green plants, either fresh or permanent, are often used. They will help to make the flowers stand out. The flowers, greenery, and candles in the background should not be so high that they seem detached from, nor so low that they are obscured by, the wedding party. If the bride is wearing a colored gown, the flowers in the decoration should be in a similar color so that there will be continuity. If she is in white, the central flowers in the background should be in white. The flanking flowers may be white, or they may pick up the colors worn by the attendants.

At the reception, a background must also be provided for the flowers and the wedding party. Again greens are often used. If there is a special arrangement in the home or club, it might have a black background to make the flowers stand out to their fullest. Never put flowers in front of a window, tapestry, or flowered wallpaper—these are very poor backgrounds. A bold silhouette arrangement is the only exception to not putting flowers in front of a window. Not just for weddings, but wherever flowers are displayed, they should have the proper background to enhance their beauty rather than detract from it.

   Weddings must be handled systematically with order sheets used for the preparations as well as the removal of wedding materials. Figure the cost as accurately as you can. A happy wedding, for the florist, is a profitable one. A well done wedding which is pleasing to the family and guests will also bring more business. When they think of flowers for other occasions, they will naturally think of your shop. The handling and servicing of weddings can be profitable for retail florists if they plan them well and charge enough for each item to make a profit.

 PART THREE

SPECIAL ASPECTS

Chapter 36

FOLIAGE PLANTS—
PLANT ARRANGEMENTS

One firm builds a new structure—an office complex, a mall, a bank, or a hotel—and wants to make the interior come alive. Another firm decides that its building needs a new look, a different appearance.

They consult with their architect and/or their interior designer and decide that the building needs green plants. But they neither want nor need the hassles of maintenance; they're simply seeking permanently good looking green plants.

They're looking for you, the florist—the professional plant expert who has a reputation for quality goods, quality maintenance services, and a solid, forthright method of conducting business.

The sale and use of foliage plants has been increasing each year and is now accounting for a good percentage of the retail florist business.

Finding out what the consumer buys and what the consumer will pay is of utmost importance to growers and retail florists. A more complete understanding of the consumer would greatly aid the seller in increasing sales. What does the consumer look for in plants? What uses do these plants have for the consumer? What does the consumer know about these plants? All are questions that must be answered for the seller to evaluate effectively the market potential.

Consumer preference studies have definitely shown that consumers do want, and will use, foliage plants rather extensively if they can secure high quality plants, properly identified, and with accurate information on their habit of growth, care, and use in the home. Much of this will be demanded by consumers to satisfy the increasing desires of collectors for various groups of plants. The main concerns of a consumer are how long the plants will stay in good condition in the home and how to take care of them.

The broad field of the use of decorative foliage plants has perhaps presented to every florist the greatest challenge in the entire history of the florist industry. The group of plants included in the classification "foliage plants" is made up, for the most part, of ornamental herbaceous perennials that are characteristic of the tropics. The majority of these plants are grown for their ornamental foliage, but some bear attractive flowers as well, according to Professor A. F. DeWerth.

The development of modern-day architectural styles, along with the tendency of architects to show foliage plants in their sketches and plans of modern buildings to enchance and give life to the severe lines and cold, austere appearance of the rooms, has led to a revived interest in foliage plants. As a result, these plants are now featured more frequently than ever before by the architects and decorators in their plans for homes, offices, hotel lobbies, and public buildings. These developments have created a golden opportunity for the retail florist.

The increase in apartment dwelling in urban areas has increased the demand for durable, less spectacular, small planters, and potted foliage plants.

In Indiana a telephone survey was conducted wherein half of the people questioned lived in apartments, the other half lived in houses. People in houses mainly buy plants for gifts (46 per cent) and only secondarily (24 per cent) for decorating purposes. The converse is true for apartment dwellers—48 per cent said they buy plants for decorating purposes and 30 per cent for gifts. This survey also showed that 62 per cent of the people questioned buy their plants in retail florist shops. This suggests that people buying plants for their personal use are interested in the service and quality found in a florist shop and are willing to pay for it.

A list of the major points of information gained from the above survey follow:

- The main reasons people buy house plants are for gifts and decorating purposes.
- Consumers buy plants mostly from florist shops and garden centers.
- Smaller plants (less than 6 inches) were liked best; large ones (more than 12 inches tall) were liked the least.
- Plants of spreading and upright growth habit were preferred over vining plants.
- Fresh or live foliage and flowering house plants were liked and bought most.

The rooms in the dwelling containing house plants are mainly the kitchen and living room.

Generally, people do not know the correct methods to use when watering, do not adequately use fertilizer, do not raise

Figure 36-1. Pole philodendron decorated with artificial fruit for a holiday.

the humidity around their plants in the winter, do not give supplemental lighting, and do not know the significance of window direction.

- ⋖ People turn to books, friends, or relatives, and magazines, but do not rely heavily upon gaining help from the seller, when plants are in trouble.
- ⋖ A small percentage of the population does not buy plants, mainly because they are received as gifts or propagated at home or because of problems in the home environment.

One new concept of florist marketing—plants for every home—finds its most fertile field with foliage plants. Proper handling of this group of plants by the florist industry can continue to produce and develop a market using a tremendous volume of plants.

If you do not have the necessary facilities or personnel to do more than small dish gardens in your own shop, it should be considered good business to refer customers to someone who is equipped to do this type of work. The use of several good large specimens for display can serve as samples, and plants can then be ordered from a grower for later delivery to the customer. The sale of plants by any florist carries with it definite obligations. This is especially true of the foliage plants. You should know the names and varieties and how to care for them, and be able to tell your customers how to handle them.

CARE OF PLANTS

Pot plants of all kinds provide lasting satisfaction to the customer, and they would receive a much more prominent place in the florist business if the average florist knew more about them and their proper care.

In general, the atmosphere of the average florist shop is too dry and too warm. This is especially true in the winter months in shops where artificial heat is used. Always keep the plants in the coolest, most humid part of the shop. When humidifiers are not used, place the plants on gravel in pans. Keep the gravel moist without water standing in the pans. Syringing the plants twice a day is advantageous to freshen the foliage. A small conservatory or greenhouse is of tremendous help in keeping foliage plants in good condition.

Improper watering causes a greater loss of foliage plants than any other factor, both in the shop and in the home. Customers frequently ask, "How much water does this plant need and how often should I water it?" There is no set rule that can be given, because humidity and temperature vary in each home. Never water by a rule-of-thumb, such as one cupful every day or every two days. *The best advice is to water the plant only when necessary.*

Overwatering is as detrimental as underwatering. When the lowest leaves on the plant turn yellow and fall off, the plant has probably been overwatered. Never allow a plant to stand in water. Never water foliage plants with water colder than room temperature if it can be avoided. In pots, containers, or plant beds that do not have drainage openings and are more or less waterproof, place a liberal layer of broken pots or gravel in the bottom for drainage.

You should have a knowledge of soil and fertilizer requirements of foliage plants, because, more and more, you will be called upon to replace the plants in interior plantings and because customers who have had foliage plants for several months usually seek the florists' advice on repotting and fertilizing. In most cases these plants would not benefit from either process. Plants in most interior plantings are ruined by the use of too much fertilizer. When the majority of the foliage plants used by florists today are not in good healthy condition, they usually need a more healthy growing environment, not fertilizer. When fertilizer is necessary, be certain it is never applied when the soil is dry or the leaves will be burned. A 2-1-2 ratio is most satisfactory, and a soluble fertilizer (liquid) has been found to be the best to apply. Foliage plants do not require frequent soil changes and repotting. They present their best appearance in containers which hold a limited amount of soil.

Every customer should be intelligently informed as to how to take care of the plants purchased and told truthfully what reasonably may be expected from them. Today, with the increased interest in foliage plants, the customer is often oversold on the possibilities due to a lack of plant knowledge on the part of architects and decorators and a lack of know-how on the part of some retail florists. This leads to dissatisfied customers and complaints, rather than continued interest in these plants and repeated sales. Replanting or replacing every six months to a year is often recommended, depending on the species of plant.

ACCLIMATIZATION

You, as a retail florist shop manager, are faced with most of the problems experienced by consumers when they maintain foliage plants under interior conditions. Those most frequently encountered are foliar yellowing, or chlorosis, leaf loss, tip burn, and general loss of quality. This is where acclimatization becomes important. Webster defines acclimatization as "The climatic adaptation of an organism, especially a plant, that has been moved to a new environment." Research has shown that this process prior to placement indoors is definitely beneficial for some plants. The length of the acclimatization period, as well as the type of acclimatization required for plants growing under different conditions, varies. The need for adaptation of plants to varying light intensities has been known for years. High light produces smaller, thicker foliage. A plant grown under high light intensity has a higher compensation point than it would have if grown at heavy shade. Therefore, even though 100 foot-candles of light may be sufficient for a shade-grown plant when it is moved indoors, had the plant been grown in the sun, 200 foot-candles may not be sufficient.

Whether or not plants are acclimatized, sufficient intensity, duration, and quality of indoor lighting will greatly improve maintenance of plant quality. It should be remembered that little growth is desired in most indoor situations.

PLANTERS

One of the greatest difficulties for the retail florist arises from the use of plants in large interior planting beds or boxes; yet this is a very lucrative field. These boxes or beds should never be filled with soil and then planted by knocking the plants out of the pots and planting them in these areas. By this method, they are always overwatered and roots fail to develop, because good drainage is impossible to obtain, and every person has a tendency to overwater rather than underwater. The best procedure to follow is to place a layer of gravel on the bottom of the bed or planter and then place the plants in on top of this layer, in the pots, and water them well. Fill the entire bed or box with a coarse grade vermiculite or peat moss, covering the pots about one inch above the rim. The material can be watered at regular intervals and the plants will remain in good condition for three or four times as long as when planted in soil. Individual plants are easily removed and replaced without disturbing the other plants in the planter. This makes replacement easy, clean, and much less costly. It also provides for ready sales of blooming plants for special displays in these areas. Planters should be designed just as carefully as a flower arrangement.

Planter arrangements are at home anywhere: in private homes, public rooms, lobbies, and hospitals, and always provide a decorative accent. Planter arrangements are interesting only in proportion to the care taken by the designer. Too often a dish garden may be dull and lifeless, with no real design to it.

Figure 36-2. An artistically designed dish garden with a flower focal point.

There is no limit to the number of foliage plants that can be sold if the sale of this group of plants is undertaken as a business opportunity. In addition to large interior planters and decorative specimens, almost all apartment dwellers as well as home owners have small foliage plants as part of their interior decorations. They will often bring them in to the florist every three or four months for replacement. Often frequent replacements are necessary because the plants are used in positions where proper light and temperature do not prevail.

Arrangement of Planters

Incorporation of fresh flowers into a planter arrangement adds continuing interest as well as color. When the flowers in water tubes of a dish garden or water garden have passed their prime, the design may look unfinished until the owner replaces the flowers with fresh blooms. This fact can be pointed out to the customer when the planter is sold, with the suggestion that the customer may wish to arrange for replacements on a definite basis with the florist. This is an excellent way to get repeat business, or see that the customer will come into the shop each week.

Since 1975 there has been a ten per cent increase in the average wholesale amount spent each year on plants to decorate the homes of America, currently a total of $205,700,000. This is not a small amount of money to add to the gross income for flowers, and most of it can go to retail florists if they will promote these sales and compete favorably with variety and five-and-ten-cent stores. The majority of florists who handle foliage plants must make them appealing to the customer. The display of foliage plants in florist shops must be attractive. Displaying pot plants that look as good or better than those of a competitor is not enough if the florist is to get a fair share of the $205,700,000 mentioned previously. Customers should be shown all the places in the home where foliage plants, planters, and water gardens can be used. These include the coffee table, mantel, centerpieces, bookcase, television (be careful watering), side tables, and even on the floor or hearth. The modern home provides countless places where planter arrangements, styled specifically for a known location, can serve a long-lived purpose in the decorative scheme.

A planter arrangement should be planned as carefully as a cut flower arrangement. It needs line, rhythm, color, and mass. Texture makes a contribution to one or more of these design elements. Shape and texture of foliages is the first consideration in planning an arrangement for a given planter. The angularity of a rectangular planter suggests that the major elements in the plant groupings should be somewhat curved for contrast.

"European gardens" are a new type of dish garden. To plant one, center a tall plant in a flat, round container. Surround it with progressively smaller plants, possibly including a few trailing varieties extending over the edge, to create a symmetrical arrangement of plants.

Designed for specific locations, planters take on a look of individual personality and become a contributing factor in home décor. Two different types of philodendron might be accented with pine cone roses—made simply by slicing pine cones and giving them wire stems. This design would complement a den, especially if its walls are pine-paneled and the room needs a touch of green.

A small flowering plant for a lamp table will leave the table surface uncrowded, free for its purpose of holding accessories and whatever falls onto it. A kitchen arrangement can be backed with a metal tray and accented with a gay reclining pixie. For a child's room a pedestal bowl planted with a philodendron on a totem pole, accented with fresh or permanent flowers and gay little elves will amuse the small fry.

Plants have become an integral part of the decorator's plan. They can no longer be assembled without thought, either for the design picture they create, nor for the contribution they make to home décor. Both plants and containers should be chosen to complement their ultimate home location.

Bonsai trees are a real money-maker for many retail florists. Also many retail florists feel that the real profit in this field is in selling accessories such as jardinieres, tubs, plant stands, bark, totem poles, fertilizers, and other materials.

Another area where you can make a profit is in the servicing of foliage plants in the home and places of business. Figure your costs on this and charge enough to make a profit.

Make your guarantee policy clear so that the customer will understand it.

Water Gardens

A water garden is a dish garden in which the plants are growing in water, not soil. They are designed, not just planted. The same principles of design apply in planning a water garden as apply in

Figure 36-3. A water garden designed by Gil Whitten, Vero Beach, Fla.

flower arranging. An attractive water garden arrangement may be styled in a classical symmetrical or asymmetrical triangle of plant materials growing in water. It is done in a shallow container which would not hold enough soil for growing the plants, but is perfect when the plants are attached to a pinholder set in water. By using a pinholder and just enough water to cover the root system of the foliage plants used, you can achieve a graceful, stately design. Plants should be selected in proportion to the size and shape of the container, and for a variety of shades of greens.

Water gardens have the advantage of needing very little care, less light than is required for the same plants if planted in soil, and the possibility of combining plants that like different types of soil and environment, but will thrive together in water. (See Section I, Table 36-1.)

Bamboo place mats make an interesting background for either dish gardens or water gardens, which can be augmented by a Chinese figurine to carry out an Oriental motif.

Specific Plants

There are many plants which can be grown in our homes under

various conditions. A partial list of the more common ones is shown in Table 36-1.

Many varieties of philodendrons, peperomias, dieffenbachias, dracaenas, crotons, caladiums, episcias, and bromeliads afford a fascinating range of plants that are easy to grow, and that are available to any indoor gardener who has a desire for improving home conditions by the use of living plants.

The leading colorful foliage plant today is the croton. It requires a warm temperature (60° F.), plenty of light, and moisture. At temperatures below 50° F., or in a dry atmosphere, it will drop its lower leaves. It requires light to retain its high color. A location in a bright east or south window is ideal. New leaves are usually green, but will color up as they reach maturity.

Another highly colored plant that lends itself well to interior decoration is the fancy-leaved caladium. It requires the same conditions necessary for the croton to keep its high color.

The episcias form a group of small plants that provide colorful effects for use on coffee tables, or in small areas that are in shady locations in the room. They do well in the same locations that are suitable for African violets and are often misnamed the "red African violet." They need filtered light and constant moisture. They should be fed with a liquid fertilizer once a month. They are trailing in nature, and must be kept warm like the crotons and caladiums. The leaves will quickly discolor at temperatures of 50° F. or lower.

The most versatile foliage plants for use in interior decoration today are the many types of philodendron. The large-leaved types, such as hastatum, dubia, pertusum, and mandianum, are ideal for totem poles and trained specimens. The most trustworthy vine for interior decoration in any situation is the common Philodendron *cordatum* (*oxycardium*). Many philodendrons, such as lacineatum, panduraeforme, and pertusum, have interesting patterns.

Bromeliads are especially well adapted to present-day interior decoration. They have foliage of a tough leathery nature and grow so that the leaves can hold water in their centers, and thus do not dry out readily, or are not as susceptible to low humidity as other foliage plants. The plants grow in light or shade, but the colors are more intense in sunny locations. In the foliage of the various species of bromeliads, there is a wide variation of color patterns, including stripes, blotches, or patches. These plants actually present a sculptured appearance and are ideally suited to interior decoration where conditions are especially trying, or where the interior decoration is in the contemporary manner.

Table 36-1. A Selected List of Various Common
House Plants Grown Mainly for Their Foliage[1]

Scientific Name	Common Name
I. Plants That Will Grow in Water and Soil	
Aglaonema modestum	Chinese evergreen
Coleus blumei	coleus
Crassula arborescens	jade plant
Dieffenbachia (all varieties)	dumbcane
Hedera helix (all varieties)	English ivy
Hemigraphis colorata	hemigraphis
Nephthytis afzeli	arrowhead
Philodendron cordatum	philodendron
Sansevieria zeylanica	sansevieria
Scindapsus aureus	devil's ivy
Tradescantia (all varieties)	wandering Jew
II. Plants That Will Withstand Most Adverse House Conditions and Abuse	
Aglaonema modestum	Chinese evergreen
Aspidistra elatior	iron plant
Cissus rhombifolia	grape ivy
Crassula arborescens	jade plant
Dieffenbachia amoena	dumbcane
Dracaena fragrans massangeana	dracaena
Euphorbia mili	crown of thorns
Ficus elastica	Indian rubber
Ficus pandurata	fiddleleaf fig
Hemigraphis colorata	hemigraphis
Howea belmoreana	Kentia palm
Nephthytis afzeli	arrowhead
Pandanus veitchi	screwpine
Paradises liliastrum	paradise lily
Peperomia obtusifolium	peperomia
Philodendron cordatum	philodendron
Sansevieria trifasciata laurenti	golden stripe sansevieria
Sansevieria zeylanica	snakeplant
Scindapsus aureus	devil's ivy
III. Plants That Do Well Under Average Home Conditions	
Acanthus montanus	mountain acanthus
Aechmea orlandiana	aechmea
Araucaria excelsa	Norfolk Island pine
Asparagus densiflorus Sprengeri	Sprenger asparagus
Begonia semperflorens	everblooming begonia

(Continued)

Table 36-1 (Continued)

Scientific Name	Common Name
Begonia ulmifolia	elm-leaved begonia
Beloperone guttata	shrimp plant
Caladium bicolor	fancy-leaved caladium
Cissus rhombifolia	grape ivy
Codiaeum variegatum	croton
Cryptanthus acaulis	cryptanthus
Cyrtomium falcatum	holly fern
Dieffenbachia bausei	dumbcane
Dieffenbachia picta	dumbcane
Dieffenbachia picta Rudolph Roehrs	dumbcane
Fatsia japonica	Japanese fatsia
Fatshedera lizei	botanical wonder
Hedera helix (and varieties)	English ivy
Nephthytis Emerald Gem	arrowhead
Peperomia crassifolia	leatherleaf peperomia
Peperomia obtusifolia variegata	variegated peperomia
Peperomia sandersi	watermelon peperomia
Philodendron cordatum	heartleaf philodendron
Philodendron dubia	splitleaf philodendron
Philodendron giganteum	giant philodendron
Philodendron scandens	redleaf philodendron
Philodendron selloum	philodendron
Philodendron tripartitum	trileaf philodendron
Philodendron wendlandi	philodendron
Pilea involucrata	artillery plant
Piper nigrum	black pepper
Piper ornatum	Celebes pepper
Polyscias filicifolia	fernleaf aralia
Polyscias paniculata	jagged-leaf aralia
Rhoeo discolor	three men in a boat
Saxifraga sarmentosa	strawberry geranium
Schizmatoglottis picta	painted tongue
Spathyphllum clevelandi	white anthurium
Vanilla planifolium	vanilla

IV. Plants Well Suited for Large Tubbed Decorative Specimens

Acanthus mollis	artists acanthus
Acanthus montanus	mountain acanthus
Alsophila australis	Australian tree fern
Codiaeum variegatum	croton

(Continued)

Table 36-1 (Continued)

Scientific Name	Common Name
Dieffenbachia amoena	spotted dumbcane
Fatshedera japonica	botanical wonder
Ficus elastica variegata	variegated Indian rubber
Ficus pandurata	fiddleleaf fig
Monstera deliciosa	cutleaf philodendron
Pandanus veitchi	screwpine
Philodendron dubia	splitleaf philodendron
Philodendron giganteum	giant philodendron
Philodendron selloum	philodendron
Polyscias paniculata	jagged-leaf aralia
Schefflera actinophylla	schefflera
Strelitzia reginae	bird-of-paradise

V. Vines and Trailing Plants for Totem Poles and Trained Plants

Cissus antarctica	kangaroo vine
Cissus rhombifolia	grape ivy
Ficus pumila	creeping fig
Hemigraphis colorata	hemigraphis
Hoya carnosa	wax plant
Monstera deliciosa	cutleaf philodendron
Nephthytis afzeli	arrowhead
Philodendron (all climbing types)	philodendron
Piper nigrum	black pepper
Piper ornatum	Celebes pepper
Scindapsus aureus	devil's ivy
Scindapsus pictus	painted devil's ivy
Stephanotis floribunda	stephanotis

VI. Low Creeping Plants for Ground Covers in Interior Planting Boxes

Episcia cupreata	episcia
Ficus pumila	creeping fig
Ficus radicans	climbing fig
Fittonia vershafelti Silvernerve	silver fittonia
Hedera helix Hahn's Star	Hahn's Star English ivy
Helzine soleroi	baby's tears
Hemigraphis colorata	hemigraphis
Pellionia daveauana	pellionia
Philodendron cordatum	heartleaf philodendron
Pilea nummulariaefolia	creeping artillery plant
Saxifraga sarmentosa	strawberry geranium
Scindapsus aureus	devil's ivy
Tradescantia	wandering Jew

[1]Compiled from material by Professor A. F. DeWerth, Texas A&M University.

Foliage plants offer a diversion for even the most conservative person. Plants are important to everyday living, and perform a real function in modern interior decoration. Their care is so simple and easy that no home, room, or building should be without one.

Specific suggestions for consumers are as follows:

1. Air conditioning is not detrimental to foliage plants.
2. Plants, except for crotons and caladiums, should not be placed in direct sunlight.
3. Plants should be grown in an average temperature of 60° F. or above.
4. Plants should be fertilized only lightly and infrequently.
5. Trained plants such as totem poles and baskets should have the tips pinched occasionally if the proper shape is to be maintained.
6. When and if spindly weak growth occurs, it should be removed.
7. Overwatering is the greatest fault of most customers in taking care of foliage plants. They should only be watered when necessary.

Table 36-2 shows a list of cultural recommendations for florists and their customers so that they may combine plants in planters that have similar light and water requirements.

INTERIOR LANDSCAPING

It has been estimated that we spend as much as 80 per cent of our life inside; yet, it has been only recently that plants have begun to play a significant role in the non-home interior landscape.

The interior landscape provides the same functions as the conventional exterior landscape in that it softens architectural lines, adds beauty to the setting, and creates a comfortable environment for those using the buildings. Psychologists argue that people have an instinctive need to associate with plants, and that plants in the interior landscape help meet this need.

Interior landscape firms to date have been centered largely in the more metropolitan sections of the country. However, in the past few years a diffusion of these firms to the smaller population centers seems to be occurring. In the smaller communities these interior landscape firms frequently are engaged in growing, retail sales, or both.

Table 36-2. A Selected List of Exotic Plants and Their Adaptability to Building Interiors[1]

Key to Maintenance Requirements

Light Requirements:

High—Bright Light or Full Sun:
    Preference: 5000 to 8000 foot-candles for average length of day.
    Tolerance: 1000 to 2000 foot-candles with 12-hour illumination.

Medium—Diffused or Filtered Light:
    Preference: 1000 to 5000 foot-candles for average length of day.
    Tolerance: 500 to 1000 foot-candles with 12-hour illumination.
    Simple Test: When hand is passed over plants between them and light source, shadow cast by hand should be barely visible.

Low—No Direct Light:
    Preference: 100 to 500 foot-candles for average length of day.
    Tolerance: 50 to 100 foot-candles with 12-hour illumination.

Soil Moisture Requirements:

Dry: Soil should be dry for best growth; only occasional light waterings should be given to moisten soil thoroughly at three- or four-week intervals. Dry, sandy, well-drained soil should be used. Examples: Cacti and other succulents, peperomias, and sansevierias.

Moist: Soil should be kept uniformly moist but never wet. Allow soil to become moderately dry before watering and then water thoroughly. Plants have delicate fine roots which will rot when soil is wet.

Wet: Soil should never be allowed to become dry. Excellent drainage should be provided in containers so that air is available in soil. Water should never be allowed to stand in saucers under containers.

Plant Use Requirements:

Tub Plants: Plants which develop into large specimens suitable for lobby decorations in public buildings or for placement on floors in homes for interior decoration.

Vines: Plants that require support such as trellises or totem poles or that can be used for ground covers in interior planter boxes or as trailing plants on ledges or over the edges of interior planter boxes.

Scientific Name of Plant	Light			Soil Moisture			Uses		
	High	Med	Low	Dry	Moist	Wet	Tub	Vine	Small Planters
Aglaonema commutatum		x			x		x		x
Aglaonema modestum		x			x				x
Aloe variegata	x			x			x		x
Asplenium nidis			x			x	x		x
Begonia rex		x			x				x
Caladium, fancy-leaved		x			x		x		x
Cissus rhombifolia		x			x			x	
Codiaeum elegantissima	x				x		x		
Costus speciosa		x			x		x		

(Continued)

Table 36-2 (Continued)

Scientific Name of Plant	Light			Soil Moisture			Uses		
	High	Med	Low	Dry	Moist	Wet	Tub	Vine	Small Planters
Crassula arborescens	X			X					X
Dieffenbachia amoena		X			X		X		
Dieffenbachia picta		X			X		X		
Dracaena warnecki		X			X		X		
Dracaena godseffiana		X			X				X
Dracaena marginata		X			X		X		X
Dracaena sanderiana		X			X				X
Euphorbia mili	X			X			X		X
Fatshedera lizei	X				X		X		X
Ficus benghalensis		X			X		X		
Ficus elastica		X			X		X		
Ficus elastica decora		X			X		X		
Ficus elastica variegata		X			X		X		
Ficus pandurata		X			X		X		
Hedera helix	X				X			X	X
Hedera helix Hahn's Self Branching	X				X			X	X
Hibiscus rosa-sinensis cooperi	X				X		X		X
Hoya carnosa	X			X			X	X	X
Hoya carnosa variegata	X			X			X	X	X
Kalanchoe tomentosa	X			X					X
Pandanus veitchii		X		X			X		
Peperomia obtusifolia		X		X					X
Peperomia obtusifolia variegata		X		X					X
Peperomia sandersi		X		X					X
Philodendron cordatum		X			X		X	X	
Philodendron dubia		X			X		X	X	
Philodendron erubescens		X			X		X	X	
Philodendron hastatum		X			X		X	X	
Philodendron panduriforme		X			X		X	X	
Piper ornatum		X			X		X	X	X
Polyscias paniculata		X			X		X		
Rhoeo discolor	X			X			X		X
Sansevieria trifaciata Hahni	X			X					X
Sansevieria trifaciata laurenti	X			X			X		X
Schefflera actinophylla		X		X			X		
Scindapsus aureus		X		X			X	X	X
Syngonium albo-lineata		X			X		X	X	X
Syngonium Green Gold		X			X		X	X	X
Syngonium wendlandi		X			X		X	X	X
Syngonium White Gold		X			X			X	X

[1]Professor A. F. DeWerth, Texas A&M University.

Calculating the fee to charge for a leased plant can be a difficult procedure. The successful interior landscape firm should be equally concerned with the plants and people in the landscape as with the potential net profit.

The size of the rental fee hinges on the initial cost of the plants (i.e., size, species) and the replacement factor. The installation and maintenance costs are more fixed than the preceding factors.

The components of a total package are:

1. **Design fee.** Frequently 10 to 20 per cent of the plant material and installation cost. Sometimes included in a package deal.
2. **Initial cost of the plants and containers.**
3. **Installation cost.** Frequently one to two times the cost of the plant material.
4. **Replacement cost.** It is important to minimize this cost by carefully matching acclimatized and healthy plants to a location where they would be expected to survive. Most experts in the interior landscape area feel that emphasis should be placed on plant maintenance and survival, not growth. If a plant is placed in a minimal suitable environment and receives adequate maintenance, replacement frequency can be greatly reduced. Some firms build into their pricing scheme a replacement factor of 6 months or 12 months. Such a shotgun approach may be financially rewarding, but seems a gross injustice to the client if the plant never needs replacing. Predicting the longevity of a plant in a particular location is one of the most difficult tasks of the person preparing the bid.

FOLIAGE CLEANERS

Foliage plant cleaners are used by all retail florists to shine the leaves of foliage plants before they are sent out to the customer or used for decorations. There are many commercial plant cleaning compounds on the market today which are used by the retail florists and homemakers to give a shine and gloss to the leaves of foliage plants. Many of the retail florists are aware of the aesthetic value of these materials, but few know of their effect on plant growth.

Experiments were conducted at The Pennsylvania State University during 1962 and 1964 on *Philodendron cordatum* and *Philodendron pertusum* plants. Six different commercial plant cleaning compounds were used on the plants. Some plants were left uncleaned for the period of the test and others were cleaned with plain water. The materials were used on the plants at two-week and four-week intervals. Data taken at the start of the experiment included the weight of the pot and plant, number of leaves, number of growing tips, total length of growing shoots on *cordatum,* and height of plant on *per-*

Figure 36-4. Gallery display of 37 different foliage plants for home use. (Courtesy, "EXOTICA, Pictorial Cyclopedia of Exotic Plants," Roehrs Co., Rutherford, N.J.)

tusum. The plants were double potted in a second pot of peat moss and watered as needed. They were fertilized every six weeks with a 20-20-20 liquid fertilizer applied at the rate of one tablespoon per gallon of water. Applications of the materials were made for nine months, and then further data taken on each plant at the end of the experiment. Seven different commercial products were used. Some of the materials were in liquid form, some in a spray, and some in an aerosol form. Several caused quite a bit of burning at the margins of the leaves. Most of the materials reduced the growth of the plants. *For best growth, it is still best to use water,* although the plants will not have the attractive shine as with a commercial material. One material, "Plant Shine," gave a good shine without any reduction in growth, and several gave a good shine but with a slight burning of the leaves. It is best for florists to try the various materials themselves to find which are best for their plants. Applications every two weeks are too frequent and not recommended. Aerosols and sprays as a general rule result in more injury than materials put on by hand.

Since the sale of foliage plants is increasing each year, every florist must handle them. It is more important than ever before for you to learn how to use them and take care of them properly so that you can pass the information on to your customers. Foliage plants play a large part in the commercial account business discussed in the following chapter, Chapter 37.

COMMERCIAL ACCOUNTS

One of the greatest single potential areas for increasing your business lies in the commercial field. Commercial accounts form a good year-round backbone for the retail florist business. The potential is great since orders can be expected continuously. The orders are usually large, payments are assured, and employees of the firm may become customers too.

Commercial accounts can be handled on a contract basis, whereby you supply flowers for offices, reception rooms, and customers of the firm on a weekly or monthly basis. Also important with commercial accounts is that these companies come to you for hospital arrangements, anniversaries, gifts, openings, and other special occasions. Often the best way to approach this type of business is through the secretaries who do the ordering for their bosses. Commercial accounts do not develop without initiative on the part of the florist.

According to an FTD survey of florists across the nation who have had success with business accounts, certain businesses and professions have proved especially profitable, as shown in Table 37-1.

DEVELOPMENT

To develop commercial accounts, both the owner and associates should build up a wide circle of acquaintances. It will help if you become an active member in various clubs such as Lions, Elks, Optomist, Kiwanis, Toastmasters, and the chamber of commerce. Attend the meetings, participate, and wear a flower. Participation in various community fund-raising drives is also a good way to become acquainted with future business prospects. The more people you know, the more opportunity you will have to add business firms to your list of customers.

Table 37-1. FTD Survey of Commercial Accounts

Business	Primary Use	Other Uses
Banks	Display	Gifts to patrons, employee relations, and bank functions
Insurance companies	Gifts to customers	Hospital arrangements and office display
Savings & loan companies	Display	Employee relations
Department stores	Holiday display	Employee relations
Stock brokerages	Lobby arrangement	Gifts to clients
Specialty retailers	Gifts to customers	Holiday display
Oil companies	Gifts to customers	Employee relations and office functions
Real estate brokers	Gifts to customers	Local display
Automobile dealers	Showroom display	Special promotion gifts
Photo studios	Photo backgrounds	Studio decorations
Dairies	Personnel remembrances	Employee functions
Accounting firms	Gifts to clients	Office decorations

There are some fairly substantial advantages to doing business at a commercial level. For example, in most companies people who make the flower purchases, or specify who gets the order, are willing to spend the company's money more freely than they are their own money. The commercial accounts tend to be for large-sized orders as a general rule. Where a buying habit has been established, there seems to be a greater freedom in the use of flowers and a higher frequency of purchase. Another advantage of the commercial account is that there are many more occasions in business, with its many relationships, for dignifying a remembrance or expressing sympathy with a bouquet than the average person finds in private life.

There are drawbacks, too, in developing commercial accounts. One of these is that selling one of these accounts can be somewhat difficult. In a large company there may be anywhere from 30 to 600 executives or secretaries who must be sifted through to find out who has the authority to purchase flowers. Second, the tendency to regard floral purchases as something that someone has to take care of, and is just a chore, makes it difficult. Third, since business relations are ephemeral and memories short, you must keep after the contact on a fairly regular basis to be sure you do not lose the contact. Finally, the average prospect requires repeated contact if the sale is to be consummated. It is often not signed on the first attempt.

Most florists have the opinion that commercial accounts will make them rich overnight and solve most of their financial worries. Commercial flower business has exciting possibilities, but, in itself, is not the answer to business success, according to Herb Mitchell. In many cities, there is not enough commercial flower business to support a profitable flower shop without proper emphasis in other areas. Not all retailers are capable of handling commercial accounts.

You should realize that commercial buyers are hammered at day and night by members of other industries which compete with flower sales. *Sales Management Magazine* surveyed 33,000 of its subscribers to find out their Christmas gift preferences. Flowers were not even listed in the 20 items which businesspersons spend money on for their gifts. To give an idea of the size of this business, this particular survey indicated that more than 378,000 turkeys were given to customers and employees. One company gave away 8,100 transistor radios, another 3,900 pen and pencil sets, and still a third gave 3,200 blankets. (How much sentiment is attached to a radio or blanket?)

A good commercial account is a steady month-in and month-out buyer. In addition, commercial accounts tend to generate other consumer business, as many employees buy flowers at the same place as the company does.

According to Herb Mitchell, basically there are four important points in developing commercial accounts: finding accounts, catching accounts, selling accounts, and keeping accounts.

Finding Accounts

Determine first where accounts can be found. Develop a mailing list of commercial flower buyers by using the following four steps: (1) secure a list of manufacturers in the area from the chamber of commerce, (2) add to the list all the professional people in the area from the yellow pages of the phone book, (3) add all the retailers in the area, and (4) check the city directory, and select other firms which offer a sales potential. This list will be much too big to use, so you must set up a system of selection to reduce your final mailing list to the best prospects to give the desired return on your advertising and promotion budget.

After the firms have been selected, it is important to find the proper name to whom the contact is sent. The best method is by asking. A phone call will give you the name of the person who makes the final decision on flower purchases. Often the head person does not do this, but does influence the purchases. Therefore, this person should be cultivated along with the actual purchaser. Often a flower sent to the secretary will pave the way for an interview. Thus, the first step in developing profitable commercial business is finding the market, then isolating the potential buyers by a realistic mailing list.

Catching Accounts

The second step is catching the account, and this can be done only when advertising really catches the prospect's attention and precipitates a positive, remembered reaction. It must be repeated many times. The advertisement must have a sharp impact on the potential customer. It must have a quality of drama and stand out in any crowd. The reader must remember the product being advertised and the florist advertising it. Color is one of the best attention-getters a florist has available. Size and shape of the direct mail advertising is also important. The ad must be intriguing to successfully compete with the some 560 advertisements which the average American sees in one day—but only notices 76—out of which 12 will make an impression, and only 9 will make a positive impression. Consistent repetition is necessary before the contract will be signed for the commercial account. Personal contact is needed as a follow-up to the advertising campaign.

Selling Accounts

There isn't as much difference as some people think between selling commercial accounts by advertising and selling by personal contact. However, one variance is extremely important and never should be overlooked. That is, that selling by advertising must be accomplished fast and with more accuracy. An individual selling person-to-person has the advantage of watching the prospect while talking. Advertising which convinces gives assurance with persuasiveness. Any commercial buyer who would purchase a food item, gadget, or liquor for a gift is a likely prospect for a flower gift. To reach this market, you must compete advertisingwise and must present your merchandise with more conviction than the others, and also must compete pricewise. Many commercial buyers will spend money, but they are not extravagant. Of the dollars spent for business gifts at Christmas one year (over 1.5 billion), about 70 per cent of these dollars were spent on gifts with a price tag of $15 or under.

To perk up commercial accounts, try including the firm's product or a replica of it in the floral design.

Keeping Accounts

The most important part of any advertising program is the function of keeping accounts sold. The major reason customers change florists is not dissatisfaction in service or price, but because they feel *neglected.* If you fail to let your customers know they are needed and appreciated, you are omitting one of the most important aspects of the advertising cycle. Buyers will spread their business to many florists unless there is contact constantly from one particular florist who gives good service. Many firms buy from more than one florist and spread their business around simply because they said they never heard from their florist except when they were sent a bill at the first of the month. Keeping in constant contact through advertising is more important in commercial accounts than with any other type of customer.

There are several important steps to consider in planning an advertising program which will keep commercial accounts sold: (1) Plan a consistent advertising campaign with at least four exposures during a 12-month period which ask for the business. (2) Acknowledge all new accounts promptly and preferably in person either by a visit or by phone. (3) Keep in periodic touch with a buyer customer. (4) Once a year, send a personal thank-you letter to every commercial account which has made a purchase during the year. (5) Watch the accounts which fall into inactivity and find out why. (6) Become known, by joining and participating in civic organizations, clubs, and drives.

Procedure for Development

For florists who have never tried commercial accounts, Harry Lazier has presented a set of eight simple steps as a procedure for getting started in developing commercial accounts.

Start small, and grow: (1) Advertise in the yellow pages of the phone book for business accounts, because many buyers of flowers for a business have never ordered them before. (2) Make up a list of the most desirable commercial accounts which are within walking distance from the shop. Get the name of the president of each firm. (3) Go to the business address and ask for the president's secretary. (4) Explain your florist business to the secretary and ask her for the name of the person who was specifically entrusted with the responsibility for commercial flower orders. (5) Ask to see the person who buys flowers for these orders if it is not the secretary. Explain your business to that person, and tell him how you are especially equipped to handle the orders from his firm. Tell the person that you would like to have his business, and hope he will call on you for the next order of flowers. (6) Make sure that the purchasers of flowers in this firm will remember you as the florist. Send a small bouquet and a thank-you note for the time given, to the person who does the buying. Also send the president's secretary a few flowers. (7) If the florist does not get the order, then he should call back within a month and do this for six months before giving up and turning his attention to another account. (8) The final point is that after the florist has a commercial account set up on the books, set up a specific date at least once a year to call back personally on the commercial account to check on the fact that the same person was still placing the orders, that everybody was happy, and to mention any new services which the florist has to offer.

It is important to remember that you should go after commercial accounts only if you have the ambition, energy, and facilities to do a good job. Perseverance is a must when it comes to cultivating commercial accounts, but they can be very rewarding. When you serve commercial accounts, you must provide service and lots of it.

If you have contracts for supplying foliage plants to offices, for bank and hotel lobbies, and for restaurants, it is to your advantage that the plants be in good condition all the time. They need professional care and you are just the one to give them that care. You do not just deliver an order to a commercial account and forget about it. Many florists have set up contracts with banks, hotels, businesspersons, and others to install, replace, and maintain decorations on a yearly basis. It is good business and brings in a steady revenue all year. Some decorations, such as for Christmas, may be on a bid basis. Do not be reluctant to bid on a decorating job and include a fair profit. Prepare a bid to give several alternatives, and tell the customer exactly what you will provide for the money. It may not be the lowest bid that gets the job. The important factor in bidding on these jobs is not price, but what will be done and how good it will look. Be sure to include the time involved in selling, creating, and installing the job as well as the cost of materials.

Many florists who have had good commercial accounts have lost them because they have taken them for granted and not given the accounts top quality and good design.

Here is a new angle to the working of commercial accounts— one florist reports that two commercial accounts—local banks—have asked to be notified when there is a store or business opening. The local medical society also has the florist call the secretary about a member's illness or a death in a member's family.

Commercial accounts generally fall into three categories: office and lobby decorations, employee's gifts, and customer's gifts. One or all of them can be cultivated by the florist who has the initiative, ambition, energy, and the facilities to handle these accounts properly.

Chapter 38

HOLIDAY PREPARATIONS

There are nine major florists' holidays that are important in the retail industry. These are not holidays from work, but holidays when you work harder than ever. It is the time when you do the largest volume of business in the shortest possible time. For this reason, you must plan and manage carefully so that a large profit can be realized from these holidays. This is when many florists make up for the slack summer months, which for many shops are "red-ink" months on the books. The large volume of business at a holiday gives the opportunity to realize the best profit percentage of the year.

The holidays may be just one day of sales, or extend for a week or more. The nine major holiday periods are: Christmas, Mother's Day, Valentine's Day, Easter, Sweetest Day, Secretary's Week, Thanksgiving, Memorial Day, and New Year's.

Lesser holidays which are more important for some florists than others are: St. Patrick's Day, Halloween, Washington's Birthday, and Lincoln's Birthday.

Whether the holiday be for 1 day or for 10 days, it must be planned in advance. Get your staff together and prepare a work schedule showing specific operations and activities for which each person is responsible. This should be posted on the wall ahead of time with the expected hours of work, so that employees can make their plans accordingly.

SPECIFIC HOLIDAYS

Let's take a look at each of the nine major holidays to become familiar with the length of the holiday and some of the materials to be sold.

1. **Christmas.** Planning for this holiday, which is the biggest of the year, begins in the summer when novelty items are or-

435

Figure 38-1. Planning for Christmas. (Courtesy, Evans-King Floral Co., Forty Fort, Pa.)

dered and permanent Christmas arrangements can be made up during the employees' spare time, wrapped in plastic, and stored away for the holiday. The rush of Christmas business lasts for about two weeks, from the 10th to the 24th of December when orders are taken, and plants, flowers, greens, wreaths, and door swags are sold. The business consists of gifts and home decorations. Many greens are sold and used in designs, including holly, pine, spruce, hemlock, cedar, juniper, boxwood, mistletoe, fir, and others. Wreaths, both fresh and permanent, are in demand as well as all types of fresh and permanent door swags. Cut flowers and pot plants are sold in the proportion of about 50-50. Pot plants sold at Christmas will be poinsettias, cyclamen, gloxinias, begonias, azaleas, Christmas cherries, kalanchoes, Christmas peppers, and pot mums. Cut flowers which are most popular are roses, carnations, gladioli, and snapdragons. Other plants and flowers are sold in lesser amounts. Many styrofoam and other novelties are sold along with permanent arrangements.

Figure 38-2. An attractive display of Christmas arrangements. (Courtesy, Buning The Florist, Fort Lauderdale, Fla.)

Ribbons and bows are sold in large quantities; add an extra charge of $0.50 to $1.00 for tying the bow for the customer. All work should be finished and delivered by the evening of the 24th. Pot plants are usually delivered on the 22nd and 23rd. Cemetery wreaths are placed early.

2. **Mother's Day.** Mother's Day is a one-day holiday, the second largest in most parts of the country, with most of the orders being delivered on Saturday. The florist, however, will have to remain open on Mother's Day morning for late order corsages. The business for Mother's Day will be mostly corsages, pot plants, and cut flowers along with boutonnieres and some centerpieces. Corsages and boutonnieres are the most important, so a florist must have plenty of orchids, cymbidiums, gardenias, roses, camellias, violets, and carnations on hand. The florist needs white carnations for boutonnieres for men whose mothers are deceased, and colored ones for men whose mothers are alive. Many times women will wear corsages in either a color or white to indicate their own mother as being alive or deceased. Centerpieces are very popular as a gift to mother as well as such pot plants as pot mums, azaleas, hydrangeas, gardenias, hyacinths, tulips, and daffodils.

3. **Valentine's Day.** This is a one-day holiday which slipped for several years, but was revived by advertising, promotion, and display. It is a sentimental holiday in which cut flowers, corsages, and pot plants are sold. Many red roses will be in demand because they indicate "love" to people. White roses, red and white carnations, and snapdragons will be sold along with a limited number of violets. Pot plants in demand will be hyacinths, tulips, hydrangeas, daffodils, and azaleas. Novelty hearts, lovebirds, and other items will be sold singly or in arrangements. Novelty containers will be used for some of the flower arrangements.

4. **Easter.** Easter is usually a large florist holiday, although in some areas of the country it has been replaced in volume by Mother's Day. Easter is a rush during the week from Palm Sunday until Easter Sunday with the biggest day on Easter Saturday. Florists must remain open on Easter Sunday for last minute corsages and will-call orders. The weather on Easter Saturday and Sunday will affect the volume of sales. Easter business is mostly corsages and pot plants with some orders for cut flowers. Corsages will be orchids, cymbidiums, roses, carnations, gardenias, and camellias. Cut flowers in-

Figure 38-3. An appropriate arrangement of larkspur, roses, and carnations for Mother's Day.

clude roses, carnations, and snapdragons. Most of the pot plants sold will be Easter lilies, azaleas, hyacinths, tulips, daffodils, cinerarias, calceolarias, pot mums, hydrangeas, and gardenias. This depends a lot on the part of the country where the shop is located.

5. **Sweetest Day.** This has become an important floral holiday, surpassing Memorial Day, Thanksgiving, and New Year's in

Figure 38-4. Gazebo or greenhouse structure for green or colorful blooming pot plants at holiday times in the front sales area. (Courtesy, Alexander's Flowers, Cleveland, Ohio.)

most parts of the country. It is a time to send flowers to your loved one, be it your wife, mother, girl friend, or sweetheart.

6. **Secretary's Week.** One of our newest and fastest growing holidays is this, when the boss remembers the secretary with a bud vase, floral arrangement, or potted plant during National Secretary's Week. The Wednesday of that week is usually celebrated as Secretary's Day.

7. **Thanksgiving.** This is the first holiday of the fall season and includes cut flowers, pot plants, and table centerpieces. The table decorations will be centerpieces of chrysanthemums, leaves, gourds, corn, and dried material, or else a horn-of-plenty with flowers and fruit. The most popular pot plant is the pot chrysanthemum. Preferred cut flowers are chrysanthemums, although snapdragons, gladioli, majestic daisies, and others are sold. Gourds, Indian corn, strawflowers, and other materials will be available for people who want to do their own decorating.

8. **Memorial Day.** This is a bigger holiday than Mother's Day in some sections of the country, but a minor holiday for most florists. The community and its customers will help to determine the volume of business. It is usually a one-day holiday with many orders ahead of time. The holiday is mainly one of cut flowers, pot plants, bedding plants, and cemetery wreaths. Many wreaths are sold, including both fresh and permanent. Cut flowers, arranged in cemetery vases, include gladioli and peonies, with some snapdragons and chrysanthemums. Pot plants include geraniums and pot mums. Bedding plants and combination boxes are also popular for this holiday.

9. **New Year's.** Decorations and corsages for New Year's Eve and centerpieces for New Year's Day make up the work for this holiday. It is a one-day holiday with most of the business on the day before New Year's. Many novelty items and novelty arrangements and decorations can be sold. It will only be a good florist holiday for those florists who advertise to get the business. Most people have to be reminded that it is a holiday for flowers.

Other holidays when flowers may be sent are Father's Day, Mother-in-Law's Day, and Grandparents' Day.

There are also many Jewish holidays in which flowers play an important part. The most joyous of all Jewish festivals is Hanukkah, a holiday marked by the use of blue and white flowers.

The preceding gives a very brief look at each of the floral holidays without going into detail.

TRAINING TIPS FOR HOLIDAY HELP

The personnel of a florist's shop, including extra help, should be the first thing to consider in planning for the holidays. Extra help can come from middle-aged women, retired persons, high school students, and college students home for the holidays. Forget about good friends and relatives unless they can do a good job for you. Do not hire too much extra help, but be sure to have enough so you won't have to turn down orders and can maintain an efficient organization.

One of the most important points is to have extra help come in a few days early for training and instruction, which should include the following:

- Spend enough time and have a 30-minute class of instruction every day. Three half-hour sessions are better than one session of 90 minutes.
- First things first. Tell the extra help the hours of work, wages, length of lunch hour and coffee breaks, and the accepted dress.
- Keep the training simple with as few facts as possible.
- Go over the stock and get the employees familiar with names of materials that will be sold at that holiday.
- Call attention to the posted price lists, and go over every item on the price list and ask for questions.
- Give every person a price list for his/her pocket whether that person works in sales, on the phone, or in designing.
- Give specific instructions including the following: write or print plainly, get complete address, initial all orders, do not promise "special time," suggest early delivery, encourage "will calls," do not suggest anything on display unless the manager is consulted, and do not take any order which may give trouble.
- Extra sales help should be given the following tips:
  - Smile and be pleasant.
  - Know the prices.
  - Know the system used for sales: charge or cash.
  - Show the more expensive items first as it is more flattering.

- Use different approaches, since customers are not alike.
- Do not judge by what *you* can afford to pay.
- Ask the customer to pay for it and only charge upon request.
- Be sure the customer has a charge account with this store.
- Show interest in both the customer and the merchandise.
- Always thank the customer.

STORE ARRANGEMENT

Arrange the store for action and for efficiency.

1. Decorate the window with a good window display which will really attract attention and bring people into the shop. Decorate the whole store so that people coming in will feel the festive atmosphere and get in the mood to spend money for flowers. Put your customers in a holiday mood.
2. Group the merchandise. Always display one price and variety of plants together, Group all novelty items together so that the customer can make his or her choice in one spot. Have permanent arrangements priced and displayed where they are easy to sell. Standardize the pot wraps and decorations to save time.
3. Always keep the display refrigerator clean and attractive. Use a special holiday background if possible. Show samples of corsages and arrangements, and be sure every item is priced. Do not display "hard-to-get" items. Check the display refrigerator often and keep it looking in top condition.
4. Make the operation easy for the salespeople. If the shop is large enough, have just one person responsible for the cash register. If order books are used, have plenty of them in convenient spots with room to write. Have plenty of table or counter space for salesclerks to place merchandise during the sale. Have plenty of cards available for the customer, and separated according to the occasion. Have a price tag in every pot plant.
5. Place telephones away from the noise of the store whenever possible. Phone booths are excellent for taking orders all year around. Select telephone salespersons with care—from regular employees, if possible. They must know stock and prices, and have pleasant voices. Post a price list in front of each phone.

Figure 38-5. Interior display. (Courtesy, Miller Florist, Warren, Ohio.)

6. Arrange the workroom as efficiently as possible. Be sure to have ample supplies of wire, ribbon, floratape, net, pins, etc. There should be plenty of table space for the designers so they are not crowded. Provide foam rubber mats because of the long hours they will be on their feet. One person should be in charge of the workroom. If the workroom is located away from the salesroom, there will not be so many interruptions from customers and salespeople.

7. Make sure the delivery equipment and driver properly represent the business. Both should be presentable—one of the toughest jobs at any holiday. The delivery person is often the store's only contact with the public. The delivery department is just as important as any other, particularly at holiday time. Make it a separate department, off by itself. Clearly write or type the delivery tag. Put one person in charge of all deliveries, setting up the routes and schedules and seeing that they are run smoothly and on time. Discourage C.O.D. orders at a holiday. An order slip should accompany each item to the delivery department so that the order can be double

checked. Each driver should keep a record and initial each delivery as completed.

GENERAL SUGGESTIONS

There are many suggestions for retail florists to follow when planning and executing holiday orders, such as the following: (1) Keep a diary of important facts for each particular holiday. (2) Pool deliveries with other florists when feasible. (3) Prepare bows, net, and artificial foliages in advance of the holiday. (4) Prepare all permanent arrangements during the dull or slack periods. (5) Make up corsages in advance, pack in cellophane or plastic, and refrigerate. Research has shown that cymbidiums and orchids can be made up four days prior to the holiday, carnation corsages three days ahead, and roses just one day ahead. (6) Separate all orders. (7) Keep an accurate record of all cut flowers sold. (8) Keep a record of returns and complaints. (9) Number all will-call orders. (10) Be sure to have ample stock on hand. (11) Plan to finish up and close on time the day before the holiday. (12) Have pot plants on display at least five to seven days before the holiday. (13) Try not to book any weddings at a holiday time. (14) Put a sign over each phone reading "For Business Only—Be Brief." (15) Make sure *every* order goes through the cash register.

Phoebe Floral in Allentown, Pennsylvania, has the following set of rules that are followed every Easter and can be adopted for other holidays:

- Wear name badge at all times.
- Remember that the showroom cash registers are for cash-and-carry transactions only.
- Try to get the customers to take their merchandise with them.
- The days for plant deliveries are Wednesday, Thursday, and Friday. Saturday is the delivery day for cut flowers and corsages.
- There are no special deliveries.
- Get in the habit of saying: "Will you pay for this now?"
- All cemetery orders must go through the hands of the manager.
- The only corsages we make are on the list of nine standard corsages.
- All gardenia and violet plants must be wrapped in polyethylene.
- After Thursday P.M., we will not take any new special make-up orders.

&§ Do not take any out-of-town phone orders (FTD, TELE-FLORA, etc.) for less than $12.50.

&§ Your meal orders will be given to you by your respective department heads.

&§ On every order that you write you must put the price of the order, and there are no exceptions.

&§ If a customer has a complaint, immediately turn him over to the owner or the manager.

&§ The following are the department heads and they are responsible for the smooth operation of their respective departments: (list the names and departments).

POT PLANT CARE

Retail florists can often assure future sales to the same customer by simply pointing out some of the characteristics of the plant just sold. When such information is not available on printed tags, sales personnel can be encouraged to mention a few tips regarding the plant's minimum needs. Here are some examples:

Poinsettias are sensitive plants but will last for many weeks if properly cared for. Place poinsettias in bright light (but not direct sunlight), where the air is not too dry, and in a temperature of 60° to 75°F. Reduce the thermostat at night. They should be kept out of all drafts and particularly away from the front door. They should be watered when needed (almost every day)—not allowed to dry out or to sit in water constantly.

Azaleas should be kept in a sunny location and in a cool spot while in flower. They should be watered daily, and old flowers should be removed when they have faded and died. Some varieties can be planted outdoors and will thrive in certain climates.

Cyclamen have attractive flowers and are one of the most beautiful plants for Christmas. They must be grown in the sunlight during the day and placed in a cool temperature (50° to 55°F.) at night. If they are grown properly, the 40 to 60 flower buds should open over a six-week period.

Pot chrysanthemums are now sold all year around in retail florist shops. They are very popular and will thrive in any home if kept in the sunlight and watered every day.

Easter lilies prefer partial sunlight and warmer temperatures than some of the other plants to keep the buds opening. They should be watered daily.

Hydrangeas will last for several weeks if properly cared for. They should be grown in sunlight, in a warm temperature, and be watered at least once a day and sometimes twice. If the house is hot and dry, they will need more water. If the heads droop before the flowers are dead, plunge the whole pot in a sink full of water for several hours; the plant will revive and live another five to seven days.

HOLIDAY RECORDS

Retail florists have many different systems for keeping holiday records, from writing on a calendar to using a separate file folder or drawer for each holiday. Many mainly depend on their growers to tell them what they ordered last year. This last system is all right if augmented with reports on what was sold and not sold, what prices were charged, etc.

Two of the biggest headaches for the retail florist are determining what to order and trying to remember whether or not the items on last year's invoices were sold profitably. Another big problem is trying to remember from the previous year exactly how much of the merchandise bought was for holiday business and how much was for normal business.

It is foolish and expensive to waste time compiling information that you are not able to use. Basically, any holiday report should give 10 things, according to Herb Mitchell. These are:

(1) Total sales, cash and charge. (2) A breakdown of this business into holiday and normal business, and how much in special parties or weddings. (3) A net holiday business sales figure. (4) A list of merchandise ordered. (5) A list of merchandise received. (6) A list of merchandise left over after the holiday. (7) Notes about items requested that you did not have that caused you to lose sales. (8) Comparison to last year's business. (9) Information about help as to how much and when used. (10) Accurate delivery information.

It is also advisable to keep a record of the weather on the various holiday reports. Of course, this does not give the information for planning next year, except for keeping in mind the change of Easter in terms of expected weather. However, it does help in understanding the present holiday sales. Weather is often a determining factor in cash sales for certain holidays and may affect the total volume.

Records can be as simple or as complex as you wish to make them, as long as they give all the basic information that you will need for planning next year.

The following sheets can be mimeographed and used for Christmas, and adapted for other holidays to fit your own business.

Date Written: (12/28/____)   For CHRISTMAS (19____)

19— SUMMARY

Total Sales (Dec. 18 to Dec. 25) .... _____

Inbound FTD Orders, TELEFLORA, Florafax .... _____

Outbound FTD Orders, TELEFLORA, Florafax .... _____

         Net Sales .... _____

GENERAL INFORMATION

Date	# Cash Customers	Amt. Funeral	Amt. Wedding	# of Deliveries	Weather
12/18					
12/19					
12/20					
12/21					
12/22					
12/23					
12/24					

CHURCHES

Name	Address	# of Plants

POT PLANTS

Poinsettias:

Size	Color	# Bought	# Sold	Retail Price	Supply Source	# for Next Year
_____						
_____						
_____						

Other Pot Plants:

Name	# Bought	# Sold	Supply Source	# for Next Year
Pot mums				
Begonias				
Cyclamen				
Xmas cherries				
Xmas peppers				
Kalanchoes				
Gardens				
_____				

WREATHS

Size	Price	# Pound Holly	# Pound Evergreen	# Pound Permanent
_____				
_____				
_____				

GREENS

Material	# Sold This Yr.	# Needed Next Yr.	Material	# Sold This Yr.	# Needed Next Yr.
Boxwood			Magnolia		
Mistletoe			Plumosus		
Ore. holly			Huckleberry		
Var. holly			Eucalyptus		
Laurel roping			Spiral eucalyptus		
Pine roping			Podocarpus		
Sm. bundle pine			Broom		
Lg. bundle pine			Balsam		
Juniper			Rhododendron		
Ore. cedar			Laurel		
Fir			Blankets		
Spruce			Other _____		

CUT FLOWERS

Roses Purchased: **# Doz. Roses Sold:**

	Small	Med.	Large	$10.00	$12.50	$15.00	$20.00	$30.00 up
Red								
Pink								
White								
Yellow								
Total								

Carnations Purchased: **# Doz. Carnations Sold:**

	Number	$10.00	$12.50	$20.00	$25.00	$30.00 up
Red						
White						
Pink						
Other						
Total						

OTHER CUT FLOWERS

Name	# Bought	# Sold	Supplier
Gladioli			
Snapdragons			
Pompons			
Chrysanthemums			
Heather			

CORSAGES

Name	# Ordered	# Sold
W. orchid		
L. orchid		
Cymbidium		
Gardenia		
Camellia		
Rose		
Carnation		
Other		

SUPPLIES

Name	Number
Corsage boxes	
Rose boxes	
Cut flower boxes	
Plant wraps	
Cellophane bags	
	Color
1″ Styrofoam	
2″ Styrofoam	

RIBBON

Size	Red	Green	Plastic	Gold
3				
5				
9				
40				
120				

DEER (or other novelty)

Size	Gold	Plastic	Flocked
Small			
Medium			
Large			
Giant			

CANDLES

Size	Red	White	Others
9″			
12″			
15″			
18″			
21″			

CHRISTMAS BALLS AND BELLS

Size	Type	Number
Small		
Medium		
Large		

NUMBER OF PERMANENT MATERIALS

Price	CENTERPIECE		VASE ARRANGEMENT		MANTEL ARR.	DOOR TRIM
	Xmas	Pastels	Xmas	Pastels		
$ 7.50						
10.00						
12.50						
15.00						
20.00						
25.00						
30.00						

TOTAL NUMBER EMPLOYEES (Regular and Part-Time)

	12/18	12/19	12/20	12/21	12/22	12/23	12/24
Sales:							
Design:							
Office:							
Delivery:							

EMPLOYEES' DATES AND HOURS (fill in and stagger hours)

Name	12/18	12/19	12/20	12/21	12/22	12/23	12/24
J. Doakes	(8-5)	(8-5)	(12-9)	(12-9)	(12-9)	(8-5)	(8-5)
_____							
_____							
_____							
_____							

NOTES FOR CHRISTMAS _____

Plants:
Cut flowers:
Greens:
Corsages:
Permanent items:
Wreaths:
Delivery:
Extra help:
Office records:
General remarks:

Chapter 39

PERMANENT FLOWERS

Permanent flowers include both silk flowers, which are very popular these days in many retail florist shops, and those called "artificial" by some people and "plastic" or "polyethylene" by others. Most retail florists prefer to use the term "permanent," which seems to describe them a little bit better for the general public. These include not only cut flowers but also various foliages and foliage plants which are used for permanent decorations. Some of the permanent trees reach up to 20 feet or more in height.

Up until 20 years ago, most retail florists did not handle the permanent material, and left it in the hands of five-and-ten-cent stores, department stores, and variety stores. There was some feeling that the sale of these materials would cut down on the sale of fresh flowers. The passing years have shown this to be untrue. Today, we find permanent flowers and materials in every retail florist shop in the country. Permanent flowers and plants represent about 7 per cent of florists' sales in the United States, according to a U.S. Marketing Research Report. They are especially popular for holidays when incorporated with fresh flowers in the arrangements.

The original quality of the polyethylene materials was mediocre. However, as the demand for these flowers increased, the manufacturers made terrific strides in improving the quality of their products. The flowers looked more real—almost life-like—had truer colors, could be manipulated, and, in most cases, could be washed easily under the water faucet.

Most retail florists are handling the better quality material and letting the other stores have the less expensive products.

Permanent flowers of good quality are not inexpensive. You should handle this material both as loose flowers and made-up arrangements or designs. Many customers prefer to come into the shop just to purchase a few flowers. You can sell any number without being forced by convention and wholesale prices to stick to a dozen; you need not fear dumping the few that are left once you have broken a dozen, as with cut flowers.

Silk flowers are usually more expensive than the best polyethylenes, but are well worth it. They are extremely "life-like."

Permanent arrangements bring in a high price which adds to the volume of the store and the net profit. They make attractive displays in the shop and the window. One of the greatest advantages is that they can be made up months ahead of time during the slow periods. Many florists make up their fall and Christmas permanent arrangements in July and August, price them, cover them with polyethylene bags, and store them away until needed.

The cut flowers themselves appeal to customers for everyday use in the home. Many people like to have flowers in their homes most of the time; yet, they feel they cannot afford to purchase fresh flowers every week. Thus, with a permanent arrangement they can have flowers every day. As for special occasions, the past 15 years have shown an increase in cut flower sales for the home, and surveys

Figure 39-1. Permanent materials stored in polyethylene bags to keep them clean. (Courtesy, Bonnie Brae Flowers, Denver, Colo.)

have shown that these same people with permanent flowers will still purchase fresh cut flowers for special occasions. It has not affected the retail florists' sale of fresh flowers except to increase it by making more people aware of flowers for their homes, according to several leading retail florists in the United States.

The sale of polyethylene flowers and plants tripled from 1959 to 1965, but began to drop off by 1976. However, silk flowers were becoming popular at this time and are expected to continue to be in the 1980's.

Some florists use poor quality permanent flowers simply because they do not really know good from mediocre quality. Good quality is what you should handle, because it is what your customers want.

Permanent materials are used very effectively in places other than the home. They are a natural for offices, lobbies, hotels, hospitals, apartment houses, banks, and churches. There are many places with conditions so poor that the proper growing of live plants is quite difficult, or where there is no one available to take the responsibility to care for them. These are the places where permanent materials can be used. If you provide these you will receive the profit from them that would otherwise go to someone else.

Permanent planters can be used in several ways, such as the following: to decorate office areas, to hide or screen radiators, equipment, or architectural defects; to highlight a particular feature in the office; to control walking areas; and to define the sides of stairways in the event that there is no railing.

Permanent foliages and planters can be used in dozens of places including the following list: airports, auto showrooms, balconies, banks, chambers of commerce, convention halls, country clubs, drive-ins, executive offices, exhibition halls, foyers, funeral chapels, hotels, libraries, motels, museums, patios, reception rooms, restaurants, schools, service stations, shopping centers, swimming pools, and theaters.

Take advantage of national advertising that you do not have to pay for—plastics in all forms have been widely advertised by almost every major department store and many manufacturers. Selling them is not much different from selling any other gift item.

Permanent flowers and plants are a natural sideline in the retail florist shop (Chapter 21). They can be used very profitably on a contract basis as in commercial accounts (Chapter 37).

Florists who go into the business of renting out permanent foliages on a large scale must have a big storage area and an attractive prop room. The permanents should be set up to show the effect they will create in the desired setting. The rental and maintenance of permanents is time-consuming but financially profitable.

There is a nice profit to be made by the sale of both individual cut flowers and foliages and made-up arrangements and planters. You, the retail florist, are the logical one to receive this profit. And, remember, it will not hurt the sale of fresh cut flowers and pot plants.

 *PART FOUR*

MARKETING

Chapter 40

MARKETING CHANNELS—
WHOLESALING FLOWERS

There are four groups of people involved in the marketing of cut flowers, greens, and pot plants. The first group consists of the growers who produce the merchandise for the market. They may sell directly to consumers from their greenhouses, sell directly to retailers, or may sell through wholesale commission houses. The latter is the way that most of the producers' merchandise is handled.

The second group is composed of brokers who sell to growers and retailers and often sell between one producer and another. They handle such merchandise as cuttings, bulbs, seeds, fertilizers, and other materials needed for the greenhouse production of flowers. Usually they do not handle the merchandise itself except to transfer it from one producer to another. They hire sales personnel to take the orders for material which is then shipped to the grower. They operate on a low commission and make their money on volume business.

The third group concerned with the marketing of floral products is made up of the retail florists who buy from growers or wholesalers and sell to the consumer—the general public.

The fourth group concerned with marketing cut flowers, greens, pot plants, and supplies consists of the wholesale florists. Their operation will be discussed in this chapter.

WHAT IS MARKETING?

What is marketing? Marketing is a series of services or functions performed efficiently and in an orderly sequence so as to convey the product from the producer to the consumer, where, when, and in the form wanted. The product will have particular value for the consumer, who will be induced to devote a justifiable share of income to the purchase of the product, and will return an equitable share of the consumer's dollar to the producer and the marketing agencies. Also, the marketing system should relay the desires of the consumer to the producer. This key to selling is either to please the prospective customer or to convince the consumer that the product is "necessary."

MARKETING CHANNELS

There are three primary marketing channels in the transfer of the merchandise from the grower to the consumer: (1) the grower may be what is called a retail-grower and sell directly to the consumer, (2) the grower may sell directly to the retailer who sells to the consumer, and (3) the grower may sell to the wholesale commission merchant who sells to the retail florist who in turn sells to the consumer. Figure 40-1 shows the path of florist crops handled by the various channels.

WHOLESALE FLORIST

The wholesale florist is one of the mainstays of the whole industry, serving as the intermediary between the retailer and the grower, and as the storehouse for the retailer. The wholesaler operates on a commission basis for most materials—accepting 75 to 85 per cent of the merchandise on consignment, but buying some local material or unusual items outright in order to be sure of a supply. The amount purchased outright from growers is increasing each year.

A wholesaler's primary stock in trade is service, which allows the modern flower shop to offer the buying public a wide range of perishables and non-perishables without investing excessive amounts of working capital in either freight or inventory.

The wholesaler tries to get the highest price possible for the growers while giving the retailer a fair price, without exceeding the prevailing market price. Much of the pricing is based on supply and demand. With the large demand for flowers at holiday times, the prices on flowers go considerably higher than during normal times. Prices fluctuate day-to-day and even during the day. Some of the more perishable items like roses, which cannot be kept by the wholesaler more than one day, will change during the day, going lower and lower as the day progresses. Some flowers are quite stable and change little from week to week. Most greens will remain the

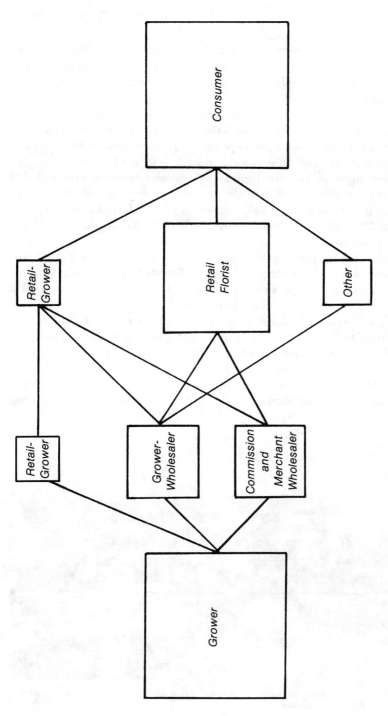

Figure 40-1. Marketing channels for florist products.

same all year. Weather conditions in certain areas of the country will also affect prices because of reduced supply. This is particularly true of a freeze in Florida which greatly affects the price of gladioli, chrysanthemums, and ferns.

Each grower has a number which is used for bookkeeping purposes. This aspect of the wholesale florist business is most important. Accurate records must be kept on all merchandise sold, as well as that dumped. The sale price for each bunch of flowers for each grower must be recorded, and each grower must be credited with the proper amount of the sale. At present the commission charged varies in different wholesale houses and on different materials from 15 to 30 per cent. Greens are normally handled at about a 100 per cent markup.

A bookkeeping system must be set up that is accurate and speedy. Some of the larger wholesale florists have set up a complete system using data processing cards, IBM machines, or one of the new computers such as the "Apple."

Each wholesale florist employs a large sales staff. Each salesperson tries to build up a list of personal customers, developing their confidence by honesty and integrity, and learning what flowers, quality, and price will appeal to each customer. If a "good buy" is available on 1,000 roses, the wholesale salesperson must know which retail florist will be interested. Often the sales staff have the authority to lower the price on certain merchandise during the day in order to make a sale.

Figure 40-2. Data processing of accounts for a wholesale florist. (Courtesy, Denver Wholesale Florists Co., Denver, Colo.)

Figure 40-3. The centralized grading of over 300,000 carnation blooms a day. (Courtesy, Denver Wholesale Florists Co., Denver, Colo.)

Figure 40-4. Wholesale refrigerated storage of 500,000 flowers. (Courtesy, Denver Wholesale Florists Co., Denver, Colo.)

Wholesalers have many excellent chances in the course of the daily business to build sales. Handling the phone, taking care of mail orders, and in-person sales give the opportunity to use real salesmanship.

The flowers should be handled very carefully by the wholesale florist. They should be put in water with a preservative and refrigerated as much as possible. Many of the larger wholesale florist establishments are air conditioned to help prolong the life of the flowers.

The flowers may be displayed on tables and benches either in cans of water, or laid out in the open. Both methods are used and will depend on the type of flower and the desires of the manager.

The growers are paid either weekly or monthly by the wholesaler (less the commission), who, in turn, is paid monthly by the retailers. One of the burdens to the business is the fact that some retail florists are slow in paying their bills, so the wholesaler must have capital on hand to pay the growers regularly. Wholesale florists need quality collection policies to make sure that money that is due them is received. If a wholesaler is operating on a net profit of 5 per cent of sales, it will take a new sale of $2,000 to offset a charge-off of $100. The wholesaler must remember that no sale is complete until the money is collected. However, it is essential to handle credit carefully, because "Yesterday's credit problems are today's good customers." With proper help, poor-paying accounts can be brought around. It may seem strange, but often the best collection policy is to improve the retailer's profit—by passing along ideas on selling, by selling what the retailer can sell fast to free cash to pay bills, by selling what the florist can pay for, and by not promoting the problem by selling too much or the wrong goods. Another burden on the wholesaler is the legal requirement that air freight and trucking charges must be paid within a week. This is often a large sum of money, particularly in the winter when up to 50 per cent of the cut flowers come in to the North and East from Florida, Colorado, and California.

The wholesale florist carries many supplies other than cut flowers, greens, and pot plants. Most wholesalers will handle a limited supply of ribbon, wire, tape, candles, foams, styrofoam materials, pottery, and many other items.

There are many things that wholesale florists must do to stay in business. Right at the top of the list is having a good collection program. The object is both to hold a customer's good will and to get the money.

Figure 40-5. The cut flower department in a wholesale florist business. (Courtesy, S. S. Pennock Co., Philadelphia, Pa.)

Figure 40-6. The rose department in a wholesale market. (Courtesy, S. S. Pennock Co., Philadelphia, Pa.)

Figure 40-7. The ribbon and supply department in a wholesale florist business. (Courtesy, S. S. Pennock Co., Philadelphia, Pa.)

Figure 40-8. Loading boxes of cut flowers from the loading platform of a wholesale florist. (Courtesy, S. S. Pennock Co., Philadelphia, Pa.)

CO-OPS AND AUCTIONS

Cut flowers are also marketed through co-ops and auctions, although in very limited quantity in this country.

In certain areas like Boston and San Francisco, the flower growers go together and rent a building with booths or stalls for each grower. They hire a manager and a small sales staff to take care of the retailers as they come to the co-op. Some growers have their own sales personnel, while others may go together to hire one salesperson to represent several growers. Some co-ops require identification to get into the building, whereas others will let in anyone who wishes to buy wholesale.

Flowers sold at auction go to the highest bidder and are sold in large quantities, often the whole lot from one grower at a time. Prices fluctuate during the day and material not sold to an exporter, wholesaler, or retailer is usually dumped.

The largest auction is at Aalsmeer, in the Netherlands, where all cut flowers are by law sold by auction. The flowers are brought by cart into the auditorium and discussed as to the grower and the quality of the merchandise. The auctioneer sets the hand on a dial like a large clock to a high price; as the hand turns, the price decreases, passing, for example, from 30¢ to 29¢, etc. When it reaches the desired price, the buyer pushes an electronic button which stops the clock and records the purchase. Buyers are wholesalers, retailers, and exporters from other European countries. Flowers not sold that day are dumped.

The wholesale commission florist, a vital link in the marketing of cut flowers and greens, must try to keep both the growers and the retailers happy—a tremendous job—as well as serve as a disseminator of information to the other two segments of the industry.

Pot plants are seldom handled by wholesale florists because of their weight and bulk, unless the wholesaler happens also to be a pot plant grower.

Chapter 41

FUTURE OF THE INDUSTRY

Most of the floricultural and economic experts are agreed that the future looks bright for the florist industry of the 1980's but will include some significant changes. One important need is the education of industry and consumers as to quality, availability, price and imports. "Americans are buying flowers in greater abundance—and variety—than ever before," so states the *Wall Street Journal* of August, 1981. For the nation's florists, business is still booming.

Florists will have to prepare for changes, and many predict that florists will have to start operating larger shops or get out of business. Expected are mergers of a number of businesses, with the big shops getting bigger and the little ones going out of business. A florist who wishes to stay in business must provide good services and quality merchandise.

The number of growers generally has been decreasing over the years, with the remainder acquiring even larger operations. The production trends of certain crops from 1970 to 1974 was as follows: standard mums, decreased; pompons, increased; carnations, decreased; gladioli, decreased; roses, increased; sweethearts, decreased; pot mums, increased; and foliage plants, increased—105 per cent.

Another change is in the growth of non-florist outlets for floricultural products, which has not been as rapid as had been predicted. M. Truman Fossum says that inter-city florist trade will continue to expand and reflect trends in total consumer expenditures for the goods and services of floriculture in all outlets.

During the past 40 years the U.S. economy has expanded at an unprecedented rate, and the social environment has undergone radical change. The florist industry, however, showed little change, according to Max E. Brunk. He has taken a critical look at the industry regarding changes for the 1980's and offers the following guidelines to florists who want to get ahead:

1. Learn to work together as an industry and learn to have confidence in, and listen to the ideas and opinions of growers, wholesalers, retailers and suppliers.
2. Identify your competitor not in terms of product handled or service rendered but in terms of consumer values offered.
3. Within your own industry, seek out ways to become distinctive, to become identified with a specific value, to serve a definite and distinguishable market segment.
4. A reasonable amount of company growth and industry growth should be planned and realized from the efforts of the firm or industry itself.
5. Evaluation of a competitor is a poor substitute for thinking and initiative.
6. Pricing is to marketing what labor efficiency is to production.
7. Recognize, analyze and capitalize on the nature of demand for your product and service.
8. The markets of the future will show several changes that will affect florists: (1) Inflation will continue at an accelerated rate. (2) Family life will be materially altered. (3) Attitudes towards females, around whom so much of the florist business is centered, are undergoing enormous changes. (4) As society becomes more affluent, man's traits, fads and customs change. (5) Quality displaces quantity and choice of variety becomes more important. (6) Long established social customs are being overturned. We are increasingly being married and buried on the run.

L. M. Berninger also predicts a new era for the florists of the 1980's. Particularly in the retailing of floriculture crops he sees chain operations coming into existence with many of our retail shops expanding in several directions. He sees the supermarkets expanding the sale of potted plants. A new concept of merchandising may arise in some of the major metropolitan areas of the country. He also predicts that the number of wholesale florists will drop.

However, contrary to predictions, Alvi Voigt, in the November 4, 1982 *Florists' Review*, states that the retail florists' market share of total floral sales moved from 53.1 per cent in 1976 to 63.3 per cent in 1980—an impressive increase of 10.2 per cent—while the supermarkets' share increased only ⅓ of 1 per cent—from 7.7 per cent in 1976 to 7.9 per cent in 1980.

Some retail florists believe that present trends indicate that new concepts and techniques in marketing practices are urgently needed to meet the demands of today's and tomorrow's free-thinking, more casual society. Looking ahead, they predict the emergence of cooperatives, where groups of retail florists merge together, maintaining their central warehouses and greenhouses from which flowers, plants, floral arrangements, and diversified items are distributed to small satellite shops. Other trends include corporate organization, less consignment in marketing, and more direct sales to retailers.

There has been considerable growth of the traditional retail florist business with a rising need for personalized service to the consumer in the way of providing knowledgeable and helpful personnel, delivery, credit, written planting and care instructions, potting of plants, plant replacement and replanting, quality accessories, and for the larger florist, landscaping advice, house calls for flower and plant problems, lawn care, fertilizing, spraying, and pruning.

American society is getting older. Counting all age levels, the average American is 28.2 years old and the age is rising. The number of persons over 65 will increase to 67 million by the year 2050. The baby boom of the 1964-1974 period accounts for the aging of the population. Should a baby boom materialize sometime during the next 10 years or so, the average aging of the population could be slowed down or arrested. The birth rate will be lowered and more diffused as to nationalities or ethnic groups over the next several years.

According to the Census Bureau, the nation's youth population peaked in 1980. Young persons between the ages of 14 and 19 numbered 23.4 million in 1981, but then are expected to fall to 22.9 million by 2000 and to 21.9 million by 2050.

The 1980's will be a period of change and growth for the retail florist industry in these ways:

1. Computers are now (and will be in the future) in the picture and will play a more significant role for all segments of the floral industry except the very small retail florists, who are already on their way out and being absorbed by larger firms.
2. In the future we can expect new firms to try to get a share of the wire order business.
3. More advertising by the producers of our product will produce more retail sales.
4. The "Chain of Life" concept will be adopted by more florists, leading to greater consumer satisfaction.

Thus, the prospects for the future seem bright for those retail florists who are willing to change and are able to plan for the future.

 BIBLIOGRAPHY

BIBLIOGRAPHY.

BIBLIOGRAPHY

Allen, Ann Dee. "Critiquing the Costs of Design," *Florists' Review* (January 17, 1980), p. 22.

American Floral Services memorandum, American Floral Services, Inc., Oklahoma City (1982).

Baker, Rolinda B. "Mini-Shops Sell Flowers and Film," *Southern Florist and Nurseryman* (December 25, 1970), pp. 8–9.

Berninger, Lou. "Better Business Involves Reacting and Keeping Competent Employees," *Florists' Review* (March 20, 1980), p. 17.

_____. *Forecasting the Future of Floriculture: A Positive Approach,* Ohio Florists' Association Bulletin 622, Columbus, Ohio: (August 1981).

_____. "What's in Store for the '70's?" *Florists' Review* (December 11, 1969), pp. 52-53.

Brunk, M. E. "Take a Critical Look at the Industry," *Florists' Review* (December 4, 1969), p. 27+.

Butler, Thomas M. "Vehicle Leasing Buys Piece of Mind," *Florist* (May 1970), pp. 38-39.

Census of Retail Trade, Washington, D.C.: U.S. Department of Commerce (1977).

Conklin, Everett. *A Guide to Interior Planting,* Montvale, New Jersey: Everett Conklin and Co., Inc. (1970), 25 pp.

Conover, Charles A. "Foliage Plants vs. Interior Conditions," *American Florist* (December 1975), pp. 30-32.

Conover, Charles A., and R. Poole. "Acclimatization of Tropical Foliage Plants," *Florists' Review* (November 27, 1975), pp. 39+.

Constantine, Clarence S. *The Chain of Life, Staby—OSU,* Bulletins 128 and 129, Massapequa Park, New York: New York State Flower Industries, Inc. (May and June 1981).

Curtis, William. "Rental Merchandise Comes to the Aid of the Party," *Teleflora Spirit* (October 1970), pp. 30-31.

Felly, Al. "Felly Flower Cutter," personal communication (November 17, 1981).

Ferrington, Ken. "Analyzing Your Sales and Using Your Balance Sheet," *Florist* (October 1981), p. 62.

————. "How to Price for Profit," *Florist* (September 1981), p. 55.

Florafax memorandum, Florafax International, Inc., Tulsa (1977).

"Florists Provide Total Green Plant Services and Make Commercial Interiors Come Alive," *Florist* (December 1975), pp. 42-47.

Florists' Transworld Delivery Association memorandum, Florists' Transworld Delivery Association, Southfield, Michigan (1982).

"Flower Shop or Variety Store," *Florist* (August 1970), pp. 50-53.

Fossum, M. T. "What's Ahead for 1970?" *Florist* (January 1970), pp. 57-59.

Golden, William P. "Selling Flowers in the European Manner," *Florist* (May 1971), pp. 54-57.

Guffey, Earle. "Holiday Record Sheets," personal interview (1977).

Hall, R., and S. M. Raleigh, Jr. *Commercial Floriculture and Related Products,* U.S. Department of Agriculture Research Report No. 855 (1969).

Heck, Bessie. "Shop Layout Geared for Efficiency," *Southern Florist and Nurseryman* (June 25, 1971), p. 11+.

"How to Build Your Commercial Accounts," *Florist* (February 1982), p. 65.

Howland, Joseph E. "Satisfied Customers Mean Higher Profits," *Florists' Review* (April 2, 1981), p. 44.

John M. E. *The Language of Flowers,* University Park, Pennsylvania: The Pennsylvania State University, 2 pp.

Kepner, Karl W. "Capturing Customers with Effective Advertising," *Florists' Review* (April 10, 1980), p. 22.

Klingaman, Gerald L. "Interior Landscapes," speech at A.I.F.D. Southern Chapter meeting, University of Arkansas (1975).

Kokus, John. "The Wonderful World of Flowers and Plants," special report, 91st Convention of SAF (July 19, 1975).

Korstad, Karl. "Interior Landscapers Plan Their Next Move," *Florists' Review* (November 5, 1981), p. 55.

Kotwick, Michael J. "Delivery Pools Cut Costs Today . . . and Maybe Save Tomorrow's Market," *Florist* (February 1976), pp. 64-67.

Kress, George. "Retail Florists—What's Happening to the Industry," *Florists' Review* (March 11, 1976), p. 25.

Major, Mike. "A Retail Florist Describes His Fruit and Flower Connection," *Florists' Review* (December 25, 1980), p. 20.

Mertes, J. E. "Site Opportunities for the Small Retailer," *Florists' Review* (July 23, 1964), p. 15+.

"Mishandling Employee Dismissal Can Be Costly to Businessmen," *Florists' and Nursery Exchange* (January 6, 1970), p. 12.

Mitchell, Herb. "Managing Your Business in Uncertain Times," *Florists' Review* (May 1, 1980), p. 17.

Mutschler, Robert G. "A Time and Motion Study in the Design Area of the Retail Flower Shop," thesis, The Pennsylvania State University (June 1966).

Norland, Jim. "Convenience Flowers," *Southern Florist and Nurseryman* (March 6, 1970), pp. 14-16.

_____. "Mass Marketers Ready for a Big Time," *Southern Florist and Nurseryman* (January 7, 1972), pp. 12-13.

Pfahl, Peter B. *Merchandising for Profit in Retail Flower Shops*, Pennsylvania Agricultural Experiment Station Bulletin 659 (August 1959), 25 pp.

_____. "Remodeling a Flower Shop, Part I," *Florists' Review* (April 25, 1963), pp. 19-20.

_____. "Remodeling the Workroom, Part II," *Florists' Review* (May 2, 1963), pp. 51-52.

Pfahl, Peter B., J. W. Mastalerz, and E. McGary. *Plant Cleaning Compounds Affect Growth of Foliage Plants*, Pennsylvania Retail Florists Bulletin 67 (October–November 1963), pp. 7-8.

"Retail Florist Product Lines," *FTD Fact Book*, Southfield, Michigan: Florists' Transworld Delivery Association (1972).

Reynolds, Marc B. "Advertising! Merchandising! Promotion! Publicity!" *Florists' Review* (November 5, 1981), p. 12.

Richards, Ed. "Total Store Planning," *Teleflora Spirit* (July 1971), pp. 18-19.

Robertson, J. L., and L. H. Chatfield. "Loose-Band Merchandising of Fresh Flowers," *Florists' Review* (September 3, 1981), pp. 14+.

Staby, George L. "Chain-of-Life," personal communication (October 29, 1981).

Stults, Marcia. "House Plants—A Survey," *Florists' Review* (September 11, 1975), p. 33+.

TELEFLORA memorandum, TELEFLORA, Inc., El Segundo, California (1982).

Tintori, Karen A. "Efficient Workrooms Increase Profits," *Florist* (July 1971), pp. 26-29.

Voigt, A. "Floriculture—¼ of 1 Per Cent of Nation's Total Personal Consumption Expenditure in 1979 per July Survey of Business for USDA," *Florists' Review* (September 24, 1981), pp. 128+.

_____. "Statistics Show Retailers Thriving," *Florists' Review*, Nov. 4, 1982.

"Weddings '80: Florists from Coast to Coast Spot Wedding Design Trends," *Florists' Review* (May 22, 1980), p. 20.

"What Is the Worth of Your Closely Held Corporation?" *Florists' Review* (September 17, 1981), pp. 34-37.

"What to Look for When You Buy Another Shop," *Florists' and Nursery Exchange* (March 5, 1966), pp. 20+.

"Where to Locate and Why," *The Exchange* (February 22, 1964), pp. 32-33.

Zeller, Cathy C. "How Florists Train and Motivate Their Salespeople," *Florist* (July 1981), p. 35.

_____. "How to Make and Market Fruit Baskets," *Florist* (December 1981), p. 39.

 GLOSSARY

GLOSSARY

Accessories—Supplementary items and objects sold in conjunction with flowers.

Acclimatization—Climatic adaptation of a plant to a new environment.

Accounts payable—A liability to the business, carried on open accounts, usually for purchase of goods and services.

Accounts receivable—Accounts of customers who owe for merchandise or services.

Adjunct—One thing added to another, such as a different type of store or merchandise.

Advertising—Supplying information to the public to induce people to buy a product.

Aesthetic—Pertaining to a sense of beauty.

Allied—A group of growers, wholesalers, and retailers in an area, contributing a percentage of their gross for the advertising and promotion of flowers.

Assets—Items of ownership belonging to the business.

Asymmetrical—Having two sides of the centerline of a flower arrangement different in appearance, but equal in visual weight, giving it stability.

Auction, flower—Sale of flowers to the highest bidder.

Backboard—A plaque designed on a piece of styrofoam to use as a background for a floral design.

Bad debts—Accounts uncollectable now and seemingly so in the future.

Balance sheet—A tabular statement of assets, liabilities, and net worth in which the debit and credit balance are equal. The financial position of a business on a specified date.

Bedding plant—Any annual flower or vegetable plant grown for resale for a home garden.

Bonsai—A tree or shrub that has been dwarfed by certain methods and grown in a pot or container.

Book value—The value of a business or property as stated in a book of accounts.

Botany—The study of the classification and processes of plants.

Boutonniere—One flower worn in a man's lapel.

Browse—To look leisurely at goods displayed for sale.

Cash-and-carry—Merchandise paid for in cash and taken by the customer. No design, delivery, package, or bookkeeping involved.

Cattleya—The most popular hybrid orchid; white or lavender in color.

Centerpiece—A flower arrangement for the center of the table.

Chenille stems—A straight wire with a fuzzy covering.

Chuppah—A 7- by 7-foot canopy under which a Jewish couple are married.

Cibotium—A type of large tree fern used for decoration.

Circulation areas—Open areas to provide freedom of movement for people in the shop.

Consignment—Merchandise sent to a wholesaler for sale to a retailer on a percentage basis.

Container—A receptable to hold flowers and greens.

Control center—The office or manager's desk from which all orders and deliveries are processed.

Co-op—The association of several growers who offer merchandise for sale to retailers under one roof.

Curly-Q—A spool of thin wire coated with plastic or enamel.

Custom service—Bouquets and decorations designed specifically for the customer.

Cut flower—A flower that is cut from the plant.

Cut-off time—A certain hour of the day after which no orders will be taken for delivery that day.

Cyclic billing—Statements sent over a 30-day period by alphabetical order.

Cymbidium—A type of orchid growing 30 to 50 flowers on a stem. Smaller than most cattleyas.

Data processing—The handling and recording of accounts by electronic equipment.

Depreciation—A decrease in value due to wear and tear, and allowed on the accounts of the business in computing the value of property for tax purposes.

Designing—The art of arranging flowers and plant material in an artistic manner.

Direct mail—Advertising and promotional materials sent by mail to a select list of customers.

Discounts—Reduced prices for materials.

Dish garden—A container in which several different low growing foliage plants are grown in soil.

Display—To visibly show merchandise to the public.

Display refrigerator—A refrigerator in the sales area with an all glass front.

Display window—Any window in the florist shop which has merchandise on view to the public.

Double spray—A funeral spray, twice the size of a normal spray with the bow of ribbon in the center. Used as a casket cover.

Dowel rod—A round piece of wood similar to a peg or table leg.

Driftwood—Old wood seasoned by water and weather used in interior decorating.

Drive-in—An area designed so the customer can transact business without leaving the car.

Drop-in—To stop in without notice; unexpected visit.

Dumpage—Material thrown out each day because it wasn't sold or is too old for sale.

Efficiency—The ability to accomplish a job with a minimum amount (expenditure) of time and effort.

Elemental operation time—The amount of time for an operator to complete each element of the operation.

Elemental transportation time—The amount of time for an operator to travel for each element of the operation.

Emblem—A funeral design, or set piece, symbolizing the loss of a loved one.

Ephemeral—Lasting a very short time.

Facets—Different aspects or phases of the business.

Far corner—The opposite corner from the main stream of traffic.

Filler—A flower or green used to fill in spaces in an arrangement. A material used in a container to hold the flowers in place in a design.

Fleurin—An international unit for medium of exchange between retail florists of different countries.

Flocked wire—A florist wire with a coating of flocked material.

Florafax—Florafax International, Inc.

Floratape—A tape used by florists to cover wire stems.

Floriculture—The producing, marketing, use, and sale of florist crops.

Flow diagram—Pictorial representation of the layout of the process and the paths of travel during the process.

Flow process chart—A graphic representation of all operations, transportations, and delays during a process or procedure.

Flower cart—An ornamental cart used to display merchandise.

Flowers-by-wire—The transmitting of orders from one city to another by phone, mail, telegraph, or computer network.

Fluctuate—To continually change from one thing to another, as in the price of flowers.

Foam—A plastic compound which absorbs water used to hold flowers in place in a design.

Foil—Roll of colored aluminum foil used to wrap pots. Also a roll of tin foil for putting around the back of wreath frames.

Foliage plant—Any pot plant grown for its foliage effect.

Foot traffic—Pedestrian traffic passing the store.

FTDA—Florists' Transworld Delivery Association.

Garden center—An area devoted to the sale of outdoor garden merchandise.

Garland—A wreath or festoon of flowers, foliage, or other plant material used as a decoration.

Gift line—A series of various colors, sizes, and shapes of the same type of a gift item.

Glut—An oversupply of a product on the market.

Greenhouse—A structure covered with glass or plastic used to produce cut flowers and pot plants.

Gross—The total amount without deductions.

Hard foliages—A group of foliages used by florists which will hold up out of water for several days if stored in a refrigerator.

Hardgoods—Staples or inventory items.

Headhouse—An enclosed structure connected to a greenhouse for potting, transplanting, and doing other jobs required in the growing of plants.

Horticulture—The science, art, and business of improving, producing, storing, and processing fruits, vegetables, flowers, and ornamental plants.

Image—The picture or idea represented in the customer's mind of a particular person or business.

Impulse sale—The purchase of an item other than that which the customer entered the store to buy.

Inventory—Staple items on hand for resale and use by the designers.

Jardinere—An ornamental receptacle or stand for holding plants or flowers.

Keeping quality—The ability of a cut flower to last as long as is normally expected of that flower.

Kimpack—An insultation material used in packing cut flowers for shipment.

Layout—The arrangement or plan of a certain area such as the design and sales areas in a retail flower shop.

Leasing—A contract for renting a piece of property for a certain period of time at a specified price.

Liabilities—Obligations owed by the business.

Make-up work—Any arrangement of flowers that must be designed.

Manzanita—A dried branch, bleached by the sun, used in decorations.

Markup—A system for determining the sale price of an item based on the cost of merchandise.

Mass display—Display of an item in a large quantity.

Mass market—Any supermarket type of operation.

Mechanical aid—Any material used in a container to make the cut flowers and greens stay in place.

Media—Means of offering merchandise for sale to the consumer.

Merchandise—Material offered for sale.

Merchandising—Offering the right merchandise, at the right price, to the right people, at the right time, and in the right place. Volume selling at a lower than normal markup.

Mossing—Placing wet spagnum moss in a frame for funeral and Christmas wreaths; set pieces.

Motivation—A state or condition of being persuaded to act. An incentive to do something.

Near corner—The location at the closest corner to the main artery of traffic.

Net worth—The net value of the business.

Non-perishable items—Merchandise other than flowers, pot plants, or plant material. May be used in design work or for sale.

Novelties—Unusual articles for sale that are chiefly decorative and often used with flowers.

Opaque—Not allowing light to pass through.

Open house—Promotion to get the general public to visit the shop to see the displays, usually prior to a major florist holiday.

Order-taker—A poor salesperson who simply writes up the orders for the customer without any salesmanship involved.

Overhead—Expenses and the general cost of running a business.

Package service—A set service for weddings with just a few selections of bouquets and decorations from which to choose.

Packaging—Wrapping arrangements and cut flowers for delivery.

P&L—Profit and Loss statement showing the condition of the business at any particular time.

Papier-mâché containers—Containers made out of paper pulp and glue pressed together; inexpensive.

Parafilm—A roll of plastic material used to cover the wire stem of a flower.

Partnership—Two or more people in business together.

Pegboard—A composition wall board with regular perforations for the insertion of hooks to hold shelves and merchandise on display.

Per capita—So much for each individual person.

Period Arrangement—An arrangement typical of an era in Western history.

Perishable—Subject to decay, short-lived.

Permanent materials—The artificial flowers and materials made out of polyethylene or silk.

Personal delay—A percentage of time allotted to accommodate the personal needs of the operator.

Physiology—The study of plants and the functions of their organisms.

Pickled flowers—Flowers which have been held too long in water in a refrigerator and are not salable.

Pinholder—A holder of steel needles used to hold flowers in place in a low container.

Planter—A watertight container for growing plants.

Plastic—Bags and other items made out of one of the synthetic materials.

"Please Omit"—An addition in death notices asking people not to send flowers to a funeral.

Polyethylene materials—The flowers and greens constructed out of a type of plastic polymer of ethylene. Also clear plastic bags used in packaging.

Pot plant—A plant grown and sold in a pot. Sometimes called a potted plant.

Preservative—A chemical preparation to make cut flowers last longer.

Promotion—The act of getting public recognition for a business or merchandise through advertising.

Proprietorship—One person as a sole owner of the business.

Prospects—Potential customers or flower buyers.

Protocol—The code of customs and regulations dealing with etiquette. Acceptable to the majority of people.

Publicity—Public notice resulting from mention in the press, radio, or other medium.

Public relations—The act of promoting good will between a business or person and the public.

Qualifications—Necessary characteristics which fit a person for a particular job.

Quality—Characteristic of a high grade of merchandise.

Random selection—A process of selection whereby each item has an equal chance of being picked. A selection without a definite aim.

Rapport—A harmonious relationship between individuals.

Receiving florist—A florist who receives a flowers-by-wire order and fills it by delivering the flowers to the proper person.

Retail-grower—A retail florist who grows some or most of his/her merchandise.

Retail-only—A retail florist who does not grow any of his/her own merchandise.

SAF—Society of American Florists.

Salesmanship—The art of selling.

Salient—Conspicuous.

Seasonal variation—Availability of certain cut flowers according to the season of the year.

Sending florist—A florist who takes an order and transmits it to a member florist in another city.

Shadow box—A rectangular frame used to display special floral designs or items of merchandise.

Shatter—Begin to lose petals due to a blow or crushing of the flower.

Sheaf—A cluster of cut flowers tied together at one end with a bow of ribbon.

Site—The place where the shop is located.

Smilax—A trailing green plant grown on twine, used for decoration, and draped as a garland.

Social-psychological behavior—The explanation of why people act the way they do in society.

Special occasion—A particular time to celebrate such as a birthday or an anniversary.

Spray—A flat horizontal funeral arrangement of flowers with the stems in some type of foundation, or tied together.

Stability—The condition of being stable—not inclined to fall over.

Standard deviation—A measure of variability in terms of the units of measurement, usually of a total population.

Staples—Non-perishable items for use and for sale, such as ribbon, wire, paper, etc.

Stock container—A container used for the cut flowers (stock) to be used by the designers, and kept in the storage refrigerator.

Stock control—An accurate account of the merchandise in the store.

Storage refrigerator—An enclosed refrigerator in which the bulk of the flowers and greens are stored.

Styrofoam—Plastic material used for novelty cut-outs and bases for dried and permanent arrangements which will not absorb water.

Swag—A sheaf of flowers and/or greens tied together for the door.

Symmetrical—Having both sides of the centerline the same in a flower arrangement.

TELEFLORA—Teleflora, Inc.

Terralite—A horticultural grade of vermiculite.

Time-motion study—The study of time and motions comprising an operation.

Time standard—The time required for an *average* operator, fully qualified and trained and working at a *normal* pace, to perform the operation.

Totem pole—A pole, bark, or frame used to support trailing types of plants.

Trade fair—A group of exhibitors of novelty and staple items from whom florists will order for the store.

Transients—People who are going by in the street; or are temporary, not permanent.

Translucent—Permitting light to pass through but diffusing so objects are not clearly visible.

Tubbed plants—Foliage or flowering pot plants grown in a wooden tub.

Tufflite—Shredded styrofoam used as a mechanical aid to hold flowers in place in a tall container.

Turnover—The number of times items are sold and reordered for sale in a given time.

Unencumbered—Not impeded or hindered; not burdened with debt.

Upsell—To persuade the customer to spend more money than intended for an item.

Values—The ideals or customs of a society held in high regard by its people.

Vermiculite—A group of platy minerals and silicates used by florists for propagation of plants and as a mechanical aid in containers.

Water garden—An arrangement of foliage plants on a pinholder in a shallow container of water.

Will calls—Orders which will be picked up by the customer.

Window box—A box for growing plants outdoors on an outside window ledge.

Wire orders—Customers' orders which are sent by one florist to another by wire, phone, mail, or computer network.

Withdrawal—Taking cash out of the business for purchases or personal needs.

Workroom—The design area in a retail flower shop.

 INDEX

INDEX